CAMBRIDGE COMPANIONS TO RELIGION
A series of companions to major topics and key figures in theology and religious studies. Each volume contains specially commissioned chapters by international scholars which provide an accessible and stimulating introduction to the subject for new readers and non-specialists.

THE CAMBRIDGE COMPANION TO JOHN CALVIN
edited by Donald K. McKim (2004)
ISBN 0 521 81647 5 hardback   ISBN 0 521 01672 x paperback

THE CAMBRIDGE COMPANION TO URS VON BALTHASAR
edited by Edward T. Oakes, SJ and David Moss (2004)
ISBN 0 521 81467 7 hardback   ISBN 0 521 89147 7 paperback

THE CAMBRIDGE COMPANION TO REFORMATION THEOLOGY
edited by David Bagchi and David Steinmetz (2004)
ISBN 0 521 77224 9 hardback   ISBN 0 521 77662 7 paperback

THE CAMBRIDGE COMPANION TO AMERICAN JUDAISM
edited by Dana Evan Kaplan (2005)
ISBN 0 521 82204 1 hardback   ISBN 0 521 52951 4 paperback

Forthcoming

THE CAMBRIDGE COMPANION TO THE GOSPELS
edited by Stephen C. Barton

THE CAMBRIDGE COMPANION TO ISLAMIC THEOLOGY
edited by Tim Winter

THE CAMBRIDGE COMPANION TO FRIEDRICH SCHLEIERMACHER
edited by Jacqueline Mariña

THE CAMBRIDGE COMPANION TO EVANGELICAL THEOLOGY
edited by Timothy Larsen and Daniel J. Treier

THE CAMBRIDGE COMPANION TO THE QUR'AN
edited by Jane Dammen McAuliffe

KARL RAHNER

Edited by Declan Marmion and Mary E. Hines

CAMBRIDGE
UNIVERSITY PRESS

CAMBRIDGE UNIVERSITY PRESS
Cambridge, New York, Melbourne, Madrid, Cape Town, Singapore,
São Paulo, Delhi, Dubai, Tokyo, Mexico City

Cambridge University Press
The Edinburgh Building, Cambridge CB2 8RU, UK

Published in the United States of America by Cambridge University Press, New York

www.cambridge.org
Information on this title: www.cambridge.org/9780521540452

First published 2005
Reprinted 2007

A catalogue record for this publication is available from the British Library

ISBN 978-0-521-83288-5 Hardback
ISBN 978-0-521-54045-2 Paperback

Contents

Notes on contributors

NICHOLAS ADAMS is a Lecturer in Theology and Ethics at the University of Edinburgh. His research area is the relationship between German philosophy and theology.

DAVID COFFEY holds the William J. Kelly Chair in Systematic Theology at Marquette University. He has written extensively on Pneumatology, Christology, and the Trinity. He is the author of *Deus Trinitas: The Doctrine of the Triune God* (New York: Oxford University Press, 1999) and has published widely on Rahner's thought.

NANCY A. DALLAVALLE is Associate Professor of Religious Studies at Fairfield University. She has served on the steering committee of the Karl Rahner Society (U.S.), and has published scholarly articles on both Rahner's trinitarian theology (*Irish Theological Quarterly*) and the meeting of feminist thought and Catholic theology (*Horizons, Modern Theology*).

DANIEL DONOVAN, a priest of the archdiocese of Toronto and Professor Emeritus of Theology at St. Michael's College in the University of Toronto, received his doctorate in theology from the University of Münster where Karl Rahner was one of his professors. He is the author of several books including *The Church as Idea and Fact* (Collegeville, MN: Michael Glazier, 1988), *What Are They Saying About the Ministerial Priesthood?* (Mahwah, NJ: Paulist, 1992), and *Distinctively Catholic: An Exploration of Catholic Identity* (Mahwah, NJ: Paulist, 1997).

STEPHEN J. DUFFY is Professor of Systematic Theology at Loyola University, New Orleans. He is the author of *The Dynamics of Grace: Perspectives in Theological Anthropology* (Collegeville, MN: Liturgical Press, 1993) and of *Graced Horizon: Nature and Grace in Modern Catholic Thought* (Collegeville, MN: Liturgical Press, 1992), and a contributor to a number of theological journals and encyclopediae.

HARVEY D. EGAN received his doctorate in theology under the direction of Karl Rahner from Westfälische Wilhelms-Universität and is currently Professor of Systematic and Mystical Theology at Boston College. His books include *Christian Mysticism: The Future of a Tradition* (Collegeville, MN: Michael Glazier, 1992), *Ignatius Loyola the Mystic* (Collegeville, MN: Liturgical Press, 1991), *An Anthology of Christian Mysticism* (Collegeville, MN: Liturgical Press, 1991) and *Karl Rahner: Mystic of Everyday Life* (New York: Crossroad, 1998).

PHILIP ENDEAN is Tutor in Theology at Campion Hall in the University of Oxford, and Editor of *The Way*, the journal of spirituality published by the British Jesuits. He has previously worked as a hospital chaplain and taught at Heythrop College, University of London. He is the author of *Karl Rahner and Ignatian Spirituality* (Oxford: Oxford University Press, 2001), and of many articles on a range of theological and spiritual topics.

JERRY T. FARMER is an Associate Professor of Theology at Xavier University in New Orleans, Louisiana. He is author of *Ministry in Community: Rahner's Vision of Ministry*, Louvain Theological and Pastoral Monographs 13 (Louvain: Peeters Press, 1992). He has been involved in California in developing a ministry formation process for laity, in both English and Spanish, and has addressed issues of popular religiosity, in both the U.S. Hispanic/Latino context as well as in Spain.

FRANCIS SCHÜSSLER FIORENZA is presently the Charles Chauncey Stillman Professor of Roman Catholic Theological Studies at Harvard Divinity School. He received his doctorate from the University of Münster, West Germany, with Karl Rahner and Johann Baptist Metz as his dissertation advisors. He has published *Foundational Theology: Jesus and the Church* (New York: Crossroad, 1984), co-authored with J. Livingston *Modern Theology: Vol. II: The Twentieth Century* (New Jersey: Prentice-Hall, 2000), co-edited with J. Galvin *Systematic Theology: Roman Catholic Perspectives*, 2 vols. (Minneapolis: Fortress, 1991), and has written over 140 essays in the areas of fundamental theology, systematic theology, and political theology.

JEANNINE HILL FLETCHER is an Assistant Professor of Theology at Fordham University, Bronx, New York. She received her Th.D. from Harvard Divinity School where she wrote her dissertation on "Ultimacy and Identity: Karl Rahner and George Lindbeck on Religious Pluralism." Her published articles include: "Shifting Identity: The Contribution of Feminist Thought to Theologies of Religious Pluralism" (*Journal of Feminist Studies in Religion*), and "Karl Rahner's Principles of Ecumenism as Resources for Contemporary Religious Pluralism" (*Theology and the Social Sciences, The Annual Publication of the College Theology Society*, 2001).

RICHARD LENNAN is Senior Lecturer in Systematic Theology at the Catholic Institute of Sydney. He has published *The Ecclesiology of Karl Rahner* (Oxford: Clarendon Press, 1995) and *Risking the Church* (Oxford: Oxford University Press, 2004), and edited *An Introduction to Catholic Theology* (Mahwah, NJ: Paulist, 1998) and *The Possibility of Belief* (Homebush, NSW: St Pauls, 2004).

BRIAN LINNANE is an Associate Professor of Religious Studies and an Assistant Dean at the College of the Holy Cross, Worcester, MA, USA.

GASPAR MARTINEZ is Associate Professor at the Diocesan Institute of Theology and Pastoral Studies in Bilbao, Spain. After studies in Bilbao and London, he received the Ph.D. degree from the University of Chicago in 1997. He has published *Confronting the Mystery of God: Political, Liberation, and Public Theologies* (New York: Continuum, 2001).

PETER C. PHAN holds three earned doctorates and is currently the Ignacio Ellacuria, S.J. Professor of Catholic Social Thought at Georgetown University, Washington, D.C. He has authored 10 books, edited 20 books, and written 250 essays for popular and scholarly journals. His writings have received several awards from theological societies. His latest writings include his trilogy: *Christianity with an Asian Face*; *In Our Tongues*; and *Being Religious Interreligiously* (Maryknoll, NY: Orbis). He is Past President of the Catholic Theological Society of America.

MICHAEL PURCELL lectures in Systematic and Philosophical Theology in the School of Divinity, University of Edinburgh, Scotland. His research interests focus on Karl Rahner's theology, the relation between phenomenology and theology, and the theological relevance of Emmanuel Levinas' ethical metaphysics. Publications include *Mystery and Method: The Other in Rahner and Levinas* (Milwaukee, WI: Marquette University Press, 1998), and various articles, inspired by Levinas' thinking, on the nature of theology, grace, liturgy and sacraments, and the Eucharist, in *Philosophy and Theology, Gregorianum, Heythrop Journal, Bijdragen,* and *Louvain Studies*. He has recently completed a book on Levinas and theology, and is currently working on the theology of death in post-modernity.

THOMAS SHEEHAN is Professor of Religious Studies, Stanford University, and Professor Emeritus of Philosophy, Loyola University, Chicago, with specialization in the work of Heidegger and Rahner. He is the author of *Karl Rahner: The Philosophical Foundations* (Ohio: Ohio University Press, 1987), *The First Coming: How the Kingdom of God Became Christianity* (New York: Random House, 1986), and editor with Richard Palmer of Edmund Husserl, *Psychological and Transcendental Phenomenology and the Confrontation with Heidegger (1927–1931)* (Boston, Dordrecht, London: Kluwer Academic Publishers, 1997).

ROMAN A. SIEBENROCK is Professor of Fundamental Theology and Director of the Karl Rahner Archives at the University of Innsbruck, Austria. He is co-author of *Der Denkweg Karl Rahners: Quellen – Entwicklungen – Perspectiven* (Mainz: Grünewald, 2004).

GESA ELSBETH THIESSEN is Reader in Theology at the Milltown Institute of Theology and Philosophy and Honorary Research Fellow of the Department of Theology and Religious Studies of the University of Wales (Lampeter). She is the author of *Theology and Modern Irish Art* (Dublin: Columba, 1999) and *Theological Aesthetics – A Reader* (London: SCM, 2004).

Chronology of Karl Rahner

1904	Born March 5, in Freiburg in Breisgau, Germany
1922	Enters the Society of Jesus (Jesuits)
1924–27	Philosophical Studies in Feldkirch (Austria) and Pullach (Munich)
1927–29	Teacher in Feldkirch
1929–33	Theological Studies in Valkenburg (Holland)
1932	Priestly Ordination in Munich
1934–36	Graduate Studies in Philosophy at Freiburg with four semesters in Martin Heidegger's seminar
1936	Undertakes and completes doctoral studies in theology at Innsbruck
1937	Habilitation in Dogmatic Theology and begins lecturing in Dogma and in the History of Dogma at Innsbruck
1938	First (German) edition of *Encounters with Silence* published
1939	Rejected doctoral thesis in philosophy published under the title, *Spirit in the World*
1941	*Hearer of the Word* published
1939–44	Work at the Diocesan Pastoral Institute in Vienna
1944	Pastoral work in Bavaria
1945–48	Lecturer in Dogma in Pullach
1954	First volume of *Theological Investigations* published
1949–64	Lecturer in Dogma and in the History of Dogma at Innsbruck; Professor in 1949
1962–65	Theological consultant (*peritus*) at the Second Vatican Council
1964–67	Succeeded Romano Guardini in the Chair of Christianity and the Philosophy of Religion at Munich
1967–71	Professor of Dogmatic Theology in Münster (Westphalia)
1969	Member of the International Theological Commission
1971–81	Emeritus in Munich
1972	Appointed Honorary Professor of Dogma and in the History of Dogma at Innsbruck
1976	*Foundations of Christian Faith* published
1981–84	Emeritus in Innsbruck
1984	Died in Innsbruck on March 30; buried in the crypt of the Jesuit Church

Glossary

Analogy: For Rahner, the term refers to the form of our knowledge and thought about God that simultaneously underscores God's transcendence and follows the Fourth Lateran Council's assertion: "For no similarity can be said to hold between Creature and creature which does not imply a greater dissimilarity between the two." (DS 432)

Anonymous Christian: A term coined by Rahner to be judiciously used by Christians to indicate the universality of God's grace beyond the confines of Christianity. Non-Christians, by virtue of God's universal salvific will and their own orientation to transcendence, can live in a Christian manner without explicitly articulating their lives in such terms.

Apophatic: A tradition of spirituality as well as a style of theologizing that underscores the transcendence of God who cannot be circumscribed by human concepts and discourse. A consistent characteristic of Rahner's theology is its apophatic insistence on the "always greater" God and on the ineffability of the divine mystery.

Categorical (Categorial): represents the concrete, historical aspect of human reality and is often contrasted by Rahner with the term "transcendental."

Concupiscence: Though this is traditionally understood as the inclination to sin, Rahner describes it in a morally neutral way in terms of the tension between what one is (nature) and what one desires to become by free decision.

Economic Trinity: refers to the actions of the divine persons as they are revealed in history, in God's plan or "economy" of salvation.

Eschatology: traditionally understood as the doctrine of the Last Things, specifically heaven, hell, death and judgment. While the individual and social aspects of eschatology have often be overly separated, theology since the 1960s (e.g., J. Moltmann) has tried to overcome such dualism by showing how human efforts to build a better world anticipate the divine future.

Existential: A term derived from Martin Heidegger to designate a characteristic of human existence or "being-in-the-world." For Rahner, these characteristics or existentials refer to the human person as transcendent, free, historical, and threatened by sin and guilt.

"Existentiell" Christology: In contrast to an abstract theoretical Christianity, the term refers to the process of personal appropriation and actualization of a Christian's personal relationship to Jesus Christ.

Extrinsicism: refers to the tendency, noted by Rahner and others, to separate grace from nature, revelation from experience, and to rely on external authorities (e.g., official teaching or the eternal divine will) as the sole warrant for theological claims.

Gnoseological Concupiscence: A term coined by Rahner to refer to a legitimate pluralism within contemporary theology where there are competing and legitimate perspectives that cannot be simply harmonized.

Ignatius of Loyola (1491–1556): Spanish (Basque) Founder of the Society of Jesus (Jesuits), famed for his *Spiritual Exercises*, a four week guided reflection aimed at discerning how one can best serve God.

Immanent Trinity: refers to the interaction between the divine persons *within* the Trinity.

Mystagogy: refers to a process of initiation into the sacred, into the experience of the mystery of God. For Rahner all forms of Christian initiation need a mystagogical dimension alongside the more doctrinal aspects.

Mystery: For Rahner, not so much to be understood negatively in terms of truths that are provisionally incomprehensible but, more positively and primordially, referring to the human person, as a being of unlimited transcendence, who is confronted by mystery, or, more precisely, by the incomprehensible mystery of God.

Nature: refers to the permanent structure or principle of a being. For Rahner, human nature, by virtue of its transcendent orientation, is open to a possible self-communication of God (grace).

Nouvelle Theólogie: A term (generally employed pejoratively in official circles) from the 1940s to describe an attempt by mainly French theologians to renew traditional theology, particularly in the light of new developments in science (e.g., evolution theories), biblical and patristic research. While official documents (e.g., the encyclical *Humani Generis*) issued warnings, the underlying aim was to render traditional Christian teachings more credible.

Phantasm: For Rahner, following Aquinas and in dialogue with Kant, all knowledge comes from the senses, or, in Thomistic terms, a turning of the intellect towards the phantasm (image).

Potentia Oboedientialis: refers to the disposition of a person to receive and accept the gift of God's self-communication, which leads to the fulfillment of his or her spiritual nature.

Transcendental: The term refers to a metahistorical, a priori disposition of the human person, who asks after the question of being, and who thereby experiences him or herself as a being with an unlimited horizon, open to the mystery of God.

Quasi-formal Causality: In God's self-communication (grace), what is really communicated is God in God's own being. Following Aristotle, formal causality makes something the kind of being it is. Rahner uses the prefix "quasi" so as not to conflate the human and the divine, while stressing that God's grace is fully given and fully efficacious in the human person.

Realsymbol: In the context of his theology of sacraments, particularly sacramental causality, Rahner shows how sacraments are intrinsically real symbols (in contrast to mere signs) genuinely effecting what they signify. Rahner also applied his anthropology of symbol to the theology of the Trinity and to Christology.

Sapiential: The sapiential task of theology aims at discovering wisdom for practical Christian living. Rahner saw all his writings as sapiential and spiritual in this sense rather than strictly scientific treatises.

Supernatural Existential: In the context of Rahner's theology of grace, this term refers not only to its gratuitous character (supernatural) as a result of God's universal salvific will, but also to a characteristic (existential) of each person's consciousness whereby they are open, or disposed, to the offer of the divine self-communication.

Uncreated Grace: refers to the self-communication of God to a person, which can be experienced; it forms part of Rahner's attempt to retrieve a more existential understanding of grace.

Vorgriff (**Pre-apprehension of Being**): A capacity of the dynamic self-movement of the spirit, whereby a particular object of knowledge in each act of cognition is grasped in its limitation and against a background of an infinite, unlimited horizon.

Abbreviations

DS   H. Denzinger and A. Schönmetzer, *Enchiridion Symbolorum* (Freiburg: Herder, 32nd edn., 1960).

FCF   K. Rahner, *Foundations of Christian Faith: An Introduction to the Idea of Christianity*. Trans. W. Dych (London: Darton, Longman & Todd, 1978).

HW   K. Rahner, *Hearer of the Word*. Trans. J. Donceel (New York: Continuum, 1994). This work exists in two German editions, the original 1941 edition and a second modified edition edited by J. B. Metz in 1963. For the first edition in English, see *Hearer of the Word*, trans. J. Donceel (New York: Continuum, 1994); for the second edition, see *Hearers of the Word*, trans. M. Richards (New York: Herder, 1969). Contributors normally refer to the 1994 edition unless otherwise indicated.

ITS   Innsbrucker Theologische Studien (Innsbruck/Vienna: Tyrolia, 1978–).

LThK   *Lexikon für Theologie und Kirche*. 10 vols. Ed. K. Rahner and J. Höfer. (Freiburg: Herder, 2nd edn., 1957–65).

SaW   *Karl-Rahner: Sämtliche Werke*. 32 vols. (approx.). Ed. K. Lehmann, J. B. Metz, K.-H. Neufeld, A. Raffelt and H. Vorgrimler (Freiburg: Herder, 1995ff.).

SM   *Sacramentum Mundi. An Encyclopedia of Theology*. 6 vols. Ed. K. Rahner, A. Darlap, et al. (New York: Herder and Herder, 1968–70).

SW   K. Rahner, *Spirit in the World*. Trans. W. Dych (New York: Herder and Herder, 1968, 2nd edn., New York: Continuum, 1994).

TI   K. Rahner, *Theological Investigations*. 23 vols. Various translators (London: Darton, Longman & Todd, 1961–84). In the US, vols. I–VI were published in Baltimore by Helicon Press; vols. VII–X in New York by Herder and Herder; vols. XI–XVI in New York by Seaburg Press; vols. XVII–XXIII in New York by Crossroad.

Introduction

DECLAN MARMION and MARY E. HINES

It is both terrible and comforting to dwell in the inconceivable
nearness of God, and so to be loved by God that the first and last gift is
infinity and inconceivability itself. But we have no choice. God is with
us. *Prayers for a Lifetime*[1]

The year 2004 marks the hundredth anniversary of the birth of Karl Rahner,
S. J., who, it is widely acknowledged, was the dominant theological voice
of the Roman Catholic Church in the twentieth century. For many, his theology has come to symbolize the Catholic Church's entry into modernity,
an event publicly and ritually celebrated at the Second Vatican Council.
Not surprisingly in the forty years since the Council and the twenty years
since the death of Rahner both the Council and the theology of Karl Rahner
have undergone some critical reappraisal, often in connection with their
relationship to modernity. With the widespread intuition that society had
moved beyond modernity into a somewhat amorphous consciousness
called "post-modern" came the need to look critically at all things labelled
"modern." On the other hand, there is also a growing concern with a tendency in some quarters to retreat into a kind of naïve pre-modern mindset
that would also call into question the vision of the Council and the theological insights of Karl Rahner. The legacy of Karl Rahner stands between this
Scylla and Charybdis. It seems, then, an appropriate time to re-examine his
theology and to introduce Karl Rahner to students of theology for whom he
has not been a formative influence.

This collection of essays brings together a number of noted Rahner
scholars from Australia, Canada, Europe, and the United States whose contributions reflect the continuing relevance of Rahner and his relationship
both to modernity and to the emerging ethos of post-modernity. The *Companion* touches the major themes of Rahner's writings, offering both an
exposition of the main lines of his thought as well as critical analysis. We
hope that the volume will serve as an introduction and companion to explore

the many dimensions of Rahner's theological thought and that it will be a contribution to the reassessment of the impact and ongoing relevance of Rahner's theological legacy to Church and world.

Karl Rahner was born on March 5, 1904, the middle child of seven, in the city of Freiburg in the Black Forest. By his own account, his childhood was unremarkable for the time. His family was middle class and thoroughly Catholic, though not overly pious. An average student at secondary school, he entered the Jesuit community after graduation, following his brother Hugo. With typical reluctance to discuss personal matters, he claimed not to recall the precise motivations that led him to the Jesuits. His years of Jesuit formation and philosophical and theological study in Austria, Germany, and Holland gave him the threads out of which he would develop his thought – in critical dialogue with the prevailing neo-scholastic theology of the time and the currents of modern German philosophy, but also deeply marked by the Ignatian spirituality into which he was being initiated.

From 1934 to 1936 he pursued graduate studies in philosophy at Freiburg and participated in Martin Heidegger's seminar. In a story that warms, or terrifies, the hearts of many graduate students, Rahner's doctoral thesis in philosophy, which became his foundational philosophical work, *Spirit in the World*, was rejected. His creative rethinking of the metaphysics of knowledge of Thomas Aquinas in relationship to the insights of modern philosophy, particularly Kant and Heidegger, was too much for his thesis director who took a more traditional scholastic approach. Rahner then went to Innsbruck where he completed a dissertation in theology that was accepted for the doctorate. A much less significant work, it was not published until very recently.

Rahner began lecturing at the theological faculty at Innsbruck in 1937 and remained until it was closed by the Nazis in 1939. During the war he did pastoral work, mostly in Vienna, taught theology briefly at Pullach, and returned to Innsbruck when the faculty reopened in 1948. He taught in Munich and Münster, and returned as emeritus to Innsbruck where he died in 1984. On the surface, this appears to be an unexceptional academic and religious life, but during those years he developed an approach to theology that offered both intellectual and spiritual reinvigoration to what had become for many a sterile and lifeless theological landscape.

The prayer quoted above offers a key to understanding the central preoccupation of Karl Rahner's life and work. It is a theme to which he returns in the final essay included in this work, a talk delivered very close to his death – God, the incomprehensible mystery, the horizon of being, who has graciously chosen to draw near to human beings, whose very essence is to be drawn to this horizon as question to answer. For Rahner, to be human is to be in relationship with God. His philosophical work reflects on the conditions for the possibility of this relationship, thus the term "transcendental." His more theological work works out the consequences of this relationship in the concrete circumstances of life. Rahner himself rejected the idea that he was a systematic theologian since he never developed a system. Nor did he articulate a theological method as did his contemporary Bernard Lonergan. Most of the numerous and eclectic theological works that he produced were in response to pressing ecclesial and social questions of the day.

Rahner's early works reveal the style of theologizing that was both to aggravate his critics and win approval from admirers. Rahner is a theologian of continuity, not looking simply to reject the recent past but to show how it could be broken open to reveal other possibilities. In the context of the nineteenth century revival of Thomism, Leo XIII in *Aeterni Patris* (1879) had declared the philosophy and theology of Thomas Aquinas to be the official theology of the Roman Catholic Church. By the beginning of the twentieth century when Rahner was studying theology, the prevalent theological approach in seminary education was what was often called a manualist approach. Students of this neo-scholastic theology studied out of textbooks that most often presented the theology of Thomas Aquinas in a dry, static, and abstract form, quite unrelated to human experience. Neo-scholasticism emphasized obedience to ecclesial authority as the primary responsibility of the Catholic Christian. Throughout his life Rahner reacted strongly against this approach, fearing that post-Enlightenment Catholics would find such an approach to faith alienating and incredible.

As Rahner began his theological career, however, there were already a number of attempts to bring Thomistic theology more into dialogue with the intellectual currents of the modern world. The Belgian Jesuit Joseph Maréchal (1878–1944) and the French Jesuit Pierre Rousselot (1878–1915) were the most influential in Rahner's own interpretation of Thomas. Many of these proponents of a "new theology" were concerned to retrieve the "real" Thomas from the deformations of his neo-scholastic interpreters and to show that there was an experiential awareness in Thomas that opened him to relationship with contemporary philosophical currents, particularly the "turn to the subject" which emphasized the role of human experience.

In neo-scholastic thought, revelation had been understood as purely extrinsic to human experience, primarily known propositionally. In his early works, Rahner is concerned to demonstrate through his transcendental method that revelation, which is in the first place God's own self-communication, is experienced unthematically as the awareness of unlimited being against which we experience all our limited categorial knowing. God is not one object among the many objects of our knowing, but the infinite and mysterious horizon against which we experience all other reality. In his second philosophical work, *Hearer of the Word*, Rahner focuses on the human being as constitutively open to the possibility of hearing God's self-communication. Thus anthropology, or reflection on the experience of being human, is the condition for the possibility of receiving God's revelation. Though no essay in this volume takes Rahner's anthropology as its explicit focus, no area of his theology can be treated without dealing with this distinctive and pervasive starting point of Rahner's theological project.

Although this transcendental method is often cited as the distinctive mark of Rahner's theology, it must be understood in relationship to the nature of the vast number of books and articles that are firmly situated in the categorial, responding to the concrete questions of the distinctive historical and ecclesial period in which he lived.

Particularly from the period just prior to the Second Vatican Council, through the Council where he was appointed as a *peritus*, until his death, Rahner was occupied with the many dimensions of ecclesial Christianity – intra Roman Catholic issues as well as questions concerning the Church's relation to culture and to the many social questions of the mid to late twentieth century. Though the mystery of God is clearly the centre of Rahner's thought, his anthropology understood human being as essentially relational, thus the transcendental necessity of the Church as the concrete locus of the human encounter with God.

After the two major philosophical works, the majority of Rahner's writings are concerned in some way with the Church, whether internally or in relation to culture. His relationship to the Church was complex. His stance was often critical, especially when he saw the church retreating into what he called a "Pian" approach (after the recent popes named Pius, with whom he identifies this approach), his shorthand for the authoritarianism of neo-scholasticism. As the Council receded in memory his vision became darker and his fears increased that there would be a retreat to a pre-Conciliar mentality. He referred to "a wintry season" and to the Church as burden. But it is clear that his critique came from a love for the Church and his conviction that it was the necessary continuation of the definitive mission and ministry of Jesus in the world. Its failings impeded that mission. His friend and sometime critic Johann Baptist Metz once said, "He has this church in his guts, and feels its failures like indigestion."[2]

Rahner's pastoral concern for the Church is demonstrative of a theological influence at least as important, and probably more important, than the theology of Thomas and the influence of German philosophy. Karl Rahner was a Jesuit priest marked deeply by the theology and spirituality of Ignatius of Loyola.

Both his engagement with the concrete questions of the Church and the mystical tendency characteristic of his theology find their roots in Ignatian spirituality. The *Spiritual Exercises* begin with the subjectivity of the human person and it can be argued that this theological insight is at least as important to Rahner's starting point as is the influence of the German philosophers.

Rahner's essay on Ignatius of Loyola[3] in which he has Ignatius speak to contemporary Jesuits is revelatory of the debt he acknowledges to Ignatius. The mystical dimension that he identifies in Ignatius presumably underlies his own spirituality. Although, as we mentioned, the Church occupies a great deal of Rahner's attention, it is not for him by any means the primary datum of faith. For him always, the center is God who enters into relationship with humans through God's own self-communication, which is his primary understanding of grace, "uncreated grace." He chides Jesuits of the past for understanding grace as something foreign to human experience and known only through an extrinsic understanding of revelation. For him, contrary to the neo-scholastic understanding of the time, grace can be experienced. He has Ignatius say, "All I say is I knew God, nameless and unfathomable, silent and yet near, bestowing himself on me in his Trinity. I knew God beyond all concrete imaginings."[4] Here again is the core of Rahner's theology. This obviously leaves him open to the critique that in the last analysis the concrete or categorial is quite secondary to him. By his own admission Rahner is not a theologian in which all the threads can be neatly tied together. In spite of this seeming relativization of the categorial he paid enormous attention to the nitty-gritty concerns of life as an ecclesial Christian. A number of the authors in the *Companion* engage this debate as to whether Rahner is primarily a theologian of the transcendental for whom the categorial is radically secondary, but it must be said that in offering his transcendental analysis he always posits the categorial. His work in Christology is illustrative of his own understanding of this approach.

In his treatment of this most explicitly Christian issue in *Foundations of Christian Faith* he says that "the two moments in Christian theology reach their closest unity and their most radical tension,"[5] i.e., the transcendental theology that develops an a priori doctrine of the God-man and the historical testimony about what happened in Jesus. But the historical and actual encounter with the God-man must come first. "At this point what is most historical is what is most essential."[6] This conviction becomes even more explicit in his later work. It is important to note here the development in Rahner's own thought. Commentators and critics often identify Rahner almost exclusively with the preoccupations and approaches of his early works, but there are important shifts that take place particularly in the years following Vatican II.

Although Rahner did historical work right from the beginning – his work on the history of spirituality and on the history of the sacrament of penance, for example – his attention to history becomes much more pronounced in the later works, perhaps in response to the critic he took most seriously, his friend and student, Johann Baptist Metz. As we have noted this development is perhaps most clear in his Christology. The early christological work such as "Current Problems in Christology"[7] begins "from above" with the christological doctrines. *Foundations* attests that "the basic and decisive point of departure, of course, lies in an encounter with the historical Jesus of Nazareth, and hence in an 'ascending Christology,'" though this affirmation is not extensively developed. The essay "The Two Basic Types of Christology"[8] brings the two approaches into dialogue and suggests that for the future a pluralism in approaches to Christology is to be expected and valued.

Parts I and II of this volume focus on significant and well-developed areas of Rahner's thought, a number of which have already been touched on. Part I deals with the spiritual, philosophical, and theological roots of Rahner's theology. Harvey Egan develops the centrality of Rahner's work on spirituality; Thomas Sheehan examines the philosophical underpinnings of Rahner's transcendental project, while Stephen Duffy deals with the radical reorienting of the understanding of grace that is so emblematic of Rahner's approach. Major theological themes are then treated in Part II. Francis Schüssler Fiorenza takes an innovative approach to Rahner's theological method and proposes that the occasional nature of Rahner's writings suggests that he is not a foundationalist but primarily a practical theologian. Daniel Donovan offers a clear exposition of his understanding of revelation and its correlative, faith. David Coffey focuses on Rahner's contribution to the renewal of trinitarian theology and Roman Siebenrock traces the chronological and theological developments in Rahner's Christology. Richard Lennan offers an analysis of Rahner's work on ecclesiology and ecumenism, while Jerry Farmer deals with the related issues of ministry and worship.

Ethics and eschatology remain to be mentioned. Rahner's ethical thought comes from his deep conviction about the unity of the love of God and love of neighbour, another key instance of his conviction of the relationship between the transcendental and the categorial. Not known primarily as an ethicist, Rahner worked with the category of "fundamental option" to offer a context for understanding moral decision making in light of one's whole disposition before God. Brian Linnane takes up the area of ethics and its relation to Christian witness.

Eschatology for Rahner was an integral part of theology. It is one of the most intriguing areas of his thought where he deals with the possibility of universal salvation, or *apokatastasis*, questions of individual and community, and the relation between the material and the spiritual. As he approached death himself, Rahner became more preoccupied with issues of how one lives into one's own death. Peter C. Phan probes this significant dimension of Rahner's thought for both its present significance and its future possibilities.

Having evoked the context, influences, and some central and well-developed themes of Rahner's theological journey, it is important to note some of the many other topics that engaged his attention through his long career. They provide an insight into the journey of the Roman Catholic Church as well as into the changing social landscape of his time. Rahner wrote on Mary, where his work also shows considerable development from the early approach of opening up the dogmas of the Immaculate Conception and the Assumption to later work that recognizes the ambiguities in the Mary tradition and a need for reconceiving the place of Marian devotion in light of the hierarchy of truths and the changed situation of contemporary women. In the context of this changed social and cultural situation Rahner also explored the role of women in ministry. He evaluated the 1976 "Declaration on the Question of the Admission of Women to the Ministerial Priesthood" as authentic but reformable teaching and encouraged further discussion of the issue.[9] Perhaps Rahner's long friendship with the German author Luise Rinser was an influence on his sympathetic attention to women's roles in Church and society. His reticence about his personal life leaves the possible influence of Luise Rinser on his theological work largely to conjecture.[10]

Rahner also wrote on the theology of revolution, on the dialogue with Islam, on religious pluralism, on atheism, on the natural sciences and their relation to faith, and on theology and popular religion. Part III of the volume takes up some of these topics of Rahner's later life which show the development in his own work and perhaps provide a bridge to today's concerns. These chapters also introduce in a more focused way some contemporary areas of critique as well as acknowledging indebtedness to Rahner's theological project as foundational to today's theological preoccupations.

Liberation and political theologies as well as feminist theologies often acknowledge Rahner for his recognition of the important role of experience as a starting point in theology. In turn they critique him for his lack of attention to specific, historical experience, the experience of the poor and marginalized, including the experience of women. Although more complex, this describes Metz's critique – a critique Rahner accepted. Although Rahner's theology did not make this move, he recognized that this was a legitimate direction for its development. Gaspar Martinez and Nancy Dallavalle explore the relationship between Rahner and liberation, political, and feminist theologies.

Rahner wrote on ecumenism, but there has been little attention to his reception in Protestant theology. Nicholas Adams offers a realistic assessment of the impact of Rahner in Protestant circles, focusing especially on the critique of George Lindbeck.

Theological aesthetics is also an area of contemporary interest where Rahner's views have been little noted. Gesa Thiessen draws attention to the importance of artistic image and poetic word as sources of Rahner's theological imagination.

One of the most widely controverted areas of Rahner's theology was his use of the phrase "anonymous Christian" to express his conviction that all human beings are touched by the grace of Jesus Christ and therefore drawn into the salvific embrace of God. Jeannine Hill Fletcher situates that discussion within the context of the prevalent exclusivist understandings to which Rahner was responding and contemporary theologies of religious pluralism. Does Rahner's inclusivist position, infelicitous as its language may have been, remain a viable theological option for understanding religious diversity?

CRITIQUES

Karl Rahner had his critics, both during his lifetime and now in a changed philosophical and ecclesial world. During his lifetime, Hans Küng, Hans Urs von Balthasar, and Johann Baptist Metz raised critiques from significantly different perspectives. Hans Küng was impatient with Rahner's insistence on showing the continuity of his approaches with the tradition rightly understood. Was a linear, positive, unfolding of the tradition inevitable? Could not the Church ever just admit mistakes?

Von Balthasar questioned Rahner's whole anthropological starting place, finding his theology too human-centered. Along with other critics from the right, he questions whether Rahner has evacuated Christianity of its categorial content in favour of a relationship with God not essentially mediated by the concrete content of faith. Metz, for his part, was concerned with an individualism or privatism which seemed to render the social and historical dimensions of Christianity quite irrelevant. In the light of Rahner's hopeful expectation of salvation the suffering, the unexpected reversals, and the interruptions of life could be overlooked.

In the context of post-modernity questions are raised about the ongoing relevance of a theology so rooted in notions of permanent truth and an anthropology presupposing a modern understanding of the self. Michael Purcell addresses the challenges of post-modernity to a theology seemingly so rooted in the ethos of modernity.

READING RAHNER

Although often considered difficult to read – and he can be – Rahner's major themes recur throughout both his academic and more popular writings. It is sometimes better to approach him first through the more popular works where the pastoral concern and mystagogical sensibility that mark all his work is unmistakable. Works such as *Encounters with Silence, The Shape of the Church to Come, Everyday Faith, Karl Rahner in Dialogue,* and *Christian at the Crossroads,* to name just a few, are excellent ways to encounter Rahner's major themes in accessible language. They reveal the deep pastoral intent of Rahner who famously said that all (real) theology is pastoral theology. Rahner had no patience with abstract theological speculation for its own sake. A brief bibliographical guide for students approaching Rahner for the first time is found at the end of the volume and a brief glossary of commonly used terms will also help first-time readers.

RAHNER'S SIGNIFICANCE FOR CONTEMPORARY THEOLOGY

Rahner started out in a theological climate that was dramatically different from today. He was dealing with a monolithic theological and philosophical system that placed obedience to external authority at its center. Philosophy was the privileged partner and interpretative companion to theology. Today radical pluralism is the situation. Along with philosophy, the social sciences, and increasingly the empirical sciences, are being brought into the dialogue searching for meaningful interpretations of humanity, God, and the cosmos. If post-modern thinkers question Rahner's understanding of truth and his understanding of the self, there exists an equally strong tendency today to return to a pre-Conciliar mentality, to an authoritarian approach to faith, to the kind of neo-scholasticism that was Rahner's nemesis. Fundamentalisms of many kinds abound and not just outside Christianity. In the light of this complex reality, Johann Baptist Metz suggests that Rahner is the ideal theologian for this post-modern period. Rahner, in Metz's view, should not be simply identified with the ethos of modernity since his work critiques problematic aspects of modernity, as well as of pre-modernity and post-modernity. "Rahner's life work has succeeded in bringing together what has long been separated, indeed set at variance: his work has brought to an end the schism between theology and life history; it has related doctrine and life, the mystical and the everyday, in the context of the irreducible complexity and anonymity of our postmodern situation."[11] For Metz, Rahner's insights, though not the last word, remain valuable in today's complex world.

The authors you encounter in this *Companion* represent a variety of perspectives on the legacy of Karl Rahner. We have not attempted to harmonize them. Their perspectives may be influenced by the philosophical and ecclesial concerns of the author's own cultures and contexts. Whether their primary concern is a retreat into pre-modernity, or a concern that a theology so grounded in Rahner's philosophical positions can in fact speak to the issues of post-modernity, they agree that Roman Catholic theology has been profoundly touched and changed by the theology of Karl Rahner. To encounter Rahner is to encounter the variety of interpretations of his thought as well as the personal, spiritual, and theological impact that he has had on generations of scholars and believers.

Notes

1 K. Rahner, *Prayers for a Lifetime* (New York: Crossroad, 1984), 3.
2 H. Vorgrimler, *Understanding Karl Rahner*, trans. J. Bowden (New York: Crossroad, 1986), 37.
3 K. Rahner and P. Imhof, *Ignatius of Loyola*, trans. R. Ockenden (New York: Collins, 1979).
4 Ibid., 11.
5 *FCF*, 176.
6 Ibid., 177.
7 "Current Problems in Christology," *TI* I, trans. C. Ernst (London: Darton, Longman & Todd, 1961), 149–200.
8 *TI* xiii, trans. D. Bourke (London: Darton, Longman & Todd, 1975), 213–23. See also K. Rahner and W. Thüsing, *A New Christology*, trans. D. Smith and V. Green (New York: Seabury, 1980).
9 "Women and the Priesthood," *TI* xx, trans. E. Quinn (London: Darton, Longman & Todd, 1981), 35–47. See also chapters 9 and 17 of this volume.
10 See L. Rinser, *Saturn auf der Sonne* (Frankfurt: S. Fischer, 1994), 208–38.
11 J. B. Metz, *A Passion for God*, trans. J. M. Ashley (New York: Paulist, 1998), 103.

Part I

Spiritual, Philosophical, and Theological Roots

1 Theology and spirituality

HARVEY D. EGAN

Karl Rahner has been rightly praised as the twentieth century "Father" of Roman Catholic theology and as "the quiet mover of the Catholic Church." His four thousand written works show his profundity as a philosopher and as a multi-faceted theological genius. They also indicate his talent as a preacher, a retreat director, and a teacher of prayer. A great ecumenist, he entered into dialogue with atheist, Buddhist, Jewish, Marxist, Muslim, Protestant, and scientific thinkers the world over.

Although this Catholic titan defies easy classification, many of Rahner's earliest commentators wrote almost exclusively about his philosophical-theological-speculative prowess. More recent studies have corrected this imbalance by accenting the spiritual dimension of even his most difficult writings, particularly as this relates to his own Jesuit and priestly life. However, this chapter will attempt to make evident the indissoluble marriage of theology and spirituality which runs throughout almost all the Rahnerian enterprise.

A SAPIENTIAL THEOLOGIAN

When praised by an interviewer for his numerous publications, Rahner replied: "I always stressed that in point of fact by profession I never claimed to be a scientific researcher either in philosophy or in theology. I never practised theology as a sort of art for art's sake. I think I can say that my publications usually grew out of pastoral concern. But in comparison to professional scholars I have remained a theological dilettante."[1] Thus, he spoke of himself only as a man, a Christian, and a priest – not as an academic scholar. When asked a few years before his death about his theology, he reiterated that his theological norm centered on pastoral problems relating to the proclamation of the gospel in ways the contemporary person can understand.

Some Rahnerian commentators contend that Rahner's profound pastoral theology flowed from his speculative genius. The medieval theological giants, to him, never viewed pastoral and spiritual theology as extrinsic additions to systematic theology but rather as aspects of the one unified theological activity from which systematic theology arises.

True, but I think a better description of Rahner's work is found in his description of Thomas Aquinas' theology. He wrote:

> Thomas's theology is his spiritual life and his spiritual life is his theology. With him we do not yet find the horrible difference between theology and spiritual life which is often found in later theology. He thinks theologically because he needs it in his spiritual life as its most essential condition, and he thinks theologically in such a way that it can become really important for life in the concrete.[2]

In other words, Rahner resolutely refused to divorce theology and spirituality into separate disciplines because of his conviction that one cannot exist without the other. Johann B. Metz states correctly that Rahner's theology is a "type of existential biography . . . a mystical biography of religious experience, of the history of a life before the veiled face of God, in the doxology of faith."[3]

Thomas Aquinas also impressed Rahner because the saint theologized on the basis of the totality of the faith and always in relationship to it. The same can be said of Rahner's architectonic grasp of Christianity and his ability to theologize in terms of Christianity's whole. His theology attempted to explicate Christianity's many truths in terms of the *one* truth, that is, God's incomprehensibility. Theology, for Rahner, must always be *salvific*, that is, focused on God's forgiving, healing, and transforming love as revealed in the long history of salvation which reached its high point in the life, death, and resurrection of Jesus Christ.

Simply stated, Christianity to Rahner is nothing more than the genuine explication and true interpretation of what resides in the ultimate depths of the human person. In essence, because Christianity is the best interpretation of what and who we are, Rahner grounded his theology in God's unending self-revelation in human *experience* as manifested in the life, death, and resurrection of Jesus Christ.

This accounts for what I would call the *sapiential* quality of Rahner's theology. By this, I mean a penetrating intellectual enterprise never removed from his spirituality, the Church's living faith, and the actual questions rooted in the hearts of those he encountered. His appeal rests not only in his skill to explain critically and precisely what the Christian faith is – coupled with giving cogent reasons for believing it – but also in his ability to offer his readers experiential union with this faith by leading them into their own deepest mystery as graced human beings.

While Rahner's theology often began and ended in prayer, he considered strenuous thinking itself as a form of prayer and spirituality. He constantly urged every priest and preacher to reflect as deeply as possible upon the preached contents of the faith. On the other hand, he never accepted the so-called "kerygmatic theology" (theology of preaching) proposed at Innsbruck and defended by his own brother, Hugo. The most "scientific" theology, to him, produced – in the long run – the most profound kerygmatic theology. In fact, one finds theology of the strictest kind both in his so-called devotional writings and in the essays in spiritual theology scattered throughout his dense *Theological Investigations*. Even his monumental *Foundations of Christian Faith* illustrates his unscientific, "first level," attempt to express the whole of Christianity and to give an honest account of it. Thus, rigorous theological reflection and Christian edification are always intrinsically linked in Rahner. For these reasons, I deem Rahner to be not an academic theologian but a sapiential or mystagogical theologian who leads us into our own deepest mystery.

INFLUENCES ON RAHNER'S SAPIENTIAL THEOLOGY

Past commentators correctly stressed the intellectual influence of Thomas Aquinas, of the great German modern philosophers (especially Kant and Hegel), Heidegger, and of Catholic manual philosophy and theology upon Rahner's thought. Rahner also studied deeply two Thomists of his era: the French Jesuit Pierre Rousselot (1878–1915) and the Belgian Jesuit Joseph Maréchal (1878–1944) who profoundly influenced the way Rahner was later to interpret St. Thomas Aquinas. In fact, Rahner attributed to Maréchal – whose contribution to the Aquinas–Kant dialogue remains unsurpassed – his first truly philosophical insight. However, many Rahnerian commentators overlook Maréchal's great interest in mysticism and mystical experience, especially how the contemporary person could experience God – a topic so dear to Rahner. As he said, "there is an *experience* of grace, and this is the real, fundamental reality of Christianity itself."[4]

Rahner stated emphatically that even during his early Jesuit training he was interested in serious theological questions in patristic mysticism, in the history of mystical piety, and especially in Bonaventure. His first serious publications – detailed studies of the asceticism and mysticism in the Church

Fathers and of notion of the "spiritual senses" in Origen and Bonaventure – bear special witness to his great interest in intense experiences of God found in the Christian spiritual-mystical tradition. Of special importance in this regard was the collaboration with his brother Hugo both on patristics and on the spirituality of St. Ignatius of Loyola – the latter indelibly influencing Rahner's theology of the experience of grace, as well as other themes. One also finds in Rahner's reflections on the mysticism of both Thomas Aquinas and Teresa of Avila further elaborations of his conviction that the experience of grace is at the heart of all human existence. This abiding interest singles out Rahner as one of the few twentieth century theologians to take seriously the mystics and their writings as theological sources.

THE FOUNDATIONS OF RAHNER'S SAPIENTIAL THEOLOGY

When asked to give the briefest possible summary of Rahner's theological enterprise, I unhesitatingly reply: his creative appropriation of Scotus' view that God creates in order to communicate *self* and that creation exists in order to be the recipient of God's free gift of self. Given sin, God's self-communication forgives, heals, and transforms the world through and into his very own life.

Rahner's understanding of the terms "supernatural existential" and its correlative, the "obediential potency," provides yet another summary. The former term refers to Rahner's emphasis upon grace as God's very own self-communication to *every* person; the latter, as the human person's natural ability to receive God's self-offer. Given the reciprocal relationship between grace and the human person, Rahner's theology is essentially anthropology; his anthropology, theocentric. Therefore, any Christian truth is simultaneously a truth of both human consciousness and experience. To my mind, Rahner's bold view that the human person somehow consciously and directly experiences this divine–human correlation provides the reason for his unusual creativity and appeal.

Despite the complete gratuity of God's self-communication, Rahner considers it to be a human "existential," that is, an aspect of the human being constituting the human person as the *event* of God's free and forgiving self-communication. To Rahner, therefore, there is no such thing as the "natural" person, because *everyone* (not merely Christians) is graced with the offer of God's self-communication even prior to any human response. This means that there was never a time or a place in which God did not offer himself to all persons. Hence, everyone must say yes or no to God's self-offer freely, with one's entire being.

Whether we are explicitly conscious of it, whether we open ourselves to it, our whole being is directed toward a holy, loving Mystery who is the basis of our existence. Even prior to baptism, either by water or by desire, *every* person is already objectively redeemed and obliged to live for his or her supernatural destiny. The supernatural existential also means that every person's consciousness is graced, which is Rahner's primary understanding of "revelation." All persons experience God, albeit often only in a hidden way. Moreover, the free, conscious, and self-conscious person experiences God constantly, not sporadically. The thrust of much of Rahner's theology aims at making intelligible this genuine experience of God – which often remains only implicit, not reflected on, and not verbalized – that is rooted in the depths of every person.

To dwell in God's incomprehensible nearness and to be so loved by God Rahner experienced as both awesome and comforting. For him, however, that God is in fact with us, we have no choice. One may be able freely to say no to God with one's entire being, but one can never separate oneself from God's self-communication. This provides the context for understanding what Rahner said, namely, that "the devout Christian of the future will either be a 'mystic,' one who has experienced 'something' [that is, God], or he will cease to be anything at all."[5]

The experience of grace – that is, God's self-communication at the heart of human existence – summarizes Rahner's entire theological enterprise. What he says about St. Ignatius must also be said of him. Both attempted to translate their "mystical" experience of God so that others might share in this grace. Rahner's sapiential theology awakens and deepens the basic experience of the triune God that haunts every person's core. Rahner is the preeminent theologian of experienced grace.

As mentioned above, the correlative to the supernatural existential is the obediential potency. Rahner understands human nature as essentially open to God's free and unmerited self-communication because the human spirit is open to all being. In fact, "human nature," to Rahner, "is an obediential potency for the radical self expression of God, which is actualised in Jesus Christ."[6] For Rahner, human nature is nothing less than the ability to be God in the world! Furthermore, if the person is really this ability and is truly the one addressed by God's self-communication, then he or she must be at least implicitly conscious of it.

Because the human person is spirit-in-world, whatever is known or loved as finite and particular ("categorical") is known and loved against the "horizon" of holy mystery, like white chalk marks against a blackboard. Moreover, in knowing or loving anything finite, the person simultaneously also implicitly knows or loves God. The "transcendental" movement of spirit, reaching beyond anything particular to an infinite horizon within which all finite realities are known, constitutes the conscious tension we are and live. We can know and love the finite only because we can know and love the infinite, and vice versa. Rahner understands this tension experienced between the finite and the infinite – which we are and live – as analogy. He wrote:

> We ourselves . . . exist analogously in and through our being grounded in this holy mystery which surpasses us. But it always constitutes us by surpassing us and by pointing us towards the concrete, individual, categorical realities which confront us within the realm of our experience. Conversely, then, these realities are the mediation of and the point of departure for our knowledge of God.[7]

That the human person as spirit-in-world *is* analogy enables the theologian to affirm, for example, that God is good in a way that any finite reality is good, and not only good in the way any finite reality is good, but supereminently good.

I maintain that this understanding of analogy which we both are and experience grounds Rahner's sapiential theology. This is also why penetrating theological thought and living spirituality remain inextricably linked in his theology. Moreover, the tendency to view analogy solely as a logical principle rather than as a principle the person is and lives accounts for the dead ends found in much of contemporary theology.

THE EXPERIENCE OF GOD AND RAHNER'S SAPIENTIAL THEOLOGY

Rahner maintains that our deepest, primordial experience is at one and the same time of a God who remains Mystery, of the Word that illuminates our spirits, and of the Love that embraces us. This is not a particular, or "categorical," experience to which we can point. As the "horizon" in which all our experiences take place, it is beyond all particular experiences.

One should not even call it *an* experience because it is "transcendental" experience, the ground of all experiences. It is the atmosphere in which we live, our basal spiritual metabolism, "more intimate to us than we are to ourselves," as the mystics were fond of saying. Just as we take our breathing, our beating hearts, or our own self-awareness for granted, so too might the ever-present experience of God remain overlooked, repressed, or even denied. In our daily lives we often overlook or take for granted the divine life we in fact dwell within and experience.

Through God's self-communication, we actually experience God-above-us (Mystery), God-with-us (enfleshed Word), and God-in-us (Holy Spirit). The call of Mystery explains why our questions never cease, why we eventually must ask ultimate questions, and why we are never satisfied totally with anything in this life. Because we are historical persons, we search incessantly for that one person or thing that will fulfil us perfectly – whom Rahner termed the "absolute saviour." The attraction of the Holy Spirit explains why our immense longing often draws us into the deepest levels of our being. Thus, we are essentially *ec*static beings drawn to God's mystery, worldly and historical beings attracted to an absolute saviour, and *en*static beings drawn to our deepest interior by the fontal fullness of the Spirit of Love.

Because of the immediate unthematic experience of God found within the unlimited breadth of our consciousness, Rahner maintained that Christianity contains a mystical component. In fact, he called experience of grace "mystical" and maintained that it grounded not only the ordinary Christian's life of faith, hope, and love but also that of anyone living according to his or her conscience. However, given the infelicitous connotations often associated with the word "mysticism," Rahner suggested that one might wish to avoid the term. Not only did he find it unimportant to designate as "mystical" the experience of God at the person's core, but he also often used the term pejoratively to designate ways of salvation which attempt to bypass the human, the historical, and the incarnate Word.

On the other hand, Rahner did identify the primordial experience of God in every human life with the mystical. From a Rahnerian perspective, the human person is *homo mysticus*, mystical man. All personal experiences contain at least an implicit, yet primordial, experience of God which tends toward an amplification directed toward something which one can call mystical. Thus, each and every human being's experience of the immense longing for complete happiness contains within itself the seeds of mysticism. Strictly speaking, therefore, everyone is at least a sleeping, distracted, or repressed mystic. To deny this experience with one's entire being – not simply with words – is to deny one's deepest self. It is damnation.

Since all genuine faith, hope, and love contain a primordial experience of God, Rahner speaks of the mysticism of everyday life. Paradoxically, this mysticism appears in the greyness and banality of daily life, in contrast to the psychologically dramatic way the mysticism of the great saints is manifested. "If, however, there is such a thing as eternal life at all," Rahner wrote,

> if it is not merely something different added to our temporal life and likewise stretching out over time, if it is truly the finality of this present life of freedom which fittingly comes to a final and definitive consummation, only then can we see the unfathomable depths and richness of our existence, of that existence which often gives the impression of consisting of nothing but banalities.[8]

To Rahner, we weave the fabric of our eternal lives out of our humdrum daily lives. A genuine Christian must have the bold, but often hidden, confidence that ordinary daily life is the stuff of authentic life and real Christianity. It is instructive to note how often the words "ordinary," "banal," "humdrum," "routine," and the like show up in Rahner's writings. For him, grace is actually experienced and has its history in the person's everyday existence.[9]

To help us root out real experiences of grace from our often banal everyday lives, Rahner offered many examples. For example, accepting with hope the experience of utter loneliness; forgiving with no expectation of the other's gratitude or even of feeling good about one's selflessness; being utterly faithful to the depths of one's conscience, even when taken as a fool; praying, even when it feels useless; maintaining faith, hope, and love – even when there are no apparent reasons for so acting; experiencing bitterly the great gulf between what we desire from life and what life actually gives us; silently hoping in the face of death; in short, courageously and totally accepting life and oneself even when everything that props up our life fails – these are ultimately experiences of the Spirit.

To Rahner, God is experienced most clearly and most intensely in our ordinary and banal everyday existence, especially when the props to our lives fall apart. God's presence becomes transparent, therefore, when the comforting lights which illuminate the tiny islands of security of our everyday life are extinguished. Rahner prefers death experiences to joyful ones because "wherever space is really left by parting, by death, by renunciation, by apparent emptiness, provided the emptiness that cannot remain such is not filled by the world, or activity, or chatter, or the deadly grief of the world – there God is."[10]

However, after listing experiences which only in their *ultimate* depths *may* be experiences of the Spirit, Rahner says: "One could go on and on like this forever, perhaps *without* coming to that experience which for this or that man is the experience of the Spirit, freedom, and grace in his life. For *every* man has that experience in accordance with the particular historical and individual situation of his specific life."[11] To my mind, Rahner is saying that one should examine one's daily life for the significant "signals of transcendence" in and through which one is summoned to appropriate a grace *already* given, a grace beyond anything particular, a grace which is really the divine ambience in which all particular experiences take place. What really matters are the experiences which awaken the person to respond freely to God's ever-present offer of self.

This interest in the experience of God permits us to understand Rahner's wish to "hear the views of the person who himself experiences most clearly and with the least distortion the relationship which exists between the human subject and the reality we call God."[12] Rahner thus looks to the experiences of God found in the Christian mystical tradition because of their special clarity, intensity, and ability to explain the *conscious* – albeit often only vague and implicit – relationship everyone has with God.

He urged that the writings of the classical mystics be transposed for contemporary use. "And such a transposition," Rahner notes, "could be fruitful, because the depth and radical nature of the experience of God which the classical authors describe are not so commonplace that we could discover in ourselves the buds and traces of this experience of God just as easily without their help as with it."[13] This transposition would also aid a sapiential theology directed to making intelligible the personal experience of God. Moreover, a theology and mystagogy drawn from the experiences of the great Christian mystics would help Christians in their dialogue with Eastern religions. Thus, one can understand why Rahner found the contemporary theological lack of interest in mystical questions so disappointing.

SALVATION HISTORY AND RAHNER'S SAPIENTIAL THEOLOGY

Rahner's creative emphasis upon salvation history and the human person's historical nature leads him to develop his sapiential theology in yet another direction. Rahner considered the mysteries of salvation history to be the keys that unlock the various levels of the one mystery of the human person. The great questions that the human person is, lives, and asks – Where did we come from? Where are we going? What is the meaning of life? Who am I? Who are we?, and so on – are answered only when the person turns to the truths of salvation history. In short, the human person resonates experientially with the truths of the faith.

In other words, Rahner sought to disclose the anthropocentric dimension of salvation history. As he wrote, "with reference to all statements of faith and theology . . . the question must be asked how and why man, in virtue of his own [graced] nature, . . . is the one with whom these statements can and must actually be concerned."[14]

Therefore, Rahner's theology sought to explain why the person, by intrinsic necessity, must turn to the mysteries of salvation history to discover who and what he or she is. Because this history intends nothing less than the forgiving, healing, and transforming perfection of the entire human person, he or she resonates experientially with it. His sapiential theology transformed a medieval theological method which sought the "necessary reasons" for the truths of salvation history – reasons, which, for Rahner, must always be intrinsic to the human being. It also skillfully employed St. Ignatius' instructions not only to contemplate the great Christian mysteries but also to ask why and how they relate to oneself. Rahner reflected consistently upon the existential dimension of historical facts, that is, how they both affect and effect our salvation.

Rahner's "searching Christology" provides one of the most salient examples of his sapiential theology. To him, the history of revelation and salvation is co-extensive with the whole of world history. Thus, revelation and salvation can and do occur not only in the religious but also in all dimensions of human existence. The Holy Spirit – always Christ's Spirit, given prior to but only in view of him – always and everywhere directs the history of revelation and salvation to its tangible, victorious, irreversible goal: the God-Man.

Rahner maintained that all grace is the grace of God and of Jesus Christ. "It is in everything," he writes, "as the secret essence of all eligible reality. [Therefore], it is not so easy to grasp at anything, without having to do with God and Christ – one way or another."[15] Moreover, Jesus Christ is present in all justifying faith because such faith always has a christological character. Rahner underscored that Christ *is* the meaning of life, the "absolute saviour," and that his humanity always was, is, and will be "the *permanent openness* of our finite being to the living God of infinite, eternal life."[16]

Rahner developed his incarnational theology in yet another way. The human person, he maintained, does not accomplish true self-emptying by techniques aimed at pure interiority but only by true Christian activity, such as dying to self through humble service to one's neighbour.

Despite Rahner's emphasis on Jesus' humanity, he never reduces Jesus to a prophet or religious reformer. "Jesus in his human lot," Rahner writes, "is *the* (not *an*!) address of God to humanity, and as such eschatologically unsurpassable."[17] Only Jesus' reality *is* God's reality in the world, God's enfleshed and ultimate Word to us.

Everywhere and always people have expected, hoped for, and searched for God's answer to the one, total question the human person is. Thus, this searching Christology is often objectified in saviour myths or projected onto historical figures who are considered savours either in a provisional or in a definitive sense. For Rahner, however, one finds only in Jesus Christ God's very own self-communication and its perfect acceptance made one by God. Jesus' human reality *is God's* self-emptying, self-expressing Word in the world. From the very moment of his existence, Jesus in his human reality is God's *kenosis* – and he now exists eternally as such.

In what may be one of the most profound statements of Rahner's high Christology, we find:

> [T]he man Jesus . . . is someone who continually accepts himself from the Father and who in all the dimensions of his existence has always given himself over to the Father totally; in this surrender he is able to accomplish through God's grace what we are not able to accomplish; he is someone whose "basic constitution" as the original unity of being and consciousness is to have his origins in God radically and completely, and to be given over to God radically and completely.[18]

It is because God has accepted our humanity in Christ that even non-Christians who accept fully their human mystery accept Christ. "Anyone," Rahner writes, "who accepts his own humanity in full – and how immeasurably hard that is, how doubtful whether we really do it! – has accepted the Son of Man, because God has accepted man in him."[19]

Insofar as every person hopes for total and absolute fulfillment – despite the futility, sin, and death which fill every human life – every person is and lives a searching Christology. In Christ, death becomes something absolutely different. What was the manifestation of sin becomes – without the darkness of total failure and death being eliminated – the revelation of his total assent to the Father's will and to the human condition – which is the negation of sin.

By its very nature as total, loving surrender, Jesus' death is subsumed into resurrection. Jesus dies into resurrection through the Father's acceptance and validation of his person and his actual history before and with

God. A searching Christology finds in the Risen Christ that for which it has always hoped, the permanent validity and confirmation of one's historical existence.

Christian faith remains inextricably linked to Jesus' *historical* existence. "When we turn to the exalted Lord in faith, in hope and in love," Rahner says,

> we find none other than the crucified Jesus, in whose *death* his whole earthly life is of course integrated . . . The risen Lord is the One who was crucified . . . We must not render trivial the identity between the earthly Jesus and the exalted Lord . . . His eternal life is rather the ultimate form of his earthly life itself . . . His life in eternity is the ultimate form of his history.[20]

Thus, Christian devotion must avoid praying to the glorious Lord in a way that dissolves his genuine earthly history. It must also avoid turning backwards in imagination to Jesus' past history to pray to him "as if" he were present as the unborn baby, infant, child, young adult, and so on. We can and must pray to the Jesus of the entire liturgical year because all the mysteries of his life and death retain their eternal reality and validity in the Risen Lord. The Risen Lord *is* the crucified One, the One who suffered, ate the Last Supper with his disciples, performed miracles, lived a hidden life, was a child, an infant, and an unborn baby. Moreover, as we contemplate the mysteries of Christ's life, death, and resurrection, they lead us into our own deepest mystery.

LITURGY OF THE WORLD AND RAHNER'S SAPIENTIAL THEOLOGY

One finds another striking example of Rahner's sapiential theology in his understanding of the Church's Eucharist. He noted that the world and its history

> are the terrible and sublime liturgy, breathing of death and sacrifice, which God celebrates and permits to be celebrated in the free history of humanity, this history which he in turn sustains in grace through his sovereign disposition. In the entire length and breadth of this immense history of birth and death, replete with crucifying superficiality, folly, inadequacy and hatred, on the one hand, and with silent submission, responsibility unto death – in dying and in joyfulness, in successes and failures, on the other hand, is the true

liturgy of the world present. It is present in such a way that the liturgy which the Son brought to its absolute fulfilment on the cross belongs intrinsically to it, emerges from it, that is, from the ultimate source of the world's grace . . .[21]

Christians, therefore, should not understand the Eucharist as a sacred ghetto in the midst of a profane, pagan world. For Rahner,

> The Mass should be understood as the explicit coming-to-awareness of this tremendous drama, full of guilt and grace, that unfolds in the whole of world history . . . in our times, and in our life. It assumes a meaning . . . in that act in which Jesus, in the incomprehensibility of his death, surrendered in total confidence to the mystery of forgiving love, to the mystery we call God.[22]

In short, there is this experiential correlation between what is happening in the world, in us, and on the cross.

CONCLUSION

When asked on his eightieth birthday what he wished to bequeath as his last will and testament, Rahner pointed unhesitatingly to the essay "Ignatius of Loyola Speaks to a Modern Jesuit."[23] In this spiritual gem, Rahner put himself in Ignatius' place to speak to contemporary Jesuits. Not only did he call this masterpiece his last will and testament, but he also considered it a résumé of his theology in general and of how he tried to live it. He wrote:

> You know that I wanted "to help souls" . . . therefore to say something about God, his grace, and about Jesus Christ, the crucified and risen one, so that their freedom would be redeemed in God's freedom . . . I [am] convinced that . . . I experienced God directly and I wish to communicate this experience to others, as well as I can . . . I mean only that I experienced God, the ineffable and unfathomable one, the silent yet near one, in his trinitarian bestowal upon me. I experienced God also and especially beyond all images – who when he thus approaches in his grace cannot be confused in any way with anything else . . . I have experienced God himself, not human words about him . . . This experience is truly grace, but for that reason it is nonetheless essentially refused to no one . . . One thing remains certain: a person can experience God's very own self . . .
>
> But now I must speak about Jesus. Did what I say before sound as if I had forgotten Jesus and his blessed Name? I have not forgotten

him. He was intimately present in everything I said before, even if the words I addressed to you . . . could not say everything at once. I say *Jesus* . . .

I never had a problem – or at most the one of loving and being a true disciple – finding in a unique way God in Jesus and Jesus in God. And I mean Jesus as he really and truly is in flesh and blood, such that love alone – not hair-splitting reason – can say in what way he should be imitated if one is his disciple. It is from being able to narrate Jesus' story that one has then narrated the history of the eternal, incomprehensible God, without dissolving this history into theory . . .

Since my conversion I knew Jesus to be God's unconditional loving condescension to the world and to me, the love in which the incomprehensibility of pure mystery is totally present and through which a person attains his or her perfection. Jesus' singularity, the necessity of seeking him in a limited treasury of events and words with the intention of finding in this limited reality the infinite and ineffable mystery – this never bothered me . . .

There is no Christianity which can bypass Jesus to find the incomprehensible God. God has willed that legions find Him because they seek Jesus – even though they do not know Jesus' name, and even though they plunge into death sharing with Jesus the experience of abandonment by God without benefit of knowing how to name this fate or how to name the One with whom they share it. God has permitted this darkness of finitude and guilt in the world only because God has made it His own in Jesus.

This Jesus I thought about, loved, and desired to follow. And this was the way in which I found the real, living God without having made Him a figment of my own unbridled speculation. A person gets beyond such speculation only by dying a real death throughout life. But this death is real only if the person, resigned with Jesus, accepts in it the abandonment by God. This is the ultimate "wayless" mysticism. In so speaking I know that I have not clarified the mystery of the unity of history and God. But it is in Jesus who surrendered to God in his crucifixion and received God in his resurrection that this unity is definitively present. It is in Jesus that this unity can be accepted in faith, hope, and love.

Thus speaks the father of my theological life and of my heart. Such is his sapiential interlocking of theology and spirituality.

Notes

1 *Faith in a Wintry Season: Interviews and Conversations with Karl Rahner in the Last Years of His Life, 1982–84,* ed. H. Biallowons, H. D. Egan, S.J., and Paul Imhof, S.J. (New York: Crossroad, 1990), 174.

2 "Thomas Aquinas: Patron of Theological Studies," *The Great Church Year: The Best of Karl Rahner's Homilies, Sermons, and Meditations,* ed. A. Raffelt and H. D. Egan, S.J. (New York: Crossroad, 1993), 316.

3 J. B. Metz, "Karl Rahner – ein theologisches Leben," *Stimmen der Zeit* 192 (1974), 308.

4 "Theology and Anthropology," *TI* IX, trans. G. Harrison (London: Darton, Longman & Todd, 1972), 41.

5 "Christian Living Formerly and Today," *TI* VII, trans. D. Bourke (London: Darton, Longman & Todd, 1971), 15.

6 K. Rahner and H. Vorgrimler, "Potentia Obedientalis," *Dictionary of Theology,* new revised edn. (New York: Crossroad, 1981), 400.

7 *FCF*, 73.

8 "Eternity from Time," *TI* XIX, trans. E. Quinn (London: Darton, Longman & Todd, 1983), 177.

9 "On the Theology of Worship," *TI* XIX, 147.

10 K. Rahner, *Biblical Homilies,* trans. D. Forristal and R. Strachan (New York: Herder and Herder, 1966), 77.

11 K. Rahner, "Experiencing the Spirit," *The Practice of Faith* (New York: Crossroad, 1983), 83.

12 "Mystical Experience and Mystical Theology," *TI* XVII, trans. M. Kohl (London: Darton, Longman & Todd, 1981), 92.

13 "Teresa of Avila: Doctor of the Church," *The Great Church Year,* 63.

14 "Foundations of Christian Faith," *TI* XIX, 8.

15 "On the Theology of the Incarnation," *TI* IV, trans. K. Smyth (London: Darton, Longman & Todd, 1966), 119.

16 "The Eternal Significance of Jesus' Humanity," *TI* III, trans. K.-H. and B. Kruger (London: Darton, Longman & Todd, 1967), 44.

17 "The Two Basic Types of Christology," *TI* XIII, 215–16.

18 *FCF*, 303.

19 "On the Theology of the Incarnation," *TI* IV, 119.

20 "On the Spirituality of the Easter Faith," *TI* XVII, 13.

21 "Considerations of the Active Role of the Person in the Sacramental Event," *TI* XVII, trans. D. Bourke (London: Darton, Longman & Todd, 1976), 169–70.

22 *Karl Rahner in Dialogue: Conversations and Interviews, 1965–1982,* ed. H. Biallowons, H. D. Egan, S.J., and P. Imhof, S.J. (New York: Crossroad, 1986), 60.

23 "Ignatius of Loyola Speaks to a Modern Jesuit," *Ignatius of Loyola,* with a historical introduction by P. Imhof, S.J., trans. R. Ockenden (Cleveland: Collins, 1978), 11–38. Unfortunately this translation is not always reliable. The following quotations, which I have emended, are from pp. 11–15 and 19–21.

Further reading

Burke, P., *Reinterpreting Rahner: A Critical Study of His Major Themes* (New York: Fordham University Press, 2002).

Egan, H. D., *Karl Rahner: Mystic of Everyday Life* (New York: Crossroad, 1998).

Egan, H. D., and A. Raffelt, eds., *The Great Church Year: The Best of Karl Rahner's Homilies, Sermons, and Meditations* (New York: Crossroad, 1993).

Lehmann, K., and A. Raffelt, eds., *The Practice of Faith: A Handbook of Contemporary Spirituality* (New York: Crossroad, 1983).

The Content of Faith: The Best of Karl Rahner's Theological Writings (New York: Crossroad, 1992).

Marmion, D., A *Spirituality of Everyday Faith: A Theological Investigation of the Notion of Spirituality in Karl Rahner* (Grand Rapids, MI: 1998).

Raffelt, A., ed., *Prayers for a Lifetime* (New York: Crossroad, 1984).

Rahner, K., *Theological Investigations*, Volumes III, VII, VIII, XVI, and XXIII.

2 Rahner's transcendental project

THOMAS SHEEHAN

Karl Rahner's accomplishment consisted in putting Catholic philosophy and theology on a transcendental footing. The undertaking spanned some fifty years, from his matriculation in philosophy at Freiburg University in 1934 to his death at Innsbruck in 1984. From beginning to end, the driving force behind the project was the seriousness with which Rahner regarded the transcendental turn in modern philosophy.

THE PROGRAM

Rahner's program unfolded in two stages, the first philosophical and the second theological. (Only the former is the focus of this essay.) The first stage occupied him from 1934 to about 1941 and found expression in two works, *Geist in Welt* (1939) and *Hörer des Wortes* (1941). The first of those two texts marshaled central elements of the work of Kant, Rousselot, Maréchal, and Heidegger for the goal of reformulating Thomism – its epistemology, philosophical anthropology, and metaphysics – as transcendental *philosophy*. In the second stage, which occupied him from the 1940s onward, Rahner used the transcendental Thomism of the first stage as the basis for rewriting Catholic doctrine as transcendental *theology.*[1]

In March of 1966 Rahner outlined his program. "Dogmatic theology today has to be theological anthropology . . . Such an anthropology must, of course, be a transcendental anthropology." This entails "the necessity of considering every theological question from a transcendental viewpoint." That is, "we must explicitly deal with the apriori conditions for knowing a given object of faith; and this reflection must determine the concepts we use to describe the theological objects."[2]

The radical import of this project may be stated in two theses. (1) Since a transcendental philosophy of human nature establishes the a priori possibilities and limits of all human experience, it also establishes the possibilities and limits of all *religious* experience. (2) Just as a transcendental philosophy of human nature is co-extensive with general metaphysics, so likewise, when employed as a theological anthropology, it is co-extensive with all that can be learned in theology.

Guiding Rahner's overall project was the classical metaphysical axiom, *operari sequitur esse*: operations are conditioned by and consonant with the ontological structure of the operator. (Or in another iteration, *qualis modus essendi talis modus operandi*: an entity's way of being determines its way of acting.) The import of these axioms is both methodological and substantive, as may be illustrated by the case of human being. As regards method: since natures are revealed by actions, we discover what human being *is* by analyzing what human beings *do*. As regards substance: once discovered, the ontological structure of human being is seen as determining the possibility, necessity, and scope of all human experience. Moreover, in Rahner's critical-transcendental approach, the human essence not only defines the structure and function of human experience but also delimits the range of objects available to that experience.

For Rahner this delimitation applies preeminently to metaphysics, not just the second-order science of metaphysics but more importantly the first-order activity of metaphysical *experience*. Like Kant before him, Rahner approaches metaphysics by (1) studying one particular human operation – predicative knowledge – for the purpose of (2) determining the structure of human being *qua* theoretical knower, for the purpose of (3) establishing the possibility, necessity, and limits of metaphysical experience, for the purpose of (4) delimiting the range of objects available to metaphysical knowledge.

Whatever operations human beings consciously perform – whether working, eating, speaking, enjoying, thinking, or whatever – those actions always take some form of *relatedness*, and that relatedness always has a bivalent structure: (1) relatedness-to-*another* (2) as relatedness-to-*oneself*. As far as one can tell, all human operations are bereft of perfect immediacy. Such immediacy, as pure coincidence-in-unity, would transcend all relatedness-to. Instead, human action is condemned to mediacy, thrown ineluctably into relatedness, but without the actor ever losing the ability to see and say "I" and "myself." Even the attempt to deny the self–other bivalence ends up replicating it.

To judge by its operations, therefore, human being is an otheredness that is always self-related, and a self-relatedness that cannot exist without being othered. Since relation-to-another is the only way humans can relate to themselves, we may define human being as *self-related otheredness*.

"Self-relatedness" means self-awareness and self-responsibility – in a word, spirit. "Otheredness" means that human beings *need* to be affected by others – but are *limited* to being affected only by this-worldly corporeal others. In Rahner's phrase, human being is a "Geist in Welt," a this-worldly spirit that cannot see beyond, or exist without – much less ever leave – this material world.

Rahner's *Geist in Welt* analyzes and interprets the operation of predicative knowledge – the act of correctly judging that predicate P pertains to subject S – for the twofold purpose of demonstrating that human being *is* what was said in the previous paragraph and drawing all the conclusions from that. Rahner's analysis is focused on a central text in Aquinas' epistemology (*Summa Theologiae*, I, q. 84, art. 7), and for the most part the text remains within the philosophical worldview and language of medieval scholasticism: abstraction of universals, conversion to the phantasm, formal and efficient causality, etc. However, Rahner's *interpretation* of that analysis propels his project out of the Middle Ages and into the modern (even Nietzschean) refusal of any metaphysics that makes pretensions to direct knowledge of otherworldly entities. For Rahner the human spirit is, for better or worse, stuck in this world with no escape; and the range of objects available to human experience – including metaphysical experience – is always and only material.

The stark outcome of *Geist in Welt* is that human knowledge is focused exclusively on the material order, with no direct access to the spiritual realm. Human being is certainly spirit (self-reflective, self-conscious, self-responsible), but the only thing such a spirit can properly know is the *meaning of things within the world*. If human being is ineluctably a this-worldly spirit with no intuition beyond the five senses, and if human knowledge is exclusively about what those senses perceive, then meta-physics – taken as the alleged knowledge of spiritual entities separate from matter – is impossible.

And along with such Platonizing meta-physics, theological entities like God and the supernatural content of revelation risk disappearing from the field of human experience. Either that – or the entire Catholic tradition of metaphysics, revelation, and theology must undergo a decisive and irreversible Copernican Revolution.

THE TRANSCENDENTAL TURN

In taking the transcendental turn, Rahner radically transformed both the field and the focus of traditional metaphysics and eventually of Catholic theology. From Aristotle to Aquinas, the subject matter of first philosophy was everything real – whatever is in being, whatever is not nothing – in a word, *ens*. And the formal aspect under which first philosophy studied *ens* was its very condition of being real, its state of having-being (*ens qua ens = ens qua habens-esse*). Classical metaphysics carried out that task by tracing all *entia* back to the first principles of their *esse*. As Aquinas put it: "All things that are composite and that participate [in being] must have their causes in things that possess being by their very essence."[3]

By contrast, the subject matter of transcendental philosophy is not objects taken by themselves (the independent-of-my-mind-out-there-now-real) or objects as supposedly meaningful of themselves. Nor is transcendental philosophy focused on subjectivity as something separated from the world. The field of transcendental philosophy is neither the subject nor the object taken by themselves, but the very *relatedness* of subject and object, knower and knowable. Strictly speaking, then, the transcendental turn is not simply a "turn to the subject" but more precisely a turn to the subject-*in-relation* – for example, the inquiring subject, which is already related (at least interrogatively) to whatever is being questioned.

Transcendental philosophy studies the a priori correlation between the meaningful and the constitution of its meaning, where "constitution" refers to the correlation's active role in establishing the meaningfulness of the known. This correlation is called "transcendental" insofar as the knowing subject necessarily "transcends itself," i.e., has already escaped from an imaginary Cartesian interiority and is always in a state of relatedness to possible objectivity as the a priori basis for knowledge. If classical metaphysics is the study of the independent-of-my-mind-out-there-now-real in terms of its mind-independent-out-there-now-realness (*ens* as material object; *habens-esse* as formal object), transcendental philosophy is the study of the meaningful in light of how it gets its meaning. The material object of a transcendental first philosophy is the *intrinsic relatedness* of the knower and the knowable; and its formal object is the *structure and source* of that correlation. In the terms of Husserlian phenomenology we would say that this material object is the outcome of a phenomenological reduction, whereas the formal object gets worked out by a transcendental reduction.

Rahner's transcendental turn is nothing short of a Copernican Revolution in Catholic thought. *Geist in Welt* marks his radical and permanent shift from an object-focused theory of being (a *Seinslehre*) to a correlation-focused theory of meaning (a *Bedeutungslehre*), from an objectivist study of the real in terms of its mind-independent realness, to a transcendental study of the meaningful in terms of the constitution of its meaning. Nonetheless, one of the challenges in understanding *Geist in Welt* is to remember that even when Rahner continues to use the pre-transcendental language of "being," he always means "meaningfulness" – that is, being as phenomenologically reduced: the intelligible in terms of the conditions constituting its intelligibility. *Geist in Welt* draws all the proper conclusions from Aristotle's and Aquinas' principle that being and meaningfulness, *einai* and *aletheia*, are interchangeable, including the phenomenological conclusions that being is known only as meaningfulness, and that meaningfulness is always transcendentally constituted.

To put it otherwise, Rahner "retrieves" from Thomas Aquinas a turn to the transcendental that is at best implicit in the Angelic Doctor. However, once in possession of that transcendental ground Rahner never retreats from it, even when *Geist in Welt* and *Hörer des Wortes* continue to use Aquinas' objectivist language of "being" (*Sein, Seiendes*). In order to underline and preserve the phenomenological gains of that retrieval, the present essay will translate Rahner's philosophical terminology from an ontological register to a transcendental one:

from:	*to*:
1. a being (*ens*)	1. the meaningful
2. the being of beings (*esse entium*)	2. the sense or meaning of the meaningful
3. being as such (*esse schlechthin*)	3. unlimited meaningfulness, or sense as such.

So, for example, instead of Rahner's "understanding the being of beings," I will speak of "making sense of things" or "being familiar with what something means." And in place of "the pre-grasp of being as such," I will speak of the human need for unlimited meaning, that is, our ontological fate of being *capax omnium*, able to make sense of whatever we encounter, and unable to encounter anything without making sense of it. These translations from the ontological register of being to the transcendental register of sense will help us see that the only infinity that human beings know is not God's, but their own finite infinity.

PRE-CRITICAL PRESUPPOSITIONS

Rahner brought to his doctoral studies in philosophy and to his drafting of *Geist in Welt* (1934–36) a set of pre-critical presuppositions garnered from his earlier reading of Aquinas, Rousselot, and Maréchal. Chief among them was the Aristotelian-Thomistic principle that the criterion of reality is not just identity but *self*-identity, subjectivity – what Aquinas calls a "return to oneself" that entails "knowing oneself" (*reditio completa in seipsum* as *cognoscere seipsum*). Laying out the traditional metaphysical grounds for that pre-critical position will require a few steps.

Aquinas shares classical philosophy's "top-down" understanding of being, specifically the conviction that the norm of reality lies in the ideal, the perfect, and the whole. In this view, metaphysics actually reads reality "downwards" (deductively) from the *de jure* perfect to the *de facto* imperfect, from the a priori to the a posteriori – rather than "upwards" (inductively) from the imperfect to the perfection it strives for. Philosophy begins with some sense of the ultimate and perfect (how else would it know anything as imperfect?) and then works backwards from the ideal to the real, from the fully achieved to what is still on-the-way, from the whole to what participates in it.

Aquinas follows Aristotle in this regard. Something is perfect (Greek, *teleion*) when it is in complete possession of itself, when "it already has its fulfillment" such that "not the least part of the thing can be found outside of it."[4] Such perfect self-possession is also called "wholeness." Something is whole (*totum*) and therefore its own when "it lacks no part of what belongs to it by its nature."[5] These ideas converge in Aquinas' terms *perfectio* and *actus*, which translate Aristotle's *en-tel-echeia*, "being-wholly-fulfilled," and *en-erg-eia*, "being a completed work [which therefore has begun *to be*]." To be perfect means to have arrived at one's essence, to have come into one's own. And since "perfection," "wholeness," and "ownness" are analogous rather than univocal terms, we must say that every entity *is* perfect *to the degree* that it is self-coincident, i.e., has arrived at its essence and come into its own.

In the Aristotelian and Thomistic universe, self-coincidence entails self-transparency. Therefore, the degree to which something knows itself is equally a measure of its degree of *habens-esse*. At the divine apex of reality, perfect being is pure self-presence and self-intuition (*Bei-sich-sein*). Knower and known are one and the same in God; in fact, God's very being is a unity of knowing and self-knowing.[6] That paradigm sets the norm for all other spiritual entities. Whether in God, angels, or human beings, the proper term of knowledge is not an external object but the knowing subject itself, along with all that this subject is and does.[7]

Therefore, the word *completa*, in the phrase *reditio completa in seipsum*, is analogical. Properly interpreted, it means "perfect," but perfection comes in various degrees. The divine returns to itself in keeping with its supreme degree of perfection, and therefore knows itself as entirely self-transparent. Human being returns to itself with its limited degree of perfection, and thus knows itself as *chiaroscuro*. In the analogically structured universe of St. Thomas, where *ens* is inseparable from other trans-categorial characteristics like *unum* and *verum*, a thing is real *to the degree* that it knows itself. *Ens* = *unum* = *verum*. The real = the self-identical = the clear (the knowable and self-knowing). A thing has as much being as it has self-transparency.

Therefore, in the great chain of being in which reality is proportionate to self-possession and self-knowledge, to be *othered* (even to be a self-related otheredness) is an index of imperfection. Human being is able to return to, possess, and know itself only by turning to, possessing, and knowing what is other than itself. Yet insofar as it is the *essence* of human being to be a self-related otheredness, that condition must have and be its own analogical perfection. To be human is to be fated to "almosting it." Almost is good enough – in fact, it's as good as it gets. "For us there is only the trying. The rest is not our business."[8]

If we compare human being with the divine, we see that whereas God is perfectly perfect, human being is *perfectly imperfect*. Both are instances of perfection, but with a difference. The divine being is whole and perfect in its unending state of pure self-possession, whereas human being is whole and perfect in its mortal condition of self-related otheredness. Ontologically, human being is going nowhere – precisely because it already *is* where it is supposed to be. It has no prospect of achieving some idealized (fantastical) non-othered perfection, such as cutting all ties with matter and living forever in heaven as a disembodied spirit. Ontologically, we have already come into our own, and that ownness consists in our perfectly imperfect (*completa*) self-presence (*reditio in seipsum*). At the level of essence, human perfection consists in its humanly specific imperfection; and at the level of existence, one's individual perfection consists in responsibly living out one's personal imperfection. Authenticity – i.e., actually *being* my own self – means always becoming existentially what I already am ontologically: a perfectly imperfect self-related otheredness.

Before we move on to *Geist in Welt*, there is one last pre-critical presupposition that guides Rahner's work, namely, that making sense of something – i.e., knowing it by understanding its meaning or being – is an index of finitude.

God and angels do not make sense of anything. They cannot, because they are unable to wonder what anything might mean. Since they are, each in its genre, a pure self-coincidence (God as perfect subsistent existence;

each angel as a perfect spiritual essence), their knowing consists not in inquiry, hypothesis, and judgment (*ratio*) but in simple and direct intuition (*intellectus*) both of themselves and of others. By contrast, meaning and mediation are human stand-ins for pure self-presence. Making-sense-of and understanding-the-meaning-of – i.e., knowing something through its meaning or being – is the task and glory of human beings. That is because our essence consists not in pure self-coincidence – literally "having our act together," *actus perfectus* – but in always *having to get* our act together, without hope of finally succeeding. We are an *actus imperfecti*, a work forever in progress. That is why human spirituality is not pure *intellectus/nous* (understanding all-at-once) but *ratio/logos* (learning-by-gathering-things-together).

Our own being is, in principle, endless self-synthesizing, and that is why we know everything that we know only by way of synthesis and judgment. *Qualis modus essendi talis modus operandi.* Fated to an endless *pulling* of ourselves together, we know whatever we know only by endlessly *putting it* together – subjects with predicates, tools with tasks, things with their meanings, ourselves with our essence. And in doing so, we have no illusions of attaining final unity, reaching the ultimate oneness that would end inquiry, abolish work, and transform each of us into the perfection of his or her essence (every she the ultimate Aphrodite, every he the absolute Apollo).

This may sound like the punishment of Sisyphus – but no, it is our essence, our perfection. Only if we were to compare this human condition to the pure self-coincidence of God and angels would we speak of "imperfection." Therefore, instead of "perfect imperfection," which is merely a stand-in term, we should rather speak of our "specifically human perfection," the perfection of *finitude*, a finite infinity that consists not in God's all-at-once-ness but in our own finite infinity: unlimited self-synthesizing, self-mediation, and self-interpretation, unlimited responsibility, knowledge, and creativity – and then we die. That is:

We *know* only by

1. relating one thing to another (this subject to that predicate) and
2. relating the whole S-and-P to ourselves ("I *adjudge* this S to be *meaningful* as P")

because we *are* only by

1. relating ourselves to ourselves (= ever becoming ourselves) and
2. relating the whole of our self-becoming to our otherness and to what it gives us.

THIS-WORLDLY SPIRIT

Rahner's *Geist in Welt* seeks to inscribe as much of the above as possible within a critical-transcendental framework, while also remaining within the language of Thomistic epistemology and psychology. Demonstrating that Aquinas was a transcendental thinker *avant la lettre* is no easy task, and Rahner is frequently compelled to admit that some of the most important interpretations he advances are "hard to capture within the usual categories of Thomas."[9] But that hardly seems to trouble Rahner, because, as he writes, "As far as I can see, the only reason to work on Thomas is for the sake of the questions that motivate my *own* philosophy and the philosophy of my times."[10]

In commenting on *Summa Theologiae* I, q. 84, art. 7, Rahner argues (1) that, lacking a pure intellectual intuition, we make sense only of material things; (2) that we do so by differentiating meanings (universals) and things (particulars) and then synthesizing them by judging (correctly or not) that they go together; and (3) that we do so because we cannot relate to anything except through meaning, and therefore can never step beyond meaning. For us, meaning has no limit; and by living in that limitlessness of meaning, we are able to make sense of everything we meet.

The first two points are relatively uncontroversial. The third should also be uncontroversial – except that some commentators believe *Geist in Welt* makes the extraordinary claim that, in order to grasp S-as-P, a person must have a "prior grasp" or "pre-grasp" (*Vorgriff*) of God as absolute being and as the perfect coincidence of knowing and known. If that were the case, Rahner would have produced an air-tight proof for the existence of God. In point of fact, however, *Geist in Welt* does not produce such a proof, because it does not claim that we have anything like a "prior grasp" of absolute being. Quite the contrary, the book demonstrates that we have no grasp of God at all, either prior or posterior.[11]

Rahner argues that we have no knowledge of God's perfect infinity, the point where knowing and known would converge absolutely. At best we have a sense of our own finite infinity and of the fact that we are ontologically fated to meet nothing of which we cannot make sense. (If we cannot make sense of it, we cannot meet it.) Our limitless gathering-together of things and their meanings – rendering the former transparent in terms of the latter – understandably lets us postulate a perfectly achieved in-gatheredness of transparency, which people call "God." But in order to make sense of any S in terms of a P, all that is required is this: that no matter how far we look, we can and must make sense of any material object we meet, by placing it within our limitless world of sense. We may choose to call that world "meaning as such" or, with Rahner, "being as such" (*das esse schlechthin*). However, *any* form of meaning or sense (any understanding of "the being of an entity") is an index of finitude. If we claim to have any intimation of a perfectly infinite God, it is only by analogy with our own finite infinity.

The argument of *Geist in Welt* is thick and brilliant. But it is also difficult; and a good deal of the difficulty lies in Rahner's insistence on using Aquinas' pre-critical language of being instead of the transcendental language of meaning. Rather than analyzing the book's complex argument about abstraction and conversion (which I have done elsewhere) and in the process replicating Rahner's language of "being," I will illustrate the core argument of the book by way of an allegory built around the idea of being as meaning, and knowledge as familiarity with the meaningful.

Imagine the biggest family reunion that the Sheehans have ever planned, set for a sunny Saturday at a large meadow in San Francisco's Golden Gate Park. The family has spent months organizing it, and this time we have decided to invite not just our close relatives, but everyone we believe is related to us – Irish, Jewish, Italian, American, Mexican – whether their names be Cullen, Sheehan, Myatt, or Rasi; Vargas, Masciaga, Wynn, or Libertini; Glovski, Del Vecchio, Schumacher, or Gasparinetti – all the clans and tribes in their scores and hundreds. We are related to them all, and hope to meet each one. And we are at least *able* to figure out where they fit on the family tree. We have our genealogical charts with us. We can speak English with some of them, Italian and Spanish with others, and invent sign language when all else fails. We are *capax omnium*, able to make sense of all those to whom we are related, once we meet them.

As our family of five drives to the Park, we ask ourselves: How will we decide who's who? How will we connect unfamiliar people with this or that family? My children suggest that, instead of asking them their names, we try *guessing* who fits into what family. They argue that we already know how a typical Myatt or Sheehan looks and acts, and we are generally familiar with what makes a Wynn and a Masciaga tick. With families whom we know less well, the photos we have seen may help us place them. And the e-mails we have exchanged with relatives we have never met will help us make those connections. It will be a matter of linking up unfamiliar faces with the family characteristics that we already know, putting the individual together with his or her *gens*, fitting people to the clans of which they are members. Not much different from what Aquinas called *compositio* and *divisio*: we come to understand the heretofore unfamiliar by taking it as a non-exhaustive instance of a general group with which we are already somewhat familiar.

We arrive at the meadow, and it is packed with hundreds of people. But we are not overwhelmed, because as *capax omnium* we realize that everyone we see is related to us and is either already familiar or able to become familiar. So we begin the guessing game.

My children are fairly good at figuring out who fits into what family, but my wife and I have mixed luck. She correctly identifies Molly as a Vargas and Bernadine as a Sheehan, even though she had not met either of them before. She also thinks that the cute guy in the tux *has* to be a Myatt because of his thick curly hair. She marks him down as such, while realizing, of course, that he is only *one* of the Myatts and does not exhaust the clan. Just as Aristotle and Aquinas would have predicted, she synthesizes *and* distinguishes "Myatt family" and "cute-guy-with-curly-hair." I do much the same with a lovely young woman I notice. I think she *must* be a Glovski, because they are all so good looking. As it turns out, the guy in the tux is actually a waiter, and the young woman is a professional photographer hired for the occasion. But whether our guesses are right or wrong, we are playing by the rules of *compositio* and *divisio*, synthesis and distinction. We are making sense of people by (1) linking up individuals whom we do not know with family characteristics that we already know (2) while realizing that each family is larger than – hence distinct from and not exhausted by – any individual. We are successfully performing acts of abstraction and conversion to the phantasm (even when our guesses are wrong) by affirming, for example, Vargas-hood *of* Molly while realizing that Molly *does not exhaust* Vargas-hood.

Then imagine that, dream-like, the cosmic video camera filming this reunion begins to pull further and further back and move higher into the sky in order to get a wider view of the meadow, the Park, the Sunset District, and the whole of San Francisco. The camera now reveals that there are not just hundreds of people gathered at the reunion, but thousands. The crowd spills out beyond Golden Gate Park, as far as Pacifica to the south, the Presidio to the north, and Potrero Hill to the east – and everyone, we presume, is related to us. And then, magically, the video camera begins to pan the entire *history* of all those people, backwards in time to the beginning, and forwards in time to forever. My family and I realize that, willy-nilly, we are somehow related to *everyone* (including the waiter and the photographer). And if given enough time, we could come to know them all and thereby make them *quoad nos* what they already are *quoad se*, namely, *familiares*, members of our clan.

We are able to know the whole human race as well as everything in the material world. Everyone is related to someone and, in the final analysis, to everyone; and everything is related to everything else. And we human beings are the only ones able to recognize and understand that. There is, in principle, no limit to our ability to make sense of, to become familiar with, everyone and everything.

CONCLUSION

We may draw some lessons from this allegory: (1) We are able to make sense of everything we encounter because we cannot *not* do that. The ability to make sense of ourselves and of all other entities is our very essence. That is what it means to be a rational animal.

(2) What we make sense of is always ourselves – along with all that we are and do. So yes, each of us is a *self*-relatedness. But even as self-related, none of us is ever a monad. We are all related to someone and something: everyone has a mother and a body. In fact, everything we can encounter is a body and therefore is actually or potentially related to every other body, because everything we can encounter (including ourselves) is othered. The uniqueness of *our* form of otheredness consists in being self-related and thus able to understand all the others. So when we say that the object of sense-making is always ourselves, we mean by "ourselves" not just our personal and social selves but also our material selves. Materiality and sociality are inseparable from human selfhood.

(3) As humans, each of us is, and struggles to sustain, our own finite measure of self-transparency. Such a *chiaroscuro* self is our consolation prize for what we are not and can never be: pure self-transparency. We certainly can dream of such transparency, but we can never be it (nor would we want to) because if *per impossibile* we did become it, there would be no "we" (no social-material-othered self-relatedness) to "be" it.

(4) Nevertheless, since we are *capax omnium*, we can make some kind of sense of such an absolute self-transparency. And hypothetically we *could* become familiar with it – but only if it were to bend itself to meet the transcendental conditions that our essence lays out for such an unlikely encounter. That is: It would have to show up within our material othered-ness by *not* showing up (because pure self-transparency cannot be othered, material, and temporal). It would have to leave us alone to live out our history without appeals for help from "the other world" (lest we lose the self-responsibility that makes us human). It would have to communicate

with us without breaking into our conversation from without. (We do not tolerate the rudeness of otherworldly interruptions.) And it would not be allowed to tempt us out of our self-related otherness, or coax us away from our happy fate of being this-worldly spirits.

Surely all that could never come to pass! It must be only a dream. And yet, like some of our best dreams, it may be trying to teach us a profound lesson. Perhaps, in the spirit of Karl Rahner, it is telling us: Give up trying to transcend yourself. Remain within this social, material world, stay with your bodily relatedness and all that it gives you. Be happy with being only human, with making sense only of the people and things you encounter – while never forgetting that the human power to make sense of this world, and to transform it, is without limit. Forget pure self-transparency, which, if it is at all, is off somewhere beyond what you could ever experience. If it wants to find you, it will; and if it does, it will certainly *not* arrive as pure self-transparency! Above all, remember that you need no faith, no religion, no church or theology that would alienate you from your this-worldly selves. Stay with yourselves, with your material, historical, and social community – the human community.

> That community does not demand anything of you that lies beyond your nature. It simply says: Ally yourself with what is genuine, with the challenging, with what demands everything of you. Have the courage to accept your perfect imperfection, your finite infinity.
>
> That community tells you: Go on, wherever you find yourself at this particular moment, follow your own light, no matter how dim, and tend the human fire lest it burn low. Live out your own personal and social becoming, even though you will never understand it completely. In doing so you will find a hope that is already blessed with fulfilment.
>
> If you set out on this path, you may find yourself far from religion, you may feel like an atheist, you may fear that you do not believe in God. Religious doctrines and morals may appear strange and even oppressive to you.
>
> But keep going, follow whatever measure of clarity you find in the depths of your heart – for this path has already arrived at the goal.

If there were a community that actually believed that – that embodied it in human language and symbols, and tried to live it out authentically – it might be worth a second look. But surely there is none, is there?[12]

Notes

1 For bibliographical details on the works of Rahner, Rousselot and Maréchal, see below. All translations in this article are my own.
2 "Theology and Anthropology," in *The Word in History*, ed. T. P. Burke (New York: Sheed and Ward, 1966), 1, 2, and 14.
3 Thomas Aquinas, *In metaphysicam Aristotlelis commentaria*, ed. M.-R. Cathala (Turin: Marietti, 1926), 102: Liber II, lectio II, no. 296, commenting on *Metaphysics* II, 1, 993b 23–29.
4 *In metaphysicam Aristotelis*, p. 324: Liber V, lectio XVIII, no. 1039, commenting on *Metaphysics* V, 16, 1021b 23–25. Ibid., p. 323, no. 1034, commenting on *Metaphysics* V, 16, 1021b 12–13.
5 *In metaphysicam Aristotelis*, p. 339: Liber V, lectio XXI, no. 1098, commenting on *Metaphysics* V, 26, 1023b 26–27.
6 Thomas Aquinas, *Summa Theologiae*, I, 14, 4, c. Cf. Aristotle, *Metaphysics* XII, 9, 1075a 3–5 with 1074b 34–35.
7 Cf. *Summa Theologiae*, I, 14, 2, c. abd I, 14, 4, c, ad 1, and ad 3.
8 Regarding "almosting it," see James Joyce, *Ulysses* (New York: The Modern Library, 1961), 47, line 6. Regarding "For us there is only the trying," see T. S. Eliot, *Four Quartets*, "East Coker," v, in *The Complete Poems and Plays of T. S. Eliot*, ed. V. Eliot (London: Faber and Faber, 1969), 182.
9 *SW*, 342.
10 Ibid., lii.
11 *FCF*, 64–65 (translation amended): "[The divine] is given to us only in the form of a distance that refers us to what is other than itself [*im Modus der abweisende Ferne*]. We never have direct access to it, nor can we grasp it immediately. It is given only by silently referring us to something other than itself, something finite that is the object of our direct intuition and action."
12 Regarding the indented paragraphs: compare Rahner's "Thoughts on the Possibility of Belief Today," *TI* v, trans. K.-H. Kruger (London: Darton, Longman & Todd, 1966), 21.

Further reading

Maréchal, J., *Le point de départ de la métaphysique. Lecons sur le développement historique et théorique du probléme de la connaissance* (Paris: Desclée de Brouwer, and Brussels: L'Édition Universelle, 1922–47), Cahier v: *Le thomisme devant la philosophie critique* (Louvain, 1926).

Rahner, K., *Geist in Welt. Zur Metaphysik der endlichen Erkenntnis bei Thomas von Aquin* (Innsbruck and Leipzig: Felizian Rauch, 1939; 2nd edn., expanded and reworked by J. B. Metz, Munich: Kösel, 1957) [= *Spirit in the World (SW)*].

   Hörer des Wortes. Zur Grundlegung einer Religionsphilosophie (Munich: Kösel-Pustet, 1941; 2nd edn., reworked by J. B. Metz, Munich: Kösel, 1963).

   Grundkurs des Glaubens. Einführung in den Begriff des Christentums (Freiburg, Basel, Vienna: Herder, 1976) [= *Foundations of Christian Faith (FCF)*].

Rousselot, P., *L'Intellectualisme de saint Thomas*, 2nd edn. (Paris: Beauchesne, 1924), p. xvii; cf. 56–57. (ET by A. Tallon, *Intelligence: Sense of Being, Faculty of God* [Milwaukee: Marquette University Press, 1999].)

3 Experience of grace

STEPHEN J. DUFFY

Employing the riches of the Christian tradition, Karl Rahner developed a comprehensive theological vision that brought disparate doctrinal elements together as facets of a central mystery, the grace that is God's self-communication to the world. The heart of Rahner's theology is the divine self-gift evolving in history from creation to covenant to incarnation to vision and unfolding a "world of grace." Rahner attempted to integrate the essentials of faith into a unified whole, drawing new life and unrealized meaning from the tradition. His vision toppled the neo-scholasticism that dominated Catholic theology since the mid nineteenth century and contributed to unleashing a Catholic theological renaissance. Rahner retrieved much that theology had come to overlook in its history of forgetting.

Influenced by Heidegger, Kant, and Maréchal, Rahner was rereading Scripture, the Fathers, and especially Aquinas, in light of the modern "turn to the subject." In a radical inversion of Feuerbach, Rahner saw that if theology is anthropology, correlatively, anthropology is theology, since God's incarnation forever united humanity and divinity. We cannot speak of God or humanity without at least implicitly speaking of both. The turn to the subject, then, is not inimical to Christian proclamation of human fulfillment as union with God. One finds in Christianity the fullest affirmation of the human as finite spirit open to holy mystery. In its thrusting toward this mystery the human person in freedom creates itself. Anthropology becomes the point of entry to the whole of theology. Theology will be taken seriously, Rahner thought, to the extent that it can show that humanity has to do with the question of transcendence.

GRACE AS DIVINE SELF-COMMUNICATION

That God is the obliquely anticipated whereunto (*das Woraufhin*) of human knowing and loving is derived by Rahner from his transcendental analysis of human being. But left to itself philosophical analysis comes up short. At best, it shows God is possibly the goal that all cognition and affectivity approach asymptotically; humans could only question whether, or hope that, their striving for the good and for truth would end in fulfillment rather than frustration. Christian faith, however, proclaims in the light of the incarnation that God is not merely the remote, ever-receding horizon and *telos* of human transcendence but is absolutely close, engaged in a self-communication to humans that brings them fulfillment in the love they seek and the forgiveness they need. God is free self-giving love. This is not a metaphysically self-evident truth but the incomprehensible wonder revealed in Christ. Thus grace, for Rahner, is first and foremost God in self-communication. Not only are humans open to and in quest of the infinite, they are drawn by it in self-bestowal. Herein lies the foundation of Christian life, the pattern of history itself. The Mystery grounding all human striving does not remain aloof but goes out of itself to lavish itself on humanity. Even in God love is *ecstasis*. The self-giving Godhead constitutes itself the innermost entelechy of history, its source, driving force, and fulfillment. Sounding Hegelian, Rahner can say: "The primordial phenomenon is the self-alienation, the becoming, the kenosis and genesis of God."[1] Love is God's primordial possibility and act. This seminal theme contains what he will say of creation, incarnation, anthropology, the Trinity, ecclesiology, and eschatology. He explicitly employs categories of love, personal relationship, forgiving intimacy in his theology of grace rather than ontic categories derived from our experience of things, not persons in relationship, that served as the armature of school theology, e.g., accident, quality, and habit.[2] Yet divine closeness notwithstanding, God remains the incomprehensible mystery that brings language to the breaking point.

This self-communication is not merely transmission of information about God, but the giving of God's own self. The giver is the gift given. Rahner reverts to the scholastic category of "uncreated grace" and contends that school theology left behind its biblical and patristic heritage by stressing "created grace," called by the medievals "habitual grace," a precondition of uncreated grace, i.e., the ontic change that must precede and dispose one for the indwelling Spirit. But for Rahner, grace is primarily the divine self-gift. Effected by God, created grace is at once proximate ordination to and consequence of uncreated grace. Grace is God's transforming presence enabling divinization of humans and their participation in the divine life. Paradoxically, the addressee of the self-offering God comes to humanization by divinization. The two are not competing alternatives. Grace is neither detraction from, nor alien addition to, the authentically human, but fulfillment of the openness to the mystery energizing the heart's drive to self-realization. Grace is ground, polestar, and goal of the human journey.

In light of this, creation is the condition of the possibility of divine self-communication. Incarnation and grace are not divine afterthoughts. God willed to create because God first willed self-communication in free love, realized primordially in the self-gift of the incarnation. For Rahner, grace and nature, the divine self-gift and humans and their world, are related as the contingently-is and the hypothetically-necessary. Nature must be if divine self-giving is to have an addressee. Creation is grounded in God's gracing love. Nature exists for grace, never apart from grace. The incarnation is the goal of creation's movement, the conditions of its possibility. "When God wills to be non-divine, the human person comes to be."[3] With far-reaching anthropological implications, Rahner contends that human nature is the grammar of God's self-utterance. Sublimely transcending Aristotle's human as the rational animal, he views humanity as the cipher of God. In *ecstasis* God moves out of Godself into what is not Godself, into history through creation, incarnation, and the Spirit's divinizing work. Both creation and gracing are ordered to Christ, who is at once God's self-offer and humanity's fullest response.

From scholastic Aristotelianism, Rahner drew a model apt to express the dynamics of grace, that of formal causality, by which "a principle of being is a constitutive moment in another subject, such that it communicates itself to this subject and does not simply effect something different from itself."[4] But Rahner adapts the model to the uniqueness of the divine–human relationship. In becoming an inner co-constitutive principle of humanity in free grace God does not cease being transcendent. Paradoxically, the innermost moment of historical humanity, through which, in which, and for which it exists, is not a moment of its essence *as such*, but pure grace. Therefore Rahner appends a qualifier, not to withdraw his claim that God's self-offering presence is an inner constituent of human being, but to safeguard divine transcendence and point up the analogical character of God-talk. Uncreated grace is the *quasi*-formal cause of concrete humanity in its transcendentality. By creation God gives human being to itself (efficient causality); in grace, God gives Godself to humans (quasi-formal causality). "The essential and radical distinction between nature and the supernatural is unambiguously grounded in this distinction between the efficient and quasi-formal causality of God."[5] God "in his most proper reality makes himself the innermost constitutive element of man."[6] Formal causality connotes abiding, active, being-present-to and constituting a being the reality it is. This prevenient union with God in self-donation envisioned in terms of quasi-formal causality is not an inborn potentiality of nature as such. It is a supernatural existential.

THE SUPERNATURAL EXISTENTIAL

In the 1950s, Rahner spelled out the anthropological implications of his assertion that the whereunto humans intend in their cognitive and affective lives and anticipatorily grasp (der Vorgriff) is God in self-communication and summons. Adapting Heidegger's terminology, Rahner minted the term "supernatural existential" (das übernatürliche Existential) to describe the transformation of human transcendentality: "supernatural" because it is the initial step in God's gratuitous self-communication, and "existential" because, abidingly present to all, it permeates the totality of life.[7] The grace of God's self-offer is not the exclusive privilege of Christians. Nor does the impossibility of deducing it as an a priori constituent of humanity imply it is purely an accidental addition. According to Rahner, baroque scholasticism's extrinsicism led many to consider grace scarce, coming from without to pure nature, a self-sufficient, self-contained Aristotelian nature, as an accidental appendage super-imposing a second level on human nature, the super-natural, which lay beyond our experience. The nature–grace relationship depended on a non-repugnance in nature understood in scholastic terms as an "obediential potency," a capacity to receive gifts not incompatible with nature. Yet, it is difficult to conceive the desirability of such gifts to a nature already complete in itself without grace.

Rahner dismantled this two-storied world and exorcised the dualism bedevilling Catholic life and thought by constructing a theology of nature and grace that related the two as a unity in distinction. Grace, though an intrinsic constituent, an ontological determination of historical humanity, remains gratuitous. "Man is the event (das Ereignis) of the absolute self communication of God."[8] Universality does not diminish gratuity. Now common currency in Catholic theology, the term "supernatural existential" refers to God present and bestowing Godself upon humans in forgiving love. This gratuitous elevation of human transcendentality in its dynamism of knowledge and love is synonymous with transcendental revelation, uncreated grace, divine indwelling, and objective justification.[9] Human being is grasped from within, oriented to the self-bestowing God who is its finality, so that transcendentality is not merely the condition of the possibility of knowing and loving but transcendentality toward the holy mystery that lures it.

The existential initiates divine self-communication, looks to our acceptance of it and justification by faith and to consummation in vision. Even in the absence of reflexive awareness of the existential, humans remain, nonetheless, always graced by an inner dynamism thrusting toward the God who calls and gives Godself. Engracement is a gift, not an accomplishment. The existential does not accrue by reason of human choice or action; it is not an *existentiell*. Humanity is always more than nature. The existential endows historical human being with a finality unowed to it as such, therefore "supernatural," and not merely by reason of humanity's fallenness. Here Rahner echoes Aquinas and the Catholic tradition's stress on grace as elevating (*elevans*), not merely healing (*sanans*).

Because the initial opening and disposition of human transcendence to God's self-communicating presence is already revelation, implying the possibility of a response in faith, Rahner does not view revelation as restricted to Israel and the Christ event, but as co-extensive with history's sweep. Where humanity is, there is grace, hence transcendental revelation. God addresses all in self-communicating love. No purely natural order has ever existed. All human acts, even those appearing secular, are religious, for, ultimately, all are decisions to pursue or spurn the truth and authentic good, the God who calls. A special or categorical revelation in history is required, however, for knowledge not only of the fact but of the very possibility of graced existence. Conversely, transcendental revelation is the condition of the possibility of a response to categorical revelation, one more example of the oscillating, dialectical movement characterizing Rahnerian thought[10] as it holds together in unity distinct realities, a trait of Catholic analogical imagination.

THE EXPERIENCE OF GRACED HUMANITY

Post-Tridentine scholasticism, working with the concept of pure nature, considered grace an accident inhering in the soul and inaccessible to conscious experience. Humans experience their world simply as nature. Grace does not enter everyday experience. Rahner, however, harked back to the Thomist view that grace brings a supernatural formal object, a new a priori horizon of consciousness arising from the love of God poured forth in the heart by the Spirit (Romans 5:5). Divine self-communication provides consciousness of our transcendentality with a radically new specification. Nevertheless, Rahner considers grace and nature so bound in unity and the capacity for self-analysis so feeble that one cannot experientially distinguish with certainty between our orientation to being as such and our grace-given orientation to union with God. One can never easily say what in humanity is of nature, what of grace.[11] Nor are the contours of our lives sure indicators that we stand righteous before God. Like Augustine and Freud, Rahner recognizes that humanity's depths and its mix of motivations are not easily plumbed. Nonetheless, Rahner limns a phenomenology of grace in situations where the presence of God enters our experience as joy and consolation, even in suffering; as empowerment to love, to follow conscience in adversity; as infinite longing, radical hope, restless discontent at the insufficiency of everything attainable, rage against death.[12] Grace, therefore, is experienced, though not as grace, for it is psychologically indistinguishable from the stirrings of human transcendentality. Grace so permeates nature that it cannot be distilled off in chemically pure condition. Nor can what is of nature. Nature and grace are distinct but inseparable, interpenetrating, dimensions of our being and experience. We experience grace not as we do things in the quotidian round, but as an unthematic horizon of transcendence, as *a priori* condition of all experience and activity. At times, this ground of our being may surface into consciousness, there to be caught in the corner of the mind's eye as the alluring horizon of our lives, the illumination and inspiration making possible all cognition and affectivity, yet never to be encapsulated conceptually.

In terms of Rahner's philosophical foundations, "God" is the objective pole of the transcendental experience within which all reality and one's own being are presented. The infinite horizon affirmed in all knowing and loving is nothing other than the absolute being of God. In our anticipatory thrusting toward God, the goal of human transcendence, we are forever "almosting it." Transcendental experience of the subject's return to itself in its encounters with finite realities and relationships is simultaneously experience of and relationship to God. Not in a privileged sanctuary, but in the mundane we encounter the mystery in self-communication and respond with acceptance or rejection. Experience of God is not esoteric, marginal, restricted to mystics; it is constitutive of human being, not one more experience among others but wellspring and depth of all experience. God and self are the objective and subjective poles of the original experience of transcendence, wherein God is given objectively though not as an object. The primordial knowing of God in this experience is transcendental because incomparable to other kinds of knowing; it is the condition grounding cognition's very possibility.

Eschewing ontologism, which holds to an innate, immediate intuition of divinity, Rahner maintains there can be only *a posteriori* knowledge and experience of God through passage out of self into the world. God is experienced, co-known as horizon of all knowing in and through knowledge of the world. Humans do not discover and experience God as they might some galaxy. The thrust of all knowing of finite realities to final coherence is a drive toward the absolute, the horizon within which alone all knowing and desiring are fulfilled. Herein lies the paradox of mind and heart: the finite is comprehensible only in terms of the incomprehensible mystery that draws us. All finite realities speak of the mystery; none can deliver it.[13] Generally pre-reflexive this primal awareness of God may be ignored, suppressed, even denied, which easily happens since it comes in spatio-temporal experience whose depth may elude us. One can immerse oneself in a sea of cares, the horizon beyond lost to sight. Yet the experience persists in the lostness of the everyday. Human being is always a quest for God. Emptiness, love, tragedy may rescue one from drowning in the clutter and chatter that suffocates openness to and experience of transcendence.

THE RELATIONSHIP BETWEEN NATURE AND GRACE

In the 1940s, a firestorm erupted among Catholic theologians and raged through the 1950s. At issue was the nature/grace relationship. Ground zero of the debate was Henri de Lubac's seminal work, *Surnaturel*.[14] The debate occasioned Rahner's development of his approach to the relationship of nature and grace. For de Lubac, nature is created for grace and is unintelligible without it. The human spirit is desire for God and this desire is the most absolute of desires. Nature and grace, sacred and profane are distinct, but a two-zone division is pure abstraction. The nature/grace relationship is anything but an arcane topic for theological debate. The debate, de Lubac argued, had to do with whether Church and theology were to remain peripheral to culture or have a role within it. Too often, he contended, we are fearful of confusing realities when we should fear not uniting them. Simplistic divisions come to us more easily than analogical imagination and unity in distinction. Hence distinction became separation, loss of intimate relationship and of the finality of nature in grace. It was a shabby theology that kept the supernatural supernatural by making it an accidental add-on to a nature integral in itself. Grace was severed from its root in the heart and a wedge driven between secular and religious, hence the dualism that ravaged Catholic life. Nature was related to grace only extrinsically, by divine decree, and negatively, by a non-repugnance similar to the obediential potency for speech in Balaam's ass. As one might place a variety of caps on a bottle, all leaving it unchanged, so no matter what destiny God assigned human nature, it would remain the same.

God is, however, author of both nature and grace, and of nature only in view of grace. But theologians, said de Lubac, forsaking tradition for their over-rationalized theology, reduced the human spirit to one more nature whose desires are determined by metaphysical law and cannot surpass spirit-nature's measured capacities. The gratuity of grace, however, should be articulated not in reference to the closed, static, Aristotelian, pure nature of the Thomists, who corrupted Thomas' text (though Thomas prepared the way for reifying pure nature), but in terms of its own intrinsic character. Theologians need not hypothesize about how things could or might have been. They should account for the world as it actually is, a graced order. Here was a shot heard round the Catholic world. Debate, often bitter, ensued. *Surnaturel* argued that "pure nature," an abstract possibility, a heuristic to safeguard gratuity, had become a reality in its own right, that it was a misleading, expendable concept. But de Lubac's position, while valid at many points, was not without difficulties. Many construed it as an intrinsicism negating the gratuity of grace. De Lubac disagreed. If desire for the vision of God is woven into our humanity, it is God's gift. Of itself it can lay no claim to fulfillment. But had de Lubac reduced the double gratuity of creation and grace to the single gratuity of creation? Rahner, after analyzing de Lubac's views, formulated his own theology of nature and grace.[15]

Rahner's problem was this: How can human nature be conceivable without grace, yet be completely fulfilled only by God's gracing presence? How preserve divine freedom and gratuity while avoiding an extrinsicist dualism that renders grace alien to human being? Rahner, too, rejected the double-decker world (*duplex ordo*) of extrinsicism. Grace is no accidental garnish to a nature complete and self-contained. In the concrete order nature and grace are inseparable. If God calls, God's word does not return empty but affects humanity's inner core; humans are as they are because of their supernatural finality. But Rahner would not jettison the notion of pure, ungraced nature as a needed heuristic for understanding humanity on an essential, not an existential, level. Is the inner orientation to grace so constitutive of nature as such that it is inconceivable without it? An affirmative answer levels the orders of creation and gracing, since God could not create humanity except as an unconditioned desire for beatific vision that must be fulfilled. De Lubac appeared to be saying that this orientation to vision and union is so inherent in human nature that its frustration would contradict divine wisdom. This position could not stand, though Rahner shared de Lubac's desire to shed extrinsicism, which assumes workaday life is played out in the realm of nature, while grace moves in an orbit beyond everyday concerns. But were grace an alien superstructure imposed on self-enclosed nature from outside history and experience by divine decree, it could only appear as an intrusion responding to no felt need or yearning in humanity. For Rahner, as for the Augustinian tradition, human being as it now exists bears an intrinsic orientation to God which, far from being a mere non-repugnance to grace, is an openness to, a hunger for, God. Humanity is unrestricted desire for God. Nevertheless, de Lubac's stance jeopardized the special gratuity of grace by reducing it to the gratuity of creation. Grace cannot be unexacted if the existential that is unconditional orientation to God's self-communication is a necessary constituent of nature as such. Against extrinsicism the immanence of grace must be maintained, but not at the cost of gratuity, so that grace is no longer grace.

Nature is not nor has it ever been pure nature. Grace permeates our experience. Life in all its dimensions stands inextricably within a world of grace, whose presence and offer render humanity wholly other than it might be. No clear division can be drawn between "natural" and "supernatural" or "secular" and "religious." Still, this order is not the sole conceivable order, for humans could, Rahner thinks, lead meaningful lives in an ungraced order where they meet only divine silence. Yet pure nature refers to no actually existing situation. And given our present situation, nature apart from grace is not easily delineated. Nature is *ein Restbegriff*, a residual concept, what is left if we mentally bracket the supernatural existential. We can neither experience nor describe nature as such. It never existed in a time before grace was "added to it." Nonetheless, "nature" remains an important conceptual construct pointing up the gratuity of grace by calling to mind a graceless order that could be had God willed. While nature and grace cannot be relegated to separate realms, nature and the supernatural existential, an element of concrete existence, not of nature as such, remain distinct in the quiddity of humans. Otherwise, grace becomes intrinsically constitutive of nature as such, hence owed and exacted.

Rahner navigated around the Scylla of extrinsicism and dualism and the Charybdis of de Lubac's enticing intrinsicism. If grace is the event of God's wondrous love, human being must be open to, related to, God in some way, for the dynamics of grace require a subject sufficiently autonomous to freely accept the gift of self God is not obligated to offer. Because created spirit is boundless thrusting toward being, nature is in continuity with and positively open to grace. The formal object of nature as such, being in general, and the new formal object the existential brings are not mutually opposed. The former is sublated in the latter, ontologically elevated and borne by grace. As absolute radicalization of human transcendentality, grace lies on a trajectory in line with nature. The supernatural existential, the initial disposition to graced union with God, which alone brings the completeness humans desire, is humanity's most intimate dimension, source and center of what human personhood is called to be. Because God calls humans to a supernatural finality, human existence is other than it might have been without that summons.[16] Rahner thus complements a "gratuity from above" with a "gratuity from below." A "creaturely theology" will retain the formal concept of pure nature, nature as such, to recall humanity's creaturehood before its creator and lover who makes of servants friends. Any inner exigency for grace is itself a grace.

ANONYMOUS CHRISTIANITY

Human transcendentality does not reside above history. Though hidden in history, God's inner word never remains purely interior and personal but is embodied in social forms, including the world's religions. Rahner's transposition of his theology of nature and grace into the arena of history leads to unification of the distinct but inseparable orders of creation and redemption. The history of salvation unfolds within the one history of humankind. Formally distinct, they are, nonetheless, materially identical, co-extensive and inseparable. The history of salvation plays out not just in biblical events; it is the history of grace active in all times. There is but one creative intention: God's redeeming self-communication. Grace and revelation range as far and wide as God's universal saving will. All this is corollary to Rahner's theology of nature and grace and his distinction between unthematic, transcendental, and thematic, categorical, modes of grace and revelation. Categorical revelation appears in the history of Israel and the person of Jesus. Therein are the paradigmatic events bringing awareness of the horizon encompassing humanity. The "natural"/"supernatural" disjunction led to the view that religions beyond the pale of Judaism and Christianity were at best to be tolerated, benignly neglected, or at worst eliminated. Rahner, however, focuses on the transcendental mode of God's presence rather than on the phenomenal objectifications of the religions. Comparative study of doctrines and forms of life, while necessary, is a function of the transcendental experience.[17] "Religion" is an abstraction expressing the varied ways humans have lived their lives within the horizon of grace and sin. The great religious traditions derive from reflection on and mediation of transcendental revelation in myths, doctrines, rites, and practices. These mediations can be insightful and fruitful. But sin and guilt darken and corrupt every segment of life. Attempts at mediation of God's self-communicating presence are not exempt. Affirmation of graced, supernatural elements in non-Christian religions does not imply, for Rahner, wholesale endorsement of all religions as equivalent.

Of grace incarnated in history Jesus is the paradigm. But grace for the most part works anonymously in history. Even when recognized, God's gracing presence may appear never to accomplish anything lasting, its redemptive victories subject to history's stronger law of dissolution and death.[18] Nonetheless, the graced horizon continues to draw us. People seek salvation in their own religious worlds. Where else could they turn if not to religions within their own culture? Grace is not restricted to mediation through one religion exclusively. God is present to all in their culture and its religions. Non-Christians cannot come into saving relationship with God in a religion physically or psychologically inaccessible. One "can live his proffered relationship to God only in society and must have the right, and indeed the duty, to live this relationship to God within the religious and social realities offered him in his particular historical situation."[19] The world religions are divinely willed positive means to such a relationship, part of salvation history. It is a limited view of God that hurls at non-Christian religions the false dilemma that a religion must either come from God in its entirety to be part of the divine plan or be nothing more than a non-salvific human construct. No religion is wholly of God. Every tradition lives within the vectors of grace and sin.

Christianity, claims Rahner, recognizes devotees of other faiths as persons who, because they may be living lives of implicit faith, can and often should be regarded as "anonymous Christians,"[20] a Rahnerian coinage. His inclusivist position rests on three tenets. First, because of God's universal salvific will the possibility of salvation and faith must be granted non-Christians even if they never become Christians. Second, there is a unity between love of God and love of neighbour. The latter is not merely a means to the former. Humanity is marked by an a priori openness to the other. This openness is an essential inner moment of our transcendentality; when one gives oneself to the other in selfless love, there is God, object and ground of love. Third, salvation cannot be gained without reference to God in Christ, since the origin, history, and fulfillment of salvation is theocentric and christological in character. Anonymous Christianity has to do with the contrast between thematic and prethematic experience of God in Christ, a distinction rooted in gradations of awareness concerning self and history.[21] Because of their role in salvation history, the religions are swept up in history's movement toward the total Christ. The notion of anonymous

Christianity is key to resolving tensions between the particularity of Christianity and God's universal saving will. It respects the depths of personal experience, which are not easily probed in reflection. One remains largely anonymous to oneself. As symbol-makers we enflesh our graced condition in words, rites, institutions, and forms of life. But even Christian discourse cannot adequately capture the experience of transcendence, only traces of it, despite tendencies to think we have caught it in our theologies and life forms.

Anonymous Christianity encodes the fact that Christ is the great sacrament (*Ursakrament*) in whom the universal possibility of salvation is revealed, made actual and effective. Rahner's anonymous Christianity has roots not only in his theology of grace but also in his "Christology of quest." Humans are searching history for a salvation-bearer. The sincere seeker may not see that what is sought is there in Christ. Yet such a seeker stands ready "to accept the goal wherever and however it may be found."[22] Rahner can find precedent in thinkers such as Justin the Apologist (*c.* 165), who saw the Logos present in history among the Greek philosophers and Israel's great figures, who were "Christians before Christ." Rahner's dialectical theology builds upon a correlation of Christian faith with the structures of existence. "To be a Christian is simply to be an authentic human being, one who knows that this life he or she is living can also be lived even by a person who is not a Christian explicitly and does not know in a reflexive way that he is a Christian."[23] Rahner is not claiming that every non-Christian is an anonymous Christian. But one who lives in accord with the graced impulses of one's being in its directedness to God in effect accepts in faith God's revelation, however implicit and anonymous such faith might be. To pursue truth and goodness, no matter the cost, is commitment to the God of Jesus Christ[24] that carries within itself an orientation to inclusion in the Christian community. Implicit faith leads to salvation, even if a believer has not embraced Christianity's thematization of transcendental revelation or has explicitly rejected it, claimed identity as devotee of another religion or no religion at all. The contrast between Christianity and the other religions is not in the presence of grace in the former, its absence in the latter; rather, the contrast runs along the axis of explicit and implicit faith.

Critics have variously viewed anonymous Christianity as negating the uniqueness of Jesus, as a form of relativism, or as Christian imperialism.[25] For Rahner, however, anonymous Christianity is a category for theological understanding, not for polemical or evangelizing purposes. It bespeaks recognition of the God at work in worlds beyond Christianity. Non-Christians are not in quest of a different salvation. Humanity shares a common origin, existence, and destiny. Non-Christians may be living at the same supernatural level as Christians. There are not two kinds of divine presence, one for Christians, another for non-Christians. This does not relativize revelation occurring in the biblical events. Jesus Christ is not simply one more representative of an always, everywhere, given in history. He is the constitutive event and cause of divine self-communication and its full human acceptance. Rahner does not so slacken tension between the universal and the particular as to collapse the paradoxical uniqueness yet universal normativeness of the particular.

CROOKED TIMBER

One might consider Rahner's anthropology too roseate, resting, as it seems, on a facile integration of matter and spirit in the pre-apprehension of God as ground and goal. His anthropology, however, is anything but naïvely optimistic. Beyond "essential," integral, human being Rahner sees the existential human being, whose integrity is won only by moral struggle, threatened as it is by its own fallibility within, and a history of sin and guilt without. In a seminal essay on concupiscence, Rahner put forward his view of a morally neutral concupiscence, asserting both the vulnerability of spirit in the world and the goodness of nature and its appetites.[26] Rahner retrieved as newly relevant the concept of concupiscence, which previously had been considered only in connection with sinfulness. Freedom is inescapably influenced for good and ill by the involuntary, impersonal elements at work in structures and forces internal and external to the individual. Spirit encompasses what is personal and free, represented in decisions and choice. But decisions about finite objects are the disposition of self as before God. Every decision tends toward total self-disposition and self-enactment. Concupiscence is the influence of nature on spirit. Comprehending the spontaneous movements of appetites, it is somewhat akin to Freud's id. These erupting appetites are non-free, pre-moral. Their presence influences personal disposal of oneself in free decisions.

To the decision/concupiscence duality Rahner adds person/nature and spirituality/sensibility, though here not using "nature" as in the nature/grace couplet. "Nature" refers to what we have become through the exercise of freedom and to all in the human being that is given prior to free disposal of oneself, the psycho-physical and social determinants given as its object and the condition of its empowerment or impoverishment. "Person" refers to all we can become, the possibility of being more than we are. In each pairing the poles are distinct but not necessarily opposed, though the tension in each leads to conflict and a divided self. The first two dualities are roughly equivalent, their relationship tracing to their metaphysical source, and the dialectic of matter/spirit or sensibility/spirituality. Thus a double rift appears in human being: its distance from the ultimate term of its becoming as person, and the internal tension between spirit and matter. Nature, the structures of circumstance and situation, the spontaneities of appetite, the "matter" that spirit copes with, can be a source of power for personal becoming but also of inertia and resistance to it. Frequently, spontaneity is off on its own, not implementing freedom in its impulse to the good. Because the goal is integration of the self in free option for truth and goodness, ideally everything in the human as nature, including the involuntary, should manifest, express what the human as person intends. Free decision should embrace and transform the spontaneous elements so they do not remain merely "natural" but become personal. Yet we rarely if ever achieve full integration or successfully dispose the total self to truth and goodness, to God. Tension reigns between what one is (as nature) and what one desires to become by free election (as person). Person never absorbs nature; ineluctably, life remains concupiscent. While concupiscence is not itself evil, it remains a precondition of sin's possibility. Yet it may at times be on the side of the angels, since nature can resist not only morally good decisions, but immoral ones as well.

What concupiscence entails is the impossibility of total conversion to good or evil. Evil resides not in concupiscence as such but in failure to integrate it with freedom. Evil is in lack of wholeness, integral goodness, the "out-of-synchness" of freedom and *eros*: decisions with spontaneity left in the cold, or spontaneity with decisions rendered mere velleity. We remain unintegrated. There is dread of the whole self coming together in a total "yes" to the mystery that draws us. Desire and dread, grace and sin cohabit. In the poet Donne's words, "Look, Lord, and find Both Adams met in me." Where wholeness lacks, freedom constricts to superficial choices and does not run deeper, where the self meets the question of God and the person it wants to become. The extent to which one achieves integration carries a coefficient of ambiguity. Given the murkiness of self-reflection, one cannot gauge the extent to which spontaneities are integrated with decision or remain undissolved residues or blockages. We are always more than we can enact; much in us remains impersonal. We are never wholly absorbed in good or evil. Because of our "materiality" we are never wholly autonomous and integral. We are ever-unfinished persons. What integration subjectivity comes to is a work of grace that humanizes by divinizing. The grace of self-maintenance is required not merely because humans are sinners, but also because persons are perduringly concupiscent.

Transcending the view of concupiscence merely as enticement to sin, Rahner highlights important facets of finitude that contribute to a more adequate anthropology. Freedom is active but also receptive; disposal is disposed of; something done is also something undergone; action is reaction; voluntary and involuntary interpenetrate. Contrary to much naïvely optimistic post-Enlightenment anthropology, there are no completely autonomous agents so transcending nature's determinations that spirit wholly masters the self. To consider human agency capable of transcending nature and world is to question the goodness of bodily existence by implying that humans are not authentically human until they angelically soar beyond finitude, which is an onus to be overcome. But both nature and person are God's good creation.

The struggle for integration under grace is made difficult, however, not only by seduction of dark psychic powers within, but also by a history of sin and guilt without. Inevitably, we exercise freedom within the constraints of a situation given prior to us and our choices.[27] Nor is the situation purely extrinsic to us, for the currents of sinful history and culture flow through us, not around us. One's situation is created by the history of the freedom of all who have preceded and of all contemporaries. Their legacy of sin and guilt has lasting effect and shapes the pre-personal predicament before the individual's freedom dawns. In varying degrees, the shared situation becomes an intrinsic moment in decisions that follow. The sin of each is the sin of all, the sin of all the sin of each. And the sin and guilt permeating the situation has a power exceeding the sum of individual sins. The history of sin so plays upon all life's registers – love, work, civic and political life, sickness, death – that what experience of them would be in a guilt-free world we cannot say. What we do with our freedom depends upon what we are, which depends upon the history of our choices and of choices others have made before and for us. Situated in sinful solidarity, freedom constricts and moral impotence dogs us. Strive to purge evil from the world we must. But expect no final victory in history. The Christian is no naïve optimist.[28] Evil's opacity cannot be rationalistically dissipated, nor its effects eliminated. Still, Christians must strive to shape a future of justice and love as manifestation of the presence of grace in history.

Privation of the graced life meant to be channelled through human descent and interaction constitutes a state of sinfulness due to its rejection by beings ordered to it in the depth of their being. Such privation is not

comparable to lack of some finite good. Vocation and predicament conflict. This state of sinfulness is an abiding existential, antecedent to free
self-disposition. Freedom is conditioned by its communal past and by concupiscence. We are snared in a web of corruption, oppression, greed, and
violence woven by a history of sin. To be in history is to be complicit in
a sinful situation. Rahner might reservedly agree with Kant's Augustinian
lament: "Out of timber as crooked as that from which man is made, nothing
entirely straight can be built."[29] Yet despite eons of guilt, grace remains
an ever more radical existential than its counter-existential, sin, which is
surpassed by God's redeeming will. A demonic power, sin enters the world,
abounds, reigns. Yet grace abounds all the more (Romans 5). History is
not merely a story of perdition, but of salvation, primordially so, for history is drawn by the stronger vector, grace. Grace, not hamartialogy, is the
axis of soteriology. The significance of Christ's grace derives not from sin.
Things stand the other way round. Against a graced horizon, sin is less
lost innocence than betrayal of the dynamism of one's being, alienation,
incompleteness, the measure of one's distance from Christ and authentic
selfhood. Existence oscillates between grace and sin. But grace is eschatologically victorious. The mystery of iniquity is swallowed up in the anomaly
of the good.

THE RAHNERIAN LEGACY

Rahner's theology of grace, grounded in the supernatural existential, has
implications for all areas of theology. With his interpretation of transcendental philosophy as underpinning he broke through the essentialist linguistic
and conceptual world of a neo-scholasticism set against and closed to the
world. Study under Heidegger and his reading of Rousselot, Maréchal, and
Blondel opened the possibility of interpreting tradition in a way that linked
it to modern life and thought. Resonating through Rahner is Blondel's recognition of a transcendental ground in modernity's quest for self-realization,
in which lay an opening to revelation. Affirmation of this openness was
Rahner's theological wellspring. Contrary to neo-scholastic theology the
accent would rest on grace as God's personal presence (uncreated grace), not
as accidental habit qualifying one's mode of being (created grace); on grace
at the center of ordinary life, not as hovering on the margin of another
world; on grace as the self-realization of persons, not as merely healing
fallen nature's wounds; on grace as permeating personal and social life
and not easily distinguishable in itself, not as separate from nature and
wholly eluding consciousness; on grace as God's self-offer permanently,

universally present in the quotidian, not as scarce, offered intermittently in privileged sacramental enclaves. Rahner replaced the dualisms of the past – Church/world, philosophy/theology, liturgy/life – with "a world of grace." And his existential opened a door to dialogue with other traditions and mutual enrichment.

Rahner's theology of grace is not the last word. Rahner draws from many wells, among them Kant and Heidegger. With Heidegger he holds to the historicity of personal existence. Yet with Kant his theological positions track back to the transcendental structures of the subject residing above the particularities of history. Rahner is forever seeking the conditions that must obtain in the structures of consciousness for revelation to be received. The risk is that historical reality is not fully attended to but absorbed by historicality, a category of existence, and that the subject theology must deal with, viz. the time-bound subject shaped by history, is trumped by abstract spirit in the world, an idealized subject. Rahner's predilection for the transcendental and prethematic risks diminishing the categorical, the events and language occurring in history, where transcendence is manifested.[30] Probably at work here are Rahner's apologetic and pastoral concerns. Seeing many estranged from God, biblical and church teaching, he appeals to the transcendental experience of the subject to show how the Christian message isomorphically conforms to the inmost aspirations of humankind. Lock and key, the two are a fit. From the beginning humanity was disposed to divine self-communicating love. However, when God's graciousness appears in history, it does not automatically fulfill our deepest needs and yearnings. Exceeding our profoundest hopes and desires, it meets not merely with satisfaction but with awe at a love beyond boldest expectation. But the word in history is also judgment on our folly; hence it also meets with rejection and crucifixion. The point is that the divine self-gift appearing in history must be permitted to speak for itself, not simply conformed to and verified in human subjectivity. The height and depth of God's self-communication cannot be contained by a theological *a priori*. The particularity of divine love is determined solely by the logic of divine freedom. Any turn to the subject that diminishes the turn to the manifesting object betrays Rahner's own ontology.

As all his theology, Rahner's theology of grace stands unfinished. So it must, for Rahner knows that on the other side of its stammering talk about God, theology can only end in awe-struck silence before a graced horizon beyond all telling. Rahner's is a theology born of ardour but steeled by judgment. What difficulties it may entail cannot detract from its achievement, which so opened and enriched Christian life and thought.

Notes

1 "On the Theology of the Incarnation," *TI* iv, 114–15; "Christology in the Setting of Modern Man's Understanding of Himself and of His World," *TI* xi, trans. D. Bourke (London: Darton, Longman & Todd, 1974), 226.

2 "Concerning the Relationship between Nature and Grace," *TI* i, 316. See also *FCF*, 131.

3 "On the Theology of the Incarnation," *TI* iv, 116; *FCF*, 120–22.

4 *FCF*, 121.

5 "The Concept of Mystery in Catholic Theology," *TI* iv, 65–66. See also "Some Implications on the Concept of Uncreated Grace," *TI* i, 328–31.

6 *FCF*, 116.

7 "Existential" is distinguished from *existentiell*. "Existential" refers to constitutive structural dimensions of *Dasein* prior to free activity or, better, to the horizon within which concrete *existentiell* possibilities of *Dasein* fall. The existentials (e.g., historicality, sociality) are not deducible from abstract concepts, nor are they contingencies that may or may not characterize concrete being. *Existentiell* refers to a person's concrete situation and free decisions or to one's self-understanding and self-appropriation. See M. Heidegger, *Being and Time* (New York: Harper and Row, 1962), 32–5, 70.

8 "Concerning the Relationship between Nature and Grace," *TI* i, 298. See also *FCF*, 126–27.

9 Rahner's early work focused on the existential as an effect in human nature resulting from God's intention of self-donation, his later work on the divine call itself and the historical and existential situation it effects. See D. Coffey, "The Whole Rahner on the Supernatural Existential," *Theological Studies* 65 (2004), 95–118.

10 "Atheism and Explicit Christianity," *TI* ix, 162. See also *FCF*, 130, 142–52.

11 "Nature and Grace," *TI* iv, 165–68, 177–79; "Reflections on the Experience of Grace," *TI* iii, 86–90.

12 "The Experience of God Today," *TI* xi, 149–65. See also "Religious Enthusiasm and the Experience of Grace," *TI* xvi, trans. D. Morland (London: Darton, Longman & Todd, 1979), 35–51.

13 *FCF*, 44–53; "The Concept of Mystery in Catholic Theology," *TI* iv, 49–50.

14 H. de Lubac, *Surnaturel: Etudes historiques* (Paris: Aubier, 1946, revised edn., Paris: Desclée de Brouwer, 1991). On the debate see S. Duffy, *The Graced Horizon: Nature and Grace in Modern Catholic Thought* (Collegeville, MN: Liturgical Press, 1992).

15 A first approach to his theology of nature and grace appeared in "Eine Antwort," *Orientierung* 14 (1950), 141–45. "Concerning the Relationship between Nature and Grace," *TI* i, 297–317, presents the earlier attempt in redacted form.

16 "Nature and Grace," *TI* iv, 178–80, 183–85. See also *FCF*, 142–52.

17 "History of the World and Salvation History," *TI* v, 97–114. See also *FCF* 164, 167, 138ff.

18 "History of the World and Salvation History," *TI* v, 100–02; 114.

19 "Christianity and the Non-Christian Religions," *TI* v, 128–30.

20 Essays germane to this topic include: "Christianity and the Non-Christian Religions," *TI* v, 115–34; "Reflections on the Unity of the Love of Neighbour and

the Love of God," *TI* VI, trans. K.-H. and B. Kruger (London: Darton, Longman & Todd, 1969), 231–49; "Anonymous Christians," *TI* VI, 390–98; "Atheism and Implicit Christianity," *TI* IX, 145–64; "Anonymous Christianity and the Missionary Task of the Church," *TI* XII, trans. D. Bourke (London: Darton, Longman & Todd, 1974), 161–78; "Observations on the Problem of the 'Anonymous Christian'," *TI* XIV, 280–94; "Anonymous and Explicit Faith," *TI* XVI, 52–59; "The One Christ and the Universality of Salvation," *TI* XVI, 199–224; "Jesus Christ in Non-Christian Religions," *TI* XVII, 39–50; "On the Importance of the Non-Christian Religions for Salvation," *TI* XVIII, trans. E. Quinn (London: Darton, Longman & Todd, 1983), 288–95. See also the essay by J. Fletcher Hill in this volume.

21 "The One Christ and the Universality of Salvation," *TI* XVI, 218–20.

22 Ibid., *TI* XVI, 222.

23 *FCF*, 430. On Rahner's dialectic, see J. McDermott, "Dialectical Analogy: The Oscillating Centre of Rahner's Thought," *Gregorianum* 75 (1994), 675–703.

24 "History of the World and Salvation History," *TI* V, 104.

25 Representative reactions to Rahner's anonymous Christianity include: H. U. von Balthasar, *The Moment of Christian Witness* (San Francisco: Ignatius Press, 1994), a translation of his *Cordula*; H. de Lubac, *Paradoxe et mystère de l'église* (Paris: Auber-Montaigne, 1967), 153–6; H. Küng, "Anonyme Christen – Wozu?" *Orientierung* 39 (1975), 214–16; G. D'Costa, "Karl Rahner's Anonymous Christianity," *Modern Theology* 1 (1985), 131–48; L. Lamadrid, "Anonymous or Analogous Christians? Rahner and von Balthasar on Naming the non-Christians," *Modern Theology* 11 (1995), 363–84.

26 "The Theological Concept of Concupiscentia," *TI* I, 347–82. See also "Theological Remarks on the Problem of Leisure," *TI* IV, 368–91.

27 *FCF*, 106–16.

28 See Rahner's darker essays, "Christian Pessimism," *TI* XXII, trans. J. Donceel (London: Darton, Longman & Todd, 1991), 155–62 and "Utopia and Reality," *Theology Digest* 32 (1985), 139–44.

29 I. Kant, "Idee zu einer allgemeinen Geschichte in Weltbürgerlicher Absicht," in *Kants Werke* VIII (Berlin: W. de Gruyter, 1968), 23.

30 For critiques of Rahner on this, see, e.g., H. U. von Balthasar, "Current Trends in Catholic Theology," *Communio* 5 (1978), 77–85, and J. B. Metz, *Faith in History and Society: Toward a Practical Fundamental Theology* (New York: Seabury, 1980). R. Williams, "Balthasar and Rahner," in J. Riches, ed., *The Analogy of Beauty: The Theology of Hans Urs von Balthasar* (Edinburgh: T&T Clark, 1986), 11–34, captures the seriousness of the split between Rahner and Balthasar.

Further reading

Burke, P., *Reinterpreting Rahner: A Critical Study of His Major Themes* (New York: Fordham University Press, 2002).

Duffy, S. J., *The Graced Horizon: Nature and Grace in Modern Catholic Thought* (Collegeville, MN: Liturgical Press, 1992).

The Dynamics of Grace: Perspectives in Theological Anthropology (Collegeville, MN: Liturgical Press, 1993), 261–341.

Dych, W., *Karl Rahner* (London: Geoffrey Chapman, 1992).

Lamadrid, L., "Anonymous or Analogous Christians," *Modern Theology* 11 (1995), 363–85.
Losinger, A., *The Anthropological Turn: The Human Orientation of the Theology of Karl Rahner* (New York: Fordham University Press, 2000).
Maher, M. V., "Rahner on the Human experience of God: Idealist Tautology or Christian Theology?" *Philosophy and Theology* 7 (1992), 127–64.

Part II

Theological Investigations

4 Method in theology

FRANCIS SCHÜSSLER FIORENZA

Karl Rahner developed his theology and method within the shift taking place in theology between Vatican I and Vatican II. In that period, neo-Thomist theology permeated much of academic theology. The growing influence of scriptural, patristic, liturgical, and philosophical studies began to dismantle the neo-Thomist approach and to prepare the way for Vatican II. Karl Rahner was both influenced by these advances and was a leading figure in their development in the period before and after the Council. Today, however, another significant shift is taking place. The aftermath of the Second Vatican Council saw not only the implementations of the Council, but also many multi-sided criticisms. The Right maintained that the Council went too far, whereas the Left claimed that the Council did not go far enough. From the perspective of post-liberalism, Vatican II went too far, was too progressive, and surrendered too much of the tradition for the sake of modernity. From the perspective of the various liberation, feminist, post-colonial, and pluralist theologies, the Council was too embedded within a European mentality whose patriarchalism and colonialism constitute the undersides of Western modernity. Consequently, the current scene is one of theological conflict, disagreement, and controversy.

These shifts are important for interpreting Karl Rahner's method. As the cultural climate has changed from an openness to modern philosophical values to a critical caution toward modernity and to an embrace of postmodern values, so too the assessment of Karl Rahner's method has changed.

At the time of the Second Vatican Council, Rahner's method was welcomed precisely because of its anthropological starting point and its endeavor to bring Thomist philosophy into dialogue with modern philosophy. Rahner's theology of freedom and his advocacy of free speech within the Church was seen as opening the windows of the Church to let in the fresh air of modernity. Today, however, his method is challenged on these very points. His anthropological starting point is criticized as a reductive anthropocentrism, his advocacy of freedom is denounced for mirroring the self-centred autonomy of the Enlightenment, and his existential orientation is attacked as a privatizing of religion that lacks social and political force. In addition, post-modern and post-liberal critics argue that Rahner's method continues the very errors of a modernist method in theology when that modernism is increasingly challenged.

CHALLENGES TO RAHNER'S THEOLOGICAL METHOD

Any analysis of Karl Rahner's method should consider the criticisms that have been brought against his method and its theological implications. These criticisms are diverse. One critique argues that Rahner's method has a philosophical anthropological basis, another suspects it of a false universalism, and a third questions its insufficient political basis. These criticisms are directed less against specific opinions or doctrines than against the very basis of Rahner's method, which they view as flawed. Each of these criticisms raises two basic questions. First, does the criticism do adequate justice to Rahner's theology or does it represent a caricature, distortion, misunderstanding, or partial understanding of his theology? The second question concerns the theological vision at stake. The criticisms are obviously made from different philosophical and theological presuppositions. The methodological questions, independent of any interpretative issues, are: Is Rahner correct or are his critics correct? Which theological approach is more adequate to the criteria and demands of theology?

Foundationalist method

Rowan Williams maintains along with von Balthasar and others that Karl Rahner's theology is so dependent upon philosophy that it shares the apriority, rationalism, and transcendentalism of the Kantian philosophy upon which it is built.[1] Fergus Kerr has charged that "Rahner's most characteristic theological profundities are embedded in an extremely mentalist-individualist epistemology of unmistakably Cartesian provenance," and he concludes that "it is not surprising if this mentalist-individualist conception of the self seems difficult to reconcile with the insistence on hierarchy and tradition that marks Rahner's Roman Catholic ecclesiology."[2] In a similar manner, Kevin Hart contends that Rahner does not allow sufficient room for the experience of God to influence his understanding of the human self. In his view, "the rapport between the transcendental and categorical schemas" and the "emphasis on self-transcendence minimises the attention to the transcendence of the self."[3] George Lindbeck sees Rahner's transcendental theology as an expressive experiential viewpoint that asserts a religious universalism to the neglect of the cultural linguistic particularity of Christianity.[4]

Rahner's method neglects the historical and the specific

Hans Urs von Balthasar has criticized Karl Rahner's interpretation of Christianity on several points. He asks whether it represents a one-sided interpretation of Johannine Christology and interpretation of God's love as a universal salvific that minimizes the cross and relativizes the uniqueness of Christianity. At the heart of von Balthasar's criticisms, however, is a basic theological concern: Does Rahner's method sufficiently attend to the historical singularity of the Christ event and the death of Christ? Does his method thereby relativize historical Christianity and make possible other religions as avenues of salvation?[5] Similarly, influenced by Karl Barth and George Lindbeck, Bruce Marshall criticizes Karl Rahner's Christology for understanding Christ primarily as the example of a generic. Christ is primarily an example rather than a historically unique and singular individual. What is at stake is the singularity of the Christian revelation in the face of a more universal natural and transcendental theology.[6]

Rahner's method is insufficiently political

Jürgen Moltmann's *Theology of Hope* had criticized the transcendental subjectivity of Barth and the existential hermeneutic of Rudolf Bultmann. Johann Baptist Metz, a student and life-long friend of Karl Rahner, applies the same criticism to Rahner's approach to theology. Metz questions whether it reduces salvation to a private individual affair and fails to explore the social and political dimensions of salvation history.[7] Metz's political theology seeks to provide a critical corrective to such a privatization of religion insofar as he draws out the consequences of the Christian eschatological message for the theory and practice of Christianity in modern society. Since Metz is both a critic of Rahner as well as his student, an appropriate question is: To what extent does the development of political theology and liberation theology result not just from criticisms of Rahner, but from some basic impulses that are present in Rahner's theology?

HOW NOT TO READ RAHNER ON METHOD

Although Karl Rahner has explicitly written and reflected on methodological issues within theology, method has not been as central to his work as it has been for Bernard Lonergan. Lonergan's early philosophical work on epistemology (*Insight*) and his mature work (*Method in Theology*) stand as his major achievements.[8] In contrast, after his first two books, Rahner's major writings have focused on concrete issues of theology and Church. This difference has consequences for interpreting his theology and method. Rahner should not be interpreted primarily as a philosophical epistemologist. Nor should his early publications on the philosophy of religion be understood as if they provided the methodological foundation of his future theological work or as if they constituted his mature conception of method in theology.

Instead, Rahner's concrete writings have to be examined in their diverse literary forms and in their ad hoc rhetorical situations. A distinctive characteristic of his work is the diversity of the literary genres in which he develops his theological views. These genres often correspond to the subject matter at hand. They therefore have to be read and interpreted by taking into account the pastoral and rhetorical situation and by considering the literary genre as examples of his theology in practice. His work is not dominated by the philosophy of religion. Rather, the essays in the twenty-three volumes of *Theological Investigations* deal with concrete pastoral issues in the Church, as do the innumerable encyclopedia articles, his handbook of pastoral theology, the small monographs of disputed questions, various meditations and prayers, as well as a commentary on the *Exercises of Ignatius*. In each of these diverse literary forms, Rahner shows a variety of approaches and methods that demonstrate the significance of ecclesial praxis, religious experience, and "spirituality" for his theology in ways that go beyond his early writings on the theory of knowledge.

One should read Rahner primarily as a practical theologian. He adopts as well as adapts his method to concrete theological and pastoral issues. Rahner's method is in part ad hoc and worked out in concrete cases rather than cast in stone prior to his theological essays. Yet quite often the opposite approach is taken: Rahner's method is analyzed almost exclusively in relation to its philosophical foundations in *Spirit in the World* and *Hearers of the Word* and with reference to Kant and Heidegger's philosophy.[9] Such approaches disregard significant innovations within Rahner's theological writings in the ensuing decades.

SHIFTS IN RAHNER'S METHOD

In addition, such approaches overlook the significant shifts that took place between the early philosophical writings and the later theological, pastoral, and spiritual writings. These shifts involve a theological and historical turn that seeks to take seriously the historical condition of human existence, a transition from an emphasis on intelligibility to an emphasis on mystery, and a reciprocal method by which Christology determines human nature. In addition to these three shifts, Rahner increasingly moves practical reason and pluralism to the center of his reflections on method.

A theological and historical turn

One change involves a much more theological and historical shift. The epistemological writings give a philosophical analysis of religion and deal with the possibility of revelation. They project the anthropological possibilities that spell out in advance the epistemological pre-requisites of a possible revelation. Rahner's later theological writings, however, emphasize much more strongly the historicity of Christian existence as it flows from the experience of grace and its articulation within salvation history. The de facto historical elements of the Christian narrative become much more central to his method. Even though Rahner's early work shows the influence of Heidegger's understanding of human existence as historically given, Rahner's later development accentuates this historicity even further. He focuses not only on the context of God's salvific offer of grace, but also on the contemporary situation of the Church in the world. These writings take into account in a way that the early philosophical writings do not that "the supernatural ordination to grace is not simply an external, juridical decree of God," but is "a real ontological existential of human nature that qualifies human persons really and intrinsically."[10] Therefore, reflection on human experience is not reflection on an abstract human nature that exists independently of the divine presence in grace and revelation, but rather from the very beginning of the human world one is concretely dealing with a historical presence.

From intelligibility to mystery

In addition to this fundamental shift Rahner moves from the language of being in his early philosophical writings to the language of mystery. Whereas his early philosophical writings emphasized the intelligibility of being, his theological writings underscore the mystery of God. In addition, they interpret the whither of the human question much more as a question and as one facing the mystery of meaning. They also point to the inadequacy of the notion of being as applicable to God. Moreover, the correlation between anthropology and God is not a correlation between what is clearly and distinctively known as an object of knowledge and what is unknown, so that the known then controls what is unknown but seeks to correlate what is open with what is fundamentally a mystery. Just as our language or knowledge about God is a negative theology insofar as it expresses more what God is not than what God is, so likewise Rahner develops a negative anthropology that expresses much more what human persons are not than it brings the human person into adequate concepts and categories.

Christological center

Rahner relates the transcendental quest for meaning and transcendence in history to salvation history. As Rahner develops his Christology, he develops the reciprocal nature of this relationship and it becomes increasingly clear that Christology determines anthropology. The formula that Christology is perfect anthropology or anthropology is imperfect Christology is an abstract and formal formula that only receives its content through an analysis of his Christology. Consequently, in understanding human freedom, Rahner interprets this freedom not in relation to some abstract conception of human nature, but in relation to the interpretation of God's self-communication in Christ. It is from the paradigmatic action of Jesus, his love and solidarity with humans, and his acceptance of his finitude in accepting his death that one gains insight into the meaning of human freedom.

Because Rahner's Christology influences his view of human existence, his concept of human freedom is far from a modern emphasis on self-interestedness or self-centeredness. Rahner underscores that "by freely accepting the fate of death Jesus surrenders himself precisely to the unforeseen and incalculable possibilities of his existence"[11] and maintains in his death the hope of God's salvific will. In this way, Jesus as human is God's self-revelation not just through his word, but through his humanity as the expression of the meaning both of God and of human nature.[12] Notions of self-surrender, solidarity, and love enter into his understanding of human nature. The paradigm of Jesus' life as a life for others illuminates Rahner's interpretation of religious obedience and discipleship. The acceptance of finitude and the acceptance of death are so central to Rahner's christological understanding of human nature that one can in no way attribute to him a Hobbesian understanding of human nature as self-interested or a notion of human autonomy as mastery over nature. Rahner's method is such that he does not take a secular modern vision of humanity and project it back to Christology, but rather makes the concrete existence of Jesus the norm for understanding Christian existence. This norm of human existence is constituted by an openness to what is incalculable, unforeseen, and ultimately mystery.

Rahner himself explicitly demarcates his view from any secular humanism:

> Christianity's *concretissimum* for which alone it stands, is Jesus Christ, who in accepting death and suffering *for us* (and in no other way) has created our relationship of immediacy before God, and the Church, which looks for the Kingdom which is yet to be fulfilled and which is not identical with the humanism we ourselves have produced or shall produce in the near future.[13]

This christological center shows the influence of the historical within Rahner's method. It is overlooked when his theology is reduced to an abstract transcendental emphasis on freedom and autonomy. His method requires that the meaning of human existence be specified from the historical individuality of Jesus' existence rather than from abstract a priori reflection.

PHILOSOPHY AND THE FOUNDATIONS OF THEOLOGY

Karl Rahner's view of method in theology entails a dual affirmation of the relationship between philosophy and theology. Theology necessarily engages in philosophical reflection. Nevertheless, there is no ready-made or pre-existing philosophy that can serve as the tool or "ancilla" of theology in distinction to the neo-scholastic view. This view of the relation between philosophy and theology has implications for Rahner's understanding of the relation between fundamental theology and systematic theology and it also explains why, in a preface to a book on his work, he can write that it "deals with my theology and (as far as something can even be found) my philosophy."[14] The philosophical reflection takes place in Rahner's work within his theology and as an integral part of his theological reflection and not as something providing an external foundation.

RELATION BETWEEN PHILOSOPHY AND THEOLOGY

In outlining his conception of theology, Rahner clearly demarcates theology from a Biblicism or a dogmatic or magisterial positivism – a tendency more prevalent in some Roman Catholic circles.[15] The doing of theology does not consist mainly in ordering or structuring biblical statements as if systematic theology were equivalent to the interpretation of the Christian Scriptures. Likewise, doing theology is more than the mere exposition or interpretation of magisterial pronouncements or doctrinal statements. Such an approach overlooks the historical rationality and context of magisterial doctrinal statements and of biblical or even New Testament theologies.

Through the second affirmation, Rahner differentiates the role of philosophy from neo-scholastic views that sought to rely on neo-scholastic philosophy as the ready-made instrument of theology. Rahner argues that such a monolithic and instrumental view of philosophy is no longer the case – not even for neo-scholasticism itself. He maintains that even though neo-scholasticism sought to maintain continuity with medieval and baroque scholastic philosophy, as a result of the encounter with the profusion of the many different challenges and problems, it too has become very diverse and no longer exists as a single circumscribed philosophy. Consequently, Rahner concludes – and even italicizes his concluding summary so as to underscore its importance: *"there no longer exists today any philosophy which can be assumed as ready-made and already adapted to the needs of theology. This applies equally to the Catholic Christian."*[16] Rahner's affirmation of the radical pluralism of philosophy shows his avoidance of foundationalism. In Rahner's view theology needs to take this pluralism into account and to become aware that this pluralism is not something that should – or could – be overcome. The plurality of philosophies cannot be synthesized into a foundational philosophy that would then serve as the foundation of theology.

Philosophia negativa

Rahner introduces almost as a technical term the notion of *philosophia negativa* (negative philosophy) – a term reminiscent of the classic term *theologia negativa*. There is, indeed, a parallelism between the classic term of negative theology and Rahner's coinage of the term *philosophia negativa*. Classical theology in its awareness of the transcendence of God underscored the limitations of statements about God. Such statements were made by way of affirmation, negation, and eminence. In affirming God as wise, one must correctly understand that God's wisdom should not be equated with human wisdom (negation) and that God's wisdom excels all notions of human wisdom (eminence). The category of *theologia negativa* affirmed the inadequacy of applying human categories and concepts directly to God so that human statements about God are more unlike God than like God.

Rahner introduces the category of *philosophia negativa* to underscore the limitations of all philosophical categories to express adequately human experience and reality. The conceptual inadequacy of philosophy means that philosophy cannot serve as a foundational instrument for theology. This inability has, in Rahner's view, various causes. It stems from the pluralism of philosophies evident in the mutual confrontation of a plurality of cultures in our contemporary cosmopolitan world. It arises from the growing complexity and specialization within philosophy in which individual philosophers are increasingly expert in only one specific branch or subspecialty of philosophy. Most importantly, it results from the richness and pluralism of the human source of experience that can never be adequately conceptualized or instrumentalized in philosophy. A theology that engages in philosophy is engaging in a philosophy that is not foundationalist, but is open to the increasing pluralism of human experience and the diverse embeddedness of those experiences in and through different cultures. It is a philosophy that is done within and through theology.

FUNDAMENTAL THEOLOGY AND THEOLOGY

Rahner's reinterpretation of the role of philosophy leads to his rethinking of the relationship between fundamental theology and systematic theology. Whereas fundamental theology emerged in modernity as an independent discipline that should serve as the foundation for systematic theology, Rahner significantly rejects not only such foundationalism, but also the traditional sharp separation between fundamental and systematic theology. Instead Rahner locates fundamental theology in relation to all the treatises of systematic theology. It is part and parcel of systematic theology itself and flows from systematic theology. Even fundamental theology understood as a basic introductory course introduces one to the idea of Christianity and therefore embraces the whole of systematic theology; or as one located "from a place at the conclusion of dogmatics it could serve as a further critical reappraisal of, and reflection upon, the responsibility which our faith and our hope lays upon us."[17]

Rahner's method has been influenced by Pierre Rousselot (1878–1915) and *la nouvelle théologie* and this influence is important for his understanding of fundamental theology. Rousselot had argued in his book *The Eyes of Faith* for the cognitive importance of faith and grace.[18] He thereby reintroduced Augustinian themes into the Roman Catholic theology of the twentieth century. Rahner is convinced that Rousselot is basically correct, but suggests that he has not adequately integrated his vision into anthropology or an understanding of human nature. However, in the light of this influence, Rahner argues, fundamental theology does not demonstrate Christian faith through some universal, a priori, and neutral rational standards. Instead, it seeks to connect Christian faith and human existence in its everyday experience. The historical presence of grace as God's offer to all humans establishes an intrinsic dynamism within human nature so that there is an isomorphism between the agent who believes and what is believed. Fundamental theology is not a preliminary foundation but is an interpretation of the content of Christian beliefs that seeks to illuminate their significance and relevance.

In developing fundamental theology, Rahner explicates several important elements of method. These include the development of an "indirect method" in relation to traditional analysis of the ground faith, the transcendental dimension of theology, the importance of praxis for method in theology, and the role of pluralism and gnoseological concupiscence, and his notion of mystagogy as a training and introduction in theology.

INDIRECT METHOD

In 1964 Rahner introduced the category of "indirect method" in relation to the traditional problems of the analysis of faith and the basis or ground of faith. This indirect method can be contrasted with the "scientific" demonstration of the neo-scholastic fundamental theologies. Using the philosophical categories and the historical methods of its age, the neo-scholastic fundamental theology sought a threefold demonstration of faith that was both independent of faith and could be produced with a reasonable credibility: the demonstration of the possibility of revelation by means of a philosophy of religion; the demonstration of the truth of Christian revelation through historical arguments from the prophecies in the Hebrew Scriptures, the miracles of Christ reported in the Gospels and the New Testament testimonies to the resurrection of Jesus; and, finally, the demonstration of Catholic revelation through the historical demonstration that Jesus founded a Church with Peter as its head and that the Roman Catholic Church has maintained a legitimate succession to this Church founded by Jesus. These demonstrations were intended to establish the credibility of faith independent of faith in a way that was in principle accessible to all non-prejudiced persons.[19]

In contrast to such a "scientific demonstration," Rahner calls for an indirect method in the face of the increased knowledge and specialization necessary to make scientific judgments. Today, no single person can acquire the competency to be the judge of a whole range of questions involving the grounds of faith that were treated in traditional fundamental theology. Rahner explicitly refers to some of the central issues of fundamental theology, such as the historical foundation of the Church and the primacy of Peter, the continuity of Catholic institutional Christianity with Christ, the causes, occasion, and legitimacy of the Protestant Reformation, etc. The expertise of both an early Christian scholar and a Reformation historian would be required. Rahner observes that we experience the same increased knowledge and specialization in the natural sciences and in technology. However, in these cases one can simply assume what others tell us or we assume their truth through our practical use. For example, we can use word processing without having to understand the digitizing of language and we flip a switch to turn on the light without knowing the nature of electricity. However, a significant difference exists between scientific and technological matters, on the one hand, and religious issues of faith. Faith involves personal commitments and engagement. Hence one cannot simply presuppose their truth.

The traditional demonstration is no longer a practical possibility for most. Persons are faced with making personal decisions before they can have an exhaustive consideration of all the factors involved. Such decisions take place in many aspects of life and they also take place in regard to faith. Such an indirect method calls for a reconsideration of the traditional theories of the *analysis of faith*. However, Rahner does see some support for his position in the way the traditional fundamental theology reflected on the situation of the uneducated "rudis" and in Cardinal Newman's use of the illative sense. Newman's illative sense takes into account the distinction between theoretical and practical reason so that practical reason should not be seen as derivative of theoretical reason or a mere deduction or application of theoretical reason. In emphasizing that there are not universal criteria for decision-making, Rahner underscores a uniqueness to decision-making that Newman's view does not take sufficiently into account.

In his suggestions for the reform of theological studies, Rahner calls for the indirect method as a "first stage of reflection" that should clarify the meaning that an educated person has of his or her faith without being a theological specialist. Rahner's *Foundations of Christian Faith* develops this first stage of reflection or indirect method and one chapter outlines an "indirect method for showing the legitimacy of the Catholic Church as the Church of Christ."[20] It starts out with a trusting reliance on the Christian and ecclesial existence in which one finds oneself. He develops criteria of continuity, basic substance, and objective authority, and applies these criteria to the Roman Catholic Church. On the other hand, he takes seriously the impulse of the Protestant Reformation by arguing that the emphasis on faith, grace, and Scripture are present in the Roman Catholic Church also. His indirect method invokes an experience of the spiritual power of Christianity (reminiscent of Lessing's *Power of the Spirit*) and a conviction about the substance of what constitutes Christianity. Hence Rahner writes:

[B]ecause I am convinced that the true church of Jesus Christ exists only where there is found the pneumatic reality of Christianity which I have already experienced by the power of the Spirit, for these reasons I can regard a Christian church and community as the church of Jesus only if and to the extent that it does not contradict the basic substance of Christianity which I have already experienced in my own existence.[21]

This quotation illustrates the method of Rahner's appeal to experience. He appeals neither to some abstract experience nor to some neutral philosophical viewpoint, but to an experience of the "pneumatic reality of Christianity." Rahner gives this experience weight in elaborating the criteria of theology. He argues in a similar manner for the foundation of the Church, though he also gives exegetical and historical reasons. The indirect method does not appeal to a universal or abstract anthropology, but to the concrete experience of divine grace in human life and to the historical vision of what constitutes the substance of Christianity.

TRANSCENDENTAL METHOD

Rahner is often classified as a transcendental Thomist or as a theologian employing a transcendental method. However, it is important to understand Rahner's use of "transcendental" and to locate that understanding within the context of his view of the relation between philosophy and theology. The term "transcendental" has diverse meanings. One needs to distinguish carefully between the medieval use of the term and its meaning in modern philosophy, especially Kantian philosophy. In medieval scholasticism, the term "transcendental" refers to those attributes of being that transcend the individual categories of being in distinction to the categories that could only be applied to a certain category of being. Material beings have colour or quantity, whereas spiritual beings do not. Goodness is transcendental because it can be applied across the diverse categories of being. Modern philosophy, influenced by Kant's definition of "transcendental" in the *Critique of Pure Reason*, uses "transcendental" to refer not so much to the object of knowledge but rather to "the mode of knowledge of objects insofar as this mode of knowledge is to be possible a priori."[22] Moreover, Kant sharply distinguishes the word "transcendental" from "transcendent." Whereas the transcendent refers to what is beyond experience, the transcendental refers to the conditions of experience.[23] Kant's definition underscores both the a priori and the distinction between transcendental and transcendent. In addition to the medieval and the Kantian understanding, there is Heidegger's use of transcendental in the sense of anthropological, especially in regard to the human way of existence.

Rahner's use of "transcendental" is often read exclusively in relation to Kant's use of the term transcendental. Yet this common reading must be avoided because of decisive differences. Karl Rahner's usage should be seen as combining the medieval and modern notions of transcendental. His distinction between transcendental and categorical is closer to Heidegger's usage than to Kant's. Rahner speaks of the transcendental experience as an experience of God and here he differs very much from Kant who would never speak of such an experience. Second, though Rahner refers to the a priori, he thereby refers to the historically conditioned human experience of grace. Third, Rahner's use of the term "transcendental" is frequent and diverse: transcendental experience, transcendental reflection, transcendental subject, a transcendental-anthropological way of asking questions, a transcendental method, and a transcendental experience. The breadth of his use of the term "transcendental" indicates both its centrality and a certain "looseness" in its meaning. It is better to understand "transcendental" not as a strict philosophical category in Rahner's theology but much more as a concern about the anthropological significance. It is, therefore, important to see the link between theology and anthropology as the key to understanding what he means by "transcendental theology."

Consequently, Rahner uses the transcendental method less as a specific philosophical method – such as Kant's transcendental deduction and justification – and much more as a way of questioning and relating religious beliefs to basic human questions and experiences of life. Indeed, this is one of the decisive differences between Joseph Maréchal and Karl Rahner. Whereas Maréchal relies on judgment, Rahner places the knowledge of God in relation to a questioning about the meaning and mystery of life that transcends the objects of experience but takes place within life. Rahner's method is much like Heidegger's hermeneutical circle and in its circularity is equally anti-foundational.[24] The experiences that persons have lead them to raise the question of the meaning of the totality of reality. The pre-understanding is that just as one has a life-relation to a subject matter in order to understand it, so too must one have some life-relation to understand what the proofs of God's existence are about.[25] This questioning is transcendental in the sense that it goes beyond every limited answer and beyond every empirical object. Such radical questioning is like the unlimited desire expressed in Augustine's description: our hearts do not rest except in God. In experiencing the objects of the world in knowledge and love, humans search for

what transcends them. It is this Augustinian description of the unlimited-
ness of human desire that better characterizes Rahner's understanding of
"transcendental" than Kant's notion of a transcendental deduction.

In Rahner's method, "the transcendental orientation of man to the
incomprehensible and ineffable Mystery which constitutes the enabling
condition for knowledge and freedom, and therefore for subjective life as
such, in itself implies a real, albeit a non-thematic experience of God."[26] In
elucidating the experiences of transcendence in knowledge and love, Rahner
underscores how these come to the fore in the experience of responsibility,
love for another, acceptance of one's finitude and death in a sea of mystery.
Rahner carefully underscores the limits of theology as transcendental lest
it be understood as an inadequate anthropologizing of theology or as an
absolutizing of philosophy as an independent universal norm. He asserts
that what belongs "intrinsically to transcendental theology is precisely its
conscious recognition of its own limitations."[27] These limits are several:
First, an individual cannot draw the resources for life from some abstract
metaphysics or from some philosophy. There is a difference between the
experience of life and abstract philosophical conceptuality. In Rahner's view,
a person can only accept his or her history as that which he or she must
accept and must act responsibly within and yet cannot ever adequately comprehend. The second limitation of theology as transcendental is that while
its historical origin is indebted to a transcendental philosophy, this indebtedness does not entail the mere taking over of a transcendental philosophy.
The major reason for this limitation is theological because "the true source
of any transcendental theology [is] itself genuinely theological."[28] God's self-
communication as grace and the human consciousness of history constitute
the historical existential of being human.

PRAXIS AND METHOD: THEOLOGY
AS PRACTICAL THEOLOGY

The mature Rahner, involved in the practical implementation of Vatican
II, increasingly emphasized the significance of praxis for method in theology. The term "praxis" refers back to Aristotle's distinction between practice
as a skill or a technique of making and practice as a way of life. Rahner's turn
to practice involves several significant elements of method, the rethinking
of pastoral theology as practical theology, the importance of practical over
theoretical reason, the pluralism of the contemporary situation, and what
Rahner calls "gnoseological concupiscence."

One of Rahner's major contributions to method in theology is his rethinking of "pastoral theology" as "practical theology." Instead of understanding pastoral theology as a set of skills or simply as training in ministerial skills, Rahner reformulates pastoral theology as the actualization of the Church in practice and conceives of it in a way that underscores the integrity of praxis and influence of practical reason. Theoretical reason has lost its previous primacy; instead, practical reason has taken its place. This shift to practical reason results from a changed situation and has consequences for method in theology. The world is not only becoming increasingly dynamic and changing, but it is also increasingly seen as the result of human activity. The world is no longer a static object of human contemplation, but rather the material of human activity. Such a transformation has implications for practical theology and its relation to theology itself. "Practical theology can and must be the critical conscience of the other theological disciplines."[29] Practical theology has to make the individual theological disciplines aware of the element of practice within themselves as that which the discipline has to take into account if it is to be itself. Homiletics should be concerned not just with the technical skills of oral delivery, but with the content of the message and its mediation. In this way, practical theology becomes relevant for church history, exegesis, liturgy, and the other disciplines of theology.

In developing the method of practical theology as the actualization of the Church, Rahner explicates his understanding of political theology as explicating the social and political relevance of the Church. Whereas Metz has criticized Rahner's work for its lack of a political dimension, Rahner in his later writings accepts the importance of the political and locates it in relation to the Church's realization in praxis. He indeed writes on political topics, such as the Holocaust and nuclear warfare.

CONCLUSION: "GNOSEOLOGICAL" CONCUPISCENCE AND MYSTAGOGY

In conclusion, it is clear that Rahner's method has a distinct profile when one takes into account the shifts from the intelligibility of being to mystery, from theoretical reason to practical reason, and from unity to pluralism. These shifts are summed up in two key terms: "gnoseological concupiscence" and "mystagogy." In his analysis of the function and method of theology, Rahner argues that theology has the function of being the defender of "gnoseological concupiscence." This term is central to Rahner's description of theology's methodological self-understanding. In popular vocabulary "concupiscence" is often understood as desire, often uncontrolled desire, especially sexual desire. The term denotes that human persons are not so unified that they desire only what they think best. Instead, human persons experience themselves with a multiplicity of feelings, a plurality of desires, and a diversity of thoughts that cannot be simply harmonized and brought together. "Gnoseological concupiscence," therefore, describes the contemporary situation of contemporary theology in which there are competing and legitimate ideas and it brings to the fore the centrality of pluralism to Rahner's method that seeks to reflect the unavoidable pluralism of human life.

The centrality of Rahner's emphasis on pluralism has led Joseph Cardinal Ratzinger and Hans Urs von Balthasar to criticize Rahner. Von Balthasar views Rahner's view of pluralism as a pessimism that fails to grasp that the whole of Catholic truth is a harmony.[30] In response, Rahner contends that von Balthasar's worldview in which every piece fits harmonically together elevates and almost divinizes the human good. The whole of reality may be a symphony for von Balthasar, but it is not for others. This difference of the possibility of such a symphonic harmony ultimately characterizes the basic difference between Rahner and von Balthasar in their approach to the nature of theology. Rahner argues that pluralism is such that the creeds can no longer present a unity of the world.

Nevertheless, there is a unity insofar as Rahner seeks to develop theology as a discourse that is based upon a concrete historical experience of human nature as disclosed in the history of salvation and God's dealing with the human race.[31] In speaking of the theology of the future, Rahner labels such a theology a mystagogical theology or a theology that is both "missionary and mystagogic."[32] The beliefs, practices, and traditions that were commonly accepted and were seen as essential to the good of society are no longer unquestioningly accepted as integral to society's well-being. Theology and the proclamation of the Christian message often appealed to what was generally accepted as good, true, or valuable by society in general. Today the situation is no longer the same. One cannot appeal to a neutral universal or foundational truth to ground Christianity, but one has to appeal to a concrete experience of grace and initiate Christians into this experience. "The community church will be transformed into a Church made up of those who believe as a matter of personal conviction and individual decision."[33] For theology this means that theology involves a mystagogy. This term, taken over from the Greek Fathers, especially Gregory of Nyssa, refers to the initiation into the mysteries of Christianity and expresses the mystical and spiritual aspect of Rahner's method.[34]

Notes

1 R. Williams, "Balthasar and Rahner," in J. Riches, ed., *The Analogy of Beauty* (Edinburgh: T&T Clark, 1986), 11–34. H. Urs von Balthasar, *Love Alone: The Way of Revelation* (New York: Herder and Herder, 1968).

2 F. Kerr, *Theology after Wittgenstein* (New York: Blackwell, 1986), 14.

3 K. Hart, "'Absolute Interruption': on Faith," in J. D. Caputo, M. Dooley, and M. J. Scanlon, ed., *Questioning God* (Bloomington: Indiana University Press, 2001), 186–208, at 196.

4 R. R. Reno, *The Ordinary Transformed* (Grand Rapids: W. B. Eerdmans, 1995).

5 H. Urs von Balthasar, *The Moment of Christian Witness* (San Francisco: Ignatius Press, 1969).

6 B. Marshall, *Christology in Conflict: The Identity of a Saviour in Rahner and Barth* (New York: Blackwell, 1987).

7 J. B. Metz, "Foreword" to *Spirit in the World*, xvii–xviii, and his *A Passion for God: The Mystical-Political Dimension of Christianity* (Mahwah, NJ: Paulist, 1998). See also G. Martinez, *Confronting the Mystery of God: Political, Liberation, and Public Theologies* (New York: Continuum, 2001).

8 B. Lonergan, *Insight: A Study of Human Understanding* (New York: Philosophical Library, 1956), and *Method in Theology* (New York: Crossroad, 1972).

9 T. Sheehan, *Karl Rahner: The Philosophical Foundations* (Athens, OH: Ohio University Press, 1987).

10 "The Theological Concept of Concupiscentia," *TI* I, 376 (Engl. trans. modified).

11 *FCF*, 255.

12 Ibid., 224.

13 "Christian Humanism," *TI* IX, 195.

14 K. Rahner, "Zum Geleit," in G. Neuhaus, *Transzendentale Erfahrung als Geschichtsverlust?* (Düsseldorf: Patmos, 1982), 11.

15 See M. E. Hines, *The Transformation of Dogma* (New York: Paulist, 1989).

16 "Philosophy and Philosophising in Theology," *TI* IX, 48.

17 "The Theology of the Future," *TI* XIII, 58. See also his *Zur Reform des Theologiestudiums*, Quaestiones Disputate 41 (Freiburg: Herder, 1969).

18 P. Rousselot, *The Eyes of Faith*, trans. M. Raftery (New York: Fordham University Press, 1990).

19 For a sketch of the traditional fundamental theology and its treatment of the foundation of the Church and resurrection of Jesus, see my *Foundational Theology* (New York: Crossroad, 1984).

20 *FCF*, 346–69.

21 Ibid., 355.

22 I. Kant, *Critique of Pure Reason*, A11-a12/B25, trans. N. K. Smith (London: Macmillan & Co., 1964), 58–59.

23 See I. Kant, *Prolegomena to any Future Metaphysics*, trans. P. G. Lucas (Manchester: Manchester University Press, 1966), 142–43 and *Critique of Pure Reason* A295/B352–53, 298–99.

24 F. Fiorenza, "Karl Rahner and the Kantian Problematic," in *SW*, xix–xlv. See O. Muck's agreement on this important difference, "Heidegger und Karl Rahner," *Zeitschrift für katholische Theologie* 116 (1994), 257–69. A debated issue is

Rahner's references to "unthematic" and "mediated immediacy." They show Rahner wants to underscore an immediacy but at the same time realizes that all immediacy is also mediated.

25 M. Heidegger, *Being and Time*, trans. J. Macquarrie and E. Robinson (Oxford: Blackwell, 1962), #32, 188–95.

26 "Experience of Self and Experience of God," *TI* xiii, 123.

27 "The Theology of the Future," *TI* xiii, 45.

28 Ibid., *TI* xiii, 46.

29 "The Future of Theology," *TI* xi, 134.

30 See H. Urs von Balthasar, "'Geist und Feuer:' Ein Gespräch mit Hans Urs von Balthasar," *Herder Korrespondenz* 30 (1976), 72–82, where he states that he does not believe in the pluralism of Rahner (p. 76). For an examination of von Balthasar's criticisms, see E. Conway, *The Anonymous Christian – a Relativised Christianity?: An Evaluation of Hans Urs von Balthasar's Criticisms of Karl Rahner's Theory of the Anonymous Christian* (New York: Peter Lang, 1993).

31 A. Carr, *The Theological Method of Karl Rahner* (Missoula, MT: Scholars Press, 1977), 105.

32 "The Theology of the Future," *TI* xiii, 40.

33 Ibid.

34 K. P. Fischer, *Gotteserfahrung: Mystagogie in der Theologie Karl Rahners und in der Theologie der Befreiung* (Mainz: Matthias-Grunewald-Verlag, 1986). See also D. Marmion, *A Spirituality of Everyday Faith: A Theological Investigation of the Notion of Spirituality in Karl Rahner* (Louvain: Peeters, 1998), 262–65.

Further reading

Carr, A. E., *The Theological Method of Karl Rahner* (Missoula, MT: Scholars Press, 1977).

Fiorenza, F. S., *Foundational Theology: Jesus and the Church* (New York: Crossroad, 1984).

Hines, M. E., *The Transformation of Dogma: An Introduction to Karl Rahner on Doctrine* (New York: Paulist, 1989).

Metz, J. B., *A Passion for God: The Mystical-Political Dimension of Christianity* (Mahwah, NJ: Paulist, 1998).

Neumann, K., *Der Praxisbezug der Theologie bei Karl Rahner* (Freiburg: Herder, 1980).

5 Revelation and faith

DANIEL DONOVAN

Revelation and its correlative, faith, were at the heart of Karl Rahner's life and work. As a priest and theologian, his major concern was ultimately a pastoral one, that of helping people to come to faith, to deepen their faith, to make it a life-enhancing, life-directing force in their lives. His focus was on both the content of faith and the existential appropriation of that content in the lived response of believers to it, on *fides quae* and *fides qua*.

When Rahner began his theological career issues of revelation and faith tended to be addressed primarily within the context of fundamental theology and its preoccupation with apologetics. Although new and creative developments were beginning to be made in this area, the neo-scholastic approach remained dominant. Described as a form of extrinsicism, its concern was to establish the possibility and credibility of a historical revelation by God in the history of Israel and especially in the person of Jesus. Particular emphasis was given to miracles and the fulfillment of prophecy as divine endorsement of the claims of Jesus. A further task of this kind of apologetics was to show that Jesus instituted the Church and entrusted to its teaching authority the content of revelation. The method of argumentation remained on what might be called the formal level in that it was intent on establishing the fact of revelation and the formal structures by which that revelation is handed on in the Church. No consideration was given to the content of revelation or to the actual situation of those to whom the gospel was to be preached.[1]

THE POSSIBILITY OF FAITH

As he began his own theological work, Rahner felt obliged to address some of the classic issues of apologetics. As he did so, he saw himself confronted by two extremes, which he described as a modernistic reduction of revelation to an objectification or articulation of religious experience on the one hand and neo-scholastic extrinsicism on the other. Much of his theological work can be seen as an attempt to discern a mid ground between these positions. This is certainly the case in *Hearers of the Word*, a series of lectures delivered in 1937 and first published in 1941. It offers elements of a philosophy of religion intended as a part of a rethinking of the whole task of fundamental theology. Using the philosophical anthropology developed in *Spirit in the World* and broadening it to include freedom, will, and love alongside intellect and knowledge, Rahner argues that if human beings understood themselves they would understand that they ought to be on the look-out for a possible revelation of God in history.[2]

The argument in *Hearers* is mainly philosophical. It does not develop an explicit theology of revelation, but satisfies itself with the broad category "the word of God." Although Metz and others have suggested that at this point in his career Rahner simply accepted the neo-scholastic notion of revelation as a series of propositions, that does not seem to be the case.[3] The "word" here is more than a proposition. It suggests all the ways in which God's self-revelation in Christ comes to us in the life of the Church, in its preaching and doctrine, its sacraments and ritual. The focus of the book, however, is not revelation and its mediation but rather human beings as possible hearers of God's word.

Rahner's approach at this stage has affinities with Maurice Blondel's "way of immanence."[4] Active at the time of the modernist crisis, Blondel developed a philosophy of action that sought, by a systematic reflection on the subjective experiences of choosing, willing, and acting, to open the subject to the possibility of what he called the "Christian supernatural." Rahner's attempt was similar but in developing it he used his own distinctive philosophical anthropology.

In *Hearers of the Word*, Rahner invites us to reflect on ourselves, on our knowing and questioning, on our willing and loving, and to become aware of ourselves as beings of radical openness, as beings with a capacity for the absolute and the infinite, as beings of transcendence, who, as such, are already and always in relationship with the infinite mystery we call God. In spite of this openness to God, we do not know or relate to God in the way that we know and relate to everything else that falls within our purview. We do not know God as an object among other objects, but rather as the condition of possibility for all our knowing and acting. We are spirit, but spirit in the world. Because we are in the world, in time and space, our knowledge comes to us from outside, it comes through our senses. We know and choose this and that, but we do it in ways that reveal that we are already moving beyond the particular to the infinite horizon within which the individual thing is known as such. The awareness of this horizon, of the absolute and infinite being that is the ground and the free cause of our being, awakens us to the possibility that it might reveal itself to us. The fact that we are embodied spirits, that we are in time and space and history, makes us look to history as the place of a possible revelation.

As much as Rahner over the years will modify this starting point as he becomes more explicitly theological, its basic structure and the concern it embodies will remain. From the beginning Rahner had an acute sense of the enormous challenge to faith represented by modern Western culture. Long before it became fashionable, he spoke of the growing diaspora situation of believers in the West. He recognized the challenge involved in the shift from a church of the masses to a church of individual believers. *Hearers of the Word* reveals what will be an abiding concern of Rahner: how to help people living in the modern world to recognize that faith in both the mystery of God and the message of the gospel remains for them a genuine possibility.

REVELATION AS SELF-COMMUNICATION

One of the first areas or tracts of theology that Rahner was called upon to teach at Innsbruck was grace. Over the years, he steeped himself in and made his own the great scholastic and neo-scholastic tradition on grace. Even as he did so, however, he developed it in new directions with the aid of his philosophical anthropology. Following Aquinas Rahner saw grace as the key to Christianity.[5] Whereas the tradition before him primarily understood it as a created reality, a disposition of the human spirit enabling it through faith, hope, and love to be in an intimate relationship with God, Rahner emphasized what the tradition had called uncreated grace. Grace, in this sense, is God turned to us, inviting and enabling us to share the divine life, drawing us into a dynamic and dialogical relationship with himself.[6]

For Rahner, Christianity is primarily the good news that the infinite mystery towards which, as creatures, we are open has, in freedom and love, decided to offer itself to us so that it might become the very center of our lives. This, for Rahner, is the heart of the gospel; this is what has been revealed and actualized in a unique and definitive way in the life and destiny of Jesus.

For Rahner, the self-revelation and self-communication of God are insep-arable. What is revealed in the history of salvation and in a final and defini-tive way in Jesus is God's desire to communicate Godself to us. Such self-communication always involves a self-revelation. The categories of grace and of revelation for Rahner are not only related, they are in many ways all but interchangeable, a conviction rooted ultimately in his basic understanding of the identity of being and knowing.

Grace for Rahner and for the great tradition on which he draws is supernatural, it goes beyond the capacity of nature and is the result of a free and gratuitous act on the part of God. Although Aquinas emphasized the positive connection between nature and grace, the neo-scholastic tradition took it as a given that the supernatural was by definition beyond experience. Its presence is only known to us through faith in the word of revelation. By way of contrast, Rahner argues that it is something that can be experienced in a way analogous to the way we experience ourselves as beings of openness to the infinite and holy mystery.

A third element in Rahner's developing theology of grace, and one that will be crucial for his understanding of revelation, is his conviction about its universality, a conviction rooted in his rethinking of the traditional understanding of God's universal saving will. Here Rahner appeals to classic New Testament texts, especially 1 Timothy 2:16, and then, after Vatican II, to *Lumen Gentium*, 16 and *Ad Gentes*, 7. Because salvation means a share in God's life and because that is only possible through grace, the affirmation of God's universal saving will requires that all people everywhere be confronted with the offer of grace.

The universal offer of grace entails a universal revelation. There can be no self-communication of God without a self-revelation, and there can be no revelation in the full sense of the term without faith. The external revelation that comes to us in Jesus and the Scriptures can only be heard and received by those who have been transformed from within by grace and the gift of the Spirit. Faith as a free act of a person in response to revelation is only possible because of a prior gift of God leading and disposing the subject, giving it a certain connaturality with its object. The act of faith involves the coming together in the most intimate way of God's gift and human freedom. As gift, faith creates what the scholastic tradition described as a new formal object, a new light under which things are seen. Rahner suggests that God's universal offer of grace entails a universal revelation in the sense that the offer, even before its acceptance in the form of justifying grace, creates a new situation for humans, a situation he describes as a supernatural existential.[7]

The concept of "existential" is taken over from Heidegger. It suggests a fundamental condition, a situatedness, of human life. It is something that is given and to which and about which we react in the course of our lives. Analogous "existentials" of human existence would be "being in the world" and "being unto death." Talk of a supernatural existential points to the fact that in the world as it is known to us through the gospel every human being exists in relation to the self-communicating God. There is no purely natural experience of human life. Ours is a world that is permeated by grace. The infinite horizon within which we live our lives has revealed itself in Jesus as a mystery of self-communicating love.

TRANSCENDENTAL AND CATEGORIAL REVELATION

Two fundamental terms in Rahner's philosophical epistemology are "transcendental" and "categorial." The latter points to the kind of knowledge and choices that focus on particular questions and issues and objects. It corresponds to our being in the world, our embodied existence, our historical nature. The word "transcendental" in Rahner's thought has a number of meanings. Sometimes it refers to the so-called transcendentals of traditional philosophy (e.g., unity, goodness, truth, being), things that are common to all beings as such. More often, especially in the phrase "transcendental method," the word evokes the philosophy of Kant and more immediately the transcendental Thomism of Maréchal.[8] Here it suggests a reflecting back on the subject and on the conditions of possibility for knowing and willing. Going beyond Kant with Maréchal, Rahner uses it to point to a distinguishing feature of the human spirit. Humans are said to be beings of transcendence in the sense that in them there is an inner dynamism of spirit that reaches out beyond the individual and particular object of knowledge and choice to the infinite horizon within which human life is played out.

Our ordinary knowledge is categorial knowledge. It is the kind of knowledge that comes to us through the senses and that even as intellectual is known in relation to the data they present. Transcendental knowledge, or transcendental experience as it is also called, is non-categorial, it is not a knowing of something as an object but rather the awareness we have of ourselves in our categorial knowing and willing as reaching out to the mystery that surrounds and permeates and grounds our life. It is a knowledge that accompanies categorial knowledge, a knowledge on which we can reflect and of which we can try to get some understanding but which, even as we do, continues to elude us.

Transcendental revelation is universal revelation. In the world in which we live, a world permeated by grace, it is given to every human being. Subjectively it takes the form of the supernatural existential. Objectively, it is God's self-revelation and self-communication to finite spirits. To be human, for Rahner, is to be involved with the self-revealing, self-communicating God, whether one is aware of it or not, whether one responds positively or negatively to God's offer. In that sense revelation is co-extensive with human life and human history. Revelation and our reaction to it is in fact the deepest dimension and ultimate meaning of the historical process.

Transcendental revelation is inseparable from some kind of categorial experience. We only become aware of it as we engage with mind and heart, in knowledge and love, in the world. It is for this reason that Rahner can say that all of human history is a form of categorial revelation. It is, however, a revelation that is always unclear and mixed with sin and self-destructiveness. It becomes clearer and more focused in the history of religion. The so-called special history of revelation and of salvation that we know through the Bible, the story of Israel, and especially the life and destiny of Jesus, constitutes a high point in regard to categorial revelation and as such represents the fullness of revelation.[9]

In the course of his career Rahner developed in creative and imaginative ways the implications of his understanding of God's universal saving will, the supernatural existential, and transcendental revelation. The theory of the anonymous Christian, treated elsewhere in this volume, finds its home here.[10] It simply means that whether people are aware of it or not, they are dealing in their lives with the God of grace. The fact that Rahner speaks in this case of anonymous Christianity and of the anonymous Christian underlines that for him Christ is the ultimate key to both grace and revelation.

REVELATION IN CHRIST

Appealing to the Scotist rather than the Thomist tradition, Rahner argues that even "before" the fall grace was the grace of Christ. Rahner's view of creation is christocentric. It was for Christ and in order to communicate himself in the unique and full way of the incarnation that God created humanity in the first place. Humans exist in order to be sisters and brothers of Jesus, to share in his life and grace. And so, for Rahner, the anonymous presence of grace in the lives of those who have not yet come to know Christ explicitly should be described in such a way as to make clear that what is involved here is the grace of Christ.[11]

The same basic convictions influence Rahner's reading of the history of religion. Insofar as religions represent common efforts by people to reflect on and celebrate and relate to the ultimate reality, they are privileged places in which to find how individuals and communities have struggled to understand and objectify and live the experience of God and of God's self-revelation that is at the heart of all life. Although, as human, every religion inevitably has within it a mixture of good and evil, of the highest values and their distortion, no religion is merely natural or simply human. The traditional way of seeing Christianity in relation to other religions as God's bending down to humanity, over against human efforts to reach up to God, no longer makes sense. All religions embody the human and the divine, grace and sin. All are historically conditioned, all are marked by the various cultures in which they have been born and lived. What makes Christianity unique, in Rahner's view, is the providential guidance that has been involved in its history from the beginning. To use his language, the whole of the so-called special history of salvation, the biblical history, represents a gradual unfolding and development of the categorial revelation intended by God to bring us to a recognition of its center and high point in the person and destiny of Jesus.[12]

Another chapter of the *Companion* focuses on Rahner's Christology. Important for this chapter is the simple recognition that Jesus represents, in his being as well as in his death and resurrection, the high point of, and key to, the history of salvation and the history of revelation. In him God's self-communication and the human response to it reach fulfillment. Although we continue to live in time and to move toward the absolute future which is God, in Jesus something final and definitive has taken place. He is the eschatological prophet, the absolute saviour.

There has been considerable debate among students of Rahner about the relationship in his thought between transcendental and universal revelation on the one hand and the special history of revelation and its culmination in Christ on the other. Some have argued that the emphasis on the transcendental has undermined and relativized Christian particularity. In fact, Rahner began with the biblical revelation as understood and proclaimed in the Church. This is the source of his conviction about God as a trinitarian mystery, about Christ and grace. His development of the transcendental dimension of the gospel was partly motivated by the desire to ensure that Christian believers would truly enter into it and make it their own. Rahner has a profound mistrust of religious forms that are unaccompanied by inner experience and personal appropriation. That is as true of orthodox formulas as it is of sacramental rituals.

The emphasis on the internal, on grace and experience, coupled with a heightened sense of the universality of God's saving will, led Rahner to reflect on the ways in which grace and revelation are present and operative in people who do not share the fullness of Christian revelation and of Christian life. It is this more than anything that accounts for Rahner's increasing emphasis on the transcendental dimension of revelation and of grace. It is not a question of repudiating the categorial and the explicitly Christian, but rather of deepening our understanding of its implications for a Church and world more conscious than ever before of the age and extent of humanity, and of the social, cultural, and other factors that make difficult for many today an explicit acceptance of Christianity. That Rahner himself continually returned to the Christian message and made the kind of efforts that he did to render it comprehensible and believable within the context of modern culture reveals that in his own mind the transcendental and the categorial, the universal and the particular, are not to be played off against one another. They point to a profound tension that is at the heart of all human life. For Rahner, transcendental grace and revelation have within themselves a dynamism that pushes them towards that full categorial formulation that is found only in the gospel. Nor is the embracing of such a formulation merely a question of putting an ineffable experience into somewhat more adequate words. In accepting the gospel, one recognizes with a new clarity the reality of God and God's love and what that love has done for us in Jesus. In recognizing this we are enabled to give God explicit praise and thanksgiving and to orient our lives more self-consciously on gospel values and ideals.[13]

CATEGORIAL REVELATION IN THE CHURCH

As a systematic theologian, Rahner always took the great dogmas of the Church seriously. That remained true even as, in the course of his career, he became more conscious of their historically conditional nature and of the need not only to rethink them individually within the horizon of modern culture and experience but also to approach them in new and creative ways. With time, he became ever more conscious of the inevitable pluralism of theology and of dogma, not only within Western culture but to an even greater extent in the Church's efforts to become a world church, to be at home in the various cultures and peoples of the world.

In spite, however, of the historically and culturally conditioned nature of any formulation, Rahner had great confidence in the preaching and teaching functions of the Church as well as in its sacramental actions. In and through such things, the revelation of salvation from God in Jesus is proclaimed and actualized. The word of God in human form, including the word of Scripture, the kerygmatic word of preaching, and the word embodied in the sacramental ritual, mediates in different degrees and in different ways the reality it proclaims. Through the word we encounter God's self-revelation in Christ.

For Rahner *the* great mystery of Christian revelation is the mystery of God. Revelation does not take away the mystery but deepens our awareness of it. Rahner loved to insist on the incomprehensibility of God, including in the beatific vision. Far from eliminating the mystery, revelation draws us into it in a new and more profound way. Traditional theology sometimes spoke of the revealed mysteries in the plural. For Rahner there is fundamentally only one mystery in the strict sense of the term, and that is the mystery of the self-communicating God. God's self-communication takes two related but distinct forms, in the Word and in the Spirit. This twofold dimension of the one self-communication reveals God in his relation to us and in himself as a mystery of Father, Son, and Spirit.[14]

The definition of the Assumption of Mary in 1950 provoked Rahner to address the problem of the development of dogma. An initial focus of interest was the way in which a doctrine defined in the course of church history and not present with such clarity in earlier periods could be seen as proclaiming and participating in the character of revelation. As much as Rahner defended and tried to understand the process of development as it took place in the past, a process that tended to unpack the content of revelation in ever more specific and individual propositions, he also called for a focusing on the essential, for an attempt to articulate the content of revelation in what he called short formulas of faith.[15]

Although Rahner was enormously creative in suggesting implications of the gospel for almost every area and aspect of life, he tended to focus in a particular way on anthropology and on Christology. For him, as for most of the great mystical tradition of the Church, at the heart of religion is the relation between God and human beings. Given his spiritual and philosophical starting points, Rahner put the emphasis initially on the individual. Each and every one of us is called into relationship with the God of grace. A good part of Rahner's theological effort was to help us enter into that mystery and to abandon ourselves to it. He spoke of theology as mystagogy, as a leading of people into the mystery of themselves and of the self-communicating God.[16]

FROM FUNDAMENTAL TO SYSTEMATIC THEOLOGY

While not directly a work of fundamental theology, *Hearers of the Word* was intended as an element toward such a theology. The transcendental method it involved was intended to open the subject to the question of God and to the possibility of God's self-revelation in history. The pastoral concern behind *Hearers* and its method was later carried over into various areas of systematic theology. Rahner developed, for example, what he called a transcendental Christology. The concern here is the same, the attempt to respond to the experience of and challenge to faith represented by modern Western culture. Traditional Christology with its emphasis on the descent of the Son or Word of God into human life can for many people today seem mythological. In order to overcome possible mythological misunderstandings and above all to open people in a new way to the message about Jesus and his saving significance, Rahner tried to discern in human experience elements and aspects that point toward the need for an absolute saviour.

The concern for what in the broadest sense might be called apologetics remained central to Rahner's entire project. It took a new and final form in his efforts to develop a new kind of course in the German university system, what he called a *Grundkurs*, a basic or introductory course. His rationale in doing so was typical. One could no longer assume that those coming to the study of theology in the postwar years had a solid and mature faith. In fact in many cases, they were passing through a stage of questioning, of wondering whether they were believers at all. They needed something more than the highly technical and sophisticated courses that were taken for granted in the universities at the time. They needed an initial introduction to the main content of faith as well as to the reasons for believing, an introduction which in both cases would consciously be geared to their condition and to their needs.[17]

The *Grundkurs* (ET: *Foundations of Christian Faith*) brings together much that is central to Rahner's life and work. It tries to combine fundamental and systematic theology and to do it at what is called a first level of reflection. The purpose at this level is not to try to deal in a scholarly manner with all the questions of a historical and philosophical as well as theological nature that such an introduction could entail, but rather to break open the heart of the gospel in a way that relates it to ordinary human experience.[18]

Foundations of Christian Faith begins by inviting the reader to enter into and appropriate his/her own experience of the self as engaged responsibly in the world and at the same time as open to God. God is presented above all as the Holy Mystery, the whither of human transcendence. The gospel is articulated first of all in terms of grace, in terms, that is, of God's self-communication to human openness. The central and longest part of the book is dedicated to Christology, to a transcendental Christology and to various elements and aspects of a systematic Christology the purpose of which is to bring Christ close to human experience and, to the extent possible, to make believable the great dogmatic affirmations about him and his role within an evolutionary worldview. The book ends with three examples of a short form of faith.

FAITH AS RESPONSE TO REVELATION

Although both scholasticism and neo-scholasticism viewed faith, hope, and love, the three theological virtues, as part of the one full and integrated life of intimacy with God made possible by grace, they tended to underline their distinctions. Faith was seen as an intellectual virtue by which a person is able to assent to the truth of God's revelation. While it was understood that this assent required both grace and a free act of will, the emphasis was on its intellectual character. In order for such faith to be saving, however, it had to be completed, or informed, by love.

Rahner comes out of this tradition and develops it. He puts, for example, a particular emphasis on, and develops a different understanding of, the grace of faith. He also reinforces and deepens the role of freedom in regard to it. While recognizing the importance of the intellectual dimension of our response to God's self-revelation, he insists that it must engage the whole person, and that therefore faith, hope, and love are not to be played off against one another but are to be understood in terms of what unifies them.[19]

Faith, for Rahner, is one of those great words that point to the whole of human life and its meaning, one of those key concepts that is able to evoke much that is central to Christianity. Although used analogously, faith is fundamentally our response to God's self-revelation, God's self-communication. Because Rahner does not see revelation as primarily involving a number of truths or a set of propositions, he does not see faith as an assent to such things. As a response to God's self-communication faith engages the whole of the person and does so at the deepest level. It involves both an accepting of God's offer and a giving of ourselves to God in return. Given this understanding of faith, it is not hard to see why it can only be understood in the closest possible relationship with hope and love. In different contexts, Rahner uses each of these other two words to evoke what finally faith entails.[20]

ANONYMOUS FAITH

What is perhaps most novel in Rahner's treatment of faith is what he has to say about implicit or anonymous faith. The possibility of salvation for those who have not heard or are unable to respond to the message of Christ and of God requires the possibility for them of some kind of supernatural faith. Without such faith there is no salvation.

In developing his understanding of this kind of faith, Rahner emphasizes two things. First, faith presupposes grace and with it what traditionally has been described as the light of faith. This he identifies as the supernatural existential and in particular as the new "formal object" or grace-filled transcendentality that it implies. It makes possible a person's response to God in faith. The second factor that Rahner emphasizes is that faith engages intellect and will, i.e., it engages the whole person. Here he puts the emphasis on freedom and on the moral order. Any serious moral choice, any such choice that engages us at the deepest level of our being, involves inevitably an acceptance or rejection of the Holy Mystery and its offer of itself to us in grace.

On a number of occasions Rahner argued that a genuine acceptance of oneself is the beginning of faith, and is already an act of saving faith. What is at issue here is not the relatively superficial self-acceptance of pop psychology, but rather something that involves the whole person, including one's openness to the infinite and the absolute. It is perhaps most obvious in the kind of self-acceptance that is involved in any real confrontation with death.[21]

Anonymous faith for Rahner is not simply faith in God; it also involves faith in Christ. Here as elsewhere, the christocentric nature of creation and of grace is determinative. On different occasions, Rahner points to what he calls a seeking Christology, an anonymous affirmation of Christ in the midst of ordinary and everyday life. His three favorite examples of situations in which such a Christology might well be found are death, love of neighbour, and hope. In all three cases, there can be an implicit yes to God and to Christ. It is because of God and God's saving will revealed in Christ that we are able in confronting death to entrust ourselves into the infinite mystery. The coming together of the divine and the human in Jesus justifies that kind of absolute love of neighbour that no human person could possibly justify. The manifestation of infinite love in the divine self-giving in grace and the incarnation ground our hope for the future and especially for the absolute future.[22]

FROM ANONYMOUS TO EXPLICIT FAITH

As saving as anonymous faith is for those who freely embrace it, Rahner is convinced that there is within such faith a dynamism that tends toward its full explicitation in the message of the gospel and the lived faith of the Church.

Transcendental revelation and faith are always accompanied by some categorial expression. Our engagement in the world and with one another in knowledge and love is the condition of possibility of any kind of transcendental experience. The history of religion is in some sense the history of the more or less adequate explicitation of transcendental faith and revelation.

Rahner comes back again and again to the question of explicit Christian faith and to the kind of challenges and difficulties it encounters in the contemporary world. He recognizes, for example, that many Catholics are unable to embrace the full and explicit faith proclaimed by the Church. In such cases, as in the case of non-Christians, he appeals to the reality of grace, given and experienced, and to the faith that grace implies, and as he does he encourages believers in that situation to live to the full those aspects and dimensions of the faith to which they are able to assent.[23]

Given his convictions about the universality of God's offer of grace and therefore about the very real possibility that many to whom the gospel is preached have already responded positively to it in the context of their own lives, Rahner encourages preachers and missionaries not to approach people as if what they are bringing to them is something totally new. They should try to relate the message of the gospel to what such people have already experienced in the depths of their conscience and in their everyday lives.

DEEPENING THE LIFE OF FAITH

It can be argued that the whole of Rahner's theology and activity was motivated by pastoral and spiritual concerns. He saw himself as a priest, a Jesuit, and a person of the Church. His thinking of the faith was intended to serve the Church's preaching and to help individuals to appropriate it and in doing so to enter ever more profoundly into the mystery both of their own lives and of the infinite and inexhaustible self-communicating God who has been revealed to us in Christ and in the proclamation of the Church.

It was to this end that Rahner called for a renewed fundamental theology and above all for a creative rethinking of systematic theology in order to facilitate people's hearing of the Christian message. He called for a focusing on the essence of the message and for an understanding of it that would make clear that it is the answer to the deepest questions that humans have and are. He argued that theology should ultimately serve mystagogy, that even as theology it should show how the whole of the message can lead us ever more profoundly into the infinite, healing, and transforming mystery of God. Nothing was more fundamental for this project than his creative rethinking of the notions of both revelation and of faith.

Notes

1 For debates in this area in the first half of the twentieth century, see R. Aubert, *Le Problème de l'acte de foi: données traditionelles et résultats des controverses récentes* (3rd edn., Louvain: Warny, 1958).

2 *Hearers* exists in two German editions (see Abbreviations, p. xvi).

3 On the notion of revelation presupposed in *Hearers*, see T. Mannermaa, "Eine falsche Interpretationstradition von K. Rahners *Hörer des Wortes*," *Zeitschrift für Katholische Theologie* 96 (1970), 204–09.

4 For Blondel's apologetical method, see *The Letter on Apologetics and History and Dogma*, trans. A. Dru and I. Trethowan (Grand Rapids: Eerdmans, 1994). For the connections between Blondel and Rahner, see A. Raffelt and H. Verwegen, *Karl Rahner* (Munich, 1997), 17–20 and 41ff.

5 Aquinas, *Summa theologiae*, I–II, q. 106, a. 1, where he says that Christianity or the New Law is "principally the grace of the Holy Spirit given to those who believe in Christ."

6 See "Some Implications of the Scholastic Concept of Uncreated Grace," *TI* I, 319–46. See also the chapter by Duffy in this volume.

7 For the "supernatural existential," see "Concerning the Relationship Between Nature and Grace," in *TI* I, 297–317, "Existential," III, B, *SM* II, 306–07, and *FCF*, 126–33.

8 The relative importance of the influence of Maréchal and Heidegger on Rahner continues to be debated. See M. Chojnacki, *Die Nähe des Unbegreifbaren: Der moderne philosophische Kontext der Theologie Karl Rahners und seine Konsequenzen in dieser Theologie* (Freiburg: Universitätsverlag, 1996).

9 Rahner's single most sustained treatment of revelation can be found in K. Rahner and J. Ratzinger, *Revelation and Tradition*, trans. W. J. O'Hara (Montreal: Palm, 1965), 9–25. The same material appears in a more fluent translation in *SM* v, 348–53. For a study in English, see D. R. Kull, *Karl Rahner's Theology of Revelation: A View from the Philippines* (Manila: Loyola School of Theology, 1979). For a somewhat more critical view see P. Eicher, *Offenbarung: Prinzip neuzeitlicher Theologie* (Munich: Kösel, 1977), 347–421.

10 See especially the chapters by Duffy and Hill Fletcher in this volume.

11 See "Christology Within an Evolutionary View of the World," in *TI* v, 157–92 and *FCF*, 178–203.

12 See "Christianity and the Non-Christian Religions," *TI* v, 115–34.

13 See "Anonymous and Explicit Faith," *TI* xvi, 52–59.

14 See "The Concept of Mystery in Catholic Theology," *TI* iv, 36–73.

15 On development, see "Considerations on the Development of Dogma," *TI* iv, 3–35; on short forms of faith, see "The Need for a 'Short Formula' of Christian Faith," *TI* ix, 117–26; "Reflections on the Problems Involved in Devising a Short Formula of the Faith," *TI* xi, 230–44.

16 See "Reflections on Methodology in Theology," *TI* XI, 68–114, especially the third lecture, "Reductio in unum mysterium."

17 See "Foundations of Christian Faith," *TI* XIX, 3–15.

18 See "Reflections on the New Task for Fundamental Theology," *TI* XVI, 156–66.

19 The most comprehensive work on Rahner's theology of faith is W. Schreer, *Der Begriff des Glaubens: Das Verständnis des Glaubensaktes in den Dokumenten des Vatikanum II und in den theologischen Entwürfen Karl Rahners und Hans Urs von Balthasars* (Frankfurt: Peter Lang, 1992), 187–434.

20 On faith as engaging the whole person and the role of freedom, see "Faith Between Rationality and Emotion," *TI* XVI, 60–78; on the role of love, see "Questions of Controversial Theology on Justification," *TI* IV, 189–218; on faith as hope, see "Faith as Courage," *TI* XVIII, 211–25.

21 On self-acceptance as faith, see "Anonymous Christians," *TI* VI, 390–98 and "Anonymous and Explicit Faith," *TI* XVI, 52–59.

22 On "a seeking Christology," see "Jesus Christ," IV, B, 3, *SM* III, 194–95.

23 See "On the Situation of Faith Today," *TI* XX, 13–32.

Further reading

Rahner, K., "Revelation, B Theological Interpretation," *SM* V, 348–52.

  "Questions of Controversial Theology on Justification," *TI* IV, 189–218.

  "Thoughts on the Possibility of Belief Today," *TI* V, 2–12.

  "Intellectual Honesty and Christian Faith," *TI* VII, 47–71.

  "Anonymous and Explicit Faith," *TI* XVI, 52–59.

  "On the Situation of Faith," *TI* XX, 13–32.

6 Trinity

DAVID COFFEY

For someone who never wrote a major treatise on the subject, Karl Rahner exercised a remarkable influence on the field of trinitarian theology. His main production was a chapter of eighty-five pages written in 1967 and titled "Der dreifaltige Gott als transzendenter Urgrund der Heilsgeschichte" ("The Threefold God as Transcendental Ground of Salvation History") for the second volume, *Die Heilsgeschichte vor Christus* (Salvation History Before Christ), of *Mysterium Salutis: Grundriß heilsgeschichtlicher Dogmatik* (Mystery of Salvation: Outline of a Dogmatic Theology Based on Salvation History). Two years later he wrote two substantial articles, "Trinität" and "Trinitätstheologie," for the German original of the theological encyclopedia *Sacramentum Mundi*, the first being closely modelled on "Der dreifaltige Gott." This ("Der dreifaltige Gott") was published in English translation as a separate work (a book) titled *The Trinity* in 1970; and the English versions of the above-mentioned articles, "Trinity, Divine" and "Trinity in Theology," appeared in volume VI of the English *Sacramentum Mundi* in 1970. In this chapter, the references will generally be supplied in the text so as to avoid overloading the footnotes.[1] The majority of the references will be to *The Trinity*, whose title will be abbreviated to *Trin.* Of the two articles, only the first will be quoted. Finally, apart from the conclusion, the sections of this chapter will correspond in content and relative length to those of *The Trinity*.

METHOD AND STRUCTURE

Rahner is explicit in the acknowledgment of his guiding principle in constructing a theology of the Trinity: it is the affirmation of the identity of the "economic" and the "immanent" Trinity. The economic Trinity is the Trinity as involved in the divine "economy" (plan) of salvation, that is, the Trinity as revealed immediately in the saving mission of Christ and the consequent sanctifying mission of the Holy Spirit. The immanent Trinity is the

Trinity considered in its absolute transcendence, in its independence of the world and its needs. The statement of their identity means that the three "persons" of the economic Trinity, Father, Son, and Holy Spirit, respectively, are identical with those of the immanent Trinity. Rahner formulates this "basic axiom" (*Grundaxiom*) thus: "The 'economic Trinity' is the 'immanent Trinity' and the 'immanent Trinity' is the 'economic Trinity'" (*Trin.*, 22). It implies that to the temporal missions of the Son and the Holy Spirit in the economic Trinity correspond the eternal originations, or "processions," of the same Son and Holy Spirit in the immanent Trinity.

In proposing his basic axiom, Rahner was attempting to remedy the sorry state into which in his judgment trinitarian theology had fallen. With Karl Barth on the Protestant side, he was trying to reconstitute the doctrine of the Trinity at the center of the Christian mystery of salvation. All around he saw people in his own as well as other churches who, though paying lip-service to the Trinity, were in effect little more than "mere 'monotheists'" (see *Trin.*, 10), people for whom Christ was merely "God" in human form, and not precisely the Son of God incarnate. For these people, whose thinking had been formed in the Augustinian-Thomistic tradition, the incarnation could not in itself say anything specific about the person of the Son, because either of the other divine persons, Father or Holy Spirit, could just as easily have become man. And the human nature of Christ, as a creature of God, was a divine work *ad extra* (to the outside, beyond the Godhead), and as such a product of God's undifferentiated power, common to all three divine persons. In itself, therefore, it bore no special relationship to the divine Word or Son and was unable to reveal him, except on the basis of a purely verbal conception of revelation.

For Rahner the central importance of the basic axiom consists in its guarantee of the integrity of the economy, that is, that Jesus Christ is the true incarnation of God the Son and that Christians truly possess God the Holy Spirit. Rahner expresses this truth of faith by means of the concept of the "self-communication of God," a term, he says, that "briefly and simply sums up a good part of the Christian doctrine of salvation."[2] As applied to the economy it denotes the fact that God gives *Godself* to human beings; God gives Godself as God truly is in Godself, not just some created effect of Godself (though God does this as well, with the effect serving at the same time as the foundation of the self-giving). Now according to Scripture and tradition (with the latter taking a decisive step at the Council of Nicea), this self-giving takes place in two different forms or "modalities," that is, in the incarnation of the divine Son, in Jesus Christ, and in the "indwelling" of the Holy Spirit, in Christians. But while these modalities are distinct, they are modalities of the self-giving of the *one* God of Israel, that is, of him whom Jesus called (and whom we call) "Father." The only way in which these modalities can remain distinct and yet be modalities of the self-communication of this God is if they represent a distinction that is verified not just in the economy but in the being of God himself. Otherwise they cannot be the *self*-communication of this God. But this implies (and requires) the identity of the economic and the immanent Trinity as explained above. Trinitarian theology must proceed on the hypothesis of the truth of this basic axiom, and when it has completed its task the *fact* of this truth can be deemed to be established (see *Trin.*, 22).

In the light of this it will be clear why Rahner exhibits a certain reserve toward the method that has characterized most Catholic trinitarian theology of his and earlier generations, namely, the "psychological analogy," which was introduced by St. Augustine and perfected by Thomas Aquinas. According to this approach, in which a likeness is recognized between the one God who is pure spirit and the human created spirit, the immanent processions of the Son (now called Logos or Word) and the Holy Spirit are explained in reference to the human spiritual operations of knowing and loving, respectively. Rahner does not reject the psychological analogy outright. He acknowledges its roots in the biblical theologies of the Word of God and the Spirit of God as well as its respectful acceptance in the schools. Calling it a "hypothesis" (*Trin.*, 118), he emphasizes that despite its biblical origins it does not have the status of official theology or doctrine in the strict sense. Importantly, it is unable to explain why in the Godhead the operations of knowledge and love result in distinct subsistences, while nothing comparable occurs in the case of the human analogue. His main reservation about it, apparently, is its lack of connection to the economic Trinity, which for him is the only true foundation of our knowledge of the immanent Trinity. He is therefore careful to point out that it "differs considerably" from his own preferred method (*Trin.*, 115).

An a priori objection from Western theology that Rahner needs to deal with may be expressed in syllogistic form as follows. As the works of God *ad extra* are common to all three divine persons, they cannot be revelatory of the distinct divine persons as such. But the work of salvation is clearly a divine work *ad extra*. Therefore the claim that our knowledge of the economic Trinity grounds our knowledge of the immanent Trinity is false. Traditionally, Catholic theology has ceded this objection in regard to grace: it solves the problem that the sources of revelation teach at the same time that the Holy Spirit exercises a unique function in the souls of the just *and* that all three divine persons dwell therein, by appealing to the notion of "appropriation." This is a device by which a work is acknowledged as common to all three persons but is attributed to one alone because of a perceived affinity between it and that person. It is verified in creation, which is common to all three persons but is attributed to the Father alone because he is the origin of the other two. It is the same, so it is claimed, with the Holy Spirit and grace. In the case of the incarnation, however, it is impossible to make a similar concession, for it is a truth of faith accepted by all that though this mystery involves a divine work *ad extra*, only the Son is incarnate in Jesus of Nazareth. In giving his account of this position, Rahner notes that traditional Catholic theology refused to give ground in the face of this stunning counter-example. He summarizes its argument as follows (see *Trin.*, 25). In God all is one except where there applies the opposition of the relations of origin giving rise to the persons (Council of Florence, DS 1330). Therefore the only way in which a particular divine person can have a proper relation to the world is by hypostatic union. From revelation we know that the latter has happened only in the case of the Son. But nothing proper to him can be deduced from this fact, because it is just a fact and nothing more. That is to say, either of the other divine persons could just as easily have become man.

Rahner is not moved by this argument. First, he finds it not apodictic. In fact, the most ancient tradition always supposed the opposite. That is to say, the Father, being unoriginate and in principle invisible, reveals himself only in his Word. Rahner might also have added that it is not obvious that the only way a divine person can have a proper relationship with the world is by hypostatic union. Why not also by a union of being that is less than hypostatic, in scholastic terms an "accidental" union, the very kind that today is widely held to obtain between the Holy Spirit and the just? Secondly, he finds the argument simply false, for it wrongly supposes a univocal sense of "person" among the members of the Trinity. In fact the unique way in which the Son is a person might very well indicate that only he can become man. Indeed, Rahner proposes an argument to precisely this effect. And we shall also see that he thinks that Catholic theology was mistaken in ceding the objection in regard to grace. The obvious conclusion, not drawn by Rahner, is that while salvation *includes* a work of God *ad extra*, it is not only that: it is that and more. And the fact of the incarnation stands as a telling riposte to the defenders of the traditional theology.

In all his theology Rahner looks first to the "subject," the human person, the "anonymous Christian," who is destined for fulfillment in God and who with the aid of grace finds him in the warp and woof of life. Thus, for example, in his Christology Rahner's first concern is with what he calls "transcendental" Christology, the search for (with the expectation of find-ing) "an absolute messenger of salvation."[3] Only this a priori preparation can make historical conversion to Christ as meaningful as it is actually experienced to be. So too with his theology of the Trinity. The human being who finds God in his or her life does so in an experience that on analysis reveals itself as structured along trinitarian lines, that is, to be revelatory of God precisely as Trinity. This revelation does not occur merely in words: it is essentially the experience of the self-communication of God, for which words are found only subsequently. Only thus can an explicit theology of the Trinity be appreciated as relevant and important to the human person in his or her life.

As with his Christology, Rahner is at pains to stress that he has not attempted rationalistically and reductionalistically to deduce truths of rev-elation from human experience. This is a point on which he has been much misunderstood. His transcendental theology of the Trinity, he claims, "already presupposes this self-communication as testified by revelation and as a mystery" (*Trin.*, 100, n. 18). For "between a priori deduction and a merely a posteriori gathering of random facts, there exists a middle way: the recog-nition of what is experienced aposteriorily as transcendentally necessary ..." (ibid.). While it respects the untrammelled freedom of God to communicate Godself to human beings (or not to do so), this final phrase expresses at the same time the necessary elements contained in this self-communication, namely, that God communicates Godself as God is in Godself, and to a crea-ture constitutionally able to receive God. It identifies and guarantees the necessary within the free.

OFFICIAL DOCTRINE

In his treatment of the Trinity Rahner devotes about a quarter of the space to the official teaching of the Church. Rahner covers the subject in four sections of unequal lengths. The first has to do with the Trinity as an "absolute mystery." The First Vatican Council had taught that certain mysteries of religion are known only because they are revealed by God: if they were not revealed, they could not be known at all (DS 3015). Indeed, even when revealed and thus partly understood, they remain impervious to full comprehension (DS 3016). In his 1887 censure of Rosmini, Leo XIII numbered the Trinity among these truths (DS 3025). Thus it can be styled an "absolute mystery."

The second section deals with the technical terminology of the official documents, the two most important terms being "person" and "essence." Not being defined, these are assumed to be intelligible in themselves. Rahner argues that their meanings can be deduced from the context in which they are used, namely, that while the Father is God, the Son is God, and the Holy Spirit is God, it is the one God who comes to us in them. Thus the Father, the Son, and the Holy Spirit are "persons," and the one God is "essence" (or "nature," or "substance"). Rahner asks whether here the word "person" is replaceable by some other term. This is a practical question, since "person" has changed in meaning since its original application to the Trinity, when it denoted only concrete subsistence. Now, however, it has come to imply a distinct center of consciousness and activity as well. Rahner maintains that as there is only one such center in the Godhead, the continued use of "person" in this context can encourage a tritheistic understanding of the Trinity.

Thirdly, Rahner presents the pronouncements of the magisterium on each of the divine persons. Only the Father is "unoriginate," while the Son is "begotten" of the Father, and the Holy Spirit, whose procession is *not* a begetting, is the Spirit of the Father and the Son. Surprisingly, Rahner makes no further reference to the *Filioque*. He considers he is phrasing this procession "more precisely" by saying that "the Spirit proceeds from the Father through the Son" (*Trin.*, 66). Another surprise is his statement that this procession is conceived in the documents as that of the mutual love of the Father and the Son, for which he gives the references DS 573, 3326, and 3331 (this should be 3330). The first reference is to the 16th Council of Toledo and is not relevant; the other two are to Leo XIII's encyclical *Divinum Illud* of 1897, which in fact refers three times to the Holy Spirit in this way (in nos. 4 [bis] and 8). The reason for surprise here is that Rahner holds that "there is properly no *mutual* love between Father and Son" (*Trin.*, 106).

The unicity of the divine nature requires that the persons be distinct only "relatively," and not by anything absolute (DS 528, 532, 570). While each person must be identical with the divine nature, this identity cannot be total (*re et ratione*), for then they would be identical with each other. Rahner proposes a verbal solution to this problem by adopting the Thomistic "virtual" distinction to distinguish between each person and the nature, but he stresses that this is a unique use of the distinction. All it means is that "while it is obvious that two *absolute* realities cannot be identical with a third without being really identical with each other, this disparity cannot be shown with evidence when we are dealing with two 'mere' and opposed relations which are really identical with an absolute reality (God's essence)" (*Trin.*, 70). Rahner speaks of the persons as "three relative ways of existing

(*Existenzweisen*) of the one and the same God," which invites comparison with Barth's expression "ways of being" (*Seinsweisen*) for the same realities (*Trin.*, 74).

In the fourth section, "Some Consequences for a Deeper Understanding," Rahner deals briefly with divine operations *ad extra* and the device of appropriation, and then with "notional" and "essential" realities and statements. These latter terms are traditional scholastic terminology; "essential" embracing everything to do with the divine essence as such, and "notional" the divine persons as such (via our "knowledge" [*notio*] of them). By virtue of the unicity of essence the three persons "exist in" each other (the *perichoresis*); and there are five "notions": unoriginatedness and fatherhood (characterizing the Father), sonship (this, of course, for the Son alone), active "spiration" (the Father and the Son), and passive spiration (the Holy Spirit).

SYSTEMATIC OUTLINE

In his "systematic outline" of trinitarian theology Rahner begins with the economic Trinity, the self-communication of God that takes place in the missions of Christ and the Holy Spirit. He asks how these distinct events can be shown to be the modalities of the one self-communication of God. To answer this, he mounts an elaborate and highly original argument which calls for some preliminary comment. First, the fact that it contains not a single appeal to Scripture or tradition should alert us to the fact that this is no ordinary theological argument. Rahner calls it a "systematic outline," but this does not make it systematic or dogmatic theology. It is, rather, a "fundamental" theology of the Trinity, a reflection on the relationship of human beings to the self-communicating God that prepares them for the fact that God is triune in nature. As such, it provides a good example of Rahner's anthropological, a priori, and "transcendental" theology, in which the starting point and primary datum is the human subject over against God. Secondly, the structure of the argument appears rather loose: the features of the divine–human relationship that it presents seem arbitrarily chosen. Rahner recognizes this himself, and admits that other features could have been selected, but he defends his course by pointing out that those chosen are in fact sufficient for his purpose (see *Trin.*, 88, n. 11). Finally, he emphasizes that he is not constructing a rationalistic proof of the Trinity from human experience (see *Trin.*, 100, n. 18). Rather, he is arguing backwards from the fact of the revelation of the Trinity to its necessary elements, given the bodily-spiritual nature of human beings, and presuming the identity of the economic and the immanent Trinity. This allows him to conclude to a necessary (and not just factual) connection between the two missions and to the basic unicity of the self-communication of God as the self-communication of the *Father*.

The argument sets out to show that the one self-communication of God to the human addressee necessarily takes place in two distinct but complementary ways, these ways constituting the economic Trinity. Rahner notes that this self-communication, as both given and received, reveals at least the following four pairs of features, in each of which the first member is the "opposite" (in an imprecise sense of the term) (see *Trin.*, 98) of the second: origin – future; history – transcendence; invitation – acceptance; knowledge – love. He further notes that the four first members "line up" or belong together, thus characterizing the first modality of the divine self-communication, and likewise the four second members, thus characterizing the second modality. He overcomes the obvious objection that this division is imposed by the limitations of human nature and hence cannot be predicated of the Godhead, by insisting that essential to the doctrine of the economic Trinity is that it is God himself who is communicated in Christ and the Spirit, and not just some created effects of God (in scholastic terms, God's causality is "quasi-formal" and not merely "efficient"). If it is God himself who is communicated, then it must be God *as God is in Godself*, that is, as God exists in the immanent Trinity. Therefore the single self-communication of God given in two modalities in the economic Trinity must be identical in both its unicity and duality with the self-communication of God in the immanent Trinity. In other words, the duality in unicity experienced in time in the missions of Christ and the Holy Spirit reveals and reproduces the eternal processions of the Son and the Holy Spirit within the one God of the immanent Trinity, and indeed in the same *taxis* (order). And because both the Son and the Holy Spirit draw their being from the Father, they represent modalities of the self-communication precisely of the *Father* (see *Trin.*, 84).

We now present in summary form Rahner's argument of the four pairs of features of the self-communication of God to the human subject. (He is not referring in every instance to the *identical* human subject: at times he means Christ, at other times the ordinary Christian.) The first pair is origin – future (see *Trin.*, 91). "Origin" denotes the fact that the recipient of the self-communication has a beginning, is created by God, and created precisely in view of the self-communication. "Future" indicates the process begun at the origin, that is, "the total self-communication of God." Despite the fact that God constitutes himself as the "end" of the human subject, this process does not unfold deterministically. Rather, the future is "separated by a real history of freedom" from the origin.

The second pair is history – transcendence (see *Trin.*, 91–92). "History" indicates the "real history of freedom" to which reference has just been made. It characterizes the life of the subject in the world, in which decisions about worldly objects are constantly made. "Transcendence" refers to the human (and spiritual) tendency to reach beyond the particular object and embrace the "horizon," the "whereunto" of transcendence, identical with God himself, against which these decisions are made. In Rahner's epistemology both the object and the horizon play essential roles in the human act of knowing (and loving, or choosing). He expresses their relationship thus: "Transcendence and its whereunto have their history in the object itself. And it is the unity of these two elements, as it brings about distinction, which refers to God."

If the human being is history into transcendence, he or she is free, and therefore is characterized by offer and acceptance, the third pair of features. Offer is implied in the freedom in which the self-communication of God to the world is accepted, but this acceptance characterizes the divine act as much as the human. Here we confront the impenetrable mystery of the sovereignty of God and his act in the face of human freedom, where neither is diminished by their interaction. If God's self-communication did not carry with it the divine gift of its acceptance, it would be reduced in this interaction to the level of created being, and therefore would not take place at all.

The fourth pair is knowledge, or truth, and love. If we consider that knowledge terminates in bodily action, we shall not be tempted to regard the actuation of truth simply as a "categorial" (as distinct from a "transcendental") human determination. In fact it is both, and God's self-communication is addressed to the whole human person as such. This duality in the self-communication and its reception cannot be overcome or surpassed ("completed"). It cannot be overcome, because "the true" and "the good" are originally distinct, with neither the mere moment of the other. Nor can it be surpassed, not only because it is revealed that the divine self-communication exists in two, and only two, modalities, but because there is no valid reason "for adding a third and higher power to this duality" as it exists in human beings (*Trin.*, 94).

In proceeding to the next step of the argument, Rahner claims that the unity of three of the four *first* members of the pairs, namely, origin, history, and offer, is "easily understandable" (*Trin.*, 94). He identifies this, the first in the *taxis* of the two modalities of the self-communication of God, as the anticipation (or the expectation) of what is revealed historically as the Christ event: "If the self-proffering of God to the world is a real offer, to *historic people*, then it has taken place definitively and irrevocably only when it is historically *there* in the 'absolute bringer of salvation', when the proffering of divine self-communication not only constitutes a world as the addressee of its offer, but posits itself irrevocably as historical" (*Trin.*, 94–95). He goes on to point out that this event belongs to the "origin of history" in the sense that "the latter is understood as the history of the acceptance of this offered self-communication," that is, presumably, in the Church.

Rahner still has to fit the fourth first member, truth, into this series. This he does by taking up again his earlier comment that knowledge terminates in bodily action. He asserts that "truth is not first the correct grasping of a state of affairs." Rather, "it consists first in letting our own personal essence come to the fore, positing ourselves without dissimulation, accepting ourselves and letting this authentic nature come to the fore in truth also in the presence of others" (*Trin.*, 95–96). In language reminiscent of the Bible, he calls it "fidelity," "the truth which we *do.*" This truth is our response to the divine self-communication, which reveals itself as God's truth for us, his "faithful offer" made in Christ.

Turning to the four *second* members of the pairs, Rahner admits at the outset that their unity is "not so easy to see" (*Trin.*, 96). However, understanding how two of them, namely, future and transcendence, belong together is "relatively easy," for "transcendence arises where God gives himself as the future" (*Trin.*, 97). Further, insofar as it is absolute the self-communication of God must contain its own acceptance, for otherwise it would be degraded to the level of a human a priori. It is the fourth member, love, that is difficult to fit into the scheme. "Yet," says Rahner, "the self-communication which wills itself absolutely and creates the possibility of its acceptance and this acceptance itself, is precisely what is meant by love" (*Trin.*, 97–98), that is, *divine* love, because it is the freely offered and accepted self-communication of the person of the Holy Spirit (*SM* vi, 300a). He might have added that in the perspective of the human person it is met by the self-surrender of this person to God, that is, by human love.

Rahner concludes that the self-communication of God is given in two modalities, truth and love, Christ and the Spirit. At each of the four points we have noted along the way these reveal themselves as opposites and therefore as distinct (*auseinander gehalten*) but necessarily connected, remaining at the same time "modalities" of the *single* self-communication of "the unoriginate God [the Father] who remains incomprehensible" (*Trin.*, 99). Rahner makes the transition from the economic to the immanent Trinity by emphasizing the significance of the word "self" in the phrase "self-communication of God." As stated before, the sources of divine revelation, supported by constant Christian witness, insist that in Christ and the Spirit we experience not just created reflections of God but God in his very being, as he is in himself. The economic Trinity, therefore, reveals and *is* the immanent Trinity.

Rahner ends this presentation with the three following points about the immanent Trinity. First, real distinctions exist in God between the unoriginate one who mediates himself to himself, the one uttered for himself in truth, and the one received and accepted for himself in love, that is, between Father, Son (Word), and Spirit. This necessary process in the Godhead is what makes possible the free self-communication of God to the world (in Christ and the Spirit). Secondly, this process (in the Godhead) is the original, and double, self-communication of God. In each case, *that* which is communicated is the divine "essence." And thirdly, in each case, because of the unity and identity of the essence, the bond between the original self-communicator and the originated persons is "relative," not absolute.

The remainder of Rahner's "systematic outline" is devoted to the problem presented by the word "person" in trinitarian theology and to a consideration of the traditional Catholic "psychological" approach to the doctrine. As we have addressed the latter question already, we shall not deal with it further here. In regard to the former, Rahner maintains a consistently critical attitude, and for the reason already given (see *Trin.*, 108). According to him, the temptation to conceive the divine persons as "several spiritual centres of activity, of several subjectivities and liberties" (*Trin.*, 106) is to be resisted, and this for two reasons: first, because there is only one such reality in the Godhead (namely, the divine essence); and second, because the Logos does not "utter" but rather is uttered (by the Father), nor is there a proper mutual love of the Father and the Son (because this would require two acts) (see ibid.).

WEAKNESSES AND STRENGTHS

Weaknesses

The principal weakness noted by critics of Rahner is the inadequacy of his concept of person. He constantly emphasizes the element of subsistence, independence, incommunicability, in both its ontological and psychological dimensions (the psychological equivalent of person being "subject"), to the neglect of the other element, relation. True, he dutifully presents the official teaching that the divine persons are constituted by the relations of origin (see *Trin.*, 68–72, 78), but thereafter relation scarcely features in his thinking. In one place where he has the opportunity to present it in a positive light he speaks of it disparagingly, as "the least real of all realities," though he goes on to say that in the Trinity it is "as absolutely real as anything else" (*SM* VI, 300a). What he overlooks is the fact that it is only a predicamental, accidental relation that can be described thus negatively. But as St. Augustine pointed out, the relations in the Trinity are "not accidental" (*De Trinitate*, 5, 5, 6): they constitute the real distinction of persons. This defect, more than anything else, is responsible for the charge of modalism frequently leveled against Rahner. Even if he is not guilty of it, his neglect of relation has laid him open to it. Thus, Moltmann thinks that Rahner's God has more in common with the Absolute Spirit of German Idealism than with the triune God of revelation.[4]

The most serious consequence of Rahner's inadequate concept of person is his denial of the possibility of mutual love in the Trinity and consequently of the identification of the Holy Spirit as the mutual love of the Father and the Son. This brings him into disagreement not only with other theologians Catholic and Protestant, but with the magisterium of his own Church. We have already referred to Leo XIII's twice-repeated teaching on this point in his encyclical *Divinum Illud*; since Rahner's death the same teaching has been enunciated in John Paul II's 1986 encyclical *Dominum et Vivificantem*, likewise three times (in nos. 10, 34 and 39). Here are the relevant sentences from *The Trinity* (p. 106) in my own literal translation:

> When *we today* speak of person in the plural, we think almost necessarily, because of the modern meaning of the word, of several spiritual centers of activity, spiritual subjectivities and freedoms. But there are not three of these in God. Both because there is only *one* essence and hence *one* absolute self-presence in God, and because there is only *one* self-utterance of the Father, the Logos, he is not the one who utters, but the one who is uttered; and there is properly no *mutual* love between Father and Son, which would presuppose two acts, but a loving, distinction-grounding self-acceptance of the Father (and of the Son, because of the *taxis* of knowledge and love).

Rahner is correct in saying that there is only one subjectivity in God, for "subjectivity" denotes consciousness, which is identical at the psychological level with essence at the ontological level. But this is not to say that there is only one "subject" in God, for "subject" is the equivalent of person. There are three subjects in God, and therefore in a sense three "act-centers." This is not to say that the Father and the Son as distinct act-centers love (each other) with two distinct acts, for there is only one love in God, just as there is in God only one (absolute) consciousness. But the love which we have already equivalently characterized as the mutual love of the Father and the Son, and which is one, is not *simply* this essential love of God, for insofar as it is the love of the Father and the Son for each other it is "notional," productive of the Holy Spirit. Strangely, Rahner quotes with apparent approval a passage from Lonergan which supports (without being identical with) what I have just written and which is at odds with his own position (see *Trin.*, 107, n. 29). Rahner's position, which is easily refuted from Scripture, is criticized by Moltmann[5] and Alan Torrance,[6] among others.

Finally, Rahner's neglect of the *Filioque* roughly conforms his conception of God to that of the Eastern Orthodox, whether he intended this or not. While he is lauded for this in some circles, it cannot be said that he does justice to the official Western position, which Barth himself staunchly upheld. In general it has to be admitted that Rahner's pneumatology was rather weak, even if it began to show signs of strengthening towards the end of his life. Inevitably, his trinitarian theology suffered as a result.

Strengths

Thomas F. Torrance, while reserving certain questions of his own, happily identifies the positive features of Rahner's trinitarian theology, at the heart of which he sees the concept of the self-communication of God.[7] This concept, first used of the incarnation and the sending of the Spirit, is subsequently connected to the generation of the Son and spiration of the Spirit by and from the Father. For Rahner it leads directly to the basic axiom of the identity of the economic and the immanent Trinity, thus assuming fundamental importance in his oeuvre. Torrance sees Rahner's trinitarian theology as contributing to three principal "rapprochements." The first is that of systematic theology of the Trinity and the New Testament teaching of Christ along with the latter's foundation in the Old Testament. In this Rahner promotes a connection between the Bible's presentation of Christ and the Church's proclamation and doxology of the triune God. The second rapprochement is that between Western and Eastern Christians. It results from the fact that Rahner drew Catholic theology of the Trinity away from its dependence on the psychological analogy of St. Augustine and its consequent speculativeness, and gave it a more directly applicable pastoral orientation. The third is that between Catholic and Evangelical theology, with the latter represented mainly by Barth. Thus Western Christians would come to share a common conviction of the essentially triune character of God and the normative role of the doctrine of the Trinity in all theology.

Notes

1 Publication details absent from the above are as follows. Vol. II of *Mysterium Salutis* was published by Benziger of Einsiedeln, the editors being Johannes Feiner and Magnus Löhrer. The English translator was Joseph Donceel, and his translation was published by Burns & Oates, London, and Herder and Herder, New York, and reprinted by Crossroad, New York, in 1997. The originals of the two *Sacramentum Mundi* articles are in vol. IV of the German edition.

2 Rahner, "Selbstmitteilung Gottes," *LThK* IX, 627a (my translation).

3 "Christology today," *TI* XXI, trans. H. Riley (London: Darton, Longman & Todd, 1988), 220–27.

4 See J. Moltmann, *The Trinity and the Kingdom of God* (London: SCM, 1981), 144–48.

5 See ibid., 146–47.

6 A. J. Torrance, *Persons in Communion: Trinitarian Description and Human Participation* (Edinburgh: T&T Clark, 1996), 274–80.

7 See T. F. Torrance, "Toward an Ecumenical Consensus on the Trinity," *Theologische Zeitschrift* 31 (1975), 337–50, at 337, subsequently republished in his *Trinitarian Perspectives: Toward Doctrinal Agreement* (Edinburgh: T&T Clark, 1994). See also his *The Christian Doctrine of God, One Being Three Persons* (Edinburgh: T&T Clark, 1996), 9–10.

Further reading

Burke, P., *Reinterpreting Rahner: A Critical Study of His Major Themes* (New York: Fordham University Press, 2002).

Havrilak, G., "Karl Rahner and the Greek Trinity," *St Vladimir's Theological Quarterly* 34 (1990), 61–77.

LaCugna, C. M., *God for Us: The Trinity and Christian Life* (San Francisco: HarperCollins, 1991).

Rahner, K., *The Trinity*, trans. J. Donceel, Introduction, index, and glossary by C. M. LaCugna (New York: Crossroad, 1997; orig. 1967).

Torrance, A. J., *Persons in Communion: Trinitarian Description and Human Participation* (Edinburgh: T&T Clark, 1996).

7 Christology

ROMAN A. SIEBENROCK

Christianity is first and last Christ himself. It is not, ultimately, a collection of doctrines and laws, dogmas and regulations, but a reality which is there, and which is present in our lives ever anew: Christ and his grace, the reality of God which, in Christ, becomes our own reality . . . For Christ is God's will for our salvation made historical, made flesh; God's personal, loving will does not encounter man in some unattainable, intangible 'inner realm'; since Christ, since the One who became man, all grace is Christ's grace with a body, grace dependent on the historical event that at one particular space-time point in our human history the Word became man and was crucified and rose again . . . If anything was not assumed, neither was it redeemed . . . But everything has been assumed, for Christ is true man, true son of Adam, truly lived a human life in all its breadth and height and depth . . . And hence everything, without confusion and without separation, is to enter into eternal life; there is to be not only a new heaven but a new earth. Nothing, unless it be eternally damned, can remain outside the blessing, the protection, the transfiguration of this divinization of the world which, beginning in Christ, aims at drawing everything that exists into the life of God himself, precisely in order that it may thus have eternal validity conferred upon it. This is the reality of Christ, with constitutes Christianity, the incarnate life of God in our place and our time. A reality to which belongs the word; a reality in which all human reality is called to God and blessed.[1]

In the above quotation Rahner answers the question regarding the meaning of Christianity with some key christological convictions that express the core of his faith. Christology for him is not simply one theme among others; rather, it constitutes the heart of his theology. Karl Rahner, S.J. saw himself as a *socius Jesu*, a "companion of Jesus" – the poor and marginalized one – and as a member of his religious order, the Society of Jesus.

Karl Rahner's theological work is best examined from a combination of historical and systematic perspectives. Attention to its historical development sheds light on his way of thinking, his sources and context, the underlying experiences, and the basic intuitions of his thought. We shall try to shed some light on the foundations of Rahner's theology as well as examining its ongoing validity.[2] Rahner, however, never provided a detailed systematic presentation of his various investigations of dogmatic questions. This is evident in his essay approach to Christology, an approach not unlike that of the "tapestries" or *stromata* of Clement of Alexandria. Our systematic presentation will therefore try to discern the pattern of this christological tapestry.[3]

We shall do this in three parts. The first highlights the Ignatian roots of Rahner's Christology. The second looks in chronological order at certain systematic elements in Rahner's thought. The final part comprises a brief overview leading to a synthesis of Rahner's various perspectives and raises some questions and issues that could be further developed. Rahner's Christology, it should be stressed, is closely bound up with, on the one hand, theologies of grace and revelation, and, on the other, with anthropology, trinitarian theology, and soteriology, themes treated elsewhere in this volume.

"S.J. — *SOCIUS JESU*": IGNATIAN ROOTS

Every theology has its fundamental presuppositions in the lived faith of the Church. That Rahner was a Jesuit is significant here.[4] According to Hugo Rahner,[5] the *Spiritual Exercises* are governed by a Scotist tendency. Christ is the end of creation, not God's belated "repair mechanism" after the fall. The world was made for Christ and achieves its purpose in the incarnation of the Logos. The *Exercises* cultivate a contemplation of the life of Jesus with the purpose of finding God's will in one's life. Such contemplative discernment, Rahner maintains, leads to a particular life-choice, or in other circumstances a choice for a certain course of action. But this christological contemplation is also theocentric: it is God who reveals God's will, usually in the everyday circumstances of life. There is thus in the *Exercises* a close relationship between Christology and the existential realization of the will of God that presupposes a direct engagement of the creature by the Creator (*Ex.* 15). Other aspects of this discernment exude a certain formality – Ignatius worked within the framework of the teachings of the Church – so that a dynamic tension exists in the mediation of God's will between the personal aspect and its institutional or ecclesial counterpart. Erhard Kunz suggests a double movement within the *Exercises*: God's movement to the person and the person's movement to God. Neither movement occurs in isolation from the other but take place in tandem: God's reaching out to the person so enables the person, in turn, to reach out to God.[6] This double movement, the descent of God to us (*kenosis*), and our movement to God (*ecstasis* or transcendence) constitutes a basic dynamic of Rahner's theology. It is at the point where these two movements come together that Rahner's Christology is to be situated. Indeed, this double movement finds a particularly moving expression in the "Suscipe," the closing prayer of the *Exercises*: God shares ("se communicare") Godself with us, while we respond by the commitment of our freedom, reason, will, and memory.[7]

CHARACTERISTICS OF RAHNER'S CHRISTOLOGY

Rahner's Christology developed over many years and we will distinguish three significant stages – both chronological and thematic – in his thinking.[8] At the outset it should be said that Rahner was always concerned to reconcile the claims of classical Christology, e.g., the dogma of Chalcedon, with the challenges of science and its evolutionary view of the world. Added to this was his awareness of the increasing pluralism of religions and worldviews. With this context in mind, he turns to the Chalcedonian dogma:

> We shall never cease to return to this formula, because whenever it is necessary to say briefly what it is that we encounter in the ineffable truth which is our salvation, we shall always have recourse to the modest, sober clarity of the Chalcedonian formula. But we shall only really have recourse to it . . . if it is not only our end but also our beginning.[9]

While initially concentrating on textual exegesis,[10] Rahner also took up particular themes, e.g., the self-consciousness of Jesus. This work would subsequently be developed in Münster (1967–71). Yet these historical and scientific challenges, for Rahner, always went hand in hand with the need, as he saw it, to engage in a personal or *existentiell* relationship with Jesus Christ. It is his attempts to provide a foundation and justification for such a relationship that underlie all his christological work – be it exegetical, historical, spiritual, or systematic.

FIRST STAGE (1934–1953): FOUNDATIONS

The first stage covers a period that begins with a note on an apparent reference to the "Sacred Heart" in Origen,[11] and then moves on to a key essay on the dogma of Chalcedon. In this phase, the history of spirituality and spirituality as a lived phenomenon are intertwined, and indeed are typical of Rahner's theology.

An important summary of his ideas during this period is the article "The Ignatian Mysticism of Joy in the World," with its central assertion that "the living personal God has spoken to man in Christianity, that is in Jesus Christ."[12] Despite the ecstatic or transcendent nature of human being, one remains always at the mercy of the silent God, unless God goes out to meet the person. Humanity is always tempted to create idols – creating God as a kind of *anima mundi*.

> But God is more than that. And as this more-than-the-world, God has broken in upon a person's existence and shattered the world, that which theology calls "nature." God has revealed Godself in Jesus Christ. This revelation has taken place in the dual unity of a communication of supernatural being and of the word. And the ultimate meaning of this revelation is a calling of a person out of this world into the life of God . . . This gives rise to a transcendence of a person's mission and destination.[13]

God's call breaks open the world. That is why it is part of the basic constitution of the finite human spirit to expect a free act of revelation from a personal God. There exists, then, an existential duty for every person, if one is to be true to oneself, to listen to what the Word of God might be saying to him or her. The philosophy of religion in *Hearers of the Word* is the backdrop for Rahner's Logos theology and its implicit Christology. The conclusion of *Spirit in the World* also points to Jesus: "and if Christianity is not the idea of an eternal, omnipresent spirit, but is Jesus of Nazareth, then Thomas's metaphysics of knowledge is Christian, when it summons man back into the here and now of his finite world, because the Eternal has also entered into his world so that man might find Him, and in Him might find himself anew."[14]

The most significant of Rahner's christological statements in this first period are tied up with his theology of grace.[15] While the proper title of "De Gratia" was "De Gratia Christi," it did not, Rahner notes, contain much explicit reference to Christ. His point is that we only have a Christian understanding of grace when this is conceived "not only in the most metaphysical way possible, as a divinization, but also as assimilation to Christ."[16] This orientation is crucial for Rahner's theology. The starting point for his theology of grace (and thus for all theology) is God's irrevocable self-communication to creation (the world and humankind) that constitutes their own salvation; i.e., the stress is on the priority of uncreated grace.

God's universal salvific will of salvation is the *cantus firmus* of Rahner's theology and is the title of the first chapter of his treatise "De Gratia Christi" in 1937–38.[17] This divine self-communication as the presence of God's forgiving love finds concrete historical expression in Jesus Christ, determining the real situation of every human being in the mode of an offer of salvation. God's salvific will draws us into Christ and into the Church, which, in Christ, is the "unum magnum sacramentum."[18] From here, Rahner subsequently develops his ecclesiology and sacramental theology.

As an "experience of grace" this activity of God in Jesus Christ finds concrete expression in the everyday life of people in different ways. Rahner distinguishes between thematic and unthematic, between explicit and anonymous experiences of grace – themes treated elsewhere in this volume. Following on this christological or, rather, grace-centered, model, he later developed the relationship between the categorical and transcendental aspects of revelation. The experience of grace, however, is always depicted as a participation in the life of Christ, especially in his passion. Christ is thus the goal of the entire human race. For Rahner, our supernatural life is the prolongation and unfolding of the life of Christ. Rahner's theology of grace and with it his entire theology remains incarnationally and ecclesiologically structured. He always views the salvation of humanity in terms of a relation to Christ, which is ecclesiologically and historically mediated. Christology appears thus at the heart of his understanding of grace; it is the historical realization of God's universal desire for salvation.

SECOND STAGE (1954–1968): CHALCEDON: END OR BEGINNING?

Rahner's main christological writings confirm the fact that – various twists and turns notwithstanding – his theology remains consistently anchored in his theology of grace. His 1954 essay on Chalcedon, however, is programmatic. The basic hermeneutical and methodological guiding thought here is that a dogmatic formulation is not only an end but also the beginning of a movement of entering into a deeper truth. Critical, probing questioning is also an act of piety, and so we should have the courage "to think with the mind and heart, which one actually has, and not with the mind and heart one is supposed to have."[19]

The theme of the essay concerns an appropriate understanding of the Chalcedonian doctrine. A few theses, central to Rahner's whole thinking, are worthy of mention. He maintains that "we must conceive of the relation between the Logos-Person and his human nature in just this sense, that here *both* independence *and* radical proximity equally reach a unique and qualitatively incommensurable perfection, which nevertheless remains once and for all the perfection of a relation between Creator and creature." Christology breaks through any competitive relationship between God and humanity. God is the ground of possibility and enduring guarantor of freedom, indeed of the very humanity of human beings. Rahner describes this relationship with the expression, "the mystery of that active creation." The incarnation becomes the key to anthropology, which always must be read in light of the relationship of humanity to God: "that Christology may be studied as self-transcending anthropology, and anthropology as deficient Christology."[20] That means that "Christology is at once beginning and end of anthropology, and that for all eternity such an anthropology is really theo-logy." Christology thus represents the key to anthropology and the theology of creation. Rahner's "anthropological turn" ultimately has its basis in Christology: "But if this is the case, we only radically understand ourselves for what we really are, when we grasp the fact that we are existential beings because God willed to be man, and thereby willed that we should be those in whom he as man can only encounter his own self by loving us."[21]

Theological anthropology can thus be developed from Christology, after this has been revealed to us. Christ is the archetype of humanity. The previously mentioned Scotist tendency is again apparent: the world, creation, etc. exist only with a view to the incarnation, the hypostatic union, and Jesus Christ. Scholastic theology would say that Christ is the "final cause" of creation. In more biblical language we could say the covenant is the goal of creation. Rahner tries in this way to translate the more formal, ontological categories of dogma into ontological, existential terms. On the one hand, he is concerned with the true humanity of Jesus; on the other hand, he sees in anthropology the possibility of leading people to Christ, or rather of illuminating their already existing relationship to Christ. Putting it the other way around, Rahner also maintains that every existential claim implies an ontological one. To a "Christology from below" there is a corresponding "Christology from above." Only a correlation between Christology and belief in Christ, between inner experience and external proclamation, can refute the suspicion that the gospel is nothing more than mythology. Thus Rahner can claim that "faith comes by hearing *and* by the grace, which rises in the innermost centre of the heart."[22]

Rahner recommends, therefore, a theological phenomenology of the religious relationship to Christ, or what he calls an incarnational spirituality. Moreover, in his attempt to link Christology with a general history of religion, we find the first mention of a "searching" Christology.[23] Rahner's

Christology during this phase would develop further along the lines we have outlined and we shall now turn to some of its more significant aspects.

THEOLOGY OF THE INCARNATION

Rahner consistently maintains God's immutability and, following on from this, God's impassability. In this light an urgent issue becomes how best to understand the incarnation of God. His claim is that "God can become something, he who is unchangeable in himself can *himself* become subject to change *in something else*."[24] This presupposes that the world and humanity are understood from the perspective of God's plan in the incarnation. Further, the immanent self-expression of God, or the eternal generation of the Son in the immanent Trinity, is the precursor of God's self-expression *ad extra*, an event of grace manifested in history. Humanity is not to be seen as predetermined by the incarnation, however, but is "that which comes to be and is constituted in essence and existence when and in so far as the Logos empties himself." The incarnation is thus not understood as the assumption of a form of being that has no christological reference. In the Logos, humanity also comes into being. In other words, the human being can be said to be christologically determined:

> We could now define man . . . as that which ensues when God's self-utterance, his Word, is given out lovingly into the void of god-less nothing. Indeed, the Logos made man has been called the abbreviated Word of God. This abbreviation, this code word for God is man, that is, the Son of Man and men, who exist ultimately because the Son of Man was to exist . . . If God wills to become non-God, man comes to be . . . And if God himself is man and remains so for ever, if all theology is therefore eternally an anthropology . . . and if God remains the insoluble mystery, man is for ever the articulate mystery of God.[25]

From this it follows:

> Christology is the end and beginning of anthropology. And this anthropology, when most thoroughly realised in Christology, is eternally theology. It is the theology which God himself has taught, by speaking out his Word, as our flesh, into the void of the non-divine and sinful. It is also the theology which we pursue in faith, unless we think that we could find God without the man Christ, and so without man at all.[26]

Rahner sees the relationship between God and humanity as grounded in the Chalcedonian dogma and its assertion of the divine and human natures in Christ. Even here, though, the term "is" in the dogma does not imply an identity of natures but a unique, unsurpassable unity. Finally, Rahner sees the christological unity of the dogma reflected historically in the dramatic and dual movement that takes place between God and humankind.

CHRISTOLOGY WITHIN AN EVOLUTIONARY CONTEXT

Responding to the challenges of modern science, Rahner develops a cosmological and historical vision of Christology against the background of an evolutionary (i.e., historically developing) understanding of nature and society. The whole movement of creation reaches its goal in the free and self-conscious human person. In a certain sense, the human person sums up creation. Rahner sees an essential unity in creation – an important fact when it comes to the full soteriological implications of the Christ event. A key concept here is the term "active self-transcendence," by which Rahner, not unlike Teilhard de Chardin, means a real becoming in creation (i.e., development and progress) without negating previous stages of the evolutionary process.

The goal of the transcendent movement of creation, however, is not a self-enclosed, self-sufficient human person, but one who is radically open to the absolute nature of reality. Indeed, the human person is an indefinable being, even to him or herself. Rahner's Christology will find its systematic locus where the two movements – from above and from below – come together. "When God brings about man's self-transcendence into God through his absolute self-communication to all in such a way that both elements constitute a promise to all which is irrevocable and which has already reached fulfillment in one man, then we have precisely what is signified by hypostatic union."[27]

JESUS' KNOWLEDGE AND SELF-CONSCIOUSNESS

Rahner views this topic against the backdrop of the often-controversial relationship between dogmatic theology and exegesis. Beginning with a reflection on the various kinds of knowledge, he shows how the ontological statement that Christ is true man and true God must be linked to a specific understanding of his consciousness. Excluded from the outset is any form of superficial, two-tiered psychology that too easily replaces Jesus' fear of death and sense of abandonment by God and his status as a pilgrim and believer with the concept of the beatific vision. Rather, "the direct presence to God, considered as a basic condition of Christ's soul, must be thought of as grounded in the substantial root of his created nature." Thus the beatific vision "is nothing other than the original unobjectified consciousness of divine sonship, which is present by the mere fact that there *is* a Hypostatic Union."[28]

The hypostatic union itself has a history – testified by Christ's awareness of his immediate relationship to God. If being precedes consciousness, then, Rahner insists it is possible to ascribe to Jesus a unity with God of an absolute kind from the beginning, while, at the same time, accepting a development of this original self-consciousness in history.

A few other concerns from this phase should also be mentioned. Rahner places great emphasis on the humanity of Jesus. He speaks, for example, of the eternal significance of Jesus' humanity for our relationship to God.[29] This emphasis on the humanity of Jesus may be understood as a corrective to certain monophysitist tendencies in the Christian tradition.[30] His meditations on liturgical feasts also reveal a theology of the passion and cross and a rediscovery of Holy Saturday.[31] While these meditations and prayers are still to be fully explored, they reflect an engagement with the suffering and the aftermath of the Second World War.[32] Moreover, Rahner welcomed the rediscovery of the Jewishness of Jesus, treating it with great seriousness and seeing it as an indictment of the failures of Christians through the ages.[33]

THIRD STAGE (1968–1984): HISTORICAL-CRITICAL DEVELOPMENT AND CONCERN FOR THE EXISTENTIAL APPROACH TO JESUS CHRIST

In this final stage there is a shift in Rahner from a "Christology from above" to a "Christology from below."[34] Also in this period there is the attempt to provide a rational justification for a personal relationship with Christ.[35] This interaction between personal devotion to Christ on the one hand, and concern for historical-critical questions and ecclesial dogmatic issues, on the other, is reciprocal and gives rise to a dynamic tension in Rahner's work. In his collaboration with Wilhelm Thüsing, we find an independent and sometimes unconventional treatment of the exegetical issues underlying dogmatic and fundamental theology.[36] Running through such reflections is a concern with an existential approach to Jesus as saviour of each person and of the world.

One outcome of exploring the relationship between dogmatic theology and the results of exegesis is that we should settle for a minimum of historical statements about Jesus. His intimacy with the Father, his messianic claim, his conscious entering into the conflict-laden circumstances of death, and his gathering of disciples would suffice.[37] In his theology of salvation, Rahner pleads for an inner unity of Christ's death and resurrection, his person and mission, and their connection with all of humankind. Only in what he terms the "transcendental hope of the resurrection," where we attain our definitive salvation, can the witness of the first disciples be fully understood.[38] Here too, Rahner speaks of an inner unity between personal experience and the proclamation that comes "from without."

The "appeals" that make up Rahner's "searching" Christology also have theological implications for Christianity's relations to other religions.[39] A "searching Christology" reflects our make-up as human beings – questioning and searching for meaning. It is a way of articulating in a more existential, experiential manner the inner unity of anthropology and Christology – something he previously formulated in ontological categories. Thus one finds Christ as absolute Saviour not through some process of abstract intellectual reasoning but rather in the concrete, ordinary experiences of life. His appeals are not so much definitive conclusions as an encouragement to discover anew the presence of Christ with us. In these appeals, the mystagogical tendency of Rahner's theology comes again to the fore. The three most important appeals are the call to a radical love of one's neighbour, the readiness for death, and the call to hope against all hope. He links this unconditional love to Matthew 25:

> If we do not turn the saying of Jesus that *he himself* is truly loved in every neighbour into an "as if" or merely into a theory of juridical imputation, then, when this saying is read from out of the experience of love itself, it says that an absolute love which gives itself radically and unconditionally to another person affirms Christ implicitly in faith and love.[40]

Rahner's appeals only make sense to the extent that a person is prepared to enter into and embrace the deeper dimensions – both loving and tragic – of everyday life.

The attempt to relate different life experiences to Christ finds repeated expression in this last phase, particularly in his reflections on the Easter experience, and it is here that some previously conflicting ideas are resolved.[41] The a priori transcendental structure of human hope and the a posteriori historical witness of the apostles come together. God's universal salvific will is effective in history while safeguarding human freedom in the mode of hope. As Rahner puts it:

> Nothing compels us to believe them [the apostolic witnesses], if we do not wish to, and if we remain sceptical. But there is much to justify our believing them. What is required of us is something extremely bold yet quite obvious: to venture our whole existence on its being wholly directed towards God, on its having a definite meaning, on its being capable of being saved and delivered, and on precisely this having occurred in Jesus (as the exemplary and instrumental cause), so that it is possible to believe that with regard to ourselves as the first disciples did. In them there really occurred, and absolutely, to the point of death, what we should always "like" to do, i.e., believe. And from the depth of our being we seek the objective historical facts by which such belief can come about.[42]

CHRIST AS THE CONVERGENCE OF ALL REALITY – A SYSTEMATIC OVERVIEW

Having provided an overview of the various strands of Rahner's Christology, it can still be asked whether these aspects are completely independent of each other or whether they converge to form some kind of synthesis. We have already noted a shift from a descending Christology to an ascending one, and from a metaphysical starting point to one based on a more existential relationship. In the sixth part of *Foundations* these strands are brought together but no attempt is made to bring them into a harmonious whole. Is Rahner to be faulted for this or does it not mirror our way of speaking about God, which, after all, is rooted in different scriptural approaches and testimonies to Christ? The structure of the various christological sections in *Foundations* and their preliminary character should prevent us from interpreting Rahner in too monochrome a manner. Our spirituality and current concerns should also be part of the picture. In my view, Rahner's various sketches of Christology raise the crucial issues that every Christology (and not only Christology) must deal with. By so doing he attempted to respond to the pressing questions of faith in his time – questions that continue to be asked today. This is a theology of the pilgrim. True, all dangers have not been avoided nor all challenges overcome; what is ultimately important is not to lose sight of the goal – Christ.

There are four basic areas in which Rahner seeks Christ. The first is our personal, existential relationship to Jesus Christ as Lord and saviour, a mediated relationship – mediated through different ecclesial forms of spirituality. This relationship, secondly, is founded on the dynamic unity of the historical figure of Jesus of the biblical tradition and the profession of faith of the early Christian communities. From such professions of faith grew the testimony of faith of the early Church, a faith that, thirdly, finds its normative expression in the dogma of Chalcedon. Fourthly, a universal, cosmic dimension has always pervaded Christology, a dimension we still see today in some of the early Christian basilicas and their icons of the "Pantokrator." Christology always struggles to unfold the *universale concretum* that is Christ. For Rahner, the question is how the cosmological dimension of creation can be retrieved, particularly given the huge advances in the other sciences. In all of this the image of Jesus and of Christ in the Ignatian tradition (the "IHS") remains key, since all his attempts at Christology aim at a definitive decision for Christ, expressed concretely as a life with Christ and patterned on him. These approaches can be represented schematically:

Creation	**Dogma of Chalcedon (451)**
Evolutionary	True God – True Man
Incarnation	Two natures united in one person/hypostasis
Means of salvation for all	
The Pantokrator or cosmic Christ	

The Christ of the Church's faith

IHS

Image of the invisible God
Sacrament of the universal, salvific will of God
Absolute mediator of salvation/searching (transcendental) Christology

Personal Faith	**Jesus in History**
Different forms of spirituality that reflect our operative Christology	Historical-critical exegesis
	Comparison with other historical figures
Jesus as ground of a radical trust/love	*The "historical Jesus"*
Jesus, the Lord as model/ideal	

Rahner's attempt to integrate different approaches to Christology – given the changed situation of contemporary Christianity – ultimately converges on the person of Christ. He places particular emphasis on the mutually conditioning relationship between a personal relationship with Christ and the creed of the Church. These two aspects represent a unity of existential and ontological theology. The shift in emphasis in Rahner's Christology that we noted is not primarily an exercise in ontology or in conceptual precision. His theology of creation, for example, is characterized by a historical and evolutionary consciousness due to his taking seriously the results of modern science. Our world is not static but a dynamic, developing one. Hence Rahner further developed his original metaphysical categories with the concept of "self-transcendence." Moreover, a personal relationship to Jesus cannot bypass the historical elements of the biblical narrative and its testimony to Jesus, the crucified and risen one. But even here there are challenges. Contemporary historical and scientific criticism asks whether Jesus really did correspond to such biblical testimony. Was he really like that? Is he the only saviour? Such questions are even asked by those with only a cursory knowledge of other religions. Is Jesus really the one that the dogma of the Church confesses him to be? Personal and ecclesial profession of belief in Christ is challenged both from within and from without. But we must ask ourselves such questions if our faith is not to grow stale. It is to Rahner's credit that he drew attention to such challenges; they have since only become more acute and divisive.

Whether Rahner's responses can survive in their entirety remains to be seen, particularly since he was continually reformulating his thought. His starting point steadily becomes clearer – the concrete lived experience of faith expressed in a phenomenology of his relationship with Christ. There is an ongoing tension between a personal relationship of faith and the Jesus of Scripture, between the testimony of the Church's belief in Jesus as the Christ, and our experience of a continually changing world. Christology has to operate within the Church's tradition of faith, while also engaging seriously with a growing religious and philosophical pluralism (i.e., alternative claims to salvation). Rahner's various approaches to Christology, however, converge into a basic idea, namely, in an effort to represent Christ as the heart of the world. At the same time, the mystagogical thread, the discovery and experience of Christ in everyday life and in history, is not to be underestimated. Rahner's Christology is not simply conceptualization and reflection, but also, and primarily, witness and commitment.

Though Rahner tried to engage with as many relevant questions as possible, there are some issues which, from today's perspective, are not treated in detail, if at all. Thus, the theology of Judaism and of Israel is best described as at the margins of his theology, though even here, he can surprise us from time to time with some of his comments. The Jewish roots of Jesus and Christology need to be further developed from biblical theology. Neither should a reappraisal of the various historical-critical questions regarding the person of Jesus be bypassed. Rahner's minimalism may have a value, but it too needs always to be reassessed. Also necessary is a more developed theology that engages the history of religions, where the figure of Jesus is brought into dialogue with other theories of salvation. At the same time, Rahner's warning against a biblical fundamentalism or naïveté remains as relevant as ever.

In conclusion, Rahner's project, with all its concerns and modes of expression, is significant not simply because of its enumeration of problems. His "unsystematic" approach attempts to preserve the mystery of Christ, which is what every theology strives for, even in its attempts to develop definitive formulations. At the core of his project we find a dual movement – already identified in the *Spiritual Exercises* and which is developed in his theology of grace –: the movement of God to the world and, within this, the movement of the world to God. In this dual movement, Christ appears as that reality for which all things were made and from which all things derive their meaning.

Notes

1 This early summary of Christianity and of his Christology is part of an essay on the mission of the parish priest in K. Rahner, *Mission and Grace. Essays in Pastoral Theology*, II (London/New York: Sheed and Ward, 1964), 39–42.

2 The method employed in such an investigation represents an approach to Rahner's work of a generation of theologians "after Rahner." See A. Batlogg, P. Rulands, W. Schmolly, R. Siebenrock, G. Wassilowsky, and A. Zahlauer, *Der Denkweg Karl Rahners. Quellen – Entwicklungen – Perspektiven*, 2nd edn. (Mainz: Grünewald, 2004).

3 For a collage of his christological approaches, see *FCF*, 176–321.

4 See ch. 19 of the present volume. The importance of the Ignatian tradition on Rahner is not at issue here, only how deep these roots are. See K. P. Fischer, *Der Mensch als Geheimnis. Die Anthropologie Karl Rahners* (Freiburg/Basel/Vienna: Herder, 1974); H. D. Egan, *The Spiritual Exercises and the Ignatian Mystical Horizon* (St. Louis: The Institute of Jesuit Sources, 1976); M. Schneider, "*Unterscheidung der Geister." Die ignatianischen Exerzitien in der Deutung von E. Przywara, K. Rahner und G. Fessard*, ITS 11, 2nd edn. (Innsbruck/Vienna: Tyrolia, 1987), 79–133; A. Zahlauer, *Karl Rahner und sein produktives Vorbild Ignatius von Loyola.* ITS 47 (Innsbruck/Vienna: Tyrolia, 1996); P. Endean, *Karl Rahner and Ignatian Sprituality* (Oxford: Oxford University Press, 2001); A. Batlogg, *Die Mysterien des Lebens Jesu bei Karl Rahner. Zugang zum Christusglauben.* ITS 58, 2nd edn. (Innsbruck/Vienna: Tyrolia, 2004).

5 H. Rahner, "Eucharisticon Fraternitatis," in J. B. Metz, W. Kern, A. Darlapp, and H. Vorgrimler, eds., *Gott in Welt*, II (Freiburg/Basel/Vienna: Herder, 1964), 895–99. On the Christology of the *Exercises*, see H. Rahner, *Ignatius as Theologian* (London: Chapman, 1968, 1990).

6 E. Kunz, "'Bewegt von Gottes Liebe,' Theologische Aspekte der ignatianischen Exerzitien und Merkmale jesuitischer Vorgehensweise," in M. Sievernich and

G. Switek, eds., *Ignatianisch. Eigenart und Methode der Gesellschaft Jesu* (Freiburg: Herder, 1990), 75–95, at p. 95.

7 See K. Rahner, *Spiritual Exercises* (London: Sheed and Ward, 1976), and *Meditations on Priestly Life* (London: Sheed and Ward, 1970).

8 See É. Maurice, *La Christologie de Karl Rahner* (Paris: Desclée, 1995). See also K. Lehmann and A. Raffelt, eds., *Rechenschaft des Glaubens. Karl-Rahner-Lesebuch*, 2nd ed. (Freiburg: Herder, 1982, 2004), 13*–56*, here 40*–42*).

9 "Current Problems in Christology," *TI* I, 150–51.

10 "Exegesis and Dogmatic Theology," *TI* V, 67–93.

11 "Coeur des Jésus chez Origène?," *Revue Ascetique et Mystique* 15 (1934), 171–74.

12 "The Ignatian Mysticism of Joy in the World," *TI* III, 283.

13 Ibid., *TI* III, 285.

14 *SW*, 408.

15 The experience of grace as the key to understanding Rahner's theology is also underlined by Lehmann, *Rechenschaft des Glaubens*, 36*. See also P. Rulands, *Menschsein unter dem An-spruch der Gnade. Das übernatürliche Existential und der Begriff der natura pura bei Karl Rahner*. ITS 55 (Innsbruck/Vienna, Tyrolia, 2000); and E. Farrugia, *Aussage und Zusage. Zur Indirektheit der Methode Karl Rahners veranschaulicht an seiner Christologie*. Analecta Gregoriana 245, Series Facultatis Theologiae; sectio B, n. 81 (Rome: Gregorian University Press, 1985).

16 "Current Problems in Christology," *TI* I, 199.

17 This was published solely for the private use of his students, "De Gratia Christi. Summa Praelectionum in usum privatum auditorum ordinata" (Oeniponte, 1937/38, republished or reprinted in 1950/51, 1955 and 1959).

18 Ibid., 19.

19 "Current Problems in Christology," *TI* I, 153.

20 Ibid., *TI* I, 164.

21 Ibid., *TI* I, 184.

22 "Thoughts on the Theology of Christmas," *TI* III, 28.

23 "Current Problems in Christology," *TI* I, 188–89.

24 "On the Theology of the Incarnation," *TI* IV, 113.

25 Ibid., *TI* IV, 116.

26 Ibid., *TI* IV, 117.

27 *FCF*, 201.

28 "Dogmatic Reflections on the Knowledge and Self-Consciousness of Christ," *TI* V, 207–08.

29 "The Eternal Significance of the Humanity of Jesus for our Relationship with God," *TI* III, 35–46.

30 In the discussion on the theology of cross with Moltmann and von Balthasar he said spontaneously: "Perhaps it is possible to be an orthodox Nestorian or an orthodox Monophysite. If this were the case, then I would prefer to be an orthodox Nestorian." *Karl Rahner in Dialogue: Conversations and Interviews 1965–1982*, trans. and ed. H. Biallowons, H. D. Egan, S.J., and P. Imhof, S.J. (New York: Crossroad, 1986), 127. This is not to infer that Rahner disagreed with the classical ontological expression of the two natures of Christ. (See *FCF*, 285–89.)

31 See the various articles in *TI* VII, 136–76.

32 See his *Watch and Pray with Me* (New York: Herder and Herder, 1966).

33 "Dein verkannter Bruder. Ein Jude sieht uns Christen. Einführung zu André Neher" (1961), in *SaW*, xxvii, 31–35. See also K. Rahner and P. Lapide, *Encountering Jesus – Encountering Judaism* (New York: Crossroad, 1987). For a summary of this stage of Rahner's Christology, see "Jesus Christ IV," *SM* iii, 192–209.

34 See "Gnade als Mitte menschlicher Existenz. Ein Gespräch mit und über Karl Rahner aus Anlaß seines 70. Geburtstages," *Herder Korrespondenz* 28 (1974), 77–92.

35 K. Rahner, *The Love of Jesus and the Love of Neighbour* (New York: Crossroad, 1983).

36 K. Rahner and W. Thüsing, *A New Christology* (London: Burns & Oates, 1980). See also *FCF*, 203–311.

37 "Remarks on the Importance of the History of Jesus for Catholic Dogmatics," *TI* xii, 201–12.

38 *FCF*, 264–85.

39 Ibid., 311–21.

40 *FCF*, 295.

41 W. Schmolly, "Vom letzten Wagnis des Geistes und des Herzens. Zu Karl Rahners Theologie der Ostererfahrung," in A. Batlogg, M. Delgado, and R. Siebenrock, eds., *Was den Glauben in Bewegung bringt. Fundamentaltheologie in der Spur Jesu Christi*, Festschrift for K. H. Neufeld, S.J. (Freiburg: Herder, 2004), 63–78.

42 "Resurrection," *SM* v, 331.

Further reading

Maurice, É., *La christologie de Karl Rahner* (Paris: Desclée, 1995).

Rahner, K., "Current Problems in Christology," *TI* i, 149–200.

   "The Eternal Significance of the Humanity of Jesus for our Relationship with God," *TI* iii, 35–46.

   "Remarks on the Importance of the History of Jesus for Catholic Dogmatics," *TI* xiii, 201–12.

   "The Two Basic Types of Christology," *TI* xii, 213–23.

   "Brief Observations on Systematic Christology Today," *TI* xxi, 233–34.

   Foundations of Christian Faith (*FCF*), 176–321.

Rahner, K., with W. Thüsing, *A New Christology* (London: Burns & Oates, 1980).

8 Ecclesiology and ecumenism

RICHARD LENNAN

> Since I am a human being and a Christian, it is obvious to me that I am a Christian in the Church, an ecclesial Christian.[1]

Karl Rahner's writings on "the Church" are significant in volume, in content, and in their connection to the central concerns of Rahner's life and work. For Rahner, the Church was always more than a social structure, a political force, or a site for religious activities; the Church was a genuinely theological reality. Rahner affirmed an intimate connection between the Church and the foundational elements of Christian faith: God's self-revelation in Jesus Christ; the presence of the Holy Spirit in human history; and God's promise that love, rather than sin or death, would speak the final word in that history.

Just as Rahner's emphasis on the capacity of human beings to encounter God in their everyday world resulted in a theology of eating, of laughing, and of childhood and old age, so too it ensured that the Church's relationship to history and culture was a prominent feature of his ecclesiology. For Rahner, living as an ecclesial Christian was an invitation to be part of the world in a particular way, a way that witnessed not simply to humanity's orientation to God, but to the social implications of God's self-revelation in Jesus Christ. To that end, Rahner was at pains to aid the appropriation of ecclesial faith by articulating the authentic claims and necessary boundaries of "the Church," by promoting reconciliation between Christians, and by sketching the possibilities for the Church's creative engagement with the wider world.

In addition, Rahner was not simply a student of the Church; he was a practitioner. His own faith and life, not simply his academic pursuits, were deeply engaged with the reality of the Church, with its struggle for authenticity, its failings, and its attempts to respond to the challenges that it faced as part of a rapidly changing world. Most particularly, Rahner contributed significantly to the Second Vatican Council (1962–65), which remains the most influential event in the life of the modern Church, and to the reception of the Council into its everyday life.

In attempting to capture something of the spirit of Rahner's ecclesiology, this chapter will begin by exploring how Rahner understood the connection between the Church and God's self-communication in human history. The chapter will then examine Rahner's understanding of the dynamics of faith lived within the Church, including his approach to the relationship between individual and communal faith, the hallmarks of a healthy Church, and the imperative of reconciliation between Christians for the sake of the mission of the Church.

REVELATION, SACRAMENTALITY, AND THE CHURCH

At the heart of Rahner's ecclesiology is the notion of the Church as a sacrament. Although Rahner was not the first to view the Church through the lens of sacramentality, his analysis built on his distinctive understanding of revelation and grace, which contributed significantly to the reshaping of Roman Catholic sacramental theology in the second half of the twentieth century. Most particularly, Rahner's approach marked a step in the emergence of Catholic theology from the thrall of the Reformation-era controversies.

In post-Reformation Catholic piety and theology, the stress was on the mediation of grace through the Church. By amplifying the historical and ecclesial dimensions of revelation and grace, Catholic theology sought an antidote to the excess of individualism that Catholics perceived in Protestant theologies of faith. Consequently, both the sacraments, understood as conduits of grace, and the teaching of the Church, understood as the guarantor of unimpeachable knowledge of God, loomed large in the Catholic worldview. The Catholic approach, however, had its own underside: the tendency to portray grace as quantifiable, as an object dispensed by God, in greater or lesser amounts, especially through the sacraments of the Church.

Complementing the tendency to objectify and quantify grace was the emergence in Catholic thought of a juridical approach to ecclesiology. This approach reduced "the Church" to its authoritative structures, which were responsible both for the preservation and protection of revealed truth and for enforcing the conditions necessary for the proper administration and reception of the sacraments. Bolstering the defence of the Church's authority in such matters, Catholic biblical studies concentrated on issues of apologetics, where the primary concern was with texts that "proved" Jesus to be the founder of the Church, especially its structures, and the seven sacraments.

Rahner was as committed as his contemporaries to underscoring the necessary historical and ecclesial mediation of grace, but the focus of his ecclesiology and sacramental theology differed markedly from the prevailing Catholic emphases. Thus, Rahner recognized that doing justice to the link between Jesus Christ and the Church required more than a forensic inquiry seeking to identify Jesus as the founder of the Church. Similarly, Rahner referred to grace in a dynamic and personal way, thereby expanding the role of the Holy Spirit in the Church beyond reference to the conditions necessary for the valid administration of the sacraments. In addition, Rahner's sacramental theology not only helped to popularize the language of "mystery" among Catholics, it also promoted ecumenical possibilities by highlighting the complementarity, rather than opposition, between the Bible and the sacraments.

The fruitfulness of Rahner's approach to ecclesiology owed much to what underpinned it: his theology of symbol.

In Rahner's analysis, symbols were necessary for the self-disclosure and self-realization of all beings: "the symbol strictly speaking (symbolic reality) is the self-realisation of a being in the other, which is constitutive of its essence."[2] Symbols, therefore, were more than signposts pointing to something other than themselves: they were the means by which one being could come to know another, to know what was not accessible in an immediate way. As such, symbols not only revealed the mystery of being and indicated its depth, they did so without reducing that mystery to manageable dimensions.

As the preeminent examples of his understanding of symbols, Rahner pointed to the trinitarian life of God and to the incarnation. Most particularly, Rahner understood the relationship between the Father and the Son in terms of symbol: "The Logos is the 'word' of the Father, his perfect 'image', his 'imprint', his radiance, his self-expression."[3] The Logos, then, was more than a word *about* the Father; the Logos was the word *of* the Father, distinct from the Father, but inseparable from the Father. Similarly, Rahner stressed that in the incarnation "the humanity of Christ is not to be considered as something in which God dresses up and masquerades ... The humanity is the self-disclosure of the Logos itself, so that when God, expressing himself, exteriorises himself, that very thing appears which we call the humanity of the Logos."[4]

The humanity of Jesus, therefore, is the self-expression in human history of the God of infinite mercy. Through Jesus, especially through his death and resurrection, that mercy had become irrevocable, irreversible, and indomitable. In addition, God's self-communication in Jesus meant that God's mercy had a historical shape; it was always more than a private matter in the interior life of individuals. Rahner's conclusion from those two facts was that human history must always have a symbol of God's definitive mercy in Jesus Christ. If it were to symbolize Christ, however, such a symbol would need also to be an "event," to effect what it signified. In Rahner's theology, that symbol was the Church:

> Christ is the primal sacramental word of God, uttered in the one history of mankind, in which God made known his irrevocable mercy ... and did this by effecting it in Christ and effected it by making it known. [T]he Church is the continuance, the contemporary presence, of that real, eschatologically triumphant and irrevocably established presence in the world, in Christ, of God's salvific will. The Church is the abiding presence of that primal sacramental word of definitive grace, which Christ is in the world, effecting what is uttered by uttering it in sign.[5]

As an authentically sacramental reality, the Church did more than point to grace: it existed because of God's "eschatologically victorious" grace in Jesus Christ, through the Spirit.[6] The Spirit constituted the Church as the effective symbol of grace, as "the sacrament of salvation" for the world. Although the Church neither owned the Spirit nor functioned as the exclusive community of "the saved," its very existence guaranteed the presence and efficacy of God's love in human history, even in the lives of those who would never be baptized into the Church.

The whole of Rahner's ecclesiology, everything that he believed about the mission, structure, and doctrines of the Church, derived from his sacramental approach. The remaining sections of this chapter will develop some of the implications of that approach for Rahner's theology of ecclesial faith. Before doing so, however, it is possible to summarize in six key points the impact of Rahner's sacramental ecclesiology.

First, the sacramental understanding enabled an explicitly theological, rather than a primarily juridical or apologetic, approach to the Church. The shift in Catholic thinking that the sacramental approach initiated is evident in a comparison between Vatican I (1869–70) and Vatican II (1962–65) on revelation and the Church. While the former, echoing the Council of Trent (1545–63), highlighted the divine guarantees for the truth of the Church's teaching and the legitimacy of its structures, especially the papacy, the latter, without any disregard for issues of truth or structure, showcased the language of "communication of the self," "mystery," and "sacrament."

Secondly, sacramental ecclesiology avoided contrasting the external reality of the Church – a shibboleth for Catholics – with the freedom of God's Holy Spirit – a Protestant shibboleth. The desire to hold together the two aspects of the Church was evident in Rahner's writing as early as the 1940s, when he was critical of both the juridical tone that he perceived in Pope Pius XII's *Mystici corporis Christi* (1943) and of contemporary endeavors to promote ecumenism on the basis of understanding "Church" as an invisible fellowship of believers.[7]

Thirdly, the identification of the Church as the primary sacrament of the Holy Spirit established a link between the Church and all manifestations of the Spirit. That link, which provided a stimulus both for reconciliation between the divided Christian churches and for dialogue with all those who were open to God's presence, was also the foundation of Rahner's theology of "the anonymous Christian."

Fourthly, the sacramental approach produced a dynamic ecclesiology. Since the Church's authenticity depended on its faithfulness to the Spirit, it could never outgrow the requirement that every aspect of its life remain open to the Spirit – "the church is the proclaiming bearer of the revealing word of God as God's utterance of salvation, and *at the same time*, she is the subject, harkening and believing, to whom the word of salvation of God in Christ is addressed."[8]

Fifthly, Rahner's description of the Church and its sacramental actions as "exhibitive" words that made present the grace of the Spirit demonstrated that "word" and "sacrament" were not polar opposites. If it was valid to understand sacraments as "word-events" – a fact that was most obvious in marriage and penance where words were also the sacramental "action" – it was as legitimate to characterize the biblical word as sacramental of the Spirit's presence, as an efficacious symbol that came from God.[9] In short, Rahner offered a way out of the *cul de sac* into which the Reformation-era disputes had plunged all reflection on revelation and grace.

Sixthly, the recognition of "the Church" as a sacrament, which implied that the whole community of faith, not only its structures and office-holders, shared the Holy Spirit, facilitated a shift away from a narrow focus on the institutional dimensions of the Church. In contributing to that shift, however, Rahner did not simply substitute a congregationalist understanding of the Church for an institutional one. In fact, he applied the sacramental principle in a way that affirmed the Spirit's presence in the community, the individual believer, and the Church's authoritative structures.

THE DYNAMICS AND TENSIONS OF
ECCLESIAL FAITH

Coursing through Rahner's writings on ecclesiology is the recognition of a variety of tensions: between the Church as part of history and society and as oriented beyond history; between permanence and development in the faith and structures of the Church; between the holiness of the Church and its need for reform; between individual and communal faith; between the charisms of those in authority and the charisms of all members of the Church; and between local Churches and the central authority of the Pope. Although Rahner acknowledged that the tensions made ecclesial faith challenging, he valued the tensions since they highlighted myriad implications of the Church's sacramental nature.

Had the Church been either the product of human ingenuity alone, which would have contained it within the purposes envisaged by its founders, or a theophany, which would have meant that it transcended human and historical complexity, such tensions would have been unimaginable. As a sacrament, however, the Church existed in history, but also looked for its fulfillment in Christ, through the Holy Spirit. There could be, then, no valid theologies of the Church that dealt with their subject as if it were "merely" human or "purely" divine. Rahner's commitment to doing ecclesiology in a way that avoided such "either . . . or" approaches was particularly evident in his analysis of the Church's place in the world.

In articulating how the Church might relate to the society of which it was a part, Rahner sought to avoid two extremes: one that would deny the Church's orientation to the mystery of God and concern itself only with history; the other that would withdraw the Church from the world, thereby implying that grace and salvation did not have social and historical implications. Rahner's alternative to those flawed approaches recognized that while it was true that what belonged to the world was only of relative value, when compared to the absoluteness of God, "relative value" was not tantamount to "zero" value. As a result, members of the Church could affirm the goodness of the world as an expression of God's goodness. On the other hand, members of the Church needed also to be aware of those things that hindered the realization of humanity's orientation to God. Christians, therefore, could not relinquish the obligation to protest against social policies and structures that hindered access to God's life-giving and liberating love.[10]

While Rahner was thus committed to the right of the Church to take a critical stance towards society, he opposed resolutely any attempts by members of the Church to deny the legitimate autonomy of secular society. In other words, Rahner did not want a world run by the Church. Not only was it clear to him that those in authority in the Church lacked the necessary competencies to decide all matters of social and economic policy, he believed also that a world run by the Church would not necessarily guarantee that the gospel permeated every aspect of life. Rahner, therefore, was not uneasy about the fact that the Church in the modern era existed in a "diaspora," where Christians were not only a minority group, but often a marginal group. In fact, he argued that the diaspora, more than "Christian societies," could be beneficial, as it challenged everyone in the Church to greater faithfulness and commitment in witnessing to the hope and possibility that had their foundation in Jesus Christ.[11]

Similarly, Rahner believed that only a committed focus on Christ could enable the Church to maintain the right relationship between permanence and change. In Rahner's theology, "permanence" expressed the Church's dependence on God's revelation in Jesus Christ. Since the Spirit brought the Church into being as the sacrament of what God in Christ offered to the whole of humanity, the Church was not free to substitute anything else for the centrality of Christ. The fact that the Church privileged the Scriptures, the seven ecclesial sacraments, doctrines, and hierarchical leadership as God-given and, therefore, a permanent part of its life, witnessed to the conviction that they were means through which the Spirit continued to lead the community of faith to Christ.

On the other hand, the connection to Christ and the Spirit did not mean that the permanent features of the Church were those that had least connection to human history. In fact, all of them were the products of human decisions and actions. Nonetheless, Rahner stressed that the link between the Spirit and particular historical decisions could give such decisions and actions a permanent significance. As the prime illustration of that principle, Rahner pointed to the fact that the Church could never outgrow the apostolic witness:

> . . . an essential part of God's conserving [the church] in existence consists in God having founded it at a particular moment in time. God, then, has a unique, qualitatively not transmissible relationship to the Church's first generation, one which God does not have in the same sense to other periods of the Church's history, or rather has to the latter only through the former.[12]

It was, however, the same combination of the Spirit and human history that convinced Rahner of the paradoxical possibility that what was permanent could change and develop. What was genuinely sacramental, he believed, would be able to facilitate a deeper encounter with the mystery of God in response to new needs. In concrete terms, this meant that doctrine could be understood in new ways and that the structures of the Church could change without being severed from the Spirit. Rahner argued that the Church could discern the right relationship between permanence and development, but denied that it was possible to separate the "unchangeable" from the "changeable" in the Church. Such a division would have implied the capacity to isolate the Spirit from its symbol.[13]

Discernment of the right relationship between permanence and development required both an awareness of the contemporary world and openness to the movement of the Spirit. Since Rahner identified the Spirit as constitutive of the Church, it might seem reasonable to conclude that he would have regarded discernment of the Spirit as a relatively simple task for the members of the Church. Such a conclusion, however, would ignore another of the tensions that Rahner regarded as characteristic of the Church: that between its holiness and its sinfulness.

When Rahner referred to the holiness of the Church, his focus was on the mystery of the Spirit's presence, which established the Church as the sacrament of God's revelation in Jesus. The presence of the Spirit in the Church manifested itself through the gospel and the sacraments, which even sinful members of the Church could not impair. In addition, it was also "the saints," those characterized by their openness to God and commitment to others, who gave shape to the Spirit's presence. On the other hand, Rahner insisted that the principle of sacramentality implied that it was legitimate to describe the Church as sinful when its members or structures witnessed to something other than the movement of the Spirit.

While thus acknowledging the sinfulness of the Church, Rahner also stressed that such sinfulness was not the equal of holiness. Just as the sinfulness of any individual could obscure the Spirit, but not annul God's desire to give life to all creation, so the sinfulness of the Church could not overcome the Spirit whose presence in the Church remained both mysterious and beyond human control. Nonetheless, sinfulness highlighted the need for the conversion of the Church, a need that embraced its office-holders and structures, as well as the individual members.

Rahner welcomed Vatican II's willingness to acknowledge the Church's sinfulness, but believed that the Council had been unnecessarily tentative in avoiding the use of "the sinful Church." He did, however, find more congenial the Council's stress on the "pilgrim" nature of the Church as that term brought into relief the Church's immersion in history, where sin and the need for conversion were inescapable. For Rahner, "the pilgrim Church" captured the complex reality of its subject in a way that exceeded other designations, such as, for example, "the mystical body," which might too readily suggest that the earthly history of the Church was unimportant.[14]

The fact that the Church even had a history showed clearly that the Spirit did not bring the Church into being as an unchangeable object. Since its history underscored the Church's struggle to trust in the Spirit, it also highlighted the fact that members of the Church could not automatically assume that trust in the Spirit was always characteristic of their lives:

> It is the Church that does not have the courage to regard the future as belonging to God in the same way as it has experienced the past as belonging to God . . . It often places more value on the bureaucratic apparatus of the Church than in the enthusiasm of the Spirit; it often loves the calm more than the storm, the old which has proved itself more than the new which is bold.[15]

While Rahner critiqued "the bureaucratic apparatus" of the Church for its tendency to stifle the freedom and hope that derived from the Spirit, he was far from concluding that a church without structures of authority would be preferable. In fact, Rahner attributed to the Spirit the existence of the Church as a structured community of faith.

In Rahner's analysis, there was an intimate link between authority and the fact that Christian faith belonged within a community of believers, rather than simply to individuals. Just as he rejected a purely private and interior "church" as irreconcilable with a sacramental understanding of revelation and grace, so Rahner was unsympathetic to any claim that the grounding and content of the Church's faith resided only in the beliefs of its individual members:

> Faith does not only mean accepting what "I" as an individual believe that I have heard. It also means accepting what the Church has heard, giving my assent to the "confession" of the Church, the Church which is not only the bearer of the message of Christ which it delivers to individuals (and which then disappears again like a postman), but is the enduring and abiding medium of faith.[16]

A church in which there was no source of authority beyond individual conviction could not do justice to either the historical reality of God's revelation in Jesus Christ or the Spirit's formation of a community to witness to Christ. For Rahner, then, it was axiomatic that Christian faith was ecclesial faith: "Christianity is the religion of a demanding God who summons my subjectivity out of itself only if it confronts me in a church which is authoritative."[17] A key element of the primacy of communal faith was its formulation and articulation by the bishops of the Church.

Since the bishops were responsible in a particular way for the Church's unity in faith and its connection to the apostolic witness, both of which were essential to the integrity of the Church and the authenticity of its witness to Christ, Rahner was in no doubt that the bishops could fulfill their role only through the Spirit. For Rahner, then, the teaching authority of the bishops was not simply an administrative necessity, still less an imposition on the freedom of believers to determine the content of faith for themselves; it was sacramental of the Spirit's care for the Church. Accordingly, Rahner had little time for purveyors of theologies that either portrayed the bishops as the enemies of the Spirit or simply neglected the episcopacy when considering the movement of the Spirit in the Church.

While Rahner privileged the communal faith of the Church, and the unique responsibility of the bishops to preside over that faith, he was no less committed to affirming the presence of the Spirit in each member of the Church:

> . . . in the Church to which charismatic elements belong, subordinates are not simply those who have to carry out orders from above. They have other commands as well to carry out: those of the Lord, who also guides God's Church directly and does not always in the first place convey God's commands and promptings to ordinary Christians through ecclesiastical authorities.[18]

Rahner's theology maintained a tension between the Spirit-given responsibility of the bishops for the Church's faith and the right, indeed obligation, of all members of the Church to respond to the particular gifts of the Spirit that they had received. This meant that there could be unity in the Church only when each member of the Church recognized that no single person had a monopoly on the Spirit. While Rahner did not believe that conflict in the Church was to be avoided at all costs, he rejected both authoritarianism and schism as equally flawed responses to the challenge of achieving unity in faith.

Rahner stressed that conflict in the Church over questions of authority or the nature of authentic faith did not suggest that the Spirit might be at war against itself. Such conflict, however, did demonstrate that genuine unity in the Church required that members of the Church place openness to the Spirit above their personal preferences. That openness required not only respect for the unique authority of bishops, but also the recognition that those outside the formal circles of authority in the Church could originate ideas and actions that were for the good of the whole Church.

The tension between the responsibilities of bishops and the movement of the Spirit in the lives of all believers was not the only form of tension that Rahner recognized as inseparable from the structures of the Church. Just as significant was that between the local churches and the central authority of the Pope.

Even before Vatican II enabled Catholics to become familiar with the concepts of "collegiality" and "the local church," Rahner was concerned with the relationship between the various elements of the Church's constitution. Without detracting from the unique role of the Pope, Rahner stressed that bishops were more than the Pope's subalterns and local churches more than branch offices of Rome:

> The bishops are "local ordinaries" not merely because the Pope for practical reasons needs administrative officials in various places for his personal rule of the Church . . . but because a bishop can fulfil the function which he has in the college of bishops and indeed for the entire Church, only when he authoritatively represents a particular member of the universal Church, in which the differentiation from other members of the Church intended by the Spirit can really exist.[19]

After Vatican II, which he regarded as the first gathering of a genuine "world-church," one in which concerns specific to particular nations were not only heard, but also accepted as relevant to the Church's mission, Rahner continued to stress the indispensable role of the local church as the venue for people's experience of "the Church."[20] While Rahner believed that the Council had opened new possibilities in the relationship between local churches and "the center," his reflections on life in the Church after Vatican II concluded that the relationship between the Pope and the bishops remained too strongly weighted in favor of the central authority. To the end of his life, therefore, Rahner continued to advocate that the Pope should take action both to limit his own authority and to give practical expression to the fact that the bishops were more than advisors to the Pope.[21]

Rahner's commitment to buttressing the role of local churches and their bishops existed alongside his insistence that the identity of all local churches derived ultimately from their communion in the one Church, not from what was exclusive to any single church. In Rahner's theology, the communion of the Church was a *sine qua non*. Like his opposition to schism and sectarianism, the emphasis on communion had its foundation in the

Spirit: since there was only the one Spirit of the one Christ, there could be only the one Church. That principle not only guided Rahner's response to conflict within the Roman Catholic Church, it also shaped his lifelong promotion of ecumenism as an obligation on all Christians.

THE CHALLENGE OF ECUMENISM

In addition to being a consequence of his understanding of God's revelation in Jesus and the Spirit, Rahner's commitment to "the one Church" also flowed from another significant aspect of his ecclesiology: the conviction that the Church's authenticity depended on its response to the challenges of history. More explicitly, Rahner believed that the Christian Church would be irrelevant to the contemporary world if members of the churches remained obsessed with the controversies of the Reformation.

Although he did not deny that there were important issues of theological truth in the disputes that arose in the sixteenth century, Rahner contended that those questions were not the ones that were crucial to the future of Christianity. In a series of articles written between the end of Vatican II in 1965 and his death in 1984, Rahner argued that if the Christian churches continued to sink their energy into the topics that had been historically divisive, the churches would become increasingly unable to address the contemporary world.[22] In that world, not only had pluralism and relativism become the norm, but "God" had even become increasingly incomprehensible. Such a world, then, had little interest in sixteenth century disputes.

Rahner was convinced that the churches could effectively address the questions and concerns of the contemporary world only if they spoke with one voice. In order to develop that one voice, the churches needed to highlight what they already shared – the life of the Spirit – rather than clinging to points of division. In addition, Rahner argued that if the members of the divided churches recognized each other as sharing a common life and common challenges, there would be a new context in which to address whatever contentious issues remained from the Reformation.

To illustrate how the relationship between the churches might find a new shape, Rahner, together with Heinrich Fries, published in 1983 *Unity of the Churches: An Actual Possibility*. That book, one of Rahner's final publications, proposed a concrete model for the reconciliation of the divided Christian churches. Taking their inspiration from Vatican II's principle of the "hierarchy of truths," Rahner and Fries encouraged the churches to seek unity by agreeing on the primary matters on Christian faith "as they are expressed in Holy Scripture, in the Apostles' Creed, and in that of Nicaea and Constantinople."[23] The churches were not to impose on each other any requirement to accept secondary points of doctrine, nor were they to reject as incompatible with Christian faith any doctrines of other churches that their own church did not accept. In so doing, Rahner envisaged that institutional unity between the churches was possible even with a pluralism of creeds. What Rahner and Fries sought was that the churches reconcile differences in order that they might preach the gospel and witness to Christ in contemporary society. In other words, their concern was genuinely evangelical, not an appeal for the churches needing to work together in the hope of ensuring their survival.

Rahner recognized the contribution that theological dialogue could make to the possibility of unity, but also urged that those in authority in the churches act in a way that demonstrated courageous trust in the Spirit. While Rahner's commitment to the Catholic tradition permeated his life and work, he was nonetheless passionate in urging a more generous response to ecumenism by Catholic leaders:

> Let the Roman Curia show bold resolution and dare to hope to achieve
> something of which the end-result cannot be calculated in advance,
> thus displaying itself in its ministries of teaching and leadership in a
> way demanded by the whole historical situation today . . . let the limits
> of the universal primacy as they arise from dogma or can be restricted
> by the papacy itself be more clearly defined.[24]

ASSESSMENT

The fruitfulness of Rahner's ecclesiology derived from his fundamental insight that the Church existed as the symbol of the Holy Spirit. It was that insight that enabled Rahner to explicate the Church's place in God's offer of life in Christ, to address the Church's relationship to history and culture, and to articulate a vision for life within the Church. In each of those areas, and in others besides, Rahner employed the sacramental understanding in order to highlight the dynamism of the Church. In so doing, he also underscored the fact that one-dimensional approaches to the Church could not capture its true identity.

Rahner sought the realization of the Church as a genuine community of faith. Such a community was possible only when each of its members played a part. Thus, Rahner defended the role of bishops, but was equally insistent that the Spirit worked through every member of the Church. While

Rahner's defense of the need for authoritative structures and the primacy of the community's faith might not appeal to those who favor a looser sense of connection to the Church, his approach was far from being an uncritical affirmation of authority in the Church. Indeed, he was particularly scathing in his analysis of those trends in the post-Vatican II period that suggested a retreat from the hope inspired by the Council. In rejecting developments that obscured the Spirit's presence and weakened the freedom that was the patrimony of every member of the Church, Rahner insisted unequivocally that only a genuinely catholic Church, one that was neither authoritarian nor individualistic, could express the Spirit.

Rahner envisaged the Church as a "spacious house with large windows from which one looks out on all spheres of humanity, all of which are encompassed by the creative power of God."[25] The realization of such a vision was possible only if all members of the Church were open to both a deeper conversion to the Spirit and a more authentic witness to the Spirit in their communal and individual lives.

Although Rahner's ecclesiology was not overtly political, its emphasis on the sacramental identity of the Church, which included the Church's mission to be a symbol of humanity's reconciliation to God in Jesus Christ, was not innocent of political implications. Rahner stressed that the Church could not live quietly with injustice, either in the wider world or within the Church itself, as such injustice was alien to the Spirit. If the Church was to be a symbol of hope for the world, it needed to be more than a pious association of believers: it needed to be a community that relied on the Spirit, focused on Jesus Christ, prized unity, and worked to incarnate justice in the world.

In the decades since Rahner's death, developments in the Church have confirmed the value of Rahner's ecclesiology. The growing emphasis in Catholic writing on the *communio* of the Church, which stresses the role of the Spirit in all believers and, consequently, a shared responsibility for the life of the Church, resonates well with Rahner's priorities, especially his rejection of both authoritarianism and sectarianism as authentic responses to the Spirit. In addition, Rahner's work continues to challenge those content with divisions within and between the churches, and those who deny the need for the Church to engage creatively and sympathetically with the wider world.

Notes

1 "Courage for an Ecclesial Christianity," *TI* xx, 9.
2 "The Theology of the Symbol," *TI* iv, 236. The article was originally published in 1959.

3 Ibid.

4 Ibid., *TI* IV, 239; see also "The Eternal Significance of the Humanity of Jesus for our Relationship with God," *TI* III, 35–46.

5 K. Rahner, *The Church and the Sacraments*, trans. W. J. O'Hara (Tunbridge Wells: Burns & Oates, 1986), 18; see also "The Church as the Subject of the Sending of the Spirit," *TI* VII, 188–89.

6 "What is a Sacrament?" *TI* XIV, 143.

7 "Membership of the Church According to the Teaching of Pius XII's Encyclical *Mystici Corporis Christi*," *TI* II, trans. K.-H. Kruger (London: Darton, Longman & Todd, 1963), 1–89. The sacramental view of the Church is also evident in other articles from the 1940s; see, for example, "Priestly Existence," *TI* III, 247–48.

8 "What is a Sacrament?" *TI* XIV, 143.

9 Ibid., *TI* XIV, 137–41; see also "Priest and Poet," *TI* III, 294–317.

10 "The Function of the Church as a Critic of Society," *TI* XII, 238–41.

11 For Rahner on the "diaspora," see, for example, "A Theological Interpretation of the Position of Christians in the Modern World," *Mission and Grace*, I, trans. C. Hastings (London: Sheed & Ward, 1963), 3–55 and "The Christian Among Unbelieving Relations," *TI* III, 355–72.

12 K. Rahner, *Inspiration in the Bible*, trans. H. Henkey and M. Palmer (New York: Herder & Herder, 1966), 45.

13 "Basic Observations on the Subject of the Changeable and Unchangeable Factors in the Church," *TI* XIV, 3–23.

14 "The Sinful Church in the Decrees of Vatican II," *TI* VI, 270–94.

15 "Thoughts on the Possibility of Belief Today," *TI* V, 16.

16 "'I Believe in the Church'," *TI* VII, 109–10, translation amended.

17 *FCF*, 344.

18 K. Rahner *The Dynamic Element in the Church*, trans. W. J. O'Hara (Freiburg/Montreal: Herder/Palm Publishers, 1964), 70.

19 K. Rahner and J. Ratzinger, *The Episcopate and the Primacy*, trans. K. Barker et al. (Freiburg/London: Herder/Burns & Oates, 1962), 108.

20 For Rahner's understanding of "the world-Church" see "Basic Theological Interpretation of the Second Vatican Council," *TI* XX, 77–89 and "The Abiding Significance of the Second Vatican Council," *TI* XX, 90–114.

21 See, for example, "Dream of the Church," *TI* XX, 133–42 and "Forgotten Dogmatic Initiatives of the Second Vatican Council," *TI* XXII, 100–03.

22 See, for example, "On the Theology of Ecumenical Discussion," *TI* XI, 24–67 and "The One Church and the Many Churches," *TI* XVII, 183–96.

23 *Unity of the Churches: An Actual Possibility*, trans. R. and E. Gritsch (Philadelphia/New York: Fortess/Paulist, 1985), 7.

24 "Unity of the Church – Unity of Mankind," *TI* XX, 171.

25 "The Christian in His World," *TI* VII, 96.

Further reading

Doyle, D., *Communion Ecclesiology* (Maryknoll, NY: Orbis, 2000).

Dulles, A., *The Catholicity of the Church* (Oxford, Clarendon Press, 1985).

Fuellenbach, J., *Church: Community for the Kingdom* (Maryknoll, NY: Orbis, 2002).

Lennan, R., *The Ecclesiology of Karl Rahner* (Oxford, Clarendon Press, 1995).

Metz, J. B., *A Passion for God: The Mystical-Political Dimension of Christianity* (Mahwah, NJ: Paulist, 1998).

Phan, P., ed., *The Gift of the Church: A Textbook on Ecclesiology* (Collegeville, MN: Michael Glazier, 2000).

9 Ministry and worship

JERRY T. FARMER

Speaking at a conference on December 7, 1968 on questions concerning the diaconate, Karl Rahner stressed that while the ministerial office (*Amt*) of the Church must always be affirmed as one, its division into different ministerial offices is much more flexible than has been imagined, particularly over the last few centuries. Less than eight years later, in July 1976, focusing on the theme of the spirituality of the priest today, he highlighted the extraordinarily complex historical dimension of ministerial office that was always a part of his theological reflection. And the following year, 1977, in an article that first appeared in the journal *Stimmen der Zeit*, he reiterated that the multiplicity of ministerial offices in the Church are fundamentally rooted and draw their meaning as part of the Church's one ministerial office.[1]

The 1966 lecture and publication, *The Meaning of Ecclesiastical Office*, is essential for understanding how Rahner views church ministry or ministerial office (*kirchliches Amt*). He explicitly states in the preface to the 1967 publication, *Knechte Christi. Meditationen zum Priestertum*, which was translated into English in 1968 as *Servants of the Lord*, that this lecture must be used as a hermeneutical key to interpret the essays, written over a thirty-year period, that have been collected in *Knechte Christi*. Ministerial office itself, he argues, can only be understood within the context of the fact that God has united God's own self in a direct way with humanity, and that this unity is necessarily historically manifested. This also provides the starting point for a correct understanding of cult or worship. In the 1966 lecture, *The Presence of the Lord in the Christian Community at Worship*, Rahner indicates that this divine self-bestowal is communicated through signs and symbols at the historical and social level, thereby providing the foundation for the entirety of cultic activity. Therefore, from the beginning, it is wrong to conceive of ministerial office as something which bridges a gulf (*Kluft*) between God and humanity. Ministerial office of the Church only comes about because God's unity with humanity occurs and this unity manifests itself historically. This had been similarly addressed by Rahner much earlier in a 1942 article entitled "Priestly Existence." The bearers of ministerial office (*Amtsinhaber*) in the Church are "never *mediators* in the sense of being empowered to initiate action as a *middle person* between God and human beings, as though previously there had been a chasm which they are now for the first time bridging; they are merely the manifestation, as it were, sacramental signs of a *medium* between God and human beings already established by Christ – and by him alone!" Likewise, the bearers of ministerial office must never presume to be able to add a new word of God because this would "negate the eschatologically definitive character of the message of Jesus." Rahner also notes the distinction between the cultic and the prophetic as evidenced in the New Testament: "the descriptions of the priestly ministerial office derive from a non-cultic linguistic field (servant, presider, elders, overseer) and on the other hand cultic names are attributed only to Christ and to the faithful in general (in their universal priesthood), and in the cult itself only the community as a whole appears expressly as its subject."[2]

In the preface to *Servants of the Lord* Rahner provides an excellent summary of how he views the priest, or in broader terms the bearer of ministerial office. It means, first of all, that one see this as service (*Dienst*) rather than privilege and authority. It means looking at ministerial office (*Amt*) in terms of the community of the Church, and not the other way around. It means thinking of ministerial office without giving it a higher class status that includes benefits and privileges. It means that one who shares in ministerial office lives one's life *with* one's fellow Christians, and not primarily as an authoritative shepherd in charge of the sheep. It means that the bearer of ministerial office is one who is sustained and supported by the faith, hope and love of everyone in the church. And it means, more than anything else, that the bearer of ministerial office shares the same burden that all believers share, namely, of encountering in one's life new challenges and questions with regard to one's faith, of experiencing suffering as one seeks answers to life's many questions. In a 1965 article, "Pastoral-Theological Observations on Episcopacy in the Teaching of Vatican II," Rahner outlines similar characteristics of ministerial office. In short, Rahner highlights, specifically referring to his article, "The Meaning of Ecclesiastical Office," that the priesthood or ministerial office does not mean a *higher* level of being a Christian but its meaning is to be found as a determined, absolutely necessary function of the Church as a sociological reality. His 1969 article, "The Point of Departure in Theology for Determining the Nature of the Priestly Office," must also be read from this context.[3]

Rahner stresses that the Church as a community finds *its very meaning* (Rahner's emphasis) in being a witness "that God triumphs by his own doing and victoriously lavishes himself on this humanity and its world." And he insists that this community of witness (*Zeugen-Gemeinde*), the Church, is not identical with the community of the children of God (*Gemeinde der Kinder Gottes*). God's children are not found only in the Church, but are "everywhere, in all ages, in a countless multitude of forms, in all colours." But because the witness or testimony of God's victorious love that the community of witness gives must be constant, that is, remaining the same, the community must be one. And for the community to be one it must have a cohesiveness and an order. This order must originate from Jesus Christ, because this community witnesses to the victory of God which is precisely accomplished in Jesus Christ. This community is the necessary manifestation of the permanence of God's victory. This community can be large or small, but it can never cease to exist. This witness to God's triumph is seen as a vocation both of the community and of each believer.[4]

On the one hand, the ministry of the word (*ministerium verbi*) spoken by the ministerial office of the Church is a word bearing witness to the world of God's victorious grace. But the "world" in need of sanctification is present not only outside the Church but also in the Church. Thus *ministerium verbi* can be understood as *the* function of the ministerial office of the Church. But on the other hand this witness to God's victorious grace is an accepted and lived witness in all the members of the Church. Moreover, this witness itself is correctly understood as the basic sacrament (*Grundsakrament*) called the Church, which is constituted for the salvation of the world – the world being understood as that which is not identical with the Church. In this way, the world experiences the self-offer of God. From this context, *ministerium verbi* can be understood in a more narrow sense as *one* particular function of the ministerial office of the Church.[5]

As shown in several articles, most particularly the 1977 article, "Structural Change in the Church of the Future," a basic premise for Rahner is that the unchangeable is always found *in* the changeable. The following are what Rahner identifies as "unchangeable" theological limits of ministry and ministerial office. First, the one who holds ministerial office in the church must exemplify a serving function. The meaning and goal of the society of the church is the self-communication of God with human beings. Therefore, the individual is most eminently a person of the church "who loves God most unselfishly, who most steadfastly carries the cross of existence as Christ's cross." Insofar as one speaks the authoritative and effective word of witness of God's triumph, this can be regarded as a closeness to God, but *the* closeness of God, that is, the self-communication of God in God's spirit, is not a privileged status of the clergy. The much-overlooked truth, which then becomes the cause of anti-clerical sentiment among the laity and anti-lay sentiment among the clergy, is this: The hierarchical structure of the *meaning* and the *purpose* of a society, the unchangeable, and the hierarchical structure of the *sociological organization* of this society, the changeable, are two different things.[6]

Secondly, clergy are not the sole bearers of the actual fulfillment and coming-to-be of the Church. Free charisms are present in the Church, charisms bestowed by God, which are aimed at the Church and its activity, and which belong to the permanent nature of the Church. The individuals who are the bearers of these charisms – a determination which is the result of the free grace-choice of God – are or can be all individuals in the church and not only the clergy. It is fundamentally the love and the patience of all in the church that is embodied in *daily Christian living* which belongs to the very life and fulfillment of the church.[7] Consequently, ministry or ministerial office is not the Lord of the Spirit and the Spirit's charisms, but its servant. And there are things that God wills and asks of the conscience of the individual specifically for the well-being, fulfillment, and coming-to-be of the Church well before there may be any indication from the ministerial office of the Church. One can think of the many reform movements in the Church's history initiated and/or inspired by those outside ministerial office. An example today, particularly in the United States, are the many laypersons – individuals and in organized groups – who, while voicing their concerns about a clericalism that does not promote transparency, have offered support to survivors of the clergy sexual abuse crisis.

A third theological limit of the ministerial office of the Church is the inadequacy and sinfulness of those who hold ministerial office. After all, the bearers of ministerial office do not *own* God as their own possession, but rather bear witness to God's victorious love. And precisely as those who bear this witness, they can be sinners. Rahner offers some examples: through avarice, slowness of heart, rashness, extinguishing the Spirit, bad example, by lovelessness, and many other types of sinfulness proceeding from the heart that one commits while at the same time denying any wrongdoing. But sin also has a significant social dimension. For example, as a result of bureaucratic routine and petty legalism, the signs of the times are not understood and so opportunities are missed. All this exemplifies an important theme for ministerial office that Rahner presents in the 1965 article "The Sinful Church in the Decrees of Vatican II," emphasizing Vatican II's description of the pilgrim Church. This article is in continuity with, as well

as further developing, his 1947 article, "Church of Sinners," with both articles published back to back in volume vi of *Theological Investigations*. One
must honestly recognize that all in the Church, both those who are bearers
of ministerial office and those who are not, make the Church the *sinful
Church of sinners*.[8]

A fourth theological limit is affirming the eschatological dimension of
ministerial office. This reality of ministerial office is itself rooted in the
provisional character of the Church, which, Rahner maintains in the 1963
article, "The Church and the Parousia of Christ," does not consist in the
fact that the Church will be abolished by history, but that history itself will
be abolished. Therefore criticism and critical public opinion are necessary
for the Church today more than ever. And, in fact, Rahner stresses in his
1968 lecture, "The Function of the Church as a Critic of Society," that this
self-criticism of the Church is necessary as the anthropological foundation
for the Church to provide a sociological critique of society.[9]

Along with this need for faithful criticism, there is the concurrent responsibility of each member of the Church to live one's faith from the deep
center of one's own life. Consequently a fifth theological limit of the ministerial office of the Church is the conscience of each person in the Church.
Every individual must take the ultimate concrete decisions of one's conscience – which are for salvation or non-salvation – in ultimate solitariness.
Rahner notes that each one must speak one's own prayer with God; the priest
at the altar cannot replace this prayer. Likewise, each one must encounter
Christ in one's neighbor, because it is worth nothing to receive the body of
the Lord at the Lord's Supper if one does not find Christ in one's sister or
brother, a theme extensively developed in the 1965 article, "Reflections on
the Unity of the Love of Neighbour and the Love of God." Similarly, each
one must die one's own death, even though the priest gives one viaticum
for one's journey into that ultimate silence, a theme already elaborated by
Rahner in his 1938 *Encounters with Silence*. And, finally, each one must be
a witness to the grace of God in one's everyday life, seen in the collection of
Rahner's prayers that was presented to him in March, 1984, for his eightieth
birthday, and exemplified in "Prayer of a Lay Person": "God's grace not only
comes to me through the sacramental signs which the clergy administer but
remains above all else at the free disposal of God, who bestows it upon all
who ask it of him."[10]

As the Second Vatican Council was preparing the document that would
be called *Gaudium et spes* (*Pastoral Constitution on the Church in the Modern
World*, 1965), Rahner published an article in 1964, "The Limits of the Official
Ministerial Church" ("Grenzen der Amtskirche"). Here he focuses on a sixth

limit of the ministerial office of the Church with respect to the responsibility of the Church for the world. He is critical of those in ministerial office, in concrete terms, the clergy, who live a type of "clerical triumphalism." It is this attitude, says Rahner, that the Second Vatican Council "deplores and opposes." He insists that it is essential to see the difference "between the function of the church as ministerial office (*Amt*) and the function of the church as the community of Christians (*Gemeinschaft der Christen*), that is, between the church as a society (*Gesellschaft*) governed by the binding authority of the ministerial office, and the church as also forming a community (*Gemeinschaft*) guided by the conscience of the individual and by the Spirit." These themes are further developed in regard to the relationship between Church and world in his 1968 article "Church and World" in the theological encyclopedia *Sacramentum Mundi*, where he affirms the Church as the basic sacrament (*Grundsakrament*) which manifests that "in the unity, activity, fraternity, etc. of the *world*, the kingdom of God is at hand."[11]

Turning to the final sections of "The Meaning of Ecclesiastical Office," Rahner stresses these conclusions. Because the Church is fundamentally one, its oneness must be ever realized. Both clergy and laity are in the same service of God. Rahner first calls upon the laity to affirm that the "community of witness" to the grace of God for the world must have an order. Secondly, they are called to affirm that there must be bearers of the ministerial office of the Church who declare this word of witness, in and through their ministerial office, to the *world*, the world that is found inside as well as outside the Church. Thirdly, and consequently, they are called to give the obedience that is due to those in ministerial office *in the area of their competence*, and give them patient, brotherly love. Rahner calls upon those who are bearers of the ministerial office of the Church to affirm that they are nothing other than servants of this word of witness, the content of which belongs to everyone in the Church. For it is God who communicates God's own self to all in grace. Further, in contrast to speaking of a bearer of ministerial office as a "priest forever," Rahner stresses that the ministerial office of the Church is not something which will last forever. The Church, referring to *Lumen gentium*, 48, is a pilgrim Church. The ministerial office of the Church will come to an end, because it has carried out its service. But that to which the ministerial office of the Church bears witness – which it mediates in the efficacious word of witness – is eternal, indeed, is God's own self.[12]

A seventh and final enduring, unchangeable element in regard to ministerial office is its collegiality. In the 1967 article, "The Relationship between the Pope and the College of Bishops," he stresses that through episcopal ordination, a bishop shares in the "one and full power which is originally present in the college of bishops as united with its head the pope." It is essential to recognize the fundamental collegial character of all ministerial and worship activity of the Church. The fact that the *potestas ordinis* (power of holiness) together with the *potestas iurisdictionis* (power of governance) are elements of the one power borne by the college of bishops emphasizes the pneumatic or sacramental character that marks the *potestas iurisdictionis* itself. Consequently, as Rahner stresses in the 1964 article, "The Episcopal Office," it is wrong to think that the priest – or the deacon – exists merely because the bishop needs help. If this were the case, it is conceivable that some bishop could decide that he does not need help, and do away with the priestly – and diaconal – ministerial offices without any problem. Rahner also points out that such a situation could be realized very easily if one were simply to ordain all priests as bishops. But the bishop "does not ordain an individual, but surrounds himself with a college." The priest is not first of all ordained as someone who can "help" the bishop be present "everywhere." The priest is rather a helper to the bishop where the bishop is, *not* where the bishop is unable to be. Theologically, the presbyterium is not the adding together and forming into a college of the pastors of all the individual local worshiping communities. It is the other way around. All the pastors of the individual local worshiping communities are drawn from the one presbyterium that surrounds the bishop.[13]

Addressing more explicitly the topic of worship, in the 1963 lecture, "The Unity of Spirit and Matter in the Christian Understanding of Faith," Rahner notes that however much the salvation history of the individual "means a unique personal decision in every case, [it] always rests in the Christian sense on the will of God for a united humanity, for the covenant, for the social communication and tangibility of salvation in the spatio-temporal history of the church and in tangible sacraments and social institutions." Similarly, in the 1976 lecture, "The Church's Redemptive Historical Provenance for the Death and Resurrection of Jesus," Rahner concurs with the position of the exegete Willi Marxsen, who, in Rahner's words, says "that Jesus must rise into the faith of those who believe in him. Not in the sense that he exists only in that faith, but if and insofar as there is not a community of faith . . . then this very Jesus does not exist at all as God's self-promise to the world." As Rahner notes in the 1976 *Foundations of Christian Faith*, "we cannot exclude communal and social intercommunication from the human being's essence even when she or he is considered as the religious subject of a relationship to God . . . Otherwise religion would become merely a private affair of a human being and would cease to be religion."

In the 1966 article, "On the Presence of Christ in the Diaspora Community According to the Teaching of the Second Vatican Council," he underscores that "the church, the one church of Christ, is present in its entirety in every local community." This was already highlighted by Rahner in his 1956 article, "Theology of the Parish," stressing the fundamental importance of the Church as event (*Ereignis*). The Church as event is necessarily the local community, particularly the altar community: "Where the church *acts* – that is, teaches, confesses, prays, offers the sacrifice of Christ, etc., it attains a higher degree of actuality than it does by its mere continuing existence . . . The church must always and again and again become event." And in the 1966 article, "The Presence of the Lord in the Christian Community at Worship," he stresses that it is in the local community through its worship or cult that the highest level of the Church's own coming-to-be is brought about. "And it is through this cult that Christ and the faithful are rendered mutually present to one another in the most actual and sublime form possible." But critical to a correct understanding of this worship or cult of the Church is the affirmation that "the interior subjective principle of the cult must be the Holy Spirit of God," for otherwise the worship of the Church would merely be the "adoration of a God who is infinitely remote and *other*." However, this is not the case, for the worship of the Church is "that communication (*commercium*) which is, in a sense, interior" to God's own self, so that the worship of the Church is sharing in the trinitarian life of God. The Spirit is the "necessary prior condition for that further presence which is achieved precisely between Christ and the church in the enactment of the cult." But the Church is a sacrament of the salvation of the world not only in and through its worship activity, but also through "every deed and suffering" of its members. But even beyond this, both in relationship to one who is a member of the Church as well as one who is not, "the Lord himself says that he is present, though, at times, unrecognized, wherever anyone shows compassion from one's heart to another."[14]

This last point is clearly one that is central in Michael Skelley's *The Liturgy of the World: Karl Rahner's Theology of Worship*. Focusing particularly on Rahner's 1979 article, "On the Theology of Worship," Skelley observes that the liturgy of the world finds its necessary social and public expression in the liturgy of the Church. Skelley draws extensively from Rahner's writings, but it would not seem that he adequately incorporates what Rahner says with regard to the relationship of the Church to the reign of God. William V. Dych, in "Karl Rahner's Theology of Eucharist," interprets Rahner's "liturgy of the world" as affirming that the Church "must exist not for its own sake, but to serve the reign of God." Lambert Leijssen, in "Rahner's Contribution to the Renewal of Sacramentology," affirms that Rahner's emphasis with regard to liturgy was "on the authentic expression of the attitude of faith and prayer in the liturgical assembly." But he identifies as a shortcoming that Rahner did not look to the Church's liturgy as the primary source for sacramental doctrine. Nevertheless, Leijssen notes that Rahner "did attach importance to the role of sacramental celebrations in the different stages of life," that he emphasized "the presence of the community in relation to the individual," stressing the community even more in his later writings, and that Rahner also showed a "relative openness in regard to the frequency of reception of the sacraments."[15]

Rahner's evolving perspectives regarding the obligation of celibacy for those who are bearers of priestly ministerial office are significant. In November, 1976, almost ten years after the expression of his own support for the continuing requirement of celibacy for secular clergy which appeared as an "Open Letter" in April, 1967, and which preceded by a few months Pope Paul VI's own reaffirmation of the obligation, Rahner, in an address, "Consecration in the Life and Reflection of the Church," was direct and unambiguous: "It cannot be denied that the right of the community to have a sacramentally ordained leader takes precedence over the efforts of the church (which certainly deserve respect) to have community leaders who accept the obligation of celibacy." And, also, in an address given a few months earlier, in July, 1976, "The Spirituality of the Priest in the Light of His Office," he says that if there are or must be pastoral assistants today who are permanent official ministerial leaders of a community that has no priest, then one should, in God's name, ordain them priests. Rahner's reason is that through ordination *one does not receive something which one otherwise did not have*; but, rather, that which is already present in an individual is fixed sacramentally and tangibly in the dimension of the Church's one ministerial office. And Rahner vociferously defends his approach by pointing to the similar situation of an individual who is living a life with God but has never been baptized. The reason for the baptism, declares Rahner, is so that the life the person is already living manifests itself expressly in the dimension of the sociological and historical tangibility of the Church.[16]

The reality of pastoral assistants who are leaders in communities that do not have a priest also leads Rahner to highlight the importance of not seeing the priest as one defined principally in terms of cultic or worship activity. Theologically this presents problems, first, because the priest tends to be described and delineated only in terms of leading the Eucharist and administering the sacrament of penance. This is an unacceptable conception of the priest, however, one that is narrowly ritualistic, viewing the priest in a purely cultic way. Secondly, from the position of the pastoral assistant, if the tasks and functions of being appointed permanently to lead a community are indeed more important and more comprehensive than that of the deacon, then the permanent appointment of a pastoral assistant should be recognized as sacramental.[17]

In the 1970 article, "On the Structure of the People of the Church Today," Rahner notes that another reason why the priest cannot be restricted to cultic activity is due to what occurs today at the level of the local worshiping community. In the past the structure of the parish was able to clearly presuppose an already established and integrated local social structure, particularly at the level of the village or small town. But this is no longer the case. Therefore, the worshiping community, without an already given sociological structure, itself becomes ideological. And consequently the Church must fashion the human sociological framework that will allow the local worshiping community not to remain on the level of ideology. If the local worshiping community is led by someone, out of "necessity," who is not a priest, then the sacramental-liturgical cultic activity of the priest who comes to the community as an "outsider" contributes to both the community and the priest becoming ideological.[18]

In the 1977 article, "Women and the Priesthood," Rahner focuses on the question "whether it is certain that the Christian revelation in its unchangeable substance excludes women from priestly ministerial office in the Catholic church." Besides pointing out the extremely dangerous and narrow understanding of restricting the particular tasks of the priest to the "sacramental power of consecration," he stresses that the question must be addressed from the perspective of community leadership. He concludes that the fact that women have been excluded from the priestly ministerial office is culturally and sociologically conditioned. Consequently, this stance does not possess a normative significance for all time – specifically if and inasmuch as this sociological and cultural milieu continually changes. And Rahner underscores his conclusion in spite of the fact that this position has persisted for so long and with such little opposition. Ultimately, the discussion must continue. But discussion alone is not sufficient. Historical change will decisively come about through praxis – a praxis of life and of history that occurs in freedom, action, and decision. The Church must have the courage to bring about the "historical change which is part of the fidelity which the church owes to its Lord." Always one must work and struggle for this change with patience, while acknowledging that "time passes" and one cannot wait for a hundred years for a solution to this question without real detriment to the Church.[19]

According to Herbert Vorgrimler, Rahner's first considerations on the diaconal ministerial office can be traced to 1948. This eventually led to the publication in 1962 of *Diaconia in Christo*, co-edited by Vorgrimler and Rahner. But his 1968 address, "On the Diaconate," revealed that his earlier work for a diaconate of the future did not produce the results for which he had hoped. He was particularly disappointed by those who argued that the concrete diaconate "in the present must have been in existence all along and of necessity, and must continue to exist for all time." The diaconate should be about responding to new needs, and not be simply a repetition of history. Just as with the priestly ministerial office, it must be affirmed that there can be a great deal of diversity concretely as to how the diaconal ministerial office is shaped and formed. As to the actual process of the formation of the diaconal ministerial office, Rahner underscores the fact that "practical and concrete experimentation" is absolutely essential. Pure theological reflection cannot adequately produce the concrete decisions that must be made. Praxis is essential and must include theological reflection. The Church has a fundamental task of service toward all people. Rahner describes this as a "universal Christian diakonia" for which all members of the Church have a responsibility. But there is also a special diakonia of ministerial office itself.[20]

Finally, in a 1982 article, "New Offices and Ministries in the Church," Rahner contends that the episcopal, priestly, and diaconal ministerial offices of the Church are not absolutely the only ministerial offices. There are other functions – present in the Church or conceivable – which are similar or analogous to the Church's ministerial office in its threefold differentiation. And so there may still be other new ministerial offices to fashion, as well as other already existing but anonymous ministerial offices in the Church to discover, each with its own particular spirituality. And while there is a true distinction between one who is a bearer of ministerial office and one who is not, the boundary between them is one that is constantly shifting. And determining where that boundary is, and where it ought to be, must always be determined in the context of the sociological, historical, and tangible life of the Church.[21]

From these reflections on the themes of ministry and worship, it is clear that one of Rahner's greatest contributions is his unquestionable affirmation of the debt that is owed to previous generations of believers, great and small, while at the same time insisting that the response of faith today must be ever new and so renewed. Human experience is the dynamic reality in which Rahner's theology is rooted and which in turn challenges that human experience to even greater dynamism, leading each one to the incomprehensible and inexhaustible trinitarian God.

Notes

1 K. Rahner, "On the Diaconate," *TI* xii, 65; "The Spirituality of the Priest in the Light of His Office," *TI* xix, 125; "Pastoral Ministries and Community Leadership," *TI* xix, 76. See also J. Farmer, *Ministry in Community: Rahner's Vision of Ministry* (Louvain: Peeters Press, 1993); and my "The Contribution and Influence of Karl Rahner on Ministerial Issues Following Vatican II," in M. Lamberigts and L. Kenis, eds., *Vatican II and Its Legacy* (Louvain: Louvain University Press, 2002), 487–501.

2 K. Rahner, "The Meaning of Ecclesiastical Office," in *Servants of the Lord*, trans. R. Strachan (London: Burns & Oates, 1968), 13–45; "The Presence of the Lord in the Christian Community at Worship," *TI* x, trans. D. Bourke (London: Darton, Longman & Todd, 1973), 71–83; "Priestly Existence," *TI* iii, 232–62, esp. pp. 241 and 248 (translation emended); J. Farmer, "Four Christological Themes of the Theology of Karl Rahner," in T. Merrigan and J. Haers, eds., *The Myriad Christ* (Louvain: Louvain University Press/Peeters, 2000), 433–62.

3 Rahner, *Servants of the Lord*, 7. See also his "The Point of Departure in Theology for Determining the Nature of the Priestly Office," *TI* xii, 31–8, "Pastoral-Theological Observations on Episcopacy in the Teaching of Vatican II," *TI* vi, 361–8.

4 "The Meaning of Ecclesiastical Office," 20–4 (here and in subsequent references translation emended); K. Rahner, *Theology of Pastoral Action*, trans. W. J. O'Hara and D. Morrissey (New York: Herder and Herder, 1968), 64–133.

5 "The Meaning of Ecclesiastical Office," 29.

6 Ibid., 30–33; "Structural Change in the Church of the Future," *TI* xx, 115–32; "Basic Observations on the Subject of Changeable and Unchangeable Factors in the Church," *TI* xiv, 3–23; "Pseudo-Problems in Ecumenical Discussion," *TI* xviii, 35–53.

7 "The Meaning of Ecclesiastical Office," 34–37. See also "Observations on the Factor of the Charismatic in the Church," *TI* xii, 81–97; D. Marmion, *A Spirituality of Everyday Faith: A Theological Investigation of the Notion of Spirituality in Karl Rahner* (Louvain: Peeters, 1998), 61–9; and H. D. Egan, *Karl Rahner, Mystic of Everyday Life* (New York: Crossroad, 1998), 55–79.

8 "The Meaning of Ecclesiastical Office," 39–40; "The Sinful Church in the Decrees of Vatican II," *TI* vi, 270–94; "Church of Sinners," *TI* vi, 253–69.

9 "The Function of the Church as a Critic of Society," *TI* xii, 230; "The Church and the Parousia of Christ," *TI* vi, 297.

10 "The Meaning of Ecclesiastical Office," 40–43; "Reflections on the Unity of the Love of Neighbour and the Love of God," *TI* vi, 231–49. K. Rahner, *Encounters with Silence*, trans. J. Demske (Westminster, MD: The Newman Press, 1960). A. Raffelt, ed., *Karl Rahner, Prayers for a Lifetime*, trans. E. Junger et al. (New York: Crossroad, 1984), 130–31.

11 K. Rahner, "The Church's Limits," in *The Christian of the Future*, trans. W. J. O'Hara (New York: Herder and Herder, 1967), 49–76. See also his "Church and World," *SM* I, 346–57.

12 "The Meaning of Ecclesiastical Office," 43–45.

13 "On the Relationship between the Pope and the College of Bishops," *TI* x, 50–70; "The Episcopal Office," *TI* vi, 313–60; "The Point of Departure in Theology for Determining the Nature of the Priestly Office," *TI* xii, 31–8.

14 "The Unity of Spirit and Matter in the Christian Understanding of Faith," *TI* vi, 153–77; "The Church's Redemptive Historical Provenance for the Death and Resurrection of Jesus," *TI* xix, 24–38; *FCF*, 330. See also "The Presence of the Lord in the Christian Community at Worship," *TI* x, 74–75 and 83; "Theology of the Parish," in H. Rahner, ed., *The Parish, from Theology to Practice*, trans. R. Kress (Westminster, MD: The Newman Press, 1958), 23–35; "On the Presence of Christ in the Diaspora Community According to the Teaching of the Second Vatican Council," *TI* x, 84–102; "The Word and the Eucharist," *TI* iv, 253–86.

15 M. Skelley, *The Liturgy of the World: Karl Rahner's Theology of Worship* (Collegeville, MN: Liturgical Press, 1991); "On the Theology of Worship," *TI* xix, 141–49. W. V. Dych, "Karl Rahner's Theology of Eucharist," *Philosophy & Theology* 11/1 (1998), 125–46. L. Leijssen, "Rahner's Contribution to the Renewal of Sacramentology," trans. S. Roll, *Philosophy & Theology* 9/1–2 (1995), 201–22.

16 "The Celibacy of the Secular Priest Today: An Open Letter," *Servants of the Lord*, 149–72; "The Spirituality of the Priest in the Light of His Office," *TI* xix, 117–38; "Consecration in the Life and Reflection of the Church," *TI* xix, 57–72.

17 "Pastoral Ministries and Community Leadership," *TI* xix, 73–86.

18 "On the Structure of the People of the Church Today," *TI* xii, 218–28; "Basic Communities," *TI* xix, 159–65. Farmer, "The Contribution and Influence of Karl Rahner on Ministerial Issues Following Vatican II," 487–501; and my "Sunday Celebrations in the Absence of a Priest: A Postmodern Reading," in L. Boeve and L. Leijssen, eds., *Contemporary Sacramental Contours of a God Incarnate* (Louvain: Peeters, 2001), 190–204.

19 "Women and the Priesthood," *TI* xx, 35–47.

20 K. Rahner and H. Vorgrimler, eds., *Diaconia in Christo*, Quaestiones Disputatae 15/16 (Freiburg: Herder, 1962); "The Theology of the Restoration of the Diaconate," *TI* v, 268–314; "On the Diaconate," *TI* xii, 61–80. H. Vorgrimler, *Understanding Karl Rahner*, trans. J. Bowden (London: SCM Press, 1986), 95, 143–44.

21 K. Rahner, "New Offices and Ministries in the Church," in K. Lehmann and A. Raffelt, eds., *The Practice of Faith*, trans. R. Barr (London: SCM Press, 1985), 169–71.

Further reading

Dych, W., "Karl Rahner's Theology of Eucharist," *Philosophy & Theology* 11:1 (1998), 125–46.

Farmer, J. T., "The Contribution and Influence of Karl Rahner on Ministerial Issues Following Vatican II," in M. Lamberigts and L. Kenis, eds., *Vatican II and Its Legacy* (Louvain: Louvain University Press, 2002), 487–501.

Rahner K., "The Meaning of Ecclesiastical Office," trans. R. Strachan, in *Servants of the Lord* (London: Burns & Oates, 1968), 13–45.

  Theology of Pastoral Action, trans. W. J. O'Hara and D. Morrissey, (New York: Herder and Herder, 1968), 59–133.

  "On the Diaconate," trans. D. Bourke, *TI* xii: 61–80.

  "Women and the Priesthood," trans. E. Quinn, *TI* xx: 35–47.

BRIAN LINNANE

INTRODUCTION

The implications of Karl Rahner's theological project for ethics become clear when one considers that the concept of choice is at the heart of both his transcendental anthropology and the Ignatian spiritual tradition that so richly informs all of his theology. It would be a serious mistake, however, to view the Rahnerian concept of choice and the theology of freedom that supports it as the mere capacity to select among various objects. Choice in this account is correctly understood as "the possibility of saying yes or no to oneself, the possibility of deciding for or against oneself," which is also always a decision for or against God.[1]

For Rahner, then, the human person is that self-transcending spirit who in the act of knowing or willing implicitly experiences both itself as subject (that is, free) and something of the ultimate structure of reality. The person's unthematic experience of the self as free before the gracious mystery that is God is, for Rahner, necessarily related to self-disposition. This self-disposition, known as fundamental option, involves the subject's definitive acceptance or rejection of God by means of free, moral action. This capacity for definitive choice finds its most perspicuous Christian expression, Rahner argues, in the *Spiritual Exercises* of St. Ignatius Loyola. For Rahner, these Exercises are nothing other than "practical exercises for making a vital decision, the Election."[2] It is in the light of the Ignatian Exercises that the often unthematized experience of fundamental option finds its systematic expression. This is the case because Rahner understands that the election to be made in the context of the Exercises always involves the exercitant's *conscious* acceptance or rejection of God's specific will for him or her as discerned by means of guided prayer and reflection. The human experience of transcendence is ultimately a spiritual experience, or, in Christian terms, an experience of grace. Further, Rahner understands that this Ignatian election always has an ethical character. While the election at the center of the

Ignatian Exercises has to do with vocational choice or "state of life" decisions, this methodology is also used to locate the *magis*, or greater good, with regard to particular decisions of lesser magnitude for individuals and for communities. Thus the ethical program generated by Rahner's theology, while not unconcerned with material moral norms, is fundamentally an ethics of discernment.

FUNDAMENTAL OPTION AND THE MORAL LIFE

This ethics of discernment or discipleship, grounded as it is in Rahner's account of the human person as self-transcending subject, has served to support or indeed generate the major theological and pastoral developments in Roman Catholic moral theology in the post-Vatican II period. One of the principal developments has been the shift away from an emphasis on nature or natural law to an understanding of the human person in all of its complexity as a more adequate foundation or starting point for ethical analysis. The basic dimensions of this new personalism find an early expression in an address Rahner gave to the Austrian Catholic Conference of 1952. In this paper, he highlights what he takes to be the five essential characteristics of persons, the person as spirit, as free, as an individual, as social, and as embodied.[3] This richer perspective on the human person serves, in Rahner's account, not only to ground the fundamental dignity of all persons, but also to allow for a more nuanced understanding of the role of moral obligation in a way that traditional natural law perspectives cannot. Related to this is a rejection of any moral minimalism, which suggests that the avoidance of sins is the primary goal of the moral life in favor of an ethics of discipleship, which finds its fullest expression in the wholehearted embrace of the witness of Jesus Christ – always expressed as unreserved love of neighbor.

While Rahner's account of the human person helped to provide a fundamental theological orientation for many Catholic ethicists, it is his concept of fundamental option that has served to address some of the difficult theoretical problems that faced traditional Catholic moral theology and pastoral practice in the middle of the twentieth century. One of these problems has to do with morally righteous persons who lack Christian faith, while another has to do with "flawed saints."[4] Traditional Catholic teaching held that eternal salvation depended upon explicit Christian faith exercised in communion with the Bishop of Rome. Thus even sincere non-believers and non-Catholics of heroic virtue were destined for eternal damnation. This teaching has been perceived as unfair – especially to those virtuous persons who through no fault of their own never encountered the teaching of Christ – and as inconsistent with the understanding of God as merciful and benevolent. The theory of fundamental option, insofar as it is linked to transcendental and so to universal human experience, serves to help resolve this problem. This points to Rahner's important concept of anonymous Christianity, which suggests that persons can make a whole-hearted commitment to the God of Jesus Christ by means of free moral action in history without categorical knowledge of the Christian tradition or explicit faith in the Christian God. The problem of the flawed saint refers to the effects of a single mortal sin on an otherwise holy and virtuous person. The traditional account, drawing on Aquinas' understanding of the unity of the virtues, would hold that the God–human relationship was completely severed in such a circumstance and if this person should die in such a state, he or she would be condemned to eternal punishment. As with the righteous non-believer this perspective raised troubling questions about God's justice and mercy for contemporary Christians. The fundamental option, with its more nuanced understanding of the ways in which categorical choices or actions engage transcendental freedom, allows for a more positive evaluation of moral struggle and for a more complex relationship between sin and virtue in the moral agent – one that is a more adequate reflection of human experience. Beyond addressing these problems in moral theology, however, the central achievement of Rahner's fundamental option theory is in forcefully asserting the priority of love in the Christian life. He does this by linking the transcendental experience of fundamental option with the historical experience of "dying with Christ."[5]

A positive fundamental option must always be expressed as love or *caritas* because in Rahner's view it is the only appropriate response to the holy mystery the human person encounters as love. This understanding reflects Rahner's conception of the person as "spirit" and so as "hearer of the word." As "hearer" the subject of transcendental experience is understood to be open to divine self-revelation; a divine self-revelation which always demands a response by means of categorical action. Insofar as God is expressing or revealing God's very self to the transcendental subject it is "an act of opening himself in ultimate intimacy and in free and absolute love."[6] Because God reveals God self as love there can be no neutral knowledge of God; such a revelation is necessarily, Rahner argues, an event of grace. As an event of grace, there can be no neutral response to the event of divine self-revelation. The event of grace, which reveals God as love, similarly enables the act of love in history that is the only possible positive response on the part of the transcendental subject. A fundamental option, then, has been shown to be a free, moral action in history that is also always an event of love, expressing the person's ultimate self-realization by means of an absolute commitment of the freedom encountered in the experience of transcendence. Still to be determined is whether or not there are particular sorts of moral action more capable of realizing the love that is characteristic of a fundamental option in Rahner's account.

The unselfish love of neighbor has, for Rahner, an unquestioned pride of place as an event of fundamental option. This commitment to the centrality of neighbor-love reflects Rahner's views both on the priority of *caritas* among the virtues and on the fundamental value of persons within the hierarchy of created being. It also reflects one of Rahner's basic theological insights on the essential unity of neighbour-love and the love of God.[7] Insofar as the divine–human interaction at the heart of the transcendental experience of fundamental option is a dialogue of love, it follows that the actions in history which affect the ultimate self-realization of the person must also be characterized by love. It similarly follows that because the transcendental encounter with Absolute Being that occurs in every act of knowing reveals to the knowing subject that it is a person called to relationship with the personal God, the loving action in history that expresses a positive fundamental option must be directed toward another person; that is, the neighbor. In an act of neighbor-love, then, a person responds to a being also created for loving communion with the divine. Love in this encounter is directed both to the other person and to the One with whom it is in relationship. Love of neighbor is the central human act, in Rahner's view, because it is the only act by which the person simultaneously accepts and affirms the person itself and God.

In the works of neighbor-love, or in their rejection, persons encounter the interpenetration of transcendental and historical experience. This is the case because Rahner characterizes both the transcendental experience of fundamental option and actions of neighbor-love as kenotic or self-emptying experiences. He speaks of the positive response to God in transcendental experience as "the free self-disposal" and as a transcendental form of dying.[8] It is, in Rahner's view, a complete self-surrender to the holy mystery of God and God's purposes. Neighbor-love in history has a similar quality of complete self-donation. It is by means of this type of behavior that persons "lose themselves, in order to find themselves"; to encounter, in other words, their self-realization. Authentic neighbor-love, Rahner suggests, does not keep accounts, expects no return, and ultimately welcomes and bears the "folly of the cross" on the neighbor's behalf.[9]

AN ETHIC WITHOUT CONTENT?

Concerns have been raised about the relationship between Rahner's theory of fundamental option and specific moral norms, especially the moral norms articulated by the Roman Catholic magisterium. Because Rahner's approach focuses on discernment and the commitment of transcendental freedom, it has been argued that fundamental option theory does not offer a substantive account of the moral life. Even when expressed in categorical or historical terms as neighbor-love, Rahner's fundamental option theory has been called into question for being abstract or vague. In other words, it has been argued that the theory does not provide adequate models of Christian living and behavior. Another serious criticism is the claim that the definitive commitment of the human person's transcendental freedom which is the essence of the fundamental option can be understood as being unrelated to the actual moral good or evil achieved by the agent in history. This is the case because there need not be an essential and complete connection between the exercise of categorical or historical freedom and the commitment of that fundamental freedom encountered in transcendental experience. Since a commitment of transcendental freedom is usually experienced in a prethematic manner, it is possible for a particular agent to definitively commit him or herself to a course of moral action in history without committing his or her transcendental freedom fully. Transcendental freedom would be engaged in such a categorical choice but only in a peripheral way.

John Paul II has worried that this understanding of fundamental option serves to undermine traditional notions of mortal sin,[10] while moral theologian Jean Porter has argued that it serves to detach theological and indeed salvific meaning from all of human behaviour.[11] With regard to concrete and specific moral guidance for Catholic Christians, Rahner's earlier writings would certainly suggest that the objects or matter for choice "must be indifferent or good in themselves and furthermore must remain in the teaching and practice of our holy mother the hierarchical Church."[12] This reflects a confidence that the Church's own teaching would provide unassailable guidance about behaviors or choices which are conducive or destructive of human prospects for ultimate salvation. This absolute confidence in the teaching of the hierarchical Church breaks down, however, after the papal encyclical, *Humanae Vitae*, issued in 1968 to reaffirm the prohibition against artificial birth control. Rahner's willingness to support a limited theological legitimacy for decisions of conscience contrary to official Church teaching in matters such as the use of birth control is perceived by some as weakening the usefulness of the teaching of the Church as a guide to authentic Christian life. This in turn, it has been argued, leaves the Christian without adequate resources for a thorough formation of the conscience.

Despite these and other criticisms, this essay affirms the enduring value of Karl Rahner's theological anthropology generally and the fundamental option specifically for both moral theology and the ethical deliberation of contemporary believers. At the most basic level, Rahnerian moral reflection, like all of Rahner's theology, is grounded in a commitment to the primacy of the subject's experience of God as holy and gracious mystery. While this experience – as transcendental experience – is universally available, Rahner understands that it can also be encountered in its fullness historically in the life and witness of Jesus of Nazareth. This unique witness of Jesus' radical obedience to God's will, an obedience most fully realized in his death, becomes the model which provokes and enables authentic discipleship. An emphasis on personal experience is consistent with Rahner's insight that Christian identity itself is increasingly dependent upon what he has referred to as "mysticism."[13] Rahner saw that as the social and cultural structures which supported and indeed enforced Christian identity decline dramatically in the West, a sustained commitment to a Christian way of life will require "a genuine experience of God emerging from the very heart of our existence."[14] Thus an ethics instructed by the theology of Karl Rahner is well situated to address the concerns of persons who are sceptical about moralities based upon appeals to authority or tradition alone. Such an ethic is attractive to contemporary persons because it is not perceived as external to or distinct from their own experience of God's gracious call to live a life characterized by neighbor-love. Rahner's emphasis on experience also finds expression in his vigorous defence of the dignity of conscience. Insofar as he interprets the conscience "as the voice of God,"[15] it becomes a venue for the fundamental option. This defense is consistent with the understanding of conscience developed in the Second Vatican Council (*Gaudium et Spes*, 16; *Dignitatis Humanae Personae*, 1) and with contemporary views of personal integrity and responsibility. In order to demonstrate the enduring value of Karl Rahner's theology for Christian ethical reflection it will be necessary to give a general account of his understanding of fundamental option as a "dying with Christ" and its implications for an ethics of discipleship appropriate for contemporary Christians.

FUNDAMENTAL OPTION AS DYING WITH CHRIST

It cannot be denied that Rahner's critics are correct when they argue that he fails to provide a detailed account of actions and modes of behavior that are paradigmatic of fundamental option. Unlike Aquinas, who seems to suggest that almsgiving, benevolence, and fraternal correction are actions characteristic of the virtue *caritas*,[16] Rahner makes no claim that actions of that particular type are, in themselves, essential for salvation as expressed in a positive fundamental option. This reluctance to be overly specific about the categorical dimensions of a positive fundamental option does not reflect ambivalence on Rahner's part toward these traditional conceptions of the deeds of Christian love. It is, rather, his profound commitment to the unique interaction between God and the human person in its particular historical and cultural context that prevents him from offering a clearly delineated list of activities or commitments constitutive of a positive fundamental option. Thus it seems that this hesitation on Rahner's part can be construed as a strength rather than a weakness. His position moves the God–human interaction beyond particular cultural articulations and grasps the possibility that the love at the heart of a positive fundamental option has the potential for ever-new historical expressions. Beyond these considerations, it is important to emphasize that the criticisms about the lack of material content in Rahner's account of the positive fundamental option are exaggerated. Rahner is, in fact, willing to offer specific guidance on the nature of a positive fundamental option in his extensive reflections on what it means to share in the death of Christ.

The metaphor of "dying with Christ" is particularly apt for Rahner's understanding of a person's positive fundamental option in categorical terms because it captures both the kenotic self-disposal that is the essence of a fundamental option as well as that event in history which for Christians is the defining act of *caritas*, namely the obedient acceptance of death on a cross by Jesus of Nazareth. To understand the power of this metaphor in Rahner's theology and its relevance for ethics, it is necessary to consider his theology of death and the ways in which he views the life of Jesus to be the definitively human life and so normative for Christian existence.

Human death is a topic of singular importance in the theology of Karl Rahner. Indeed, one commentator has argued persuasively that Rahner is "fascinated" by death.[17] Human death is a topic of such importance for Rahner because he understands death to be the moment of profound summation and integration in the life of each person. This is the case because in his view death is a profound mystery confronting the human person throughout its life. In this light, death underscores the reality of human finitude, limitation, and dependence. Death also underscores the reality of human freedom insofar as Rahner understands that it demands a response from each person, which in his account necessarily reflects a free choice. The individual's response to the reality of physical death – willful resistance and despair *or* trusting surrender and acceptance – ultimately reflects its transcendental response to that Mystery who is the author of creation and the ground of all being. This choice, grounded as it is in freedom, is the choice to die, and so to live, autonomously or theonomously. Autonomous death is the rejection of free liberty, the capacity for definitive self-realization, and so of its author. Theonomous death, or "good death" in Rahner's terms, involves the subject's total surrender to the inscrutable mystery of God. Because the fundamental mystery of death and so the choice between autonomous and theonomous death confronts the person throughout life, Rahner argues that every positive moral choice is an event of theonomous death. Theonomous death then becomes synonymous with positive fundamental option. It consists of those free moral actions, over the course of a lifetime, which are events of personal self-disposal toward God. This history of fundamental choice is freely ratified in a definitive manner in the event of the subject's physical death. It is in this way that Rahner is able to claim that human death is "the act of freedom."[18]

Theonomous death while indeed *the* act of human freedom is also always an event of grace. It is, in Rahner's view, available and effective only because of the death of Jesus Christ. From this perspective theonomous death and fundamental option too are always an experience of "dying with Christ." That theonomous death must be an event of grace becomes clear when one reflects on the earlier discussion of the human person as "hearer of the word." Rahner's understanding of the person as existentially open to divine self-revelation necessarily implies and presupposes the possibility of divine revelation, or, in other words, grace. Because this divine self-communication is an experience of grace any positive response to it by the human person is itself an event of grace. On the most basic level, this is the case because there would be nothing for the human person to respond to if it were not for the antecedent experience of grace. Further, Rahner understands that it would be impossible for the person as created and finite to appropriate and respond to the uncreated and infinite without divine assistance. With regard to categorical acts of moral rectitude, this view is consistent with the traditional Christian understanding of the essential relationship between divine assistance or grace and any authentic expression of neighbor-love.

This grace which enables theonomous death is, for Rahner, always the grace of Christ. Rahner's account of grace suggests that God's free self-communication, which is the event of grace, reaches its fullness in the incarnation of the second person of the Trinity. Indeed, he argues that

God's gracious self-revelation is only possible in light of the incarnation. To explain this claim fully would require an examination of the christological implications of Rahner's theology of the symbol.[19] It suffices simply to say that for Rahner the incarnate Logos is the absolute and unsurpassable symbol of God's presence in the world and that therefore any divine self-communication *ad extra* is always mediated through the second person of the Trinity. As the incarnate Logos, Jesus of Nazareth is the fullness of God's self-revelation and so his life is the productive model of full human self-realization. Grace, then, mediated as it is by Jesus Christ, is the essential link in Rahner's account between the death of Jesus and the possibility of the human experience of dying with Christ in history. The life and, most importantly, the death of Jesus of Nazareth are understood to model theonomous death in an unsurpassed manner. The death of Jesus is of central importance for Rahner because it represents Jesus' complete acceptance of the divine will and his unsurpassed love of neighbor. This crucial link between human experience of grace and the death of Jesus allows Rahner to assert that "there is an identity between the experience of the Spirit and participation in the victorious death of Jesus, in which alone the real success of our death is experienced."[20] This helps to make clear that the religious and moral power of Christ's death is not only its exemplary nature, it is the event that enables the very possibility of theonomous death. It is the exemplary nature of Christ's death in history, however, that has the greater implications for actual behavior or concrete choice and so for ethics.

To speak of Jesus' life and death as the model for Christian life is not to suggest that Rahner is proposing an ethic based upon an *imitation* of Jesus. The very notion of imitation is problematic for Rahner because it fails to take account of the unique nature of each person's relationship with God. Rahner understands that a person's response to God is necessarily shaped by the exigencies of history and culture. Attempts to imitate the history of Jesus of Nazareth are futile and potentially dangerous. "Jesus-ism," as Rahner refers to it, has the potential to be theologically dangerous because it allows persons to perceive Jesus as an example of moral values or commitments that can be affirmed independently from this example.[21] Such an example becomes dispensable if it is no longer necessary to promote or support the moral values in question. Rahner does not intend to undermine those Christian traditions which encourage the emulation of certain aspects of the life of Jesus, fervent prayer, fasting, rejecting material wealth, and the like. The difficulty is that because these practices are not unique to Jesus they cannot be essential to Christian discipleship. For Rahner,

Christian discipleship, the following of Jesus, must be lived as a participation in his crucifixion. Jesus' acceptance of death on the cross is the
definitive integration and summation of his life and ministry. It is, as we
have seen, the ultimate act of obedience to God and of love of neighbor. An
ethics informed by the theology of Karl Rahner, then, must take the history
of Jesus seriously as both the productive witness that draws persons to a life
of discipleship and as the essential model of how such a life of discipleship
is actually lived.

Participation in the death of Christ must involve the individual subject's
unique self-realization by means of free action. The formal dimensions of
this participation – obedience to God and neighbor-love – are clear. Yet, as
Rahner's critics have suggested, the complex relationship between categorical and transcendental freedom, as well as his commitment to the unique
nature of every positive fundamental option, make it difficult for him to
offer examples of behaviors which exemplify dying with Christ. The elusive
relationship between the commitment of categorical freedom in history and
the commitment of transcendental freedom characteristic of fundamental
option is consistent with the Catholic moral tradition. This tradition holds
that one can never be completely certain about the level of freedom that
particular moral actions, whether virtuous or vicious, engage and so there
can never be complete certainty about the state of one's relationship with
God. Something similar to, or at least consistent with, this insight is seen
in Rahner's understanding of the relationship between categorical freedom
exercised in history and transcendental freedom. While one can never exercise transcendental freedom apart from concrete action, even those actions
in history that the agent perceives to be an exercise of freedom may not,
in fact, engage transcendental freedom in a definitive way. Nonetheless,
Rahner is willing to offer examples of behaviors consistent with a participation in the death of Jesus; that is, that have the potential to be expressions of
a positive commitment of transcendental freedom. One example has to do
with his notion of "witness" and another has to do with fidelity to conscience
(which itself is a form of witnessing).

FUNDAMENTAL OPTION AS "WITNESS"

Rahner's understanding of what it is to be a witness serves to give some
shape to his more abstract understanding of neighbor-love as a participation
in the death of Christ. Martyrdom is the basic and most dramatic example of
witnessing in Rahner's account.[22] At the most obvious level, the Christian
martyr participates in the fate of Jesus insofar as he or she accepts death

rather than act to betray the perceived command of God. The actual opportunity for such witnessing is, of course, rather rare, especially for those persons living in North America or Western Europe. Yet Rahner would argue that persons who accept the effects of human finitude, diminishment, and disappointment with a spirit of hope and trust, or who suffer for fidelity to conscience, serve to witness in a manner not dissimilar to that of the martyr. Accepting the effects of human ageing or of illness with a spirit of hopefulness and trust can be a form of quiet, gracious cross-bearing that witnesses to the similarly hidden graciousness of the God who calls persons to faith and obedience even in the midst of the apparent meaninglessness of human limitation and brokenness. A contemporary example of this sort of witnessing might be Pope John Paul II insofar as he struggles to live out a perceived divine calling in the context of an increasingly debilitating disease.

Witnessing then has to do with a type of behavior directed toward another that has the effect of provoking similar behavior or commitments in the other person. In the witness' act of fidelity or trust, the viewer encounters his or her unrealized desire for a similarly authentic life. In Rahner's discussion of the martyr as witness he writes, ". . . how could anybody, for instance, recognise the death of the martyr, as a death demonstrating its purity and goodness, other than by living with the same attitude, by undergoing the same death spiritually . . ."[23] Insofar as the act of witnessing is always directed to the good or benefit of other persons it is an act of neighbor-love. At the most basic level, Rahner's theological understanding of the concept of witness reminds those in positions of power how their decisions or actions can affect the lives of others. Witnessing is also always a political event because the act of witnessing necessarily involves a public, social, and historical proclamation. The historical dimension of witnessing suggests that it is an activity that cannot be understood monolithically. Rather, he continues, it develops in relationship to the demands of discipleship generated by particular times and cultures.

CONSCIENCE AND RELIGIOUS DISCERNMENT

The human person's obligation to follow his or her conscience is another significant way to understand Rahner's notion of dying with Christ as a mode of behavior consistent with a positive fundamental option. Rahner does not think it an exaggeration, as has been noted, to interpret conscience as the voice of God. In this light he equates the cost of rejecting the insight of conscience with self-destruction. Therefore, submitting to the dictates of objective morality – even the moral teaching of the Catholic Church – without reference to personal conscience is, in Rahner's view, "nothing but a higher kind of dog training" that is demeaning of God and of the individual person.[24] He is not arguing for an arbitrary subjectivism or for a rejection of Church teaching as an essential and authoritative source of moral wisdom. The Church is in a privileged position to interpret and assess the moral implications of what Rahner refers to as objective reality in light of experience of diverse Christian communities. The teaching of the Church is, however, addressed to the freedom of persons and can never fully substitute for the personal process of moral reflection (which does not occur in isolation) necessary for an authentic moral choice. Because Rahner views the moral teaching of the Catholic Church to be fundamentally sound, it will be an unusual occurrence that a person with a well-formed conscience will diverge from this teaching. Nonetheless, Rahner is clear that each person must always follow the insights of conscience. Indeed, it is more important to follow the dictates of an erroneous conscience than to submit to the authority of another in a manner that undermines essential human freedom. In a world where it is so often easier to submit to authority or to social pressure, Rahner is acutely aware that fidelity to conscience can be painful and can indeed be a form of martyrdom.

Rahner's emphasis on fidelity to conscience as a form of dying with Christ serves to reaffirm the central role of discernment in an ethics informed by his theology. His discussion of conscience, its dignity, and the subject's absolute obligation to obey the dictates of conscience is closely related to his understanding of Ignatian election. For Rahner, both the experience of recognizing an obligation of conscience and making an election in the *Spiritual Exercises* is always a personal experience of God. As experiences of God in history, they are a potential locus of that acceptance of God and of self – a dynamic that is also the case with the fundamental option. It is important to emphasize that the choice to accept God's will as encountered in conscience or prayer always exacts a price from the subject; it is by no means a detached or abstract choice. Harvey Egan's Rahnerian reading of Ignatian spirituality is particularly helpful in this regard.[25] Egan has identified this spirituality as a "mysticism of service." An authentic election always moves the subject to an expression of neighbor-love. For Rahner it is clear that the mysticism which moves the agent to an election is always related to dying with Christ and neighbor-love. He writes in this regard:

> . . . in earthly man the emptying of self will not be accomplished by
> practising pure inwardness, but by the real activity which is called
> humility, service, love of our neighbour, the cross and death. One must
> descend into hell together with Christ; lose one's soul, not directly to
> the God who is above all names but in the service of one's brethren.[26]

Far from being abstract, then, this Rahnerian reading of Ignatian spirituality demonstrates that a positive fundamental option must always involve a dying to self in concrete service to the neighbor.

While a full account of Rahner's understanding of Ignatian discernment and election is beyond the scope of this essay it will be important to give the general outlines of this theory and demonstrate its basic ecclesial orientation. Election or choice, as a matter of religious experience, involves a process of testing a particular choice over a period of time. Insofar as this process results in a decision which produces "'peace,' 'tranquility,' 'quiet,' so that true gladness and spiritual joy ensues" the agent can be sure of a genuine synthesis between "pure receptivity to God (as concretely achieved, not as a theoretical principle and proposition) and the will to this limited finite object."[27] As a religious experience, election does have an affective element. However, Rahner wants to be clear that, in his view, Ignatian election of this sort is "thoroughly an operation of the 'intellect,' in the metaphysical, scholastic sense of the word, in which it is capable of apprehending values."[28] This becomes clear when one recalls that Rahner is essentially equating his own understanding of the graced experience of supernatural transcendence which accompanies each act of knowing with Loyola's concept of consolation without previous cause or the conscious, non-conceptual experience of God. This consolation or experience of transcendence is not simply a matter of feeling something; it always involves encounter with and an appropriation of truth. It is within the context of this spiritual/intellectual experience that a decision for or against God is made. For Rahner and for Loyola, a decision for God always involves a following of the crucified Christ.

It is this element of concrete love or service which also establishes the possibility for a mystical decision for God and God's will outside of the context of an explicit prayer experience. This is what has been referred to as Rahner's understanding of the mysticism of daily life, a discussion of which would help to establish that Ignatian election is not simply for mystics or a spiritual elite but rather conforms to actual Christian practice. While Rahner argued forcefully for making the *Spiritual Exercises* more widely available as an unparalleled aid to the Christian vocation, he was fully aware that most Christians do not have the capacity or resources for determining God's concrete will for them by means of formal Ignatian discernment. Nonetheless he would claim that devout Christians can and do make life decisions in a way that is congruent with Loyola's theory of election, just as a person "in the street uses logic without having studied it."[29] These decisions are made not primarily by rational analysis but by a perception that a particular state of life or course of action suits the individual and brings a sense of peace before God.

Rahner's interpretation of the Ignatian doctrine of election provides a way for the Christian to discern God's will in a way that is linked to individual experience of God, shaped by the history of Jesus of Nazareth as proclaimed and interpreted by the Church. In this sense, a Rahnerian ethic of discernment, influenced as it is by Ignatian spirituality, is deeply ecclesial and therefore communal in nature. It cannot be understood apart from the devotional, liturgical, and ethical life of the Church. The teaching of the Church plays a vital role in the formation of the "heart" that engages the search for God's will by this means. At the same time, Rahner is clear about the limits and limitations of such moral teaching. As we have seen, he argues that authoritative norms can never adequately substitute for the deliberations of conscience. The teaching of the hierarchical Church must inform and shape the believer's conscience, it can never usurp it. Further, Rahner raises important questions about the ability of any source of moral wisdom to adequately generate detailed, universally binding norms in a context of greatly accelerated social, economic, and cultural change. In light of these circumstances, it is not impossible for such detailed and specific teachings to be "simply erroneous."[30] Overly specific solutions to particular moral issues ought to be avoided therefore in favor of general ethical guidance based upon fundamental principles. This approach is, of course, consistent with much of the Church's recent teaching on social and economic matters. This moral complexity and the inability of the Church to adequately address it in detail serves to underscore the need of the people of God for the Ignatian methodology of discernment. Rahner is convinced that an Ignatian discernment can never undermine authentic Christian identity because Ignatius' *Spiritual Exercises* "arises from the basis of traditional Christianity and Roman Catholic conformity to the Church" and so "ultimately supports and embraces everything Christian and ecclesial."[31] As a Christian and ecclesial experience of God's will, it therefore necessarily leads to an expression of neighbor-love consistent with a participation in "the lot of Jesus." Its implications, then, have more to do with a method or "form" of religious or moral choice rather than with a distinctive ethical "content." Nonetheless, just as the person of conscience demonstrates the characteristic of integrity, the person of discernment gives evidence of a life of faith and intimacy with God that is productive of a life characterized by a "dying with Christ."

Notes

1 "Theology of Freedom," *TI* vi, 185.

2 K. Rahner, "The Logic of Concrete Individual Knowledge in Ignatius Loyola," in *The Dynamic Element in the Church*, trans. W. J. O'Hara (London: Burns and Oates, 1964), 95.

3 "The Dignity and Freedom of Man," *TI* ii, 239.

4 This is Jean Porter's term. See her essay, "Virtue and Sin: The Connection of the Virtues and the Case of the Flawed Saint," *The Journal of Religion* 75 (1995), 521–39.

5 K. Rahner, *On the Theology of Death*, trans. C. Henkey (New York: Herder and Herder, 1963), 82–83.

6 *FCF*, 123.

7 "Reflections on the Unity of Love of Neighbour and Love of God," *TI* vi, 241.

8 "The Spirituality of the Priest in the Light of His Office," *TI* xix, 121.

9 K. Rahner, "Who Are Your Brother and Sister?" in *The Love of Jesus and the Love of Neighbour*, trans. R. Barr (New York: Crossroad, 1985), 83–84.

10 John Paul II, *Veritatis Splendor*, n. 65.

11 J. Porter, "Moral Language and the Language of Grace: The Fundamental Option and the Virtue of Charity," *Philosophy & Theology* 10 (1997), 170.

12 Rahner, "The Logic of Concrete Individual Knowledge," 101.

13 See "The Spirituality of the Church of the Future," *TI* xx, 149.

14 Ibid.

15 "Conscience," *TI* xxii, 10.

16 Thomas Aquinas, *Summa Theologiae* II-II, 31–33. See Jean Porter on this point, "Moral Language and the Language of Grace," 184–91.

17 R. Ochs, *The Death in Every Now* (New York: Sheed and Ward, 1969), 14. See also P. Phan's discussion of Rahner's theology of death in this volume.

18 Rahner, *Theology of Death*, 92.

19 "The Theology of the Symbol," *TI* iv, 236–37.

20 "Experience of the Holy Spirit," *TI* xviii, 205–06.

21 "Brief Observations on Systematic Christology Today," *TI* xxi, 237.

22 "Christian Dying," *TI* xviii, 256.

23 Rahner, *Theology of Death*, 123.

24 "Conscience," *TI* xxii, 12.

25 H. Egan, *The Spiritual Exercises and the Ignatian Mystical Horizon* (Saint Louis: The Institute of Jesuit Sources, 1976).

26 K. Rahner, *Visions and Prophecies*, trans. C. Henkey and R. Strachan (New York: Herder and Herder, 1963), 14, n. 12.

27 "The Logic of Concrete Individual Knowledge," 158.

28 Ibid., 94–95, n. 9.

29 Ibid., 166.

30 "The Mature Christian," *TI* xxi, 123.

31 K. Rahner, "Foreword," in Egan, *The Spiritual Exercises*, xiii.

Further reading

Bresnahan, J. F., "Rahner's Ethics: Critical Natural Law in Relation to Contemporary Ethical Methodology," *Journal of Religion* 56 (1976), 36–60.

Linnane, B. F., "Dying with Christ: Rahner's Ethics of Discipleship," *Journal of Religion* 81 (2001), 228–48.

Rahner, K., "On the Question of a Formal Existential Ethics," *TI* II, 217–34.

"The Problem of Genetic Manipulation," *TI* IX, 225–52.

"The Liberty of the Sick, Theologically Considered," *TI* XVII, 100–13.

11 Eschatology

PETER C. PHAN

Eschatology, or the doctrine of the Last Things, has had a chequered history in Christian theology. Rooted in the belief concerning Christ's return (*parousia*) in glory to judge the living and the dead and his eternal kingdom and in the expectation of the universal resurrection, the Christian teaching on life everlasting occupied the central position in the theology of the early Church. Theologians of both East and West kept in the forefront of Christian consciousness the New Testament conviction about the final consummation of human history through Christ in God's reign (see 1 Corinthians 15:28). Such is the case with, for instance, Irenaeus (*c.* 130– *c.* 200) with his concept of recapitulation (*anakephalaiosis*), Origen (*c.* 185– *c.* 254) with that of universal restoration (*apocatastasis*), and Augustine (354–430) with that of the City of God (*civitas Dei*). Furthermore, during the first few centuries of the Christian era, this eschatological consciousness was also heightened by millenarianist groups such as the Gnostics and the Montanists.

Except for brief outbursts of millenarian enthusiasm with Joachim of Fiore (*c.* 1135–1202), and, much later, with the Anabaptists and the Bohemian and the Moravian Brethren during the Reformation, the Church's official consciousness of Christ's glorious return and one-thousand-year rule was gradually eclipsed, and with it the collective eschatology that discusses the meaning and destiny of human history. In late scholasticism, and subsequently in neo-scholastic manualist theology, the main focus was the post-mortem fate of the individual. The treatise on the "Four Last Things" (i.e., death, judgment, heaven, and hell), called *De novissimis* and regularly assigned to the end of the theological curriculum, presented a quasi-reportorial description of the afterlife with as much detail as possible. At the same time, under the influence of Greek philosophy, especially Platonism, eschatology was heavily spiritualized, with exclusive emphasis on the immortality of the soul and its eternal destiny, apart from the history of humanity as a whole and the fate of the cosmos itself.

With the Enlightenment Christian eschatology was historicized and secularized, especially in Hegel (1770–1831) and Marx (1818–83), and in turn fueled ideas of historical evolution and intra-mundane utopias. Scepticism infected the discussion of the afterlife, and the transcendent messianic age was transformed into either the Absolute Spirit (*Geist*) in which all antithetic movements are resolved and sublated (the "thesis-antithesis-synthesis" dialectic), or the classless society of the proletariat. Against immanentist as well as moral (along mainly Kantian lines) reduction of Christian eschatology to this-worldly utopias, theologians such as Johannes Weiss (1863–1914) and Albert Schweitzer (1875–1965) insisted that the central message of Jesus' preaching was about the kingdom of God as a transcendent reality which is still to come (a "thoroughgoing" or "consistent" eschatology), and not something already realized in history (as in C. H. Dodd's "realized eschatology") or to be brought about by human efforts. As a result, eschatology was accorded prominence in dialectical theology, which however gives it an existential-individualist cast. Both Rudolf Bultmann (1884–1976) and the early Karl Barth (1886–1968) viewed the *eschaton* as the believer's present encounter in faith with Christ, without reference to its future dimension.

Contemporary theologians, while welcoming dialectical theology's emphasis on the eschatological dimension of the Christian faith, reject its dehistoricization and insist on the critical and transformative functions as well as the political, socio-economic, and ecological implications of eschatology. In theologians such as Wolfhart Pannenberg (1928–), Jürgen Moltmann (1926–), Johann Baptist Metz (1928–), and liberation theologians of various orientations, all aspects of eschatology – personal and political, spiritual and cosmic, immanent and transcendent, present and future – are given their proper due.[1]

This rapid overview of the development of eschatology serves to contextualize Karl Rahner's eschatology. As a matter of fact, Rahner elaborates his eschatology as an explicit rejection of the neo-scholastic version and as an attempt to retrieve certain forgotten aspects of biblical eschatology in dialogue with contemporary theologians. This essay will begin with Rahner's critique of the neo-scholastic treatment of eschatology in its *De novissimis* treatise and the theological grounding for Rahner's own eschatology. It next discusses his teaching on some key issues in individual and collective eschatology. The last part will assess his eschatology in the light of contemporary eschatologies.[2]

ESCHATOLOGY AS ANTHROPOLOGY AND CHRISTOLOGY IN THE MODE OF FUTURE FULFILLMENT

As with most of his treatments of theological *loci*, Rahner's writings on eschatology begin with a critique of what he calls *Schultheologie*, that is, the kind of theology, commonly referred to as "neo-scholastic" or "neo-Thomist," which was developed after the revival of Thomism mandated by Pope Leo XIII's encyclical *Aeterni Patris* (1879) and transmitted through seminary manuals, the kind of theology which Rahner himself was taught during his theological studies at the Jesuit school of theology in Valkenburg, Holland in 1929–32.[3] With regard to neo-scholastic eschatology in particular, Rahner's complaints are several. In terms of content it is, says Rahner, thin gruel compared with the sturdy fare offered by divine revelation. Rahner suggests that in addition to the traditional themes already treated in the manuals, others should be taken up, for instance, the nature of time and eternity, the "locality" of heaven, the meaning of death and dying (as opposed to what happens after death), the abiding significance of Jesus' humanity for our eternal beatitude, the positive meaning of the inequality of the glory in heaven, beatific vision as vision of the abiding mystery of God, the relation of the heaven of the redeemed to the rejected world of the devils, the positive meaning of the persistence of evil and the nature of evil itself, the metaphysical nature of glorified corporeality, the nature of the virtue of hope, the relationship between the reign of God and secular utopias, etc. Rahner also recommends that eschatology be integrated with other treatises of dogmatic theology, in particular, protology, the theology of history, theological anthropology, Christology, soteriology, and ecclesiology. In terms of method, Rahner notes that there still lacked a sophisticated hermeneutics of eschatological assertions by which what is affirmed can be distinguished from its modes of expression.[4]

DEVELOPMENT IN RAHNER'S ESCHATOLOGY

To remedy the situation, Rahner proposes to elaborate an "eschatology of transcendental theology."[5] From a historical perspective, Rahner's elaboration of this transcendental eschatology went through three principal phases corresponding to the development of Rahner's anthropology and theology as a whole. In the first stage, which may be called "individualist-existentialist," Rahner's focus in his doctoral dissertation *Geist in Welt* is primarily on the individual knower with the metaphysics of knowledge as the object of analysis and transcendental deduction as the method. The anthropology developed in his dissertation, in virtue of the limitations imposed by the theme itself, is through the mode of cognitional analysis rather than through a metaphysics of freedom and relation. Personal becoming is presented as intrapersonal becoming, i.e., in terms of what goes on *within* the individual. At this stage, Rahner's eschatology focuses mainly on the eternal fate of the individual, especially in his volume on death and his early essays on freedom, concupiscence, purgatory and indulgences, the resurrection of the body, beatific vision, time, and the life of the dead.

Nevertheless, already in the dissertation, there is a solid foundation for a dynamic, intentional, and relational view of the person, since the person (even though the word "person" never appears therein) is understood as "spirit" in "world" or incarnate spirit or spirited matter which enacts itself (*selbst vollziehen*) through a double act of self-transcendence to the "other," that is, the self-transcendence of matter toward spirit and the self-transcendence of the thus constituted reality of spirit-in-world toward the Absolute Being.[6]

The second stage of Rahner's eschatology may be termed "existentialist-interpersonal." It began with his *Hörer des Wortes* (1941) in which the term "person" occurs for the first time and in which the *Umwelt* (the world of things) becomes the *Mitwelt* (the world of persons). The human person is not just spirit in the world but is explicitly said to be a free and historical being who is not simply constituted a person in virtue of materiality but must become personal by becoming interpersonal through acts of freedom and love in a community of persons. This stage reached its peak in Rahner's 1961 key essay on the unity of the love of God and love of neighbor.[7]

The third stage of Rahner's eschatology may be called "socio-political." Under the influence of the Second Vatican Council, Johann-Baptist Metz's political theology, and dialogue with philosophers such as Ernst Bloch, from 1965 on Rahner came to see the human person increasingly as a member of a political, legal, economic, social, cultural, and religious community. His eschatological writings began to deal with issues such as secular and Marxist ideologies, the future of human history, hope, the relation between Christianity and humanism, revolution, and liberation.

THE HERMENEUTICS OF ESCHATOLOGICAL STATEMENTS

Before examining Rahner's eschatology in detail it is necessary to discuss one of his most important contributions to this field, namely, his hermeneutics of eschatological statements.[8] As mentioned above, Rahner laments the fact that past eschatologies had not elaborated guidelines for interpreting eschatological affirmations of the Bible and as a consequence had fallen victim to the proof-text approach. Taking for granted the necessity of the historical-critical method (e.g., source criticism, form criticism, and redaction criticism), Rahner formulates seven principles of his own hermeneutics. Briefly, they can be summarized as follows:

First, the *eschata* are future events in the strictly chronological sense. Hence, Rahner rejects Bultmann's existential demythologization of eschatology as a purely present decision for or against the kerygma and the early Barth's interpretation of eschatology as God's present judgment, manifested in the cross, on sinful humanity. Secondly, God's omniscience includes knowledge of these future events and God can reveal them to human beings who therefore can have a certain knowledge of them. Thirdly, the *eschata* are hidden realities and if they are revealed to humans, this revelation takes place necessarily in the history of salvation. Fourthly, our knowledge of the future is the knowledge of the futurity of the present. Hence, fifthly, the knowledge of the future *eschata* is derived from our knowledge of the present events of the history of salvation. Sixthly, on the basis of what we now know about salvation, we must say that (1) eschatological assertions about heaven and hell are not on an equal footing; (2) eschatological statements concern both the individual person and the world as a whole; (3) there need be no opposition between imminent and distant expectation of the *parousia*; (4) Christ is the hermeneutical principle of all eschatological assertions; and (5) the contents of eschatology are determined by the present reality of salvation in Christ. Seventhly, it is possible to distinguish between form and content in eschatological assertions and to re-express the binding contents of eschatology in a new language.

Of these seven principles the most important are the fifth and the sixth, and a word on each is called for. The fifth thesis states that our knowledge of future eschatological events is derived from our present knowledge of our history of salvation. Rahner says that in "eschatology" we "project" from the present *forward* into the future (*aussagen*), as opposed to "apocalyptic," in which we "inject" from the future *back* into the present (*einsagen*). In a nutshell, eschatology is anthropology conjugated in the future sense.[9] First of all, then, the only source of Christian eschatology is therefore our *present* experience of salvation, which consists in God's trinitarian self-communication to humans in the grace of the crucified and risen Christ by the power of the Holy Spirit. Secondly, eschatology is not a historical report of what will happen beyond death or at the end of time, but an etiological account from the present situation of grace forward into its future stage of fulfillment. Thirdly, eschatology is therefore not an *additional* chapter as it were of the history of salvation but anthropology transposed into the future tense.

The sixth principle grounds eschatology as future anthropology in Christology. Like Barth's and von Balthasar's, Rahner's eschatology is decidedly christocentric, and this in two senses. First, Christology is the criterion of the hermeneutics of eschatology: Anything, says Rahner, "that cannot be read and understood as a christological assertion is not a genuine eschatological assertion."[10] Secondly, Christology determines the contents of eschatology: death, individual judgment, purgatory, heaven, hell, the *parousia*, the resurrection of the dead, universal judgment, and the transfiguration of the world – all of these eschatological themes are at root christologically determined.

THE FINAL CONSUMMATION OF THE INDIVIDUAL AND OF HUMAN HISTORY

On the basis of this anthropological and christological grounding Rahner discusses various themes traditionally associated with eschatology and many others of his own. In spite of the multiplicity of these themes Rahner insists strongly on a unified approach to eschatology. Indeed, it is very significant that the two sections of eschatology in *Foundations of Christian Faith* are entitled "The One Eschatology as Individual Eschatology" and "The One Eschatology as Collective Eschatology." This oneness of eschatology is rooted both in the ontological unity of matter (body) and spirit (soul) in the human person and in the unity between the individual's eternal destiny and the consummation of the history of the world.

DEATH AND THE DEFINITIVE AND FINAL VALIDITY OF HUMAN FREEDOM

Of all the topics of eschatology death and dying, as opposed to what comes *after* death, has received the most extensive treatment by Rahner.[11] True to his method of weaving transcendental reflection with historical analysis, Rahner combines reflections on death and dying in general with those on the death of Christ. On the basis of these Rahner makes two preliminary affirmations about death: First, death is a universal phenomenon and it affects the person as a whole. Neither affirmation is a banal platitude derived from empirical sciences; rather, both statements are grounded theologically. Death is universal not simply because humans have perishable bodies but because they are sinners, personally and through the original sin, and because they possess freedom. Secondly, death strikes the whole person because the human person is "an absolute unity which cannot simply be split up into body and soul," so that "eschatological statements about the fulfilment of the soul and the fulfilment of the body are not of such a nature that they could be completely separated from each other and assigned to different realities."[12] Death affects human beings not only in their bodies but in their souls as well, not only "at the level of the material and the biological, but on the plane of self-awareness, personhood, freedom, responsibility, love and faithfulness."[13]

Rahner clarifies these affirmations by distinguishing between the "natural" and "personal" aspects of death. As a natural event, death cannot be adequately defined as the separation of the soul from the body. Rahner recognizes that the traditional description of death as separation of the soul from the body contains an important truth about the fact that in death humans acquire a different relationship to their bodies and that their souls remain in existence in spite of the dissolution of their bodies (the "immortality of the soul"). But this understanding of death, Rahner points out, says nothing about how death affects the whole person (therefore also the soul) and about how the soul must continue to be in some ontological way related to the body and to the material world in general in order to be able to exist.[14]

More importantly, death is also a personal act. Here Rahner links death with freedom, time, and eternity. Human freedom, Rahner argues, is not simply the capacity to choose this or that (Augustine's *liberum arbitrium*) but fundamentally the capacity to determine and realize *oneself*, for good or evil, in a definitive way (*libertas*). This freedom is exercised categorically in particular choices of this or that thing and transcendentally with reference to God as the Absolute Value, as the horizon of Absolute Goodness in which a particular thing is chosen. This exercise of freedom occurs in a history that is determined both by sin ("original sin") and by God's self-communication as an offer of grace (the "supernatural existential").

To say that freedom is exercised in history is to say that it is intrinsically connected with time. Time is best understood not as measurement of some movement outside human beings but as something internal to human beings ("internal time") which enables them to exercise their freedom and in turn is given meaning by freedom. Because time is an element of the history of freedom, it has a genuine beginning, a definitive end, and an irreversible course. The function of death, Rahner suggests, is to make this freedom-in-time *definitive* and *final* by putting an end to time-in-freedom. At the end of time, what passes away is the process of becoming and not what we have become, both good and evil, which will acquire definitive validity before God. It is to be noted that

> the achieved final validity of human existence which has grown to maturity in freedom comes to be *through*, not *after* death. What has come to be is the liberated, final validity of something which was once temporal, and which came to be in spirit and freedom, and which therefore formed time in order to be, and not really in order to continue on in time.[15]

Here Rahner makes a distinction between death as "passion" and death as "action." As passion, death is a "natural" event, something imposed from outside, something "suffered" (the etymological meaning of "passion"). At the same time, death is also a "personal" act, that is, something the person can accept or reject freely and actively, something a person "does" in freedom. Either one rejects it by running away from one's being-made-for death (Heidegger's *zum Tode sein*) through amusements and distractions and thus falls into "inauthentic existence." Or one can assume death and dying with courage as the comprehensive horizon of one's historical and finite being and accept it as one's own unique possibility, as the light that illumines everything of one's existence, as one's own "project." By saying "yes" to death, a person can turn a necessary fate externally imposed on oneself into a free act: "Wherever there is real liberty, there is love for death and courage for death."[16] This yes can also take the form of daily asceticism and renunciation by which one anticipates one's death.

DYING WITH CHRIST

Rahner's reflections on death as a personal act of freedom should not obscure the fact that for him death is also a consequence and manifestation of sin, both original and personal. While death as the end of the biological life and the dissolution of the body–soul structure may be regarded as something "natural," from the Christian point of view, it must be seen as a punishment for sin. This penal character is seen in what Rahner calls the "hiddenness of death" (*die Verhülltheit des Todes*), that is, the ineluctable and unresolvable uncertainty as to whether the goal reached in death will be for the dying individual fullness of life or sheer emptiness. This hiddenness is the result of not only original sin but also personal sins – a fact, in Rahner's judgment, not sufficiently adverted to in traditional eschatology.

Ultimately, the full meaning of human death can be seen, according to Rahner, only in the light of Jesus' death. Rahner is critical of attempts to explain the redemptive value of Christ's death on the cross by means of the theory of satisfaction. Rather than elaborating on the necessity of a human-divine being repaying in an adequate manner the offense committed by humanity against an infinite God, Rahner focuses on the meaning of Christ's dying itself. Like any death, Jesus' is both passion and action, natural and personal. It too was shrouded in hiddenness, but it was also an act of supreme freedom. Jesus' death was both an experience of emptiness and abandonment by God ("My God, my God, why have you forsaken me?") and a radical acceptance of and loving obedience to God in the midst of such emptiness and powerlessness ("Father, into your hands I commend my spirit"). In dying with Christ the Christian also undergoes that same dialectical experience of remoteness from and nearness to God, of doubt and faith, despair and hope, rebellion and love. Furthermore, she and he can do this not only at the moment of death but throughout their lives, especially in the sacraments of baptism, Eucharist, and anointing.

ETERNITY IN TIME AS "TIME'S OWN MATURE FRUIT"

It is also in connection with freedom and time that Rahner elaborates his theology of eternity. He repeatedly speaks against misunderstanding it as unlimited continuation of time after death, never-ending time running on into infinity on the other side of this world. Such "eternity" would never bring happiness since on this understanding humans never arrive at their goal. Rahner suggests that the best way to understand what eternity means is to relate it to human freedom and time. Just as freedom is not a ceaseless quest to achieve ever-new changes at will but the capacity for definitive and final self-realization in death, so eternity is not an unending continuation of time but time fulfilled and made definitive and final. Whenever something is achieved with finality and definitiveness in time, either by particular acts of freedom or by the supreme act of freedom, that is, death, there eternity comes to be: "In reality, eternity comes to be in time as time's own mature fruit, an eternity which does not really continue on beyond experienced time. Rather eternity subsumes time by being liberated from the time which came to be temporarily so that freedom and something of final and definitive validity can be achieved."[17] Eternity, then, is not outside, above, after, beyond, time; rather, it is *in* and *from* time, time having acquired final and definitive validity before God through the exercise of freedom.[18]

"THE INTERMEDIATE STATE": DEFINED DOGMA OR CULTURAL METAPHOR?

The reality of the existence of the soul separated from its body between death and the resurrection (the intermediate state) seems to be an established doctrine. Nevertheless, the fact that Rahner places the expression in quotation marks in the title of his essay gives us a hint of the controversy surrounding the notion of *anima separata*.[19] The question is whether the intermediate state is a dogma defined by Pope Benedict XII in his constitution *Benedictus Deus* (1336) or whether it is merely an imaginative framework to harmonize two apparently contradictory basic truths, namely, the future resurrection of the flesh, i.e., the one and total person, and the immediate vision of God after death. Rahner argues for the latter, on the ground that the intermediate state, if taken as a doctrine, would be liable to severe challenges from contemporary philosophical anthropology which considers "time" after death (which the intermediate state postulates) as a self-contradictory concept and which maintains the metaphysical impossibility of the *anima separata*. Furthermore, from the theological perspective, an immediate resurrection in death, which would render the notion of an intermediate state nugatory, is not impossible since the dogma of the Assumption of Mary does not exclude a priori the possibility of the total glorification in both body and soul here and now of those who have died other than the Mother of God.[20]

PURGATORY AS PROCESS OF PURGATION?

A doctrine connected with the intermediate state is purgatory. Rahner is well aware of the controversial nature of the Roman Catholic Church's teaching on purgatory and of the slim basis for it in both Scripture and early tradition. To make it more comprehensible Rahner makes use of some concepts in contemporary anthropology. One of these is that humans are complex beings with many levels in their psychological and ontological make-up. Given this multi-leveled personality and multi-staged process of becoming, a decision will require time – of varying length – to penetrate and permeate the whole person. This *décalage* in personal integration occurs on at least three levels:

between an ultimate and basic decision in the core of a person and the complete integration of the total reality of the subject into this basic decision; between the fulfilment of an individual person in death and the total fulfilment of the world; and between the final and definitive validity of a person which comes with death and the total permeation and manifestation of this fulfilment in the glorification of the body which, at least in a certain sense, does not come with death as such.[21]

Within the context of a triple stage in this process of gradual personal integration it is possible, Rahner suggests, to locate "purgatory" or, better, purgation (symbolized by "fire"). Purgatory may be understood as a process of maturation and transformation "after" death, psychologically often painful, as the result of the temporal punishments for personal sins. It is not necessary to view the temporal punishment due to sin as something that is extrinsically imposed by God, conceived of as something purely vindictive, but rather as a consequence intrinsic to sin itself inasmuch as sin gives birth to its own punishment. Furthermore, it is not necessary to imagine its "duration" as temporal in a kind of a parallel time-bound universe of the afterlife. We have mentioned above that for Rahner the "intermediate state" may be simply a cultural device or, as he puts it, a "little harmless mythology." In Rahner's account, the "duration" of the person's purification is understood not in temporal terms but as the depth and intensity of the pains the person experiences in death. Finally, Rahner tantalizingly suggests that this understanding of purgatory might open space for a more positive interpretation of the widespread belief in reincarnation provided that it is not conceived as "a fate for man which will never end and will continue on forever in time."[22]

HEAVEN AS FACT AND HELL AS SERIOUS POSSIBILITY

One of Rahner's hermeneutical principles states that biblical affirmations about heaven and hell should not be taken as parallel statements about two equal alternatives offered by God for humans to choose. Rather, given God's redemptive work in Christ and the presence of the saints, heaven must be proclaimed as a factual reality. However, Rahner insists, because our present situation is one of both grace and sin, the possibilities of eternal communion with God (heaven) *and* eternal perdition (hell) must be mentioned together in eschatological discourse.

As far as heaven is concerned, Rahner relates it first of all to his understanding of eternity. As we have seen above, eternity is time made definitively and finally valid. For humans this eternity is gradually brought into being in time through our acts of freedom. For God, however, eternity is an ever-present attribute in its absolute fullness. In contrast to time, which has a genuine beginning, a definitive end, and an irreversible course with discrete and measurable moments, God's eternity has neither beginning nor end and no measurable movement. Rather, it is the timeless and immutable present which is always in fullness and in absolute possession of itself and for which, subsisting in itself, there is no such thing as "before" or "after." At the same time, however, Rahner reminds us, because of the act of creation and above all because of the incarnation of the Logos, God not only has created time but has also freely assumed it as a specification of God's own self. God, though "immutable" and "eternal" in himself, has *himself*, in the otherness of the world (what Rahner calls God's *Realsymbol*), undergone change, history, and time. In other words, the time and history of the world has become God's own time and history.

Thus, for humans to "enter into heaven," to use a popular expression, is to share in God's eternity, or to be more exact, to share in God's trinitarian life as this has been historicized in God's self-communication to the world in knowledge (the Logos) and love (the Spirit). This means that heaven has an intrinsically christological structure, that is, our eternal beatitude is mediated to us by Christ precisely in his glorified humanity. This insight is perhaps one of Rahner's most significant contributions to the theology of heaven. While acknowledging Pope Benedict XII's teaching that the souls of the blessed "see the divine essence with an intuitive vision and even face to face, without the mediation of any creature by way of object of vision" and that "the divine essence immediately manifests itself to them plainly, clearly and openly (*nude, clare, et aperte*),"[23] Rahner insists that "the humanity of Jesus is the medium through which our immediate relationship with God is achieved."[24] There is no conflict between the mediation of our beatific vision through Christ's humanity and its immediacy because, Rahner points out, mediation and immediacy in humanity's relationship to God, being transcendental, grow in direct and not inverse proportion. Furthermore, Rahner stresses that beatific vision, which traditionally is presented as vision of God's *essence*, is more accurately understood as vision of the Trinity. This is so because beatific vision is the fulfillment of God's self-communication in grace, which, as Rahner has shown in detail elsewhere, is God's self-gift in the incarnation of the Son (in terms of origin, history, invitation, and knowledge) and in the descent of the Spirit (in the correlative terms of future, transcendence, acceptance, and love).[25] Finally, heaven in terms of beatific vision is not a dissipation and elimination of the divine mystery but rather the surrendering of the human intellect, in freedom and love, to the nameless and incomprehensible mystery of God who remains forever mystery and as such is the object of our blissful love.[26]

With regard to hell, Rahner reiterates that eschatological assertions are not "advance coverage" of the beyond or of what is going to happen at the end of time. The biblical statements about eternal punishment and the various images used to describe it do not offer a preview of future punishment but should be interpreted in keeping with their literary genre of "threat-discourse." That is, they place the hearers before a decision for or against God and affirm "the possibility of the human person being finally lost and estranged from God in all the dimensions of his existence."[27] Because biblical statements on hell are not factual descriptions but a summons to personal decision for God, it is not possible to know from them whether there are people in hell or how many (whereas with regard to heaven, the Church has declared that certain people, i.e., the saints, are in heaven even now). Rahner also notes that the eternity of hell is not an additional punitive measure of God's vengeance but rather is the consequence of the inward obduracy of human beings. Lastly, Rahner points to the inner self-contradiction of the act of rejecting God, since in such a rejection there is on the one hand an explicit denial of God which is mediated in one's sinful attitude toward concrete objects of human choices, and on the other hand an implicit and necessary affirmation of God as the horizon in which such choices are made.[28]

Finally, Rahner broaches the question of whether hell should be regarded as eternal, and if not, whether the doctrine of *apocatastasis* (universal restoration and salvation) can be construed in an orthodox way. Rahner again recalls that eternal salvation and eternal perdition are not two parallel choices. The Christian faith, he points out, professes that the world and humanity as a whole will *in fact* enter into eternal life with God. Rahner is aware that the Church's magisterium has condemned the *positive* affirmation of the *apocatastasis* as heretical. To affirm *apocatastasis* absolutely as a fact would be to fail to take seriously human freedom as the capacity for definitive and final self-determination and the reality of God's justice. On the other hand, God's will is to save all humankind (1 Timothy 2:1–6). How to reconcile in a positive synthesis God's universal salvific will and God's justice is not theoretically possible. It can be done, Rahner points out, only by the virtue of hope. Faith can only proclaim God's universal salvific will as a *general principle*, or, put in scholastic terms, faith can perceive it only as "sufficient grace." *This* faith as such cannot tell me as an *individual* whether this sufficient grace will become for *me* "efficacious grace" and thus bring about my salvation in the concrete. The transformation of sufficient grace into efficacious grace occurs when God's offer of grace is personally accepted, and this happens precisely in hope. But if this hope for salvation is possible for me as an individual, there is no reason why it should not be extended to others, and indeed to all beings. As a matter of fact, Christian love impels one to have such a universal hope. For Rahner, then, the doctrine of *apocatastasis* is justified by the virtue of hope, not as a statement of fact or an apodictic prediction, but as an object of hope and prayer.

THE RESURRECTION OF JESUS AND THE RESURRECTION OF THE DEAD

True to his christological "concentration," Rahner argues that the only context in which the resurrection of the dead can be understood is the resurrection of Jesus, since the latter is the meritorious, exemplary, and instrumental cause of the former. Consequently, to understand what the resurrection of the dead means, one has to inquire into the nature of the resurrection of Jesus and then project it into the future on all humanity. For Rahner, since Jesus' bodily humanity is a permanent part of the world, Jesus' resurrection, by which his historical existence is given definitive, final, and permanent validity, constitutes the beginning of the glorious consummation of the world. Hence, the resurrection of the dead is a metaphor for the final and definitive consummation of human history and the material cosmos. As such it is intrinsically connected with what the Christian faith says about Christ's "Second Coming" (*parousia*) and the "Last Judgment." Indeed, these three expressions, i.e., resurrection of the dead, *parousia*, and Last Judgment, highlight the intrinsic and necessary unity between individual eschatology (death, individual judgment, purgatory, heaven, hell) and collective eschatology (the resurrection of the dead, Christ's Second Coming, Last Judgment, and the coming of God's reign). The collective eschatology is not a reprise of individual eschatology; rather, it is the public and universal manifestation of what has already occurred in individual eschatology, on the world's stage as it were. At the same time, individual eschatology is not yet completed as long as history still goes on; indeed, it is still being shaped by what occurs in human history and the cosmos. Hence, Rahner insists, we should speak of both individual and collective eschatologies, even though, as Rahner puts it, there is little chance of our being able to make an unambiguous statement about the more exact relationship between the fulfilment of an individual person through death, a fulfilment which is going on now continually, and the fulfilment of the human race and with it the fulfilment of the world, the world which has no other meaning to begin with except to be the realm of spiritual and personal history.[29]

IMMANENT AND TRANSCENDENT CONSUMMATION

As we have seen above, for Rahner, one of the most pressing and important themes in contemporary eschatology is the relationship between this-worldly utopias and the transcendent consummation of human history in the reign of God. To explicate this relationship Rahner has recourse to his philosophy of the human person as "spirit in the world" and to his theology of God's self-communication and revelation. Philosophically, as matter achieves its true nature by being oriented to the spirit, and as the spirit achieves its true nature by being incarnated in matter, so the immanent consummation and the transcendent consummation are brought about through each other. For human beings, the immanent consummation and the transcendent consummation are the same; they constitute the one consummation in which the one aspect implies the other.

Theologically, just as God's self-gift ("uncreated grace") is given as an intrinsic and constitutive dimension of human existence (the "supernatural existential") and is mediated in particular historical events (both in "general revelation" and in "particular revelation"), so the transcendent consummation of human history is realised in intra-mundane utopias. For Rahner, transcendent consummation is both God's gift and a task given to humanity and the Church. It is by bringing about this-worldly utopias that humans in general and Christians in particular receive God's gift of God's reign. By the same token, this-worldly utopias cannot be identified with the reign of God and vice versa.

With regard to the task of the Church in realizing these utopias, Rahner suggests that the excesses of both "integrism" and "esotericism" be avoided. By the former he means the theoretical and practical position according to which the Church must map out and control all aspects of human life according to its theological and moral principles. By the latter is meant the total removal of the Church's sphere of influence from the world since the latter is secular and sinful. Rahner suggests a synthesis of these two positions. According to him, the Church does have a positive, albeit limited, role to play in the world. It must proclaim social principles and norms for human behavior, function as a social critic by pointing out what social policy is contrary to the common good, and formulate concrete imperatives (*Weisungen*) for social action that are midway between absolutely binding principles and mere options.

HUMANITY'S JOURNEY INTO THE ABSOLUTE FUTURE

Rahner's enormous contributions to Christian eschatology have been widely acknowledged. It is a measure of his influence that many of his ideas, controversial when first enunciated, have now become part of the "received tradition" among contemporary theologians. Like any living theology, Rahner's eschatology evolved and developed, although without any radical reversal, often in response to the signs of the times and to the criticisms of his peers. Operating initially within the narrow epistemological framework of transcendental Thomism, he gradually expanded his existentialist-individualist perspective to include interpersonal and socio-political dimensions of human existence. Any fair evaluation of Rahner's eschatology must take into account this development.

Perhaps Rahner's most valuable contribution to eschatology is providing it with a coherent anthropological framework and a christological focus. As has been mentioned above, for Rahner eschatology is anthropology conjugated in the future tense on the basis of what has occurred in Jesus. Thus, for example, his theology of death and eternity is rooted in his philosophy of human freedom and time, and his theology of resurrection in his anthropology of hope. On the other hand, because the divine self-communication reached its irreversible and victorious climax in Jesus of Nazareth, what happens in Jesus' death and resurrection can and must be applied to all humans in their final, still outstanding, fulfillment.

What is Rahner's strength may arguably be his limitation. Since his anthropology is basically transcendental Thomism, his eschatology, which is based upon it, is liable to the weaknesses this anthropology entails. For example, it has been pointed out that Rahner's brand of Thomism is too indebted to Hegelian and Kantian legacies to be able to incorporate fully biblical data on various eschatological themes. For instance, his notion of freedom as the capacity for definitive and final self-determination has been criticized for not giving full scope to the biblical understanding of sin.[30] This notion has also led to Rahner's endorsement of Gisbert Greshake's controversial theory of immediate resurrection in death and to the eclipse of the biblical teaching on the resurrection as an event at the end of time. Again, Rahner's transcendental philosophy of time and freedom has produced a too narrow understanding of eternity as definitive and final validity of history rather than as participation in the fullness of divine life. Another objection to Rahner's *anthropologische Wende* is that his concept of eschatology as an "extrapolation" into the future of what has already happened in human history does not leave much room for the *novum* of the still-to-be-realized kingdom of God. Whether or not these criticisms are fully justified, it is certain that the future of Rahner's eschatology is tied with the fortune of transcendental Thomism, in particular his anthropology of freedom and time.

On the other hand, it must be acknowledged that in several aspects Rahner's eschatology, despite its roots in transcendental anthropology, is able to engage in fruitful dialogue with contemporary theological movements such as liberation theology,[31] ecological theology,[32] the theology of universal restoration,[33] and interreligious dialogue.[34]

Whatever reservations against or endorsements for Rahner's eschatology, there is no gainsaying that he has brought eschatology from its long-occupied "appendix" status to the central position in Christian theology. This is evident in the way he formulated "brief creedal statements." Disclaiming any universality and binding force, Rahner proposed a three-part creed, the first called "theological," the second "anthropological," and the third "futurologist." It is the third part that is directly relevant to eschatology: "Christianity is the religion which keeps open the question about the absolute future, which gives itself in its own reality by self-communication, and which has established this will as eschatologically irreversible in Jesus Christ, and this future is called God."[35] In light of this creedal statement, humans are seen essentially as eschatological beings on a journey that will reach its end only in God who has bestowed Godself as the Absolute Future of the world, sustaining humans with his self-communication and luring them to enter God's eternal, trinitarian life.

Notes

1 For a brief summary of different eschatologies, see P. C. Phan, *Eternity in Time: A Study of Karl Rahner's Eschatology* (Selinsgrove: Susquehanna University Press, 1988), 26–31.

2 As is well known, Rahner's preferred genre is essay and not *summa*. Even *Foundations of Christian Faith* is not a synthesis of Rahner's theology. At any rate, as far as eschatology is concerned, its short chapter IX (431–47) cannot be regarded as a summary of Rahner's eschatology.

3 On the kind of theology Rahner studied in Valkenburg, see H. Vorgrimler, *Understanding Karl Rahner: An Introduction to His Life and Thought*, trans.

J. Bowden (New York: Crossroad, 1986), 52–58. Rahner himself calls this period of the Church after Leo XIII "integralism" and "Pian monolith" ("Pian" referring to Popes Pius IX [d. 1878] – Pius XII [d. 1958]).

4 In terms of content, Rahner said in 1959 that what was given in neo-scholastic eschatology represented "at most one tenth of what we could learn from revealed sources," and in terms of method, he observed that we had "no work, at least no exact, thorough and patient work, on the rules of interpretation of eschatological utterances in the revealed sources." See "The Prospects for Dogmatic Theology," *TI* I, 11–12; *LThK* III, 1094–98; *SM* II, 242–46; and "The Second Vatican Council's Challenge to Theology," *TI* IX, 19–20. For an extended analysis of Rahner's critique of neo-scholastic eschatology, see Phan, *Eternity in Time*, 19–23, 215–21.

5 "Reflections on Methodology in Theology," *TI* XI, 98. This transcendental eschatology, as will be shown in the course of the essay, requires both the treatment of themes neglected by the neo-scholastic manuals and an explicit hermeneutics for interpreting the statements of Scripture and Tradition on the afterlife.

6 On this double self-transcendence of the human person as spirit-in-world, see A. Tallon, "Personal Becoming," *The Thomist* 43/1 (1979), 1–177.

7 "Reflections on the Unity of the Love of Neighbour and the Love of God," *TI* VI, 231–49.

8 See "The Hermeneutics of Eschatological Assertions," *TI* IV, 326–46, and Phan, *Eternity in Time*, 64–76, 228–30.

9 See *FCF*, 433: "Eschatological statements are a transposition into the future of something which a Christian person experiences in grace as his present." Rahner distinguishes between "apocalyptic" and "eschatology": the former "projects something from the future into the present," whereas in the latter "in man's experience of himself and of God in grace and in Christ we project our Christian present into its future" (ibid., 432).

10 "The Hermeneutics of Eschatological Assertions," *TI* IV, 343–44.

11 See K. Rahner, *On the Theology of Death*, trans. C. H. Henkey and W. J. O'Hara (Burns and Oates: London, 1962). Note that this book originated as an essay published in 1949. For an extensive discussion of Rahner's theology of death, see Phan, *Eternity in Time*, 79–115, 230–36.

12 *FCF*, 435–36.

13 "Theological Considerations Concerning the Moment of Death," *TI* XI, 317.

14 In this connection Rahner proposes the hypothesis of "pancosmicity," that is, in death the soul acquires a new and more comprehensive relationship to the world: it becomes all-cosmic (*all-kosmisch*). Later Rahner abandons his hypothesis of pancosmicity in favor of Gisbert Greshake's hypothesis of immediate resurrection after death. On Rahner's hypothesis of the pancosmicity of the soul, see Phan, *Eternity in Time*, 85–88.

15 *FCF*, 437.

16 Rahner, *On the Theology of Death*, 87.

17 *FCF*, 437.

18 For further discussion of Rahner's concept of eternity, see Phan, *Eternity in Time*, 53–58.

19 "'The Intermediate State'," *TI* XVII, 114–24.

20 For Rahner's discussion of the intermediate state, see Phan, *Eternity in Time*, 116–22.
21 *FCF*, 442.
22 Ibid. See also "Purgatory," *TI* xix, 181–93 and his several essays on indulgences.
23 J. Neuner and J. Dupuis, eds., *The Christian Faith in the Doctrinal Documents of the Catholic Church* (New York: Alba House, 2001), 1019.
24 "The Eternal Significance of the Humanity of Jesus for Our Relationship with God," *TI* iii, 41.
25 See Rahner, *The Trinity*, trans. J. Donceel (New York: Crossroad, 1997; orig. 1967), 91–98.
26 For a discussion of Rahner's theology of heaven, see Phan, *Eternity in Time*, 136–49.
27 K. Rahner, "Hell," *SM*, iii, 7.
28 For Rahner's discussion of hell, see Phan, *Eternity in Time*, 149–52.
29 *FCF*, 446.
30 See R. Highfield, "The Freedom to Say 'No'? Karl Rahner's Doctrine of Sin," *Theological Studies* 56 (1995), 485–505 and P. C. Phan, "Is Karl Rahner's Doctrine of Sin Orthodox?" *Philosophy & Theology* 9/1–2 (1995), 223–36.
31 See M. H. Díaz, *On Being Human: U.S. Hispanic and Rahnerian Perspectives* (Maryknoll, NY: Orbis, 2001).
32 See P. Geister, *Aufhebung zur Eigentlichkiet: Zur Problematik kosmologischer Eschatologie in der Theologie Karl Rahners* (Stockholm: Uppsala University, 1996).
33 See M. Ludlow, *Universal Salvation: Eschatology in the Thought of Gregory of Nyssa and Karl Rahner* (Oxford: Oxford University Press, 2000).
34 See J. Dupuis, *Toward a Christian Theology of Religious Pluralism* (Maryknoll, NY: Orbis, 1997).
35 *FCF*, 457.

Further reading

Ludlow, M., *Universal Salvation: Eschatology in the Thought of Gregory of Nyssa and Karl Rahner* (Oxford: Oxford University Press, 2000).

Phan, P., *Eternity in Time: A Study of Karl Rahner's Eschatology* (Selinsgrove: Susquehanna University Press, 1988).

Rahner, K., *On the Theology of Death*, trans. C. H. Henkey and W. J. O'Hara (London: Burns and Oates, 1962).

"The Hermeneutics of Eschatological Assertions," *TI* iv, 323–46.

"Marxist Utopia and the Christian Future of Man," *TI* vi, 59–68.

"Eternity from Time," *TI* xix, 169–77.

Part III

Conversations Ongoing

12 Rahner amid modernity and post-modernity
MICHAEL PURCELL

RAHNER AS A MODERN THEOLOGIAN

Rahner has "modern" credentials. Following Maréchal, he seeks to overcome the constraints which the Enlightenment project placed upon knowledge. The former ontological critique was displaced by the transcendental critique of the Enlightenment, and it was no longer possible to give an account of exteriority other than in terms of the subject. As Maréchal notes, "the ancient critique posits the ontological object, which *includes* the transcendental subject; whereas the modern critique relates to the transcendental subject, who *posits* the ontological object."[1] If, in modernity, the concern was the constituting role of the epistemic subject in knowing and the concomitant problem of the ontological status of the object, the problem in post-modernity is the displacement of the stable subject, now viewed not simply as constituting and constructing but also as constituted and constructed, and the concomitant return of the object whose exteriority disturbs and disrupts subjective frameworks and horizons. Said otherwise, the post-modern concern is for fragmented subjectivity or interiority and the return of objectivity or exteriority, and the challenge which these present to enlightened transcendentalism.

Now, Rahner himself admits "the principle that *every* philosophy, i.e. every genuine metaphysics worthy of the name must proceed along the lines of transcendental philosophy, or else it is not philosophy in this authentic sense at all."[2] For "transcendental," the "phenomenological" – which can be viewed as a continuation of the project of modernity – can also be imputed. How then might one read Rahner otherwise without such a reading being other than Rahner, and read in such a way that the orientation, or intentionality, of the Rahnerian subject toward mystery is more exposed? Such an intentionality, which is an *excessus* toward an excessive alterity, finds its counterpart in Marion's notion of the "excess" or the "saturated phenomenon." Such a reading of Rahner will push the transcendental reduction beyond and otherwise than the limits which transcendental subjectivity imposes, and by way of the intersubjective.

CRITICIZING RAHNER'S TRANSCENDENTALISM

Rahner's transcendentalism is an obvious point of departure for a reconsideration of Rahner as a thoroughly "modern" theologian. It establishes him as a theologian of the Enlightenment as, following Maréchal, he attempts to exceed the Kantian critique. Joseph O'Leary remarks that Rahner's use of the transcendental method can be seen "as representing the *ne plus ultra* of theological enlightenment."[3] Yet, O'Leary notes, Rahner tends to make the transition "from everyday reality to the infinite mystery of God" with an "assurance" which brings together the theological, the transcendental, and the phenomenological without a rigorous phenomenological method. O'Leary asks "whether the sturdy and opaque texture of the world can be so easily transcended towards its infinite foundations," and whether "the transcendental logic which engineers the transition" is reliable. Rahner's theology mystifies. It "goes hand in hand with the ahistorical mystification of his transcendentalism" by which transcendental subjectivity is absolved from practical engagement in the world and removes the human person's transcendental concerns somewhat from the flesh. In fact, Rahner tends to convince "by the appeal of his metaphysical convictions" rather than "by a concord between these convictions and the phenomenality of human existence," and his "phenomenological fleshing out of the transcendental deduction . . . always comes after the speculative fact, a varnish on its bareness . . ." Rahner displays a lack of "phenomenological restraint" and "phenomenological precision," and Rahner's subject "never becomes the focus of an autonomous phenomenological enquiry." Rahner's "transcendental system steals the show from the data and robs them of their intrinsic meaning" on account of '[t]he chronic ineffectiveness of Rahner's gestures towards phenomenology [which] can only be explained by a reluctance to relinquish the mastery over experience which his categories promise."[4] O'Leary certainly has a point. Rahner does gesture toward phenomenology, and his transcendental reduction is insufficiently intersubjective, at least with regard to its method.

Now, one can almost hear sounding in the background Dominique Janicaud's criticism of the "theological turn in French phenomenology" and the uneasy copulation of phenomenology and theology which brings forth an illegitimacy which is neither phenomenological nor theological.[5] Janicaud's criticism is directed against such phenomenological transgressors as Jean-Luc Marion, Michael Henry, and Emmanuel Levinas, but one can imagine Rahner as a prefigurement of such a criticism. For Janicaud, *"phenomenology is not theology."* They are always two, and never one. For Janicaud, phenomenology began to lose its way and depart from its disciplined and scientific Husserlian rigor when it lapsed into the existential, although this was perhaps an original failing implicated in the Husserlian project. For Janicaud, Sartre's *Transcendence of the Ego* marked an abandonment of phenomenology as a scientific discipline. Sartre "turn[ed] resolutely towards politics and an ethics of engagement" for Husserl's phenomenology was altogether too abstract, "too detached from concrete situations and socio-political struggles."[6] (Heaven forbid that either phenomenology or theology might have anything to do with the human existential!) Thus Janicaud is critical of the "philosophical aplomb" with which writers such as Levinas, Marion, and Henry affirm notions which are phenomenologically unsustainable within the narrow confines of scientific discipline and rigor. These "take liberties" with Husserl and exploit the notion of "overflowing the intentional horizon."[7] For example, the "aplomb of alterity" by which Levinas' phenomenological reduction proceeds "supposes a . . . nonphenomenological, metaphysical desire," "a metaphysico-theological montage, prior to philosophical writing," and "faith rises majestically in the background." Phenomenology's place as a "first science" is usurped and there is the theological traduction of phenomenology for pedagogical and apologetic ends, and the restoration of theology "in the most intimate dwelling of consciousness."[8] All of this seems terribly post-modern, and places in question phenomenological and theological method, and the very notion of "foundations." And, as the psalmist says, "foundations once destroyed, what can the just do?" (Psalm 11:3).

The problem of the relation between phenomenology and theology is the difficulty of intersubjective reduction, which is also the post-modern difficulty of locating a subject who might be subjected to a reduction. The place of the subject is always elsewhere, even though the "here" of consciousness is always the transcendental and phenomenological point of departure. Jeffrey Kosky, reflecting on Levinas' phenomenology of excess, summarizes well when he sounds against Janicaud's sounding:

A broader range of phenomena appear within [the] subject than its previous figure (consciousness). These phenomena include religious meanings that have traditionally been consigned to the unintelligibility of faith or else reduced to the intentions (conscious and unconscious) of the self. I argue that Levinas's ethical philosophy can be applied to a philosophy of religion which relieves theological thought of sacrificing the significance of religious notions at the threshold of intelligibility and understanding. This philosophy of religion gives significance to religious meanings by reducing them to the responsible subject where they appear. Achieved through a reduction to subjectivity, the significance of religion is accessible to those not committed to a particular religious tradition.[9]

RAHNER AND PHENOMENOLOGY

Now, this phenomenological excursus may seem to be a digression from Rahner. But it is worth reading again Rahner's *Hearer of the Word*, the subtitle of which is *Laying the Foundations for a Philosophy of Religion*. Rahner asks the question "What do we mean by philosophy of religion?"[10] The answer unfolds as a theological anthropology which is transcendental, existential, and phenomenological. The question is "How does one do theology today?" It starts from the phenomenological presupposition that, before ever it is the question of God, theology is the question about the one who is able to raise the question of God, and for whom such a question might possibly have significance. For Rahner, an existential theology would proceed from "below" to "above." In other words, it would take its point of departure in the human person, for whom faith and believing is a particular intentionality that gives a particular way of access to an exteriority which nonetheless can only ever be grasped or pre-grasped (*Vorgriff*) in terms of the human existential. Faith is a method of understanding; it is an access which encounters excess. This is the contemporary phenomenological problem. How does one attempt an adequate account of the phenomenon which is "phenomenal," which is the phenomenological aporia of the excess, or the saturated phenomenon? Rahner's analysis proceeds by way of a reduction which, though attempting a reduction of the "here" of consciousness that is transcendental, is actually phenomenological and existential. *Hearer of the Word* takes its theological point of departure in "a study of the believer" and aims at "a metaphysical analysis of 'natural' humanity," an analysis which cannot proceed "without touching on some of the most existential concerns of the human person." It is a reduction whose movement is "from ourselves and our natural knowledge, not to supernatural theology ... but to an analysis of our capacity of hearing God's revelation, a capacity that makes fully actualised human beings of us." Thus, "the philosophy of religion becomes the sole possible natural foundation for theology." Philosophy of religion, properly understood, becomes the "only pre-theological way of grounding theology."[11]

Now, O'Leary's somewhat harsh criticism of Rahner focuses on the adequacy or otherwise of a transcendental approach to the human existential. But is such a criticism wholly legitimate? Anne Carr's study of Rahner's theological method[12] opens the way to a more post-modern appreciation of Rahner's thinking. Rahner's concern with the human existential always and already goes beyond and calls into question a narrow transcendentalism, incarcerated in its Kantian confines. Carr indicates the threefold problematic which confronts any attempt at "an expository and interpretative analysis of the theology of Karl Rahner" and "his characteristic way of doing theology,"[13] indicating that the difficulty with Rahner's theological method

> is *foundational* in that it raises the question of the point of departure
> for theology, whether and in what way that grounding lies in concrete
> experience and thought. It is, implicitly at least, *philosophical*, calling
> for analysis of all that is presupposed about the human situation in
> any theological affirmation. It is, finally, a *methodological* problem for
> it asks how theology is to be done in the light of what is thus known
> about human persons and their world.[14]

What Carr points to is the need for any theology to be phenomenologically adequate, both in respect of its method and its object. Rahner's own method and style of doing theology "in the light of what is . . . known about human persons and their world" provides the beginnings of a resolution to the foundational (phenomenological) and philosophical (transcendental) problematic, and enables his thought to be advanced beyond the captive fetters of the transcendental method as he makes use of it.

FROM INTERIORITY TO EXTERIORITY (OR, A DEFENSE OF INTERIORITY ON THE BASIS OF EXCESSIVE EXTERIORITY)

The danger of reading Rahner as a "modern" theologian is that there is the presumption of an overarching transcendental method and structure which unites and synthesizes his work. Such a reading would rely heavily on *Spirit in the World* and *Hearer of the Word*. Another reading, it seems to me, can be suggested which is more in line with Rahner's theological practice. On being asked whether there might be "a short formula for what you [i.e. Rahner] propose to accomplish with your theology," Rahner responded:

> My life work, if we can call it that, has had no plan, proposed in advance, but was strongly influenced by the needs of the day, by the tasks I had as a professor, and so on. If you look at the twenty volumes of my *Theological Investigations*, you will see that they are made up of individual articles, which were mostly lectures originally.[15]

It is from Rahner's various individual "theological investigations" which respond to the fragmented "needs of the day" that his theological method is to be gleaned.

Existence in the face of excess: the supernatural existential and the saturated phenomenon

Spirit in the World and *Hearer of the Word* can be read as philosophical works which lay the foundation for a metaphysics and a theology, and here is the difficulty for those who might read these "philosophical works" as a propaedeutic for understanding Rahner's theology. Carr admits that she had to reach Rahner's method "by inference from his writings on more particular topics,"[16] and that *Spirit* and *Hearer* are, in fact, "a theology which looks like philosophy."[17] *Spirit* and *Hearer* may be considered as Rahner's initial word on his theological project but they are certainly not his last. In fact, considered in the context of his later thinking in which transcendental *experience* and the supernatural *existential* are stressed, one can ask whether in fact *Spirit* and *Hearer* should be considered as an initial word and not a particular response conditioned by a particular Kantian philosophical problematic. Beyond the transcendental framework of *Spirit* and *Hearer*, what one reads is not so much a concern to fit the human existential into a transcendental structure and system which then becomes a theological stricture; rather, there is a concern with the failure of theology to concern itself with the *hearer* of the word, with the one who is open to a possible revelation.[18] Certainly, this is a transcendental reduction, but perhaps a reduction which, like Husserl's, halts too soon. It stops *before* it reaches the other person. Nonetheless, it is a thinking which is always done before, or in the face of, the other person, and attempts to respond to "the needs of the day."

How then might one go beyond Rahner without having to say that "this is no longer Rahner"?

Let us note that in moving beyond the project undertaken in *Spirit* one begins to speak more in terms of the "hearer of revelation" rather than the "transcendental subject," even though the transcendental concern remains. The post-modern question is both the declension and the conjugation of the subject. In fact, by the time we reach *Foundations* in 1976, which is perhaps his late attempt at a theological system, Rahner draws attention to the fact of "pluralism in contemporary theology and philosophy" and "an interdisciplinary fragmentation in theology" such that

> we have not only a pluralism of philosophies which can no longer be integrated by a single individual, but in addition to this we have the fact that philosophies no longer furnish the only self-interpretation of man that is significant for theology . . . [T]heologians today . . . must necessarily enter into dialogue with a pluralism of historical, sociological, and natural sciences, a dialogue no longer mediated by philosophy.[19]

Foundations then unfolds as reflection on the human existential – a theological anthropology – which considers "the hearer of the message," the person "in the presence of Absolute Mystery," human finitude and guilt, before a consideration of salvation and revelation in Christ Jesus. In other words, the theological endeavor is one centered less on an *ego cogito*, and more one which is embraced by the dialogic capacity of the human person.

Now, the very notion of "hearer" presupposes one who is addressed by another who speaks first. In fact, by approaching the question of the human person and philosophy of religion as "the Ontology of the '*Potentia Oboedientialis*' for Revelation,"[20] Rahner has already introduced at the beginning of his inquiry the possibility of a way beyond an ontology of transcendental subjectivity through the notion of revelation, which involves a further inter-subjective reduction which considers the transcendental constitution of the subject as an openness to alterity, or otherness. The "subject is fundamentally and by its very nature pure openness for absolutely everything . . ."[21] In terms of *Spirit* and *Hearer*, what *Hearer* actually does to *Spirit* is to alter the declension of the subject from "*I*" to "*me*." The nominative of speaking the question with its immediacy and intransitivity becomes the accusative of hearing which is always mediate and transitive. The solitary subject seeking within itself the transcendental source of its question becomes the one that discovers itself *always and already to be*, prior to its own initiative, the subject of an address. The subjectivization of the subject is always and already a subjection to a prevenient other who, speaking first, enables speaking as response. More, subjectivity is construed in a different syntactical *voice*, more passive than active.

Now, Carr identifies three interrelated stages of development in Rahner's "characteristic method of thought." First, *Spirit* retrieves the Thomistic metaphysics of knowledge to demonstrate "the dialectic unity and interdependence of knowledge of the world and metaphysical knowledge in human performance."[22] It marks a movement "from an analysis of the performance of knowing into a metaphysics which encompasses more than knowledge." Although considered as a knowing subject, the subject's stretching beyond itself in the *Vorgriff* becomes "a movement of the total human spirit in its dimensions of cognition and striving," a movement "beyond the concept to experience."[23] The method which is glimpsed in *Spirit* is "basically a Kantian transcendental reflection." However, it gives equal emphasis to reduction and deduction, and it is the emphasis on the reduction of human *experience* which enables an egress from the confines of Kant's transcendental ego. "The empirical reality is analysed to show what is involved a priori; the a priori is explicated in order to state more precisely the structure of the empirical experience." *Spirit*, however, halts at the transcendental ego, and does not advance into the intersubjective.

A second stage is developed in *Hearer*. Human historicity becomes "the locus of the metaphysical question," "the place where a possible revelation might occur," for "the question of the human knower reveals not only the openness and hiddenness of being but also the historicity and freedom of human existence."[24] This means that *Hearer* is actually developed as a *philosophy of religion*. The presupposition is that it is possible to show that "listening for a possible command of God somehow belongs to human nature and really is *human* knowledge . . ." *Hearer* thus becomes "an analytic of human being (*menschlichen Seins*) as that which has the capacity to hear a revelation,"[25] as "a positive openness for a possible revelation," and this is achieved by a "transcendental reflection on the conditions for the possibility of revelation."[26]

A third stage can be identified which progresses the project of *Hearer* beyond the limited concern with knowledge into the human dimensions of willing and loving, and which enables us "to follow the development of his theological work to determine his understanding of the foundation for theology, for only in this way will his theological method be understood, not as something totally worked out beforehand and then applied to various aspects of theology, but as a method which emerges in the course of concrete theological refection."[27] This third stage is the concern with the *supernatural existential*.

What is significant about the supernatural existential is the dimension of exteriority it introduces into the constitution of subjectivity. For example, writing on "The Theological Nature of Concupiscence," Rahner stresses that the movement out of oneself toward an absolutely other is "a real onto-logical human existential which qualifies him really and intrinsically" and which "is already present in the concrete, historical order."[28] Speaking of "The Dignity and Freedom of Man" at the Austrian *Katholikentag* in 1952, he stressed that the human person is *already beyond himself* in grace and that humanity "is called to direct personal communion with God in Christ, perennially and inescapably," "is addressed by the personal revelation of the Word of God in saving history which finds its climax in Jesus Christ," and "is unquestionably situated within the offer of his interior, saving and divin-ising grace." Humanity "possesses an ontic and spiritual-personal capacity for communicating with Jesus Christ in whom God has forever made the countenance of man his own and has opened the reality of man, with an unsurpassable finality, in the direction of God."[29] Similarly, in "Experience of the Spirit and Existential Commitment," the point is made that this super-natural ordering of the human person is not only constitutive of the person, but is something which is *given* to the person. "The gift of grace through the Spirit of God is in the first instance a genuine self-communication of God to the transcendent human self and not an internal or external categorial reality of human consciousness, material, as it were, for free decisions of the human person."[30] In other words, exteriority is affirmed in its excess to consciousness, and might possibly open the way to "a defence of interiority on the basis of exteriority."

In other words, Rahner, in practice, achieves an egress from the nar-row confines of transcendental subjectivity by way of an ongoing transcen-dental reduction. Already the limits of the *ego cogito* have been breached, for there is "the radical re-ordering of his transcendent nature in knowl-edge and freedom towards the immediate reality of God through God's self-communication in grace" which becomes "a constitutive element in human transcendence." "Experience of the Spirit is experience of the radical and per-manent nature of human transcendence, which goes beyond itself towards God because it is constantly impelled by his self-communication."[31] Such a shift in perspective from *Spirit* through *Hearer* to the notion of the supernat-ural existential, which is a gradual and reductive move from interiority to exteriority, might be termed also a move from modernity to post-modernity.

We need to take this further and perhaps give some post-modern legit-imacy to what is being said.

FRAGMENTS AND FOUNDATIONS

The notion of "fragment" is quite post-modern. One speaks of the frag-mentation of society, the fragmented self. Fragments result from a whole being shattered; fragments are the remainders left over after a whole has been constructed or reconstructed. But fragments have their own force and present a particular challenge to the whole.

Maurice Blanchot considers the significance of the fragment in his reflection on the notion of the *ensemble*. The fragment can have a "shattering" (*éclatement*) effect on the whole. What is a fragment? The fragment is usually considered as a part of a whole, and its significance is understood in terms of, or in view of, the whole. However, a fragment does violence to the whole. It has its own significance which the whole cannot encapsulate or comprehend.

> Whoever says fragment ought not say simply the fragmenting of an already existent reality or the moment of a whole still to come. This is hard to envisage due to the necessity of comprehension according to which the only knowledge is knowledge of the whole, just as sight is always a view of the whole. For such comprehension, the fragment supposes an implied designation of something that has previously been or will subsequently be a whole – the severed finger refers back to the hand.[32]

What Blanchot is drawing attention to is the significance of the fragment beyond the whole, and the capacity of the fragment to disrupt the continuity of the whole. It is a "piece of meteor detached from an unknown sky and impossible to connect with anything that can be known."[33]

Attention has already been drawn to Rahner's recognition of "the interdisciplinary fragmentation in theology,"[34] and to his acknowledgment that the volumes of his *Theological Investigations* comprise individual talks and lectures which sought to respond to the needs of the day. The question of fragments and foundations can be expressed in terms of two opposing demands: the modern demand of continuity, which is synthesis and system, and the (post-)modern demand of discontinuity, which is attentive to the particular and the fragmented. The Western philosophical (and theological) tradition has as its goal a Parmenidean synthetic and symphonic unity. However, Blanchot notes,

> When it is supposed (most often implicitly) that the real is continuous, and that only knowledge or expression would introduce discontinuity, it is first of all forgotten that the "continuous" is no more than a model, a theoretical form that, through this forgetting, passes for pure experience, pure empirical affirmation. But the

"continuous" is only an ideology that is ashamed of itself, just as empiricism is merely a knowledge that repudiates itself.[35]

Should the rending of this "beautiful seamless tunic" of a continuous Parmenidean reality be viewed as a failure of comprehension and synthesis? Or, instead, might not the proper question be: "[W]hy should not man, supposing that the discontinuous is proper to him and his work, reveal that the *ground of things* – to which he must surely in some way belong – has as much to do with the demand of discontinuity as it does with that of unity?" It may be that in human knowledge "an entirely different relation announces itself – a relation that challenges the notion of being as continuity or as a unity or gathering of beings."[36]

A similar insight is evident in Michel Foucault, who draws attention to the shift that has taken place in the understanding of history. Whereas previously, the analysis of historical events sought to link the disparate and the fragmentary by establishing a succession of causes and an overall significance, today the historian's task is less an attempt at continuity and more a concern to expose the discontinuities within total history. Similarly, in the history of Ideas, the attempt at grand narratives which seek to create "vast unities like 'periods' or 'centuries'" has given way "to the phenomena of rupture and discontinuity."[37] What strikes one now is interruption and discontinuity, which places in question such notions as "the teleology of reason," "the themes of convergence and culmination," and "the possibility of creating totalities." Since discontinuity has displaced "the privilege of continuity" and is now "one of the basic elements of historical analysis," "the theme and the possibility of a *total history*" which does not "draw all phenomena around a single centre" is dispersed into various relations and interplays.[38] In short, the whole having been fractured, the doctrine of continuity is now the new historical and philosophical heresy.

But theology also belongs to the history of Ideas. However, whereas its "modern" historical concern intended the continuity and integrity of orthodoxy and orthopraxis, theology today in post-modernity can perhaps be considered as a pursuit of discontinuities and their interruptive significance. Theology increasingly takes its point of departure from the margins, and from the marginalized – from places which theology did not previously inhabit, or venture into (except perhaps in its pastoral intersubjective dimensions: one thinks, for example, of Alphonsus Liguori's *Praxis Confessarii* and its manifest concern with the fragments of human existence). For the most part, theology sought systematic wholeness and achieved this by an exclusion of the heterodox and the heteropraxic. In short, theology was an onto-theo-logy and intended a continuity, and found it difficult to think of heterology, let alone accommodate heteronomy and heteropraxis. Thus, the theological system finds itself interrupted and disturbed by recent theologies, whether they are termed "liberation," "feminist," "post-colonial," or "queer." Modern theology finds the notion of the "strange" strange, and, paradoxically, though intending the Other *par excellence*, finds the otherness of the other person difficult to accommodate. Post-modern theology might be considered as a theology of the "strange," a heterology. As Blanchot would have it, "this other person is strangely mysterious (*Cet Autrui est étrangement mysterieux*)."[39] As Foucault notes, no longer is transcendental subjectivity the base which effects a continuity and synthesis of the disparate events of experience; now there are hidden forces and influences which not only disrupt subjectivity but also call into question the continuities that subjectivity manufactures. Yet, the *demand of continuity* is so pervasive that it is "[a]s if we were afraid to conceive of the *Other* in the time of our own thought"[40] and so had to "rethink the dispersion of history in the form of the same," and reduce difference to the same by pursuing "without discontinuity the endless search for the origin."[41]

THEOLOGY AS DISCOURSE AND CONVERSATION

Is Rahner, then, a theologian of the continuous or of the discontinuous? Blanchot notes the *demand of discontinuity* within thought (*La Pensée et l'exigence de discontinuité*), and "the idea of the fragment as a form of coherence."[42] For example, what kind of discourse is teaching? It is interrogative, where *interrogation* is taken not simply as an asking but a prayer or supplication (*rogare*) in the face of the other person. Language arises at the interface of two discontinuous and radically different subjectivities. Conversation is a conversion toward the other. Discourse, like Descartes's *Discourse on Method*, is an interrogative advance upon its object, a *dis-cursus*, a "*cours désuni et interrompu.*" Simply put, speech is always in the face of an other who is speaking's ability and provocation.

Consider, for example, the structure of Aquinas' *Summa Theologiae* which proceeds not by way of a continuous narrative, but by way of a questioning advance on particular topics. There is the constant rhythm of conversation: a question is given (the *quaestio*) and explored (the *videtur* and accompanying *praeterea*); there are the possible objections (*sed contra*), before a final response (*respondeo*), which in its turn opens onto another article (*articulum*) in which the questioning advance continues. Although perceived as an attempt at theological coherence and synthesis,

Aquinas' discourse is essentially a *dis-cursus* of propositions, objections, and responses.

Similarly, with Heidegger, the discontinuity of speaking is placed at the beginning of his interrogation of being, when, in 1929, he begins his inaugural lesson in Freiburg, interrogating his audience with the question, "What is metaphysics?" (*Was ist Metaphysik?*) The question is placed at the beginning. It is the point of departure.

Such an approach and method is also that of Rahner. Despite the structures and strictures of a transcendental method, Rahner's theological approach is more responsive to the demands of discontinuity rather than the demand of continuity. Although the attempt is often made to weave together his disparate *Theological Investigations* within his transcendental framework and find methodological coherence, his writings nevertheless are by way of response to the various pastoral and secular situations in which he finds himself. This is not to say that Rahner's theology is incoherent; rather, it proceeds by way of another method in which alterity is implicated from the first, though always in need of further reduction which ultimately ends as a *reductio in mysterium*.[43] Theology takes its point of departure from the questions of the moment – fragmented and fragmentary, theological and pastoral. The transcendental framework is not imposed from the beginning; rather, the transcendental approach, which is more phenomenological than conceptual, is in the service of the human *existentiell*, which opens onto a consideration of the human *existential*. For Rahner, it is the experience of the human and its involvement with the alterity of the other which orients his theology. Like the fragmentary, the quotidian encounter with the exteriority of the other person, and ultimately the Other *par excellence*, brings about a shattering of the totality. Although, for Rahner, the orientation toward the other is expressed in terms of *being*, his transcendental and phenomenological advances on *being*, like those of Husserl, do not "constitute the ultimate event of being itself" for, as Levinas would say, *beyond being*, there is already a situation – an *ethical* encounter in which the hegemony of being has been shattered.[44] The "break up of the formal structure of thought" into events which "restore its concrete significance" is a deduction that is not guided by the ideal of objectivity which animates theoretical thought. Rather, it pursues a *transcendent intention*, outside of the *noesis-noema* structure of intentionality within which Husserlian phenomenology was confined. Thus is the strictly scientific character of phenomenology which Janicaud espouses, for example, exceeded by such as Marion, Henry, Levinas, and, one might suggest, Rahner, for whom the reduction is a reduction which verges on the absolute mystery of the other, and who can only ever be approached asymptotically. Thus is Husserlian phenomenological method exceeded, but on the basis of Husserl, as the concrete experience of the other perturbs a consciousness for which the theoretical is existentially inadequate and incomplete. As Levinas notes, "Husserlian phenomenology has made possible this passage from ethics to metaphysical exteriority."[45]

THE REDUCTION TO MYSTERY

For Rahner, the *reductio in mysterium* "expresses a methodological pointer for the theologian" and is in fact "the condition which makes all the perceptions available to the human reason possible"; indeed, theology "is to be understood as the 'science' of mystery as such." Although the methods employed by theology "apply first and foremost in the particular concrete situation of the individual" and do "not lay any claim to any permanent or universal validity," the particular concrete situation, transcendentally reduced, reveals the subject as an orientation toward mystery as such, and this mystery, "radically beyond all comprehension," is the horizon which "makes knowledge possible within its ambience, this ultimate point of reference towards which all knowledge tends." The relation to mystery, then, is the possibility condition of knowledge:

> [T]he *mysterium* reveals itself as the condition which makes it possible for us to know that which is not mysterious. The relationship in which man stands to the *mysterium* is a primary and ultimate datum of his own nature and his mode of existence, one of which, in his transcendence, he is constantly aware, though not as the object of his conscious thought, and one which cannot be deduced from any other datum as a secondary phenomenon.[46]

Again, "reason must be understood more fundamentally as precisely the capacity of the incomprehensible, as the capacity of being seized by what is always insurmountable, not essentially as the power of comprehending, of gaining the mastery and subjugating. Reason must be understood . . . as the capacity of *excessus*, as going out into the inaccessible. . . ."[47] What Rahner points to is the responsive movement of subjectivity, or subject as response to exteriority. Said otherwise and perhaps more theologically, the subject is constituted as a moment and movement of grace, which is always prevenient and which cannot be comprehended. The mystery of the other ensures the subject as a constant dynamic movement beyond itself.

And thus does the incomprehensible excess of the other provoke the movement (*excessus*) of the subject beyond itself. And thus, as Levinas argues, does interiority find its defense on the basis of an excessive exteriority.

Notes

1 J. Maréchal, *Le point de départ de la métaphysique* (Brussels: Editions Universelles, 1947), 69.
2 "Reflections on Methodology in Theology," *TI* xi, 85.
3 J. O'Leary, *Questioning Back: The Overcoming of Metaphysics in the Tradition* (Minneapolis: Seabury, 1985), 97.
4 Ibid., 88, 97, 89, 11, 90, 95, and 91.
5 See Janicaud's essay "The Theological Turn in French Phenomenology," in D. Janicaud et al., eds., *Phenomenology and the Theological Turn: The French Debate* (New York: Fordham University Press, 2001), 3–105.
6 Ibid., 22.
7 Ibid., 26.
8 Ibid., 27.
9 J. Kosky, *Levinas and the Philosophy of Religion* (Bloomington: Indiana University Press, 2001), xix.
10 *HW*, 1.
11 Ibid., 1, 6–9.
12 A. Carr, *The Theological Method of Karl Rahner* (Missoula: Scholars Press, 1977).
13 Ibid., vii.
14 Ibid., 2.
15 *Karl Rahner in Dialogue: Conversations and Interviews 1965–1982*, trans. and ed. H. Biallowons, H. D. Egan, S.J., and P. Imhof, S.J. (New York: Crossroad, 1986), 334.
16 B. Lonergan, "A Response to Father Dych's 'Method in Theology According to Karl Rahner'," in W. J. Kelly, ed., *Theology and Discovery* (Milwaukee: Marquette University Press, 1980), 54.
17 Carr, *Theological Method*, 4.
18 Ibid., 2.
19 *FCF*, 8.
20 *HW*, 1.
21 *FCF*, 20.
22 Carr, *Theological Method*, 59.
23 Ibid., 86.
24 Ibid., 87, 60, 88.
25 *HW*, 18–19, 33.
26 Carr, *Theological Method*, 92–93.
27 Ibid., 107.
28 "The Theological Concept of Concupiscence," *TI* i, 376.
29 "The Dignity and Freedom of Man," *TI* ii, 240–41.
30 "Experience of the Spirit and Existential Commitment," *TI* xvi, 24.

31 Ibid., *TI* xvi, 27–28, 26, 28.
32 M. Blanchot, *The Infinite Conversation* (Minnesota: University of Minnesota Press, 1993), 307.
33 Ibid., 308.
34 *FCF*, 8.
35 Blanchot, *Infinite Conversation*, 437, n. 7.
36 Ibid., 309, 310.
37 M. Foucault, *The Archaeology of Knowledge* (London: Routledge, 1989), 4.
38 Ibid., 7–10.
39 Blanchot, *Infinite Conversation*, 52.
40 Foucault, *Archaeology of Knowledge*, 12.
41 Ibid., 21.
42 Blanchot, *Infinite Conversation*, 4.
43 "The Concept of Mystery in Catholic Theology," *TI* iv, 62.
44 E. Levinas, *Totality and Infinity* (The Hague: M. Nijhoff, 1979), 28.
45 Ibid., 29.
46 "Reflections on Methodology in Theology," *TI* xi, 101, 75, 104, 105.
47 "The Human Quest for Meaning in the Face of the Absolute Mystery of God," *TI* xviii, 97.

Further reading

Bacik, J., *Apologetics and the Eclipse of Mystery: Mystagogy according to Karl Rahner* (Notre Dame: University of Notre Dame Press, 1980).
Egan, H. E., *Karl Rahner: Mystic of Everyday Life* (New York: Crossroad, 1998).
Lennan, R., *The Ecclesiology of Karl Rahner* (London: Clarendon Press, 1997).
Losinger, A., *The Anthropological Turn: The Human Orientation of the Theology of Karl Rahner* (New York: Fordham University Press, 2000).
Pekarske, D. T., "Abstracts of Karl Rahner's Theological Investigations, 1–23," *Philosophy and Theology* 14:1 & 2 (2002).
Rahner, K., *Hearer of the Word* (New York: Continuum, 1994).

13 Rahner's reception in twentieth century Protestant theology

NICHOLAS ADAMS

The following short essay will rehearse and critique one of the best-known Protestant engagements with Rahner: George Lindbeck's reading of Rahner in *The Nature of Doctrine*.[1] This admittedly falls some way short of a comprehensive account of "twentieth century Protestant theology." However, Lindbeck's criticisms of Rahner are probably the most important and most interesting, because of Lindbeck's influence upon Protestant theology, and because Lindbeck was an appreciative Protestant reader of Rahner.

Rahner has not been directly influential on Protestant theology, either dogmatic or philosophical, and in my judgment is unlikely to be in the future. This is not because Rahner is rejected in any emphatic way, or because his theology is deficient. It is for two reasons. One is that the problems Rahner tries to repair are often local problems: local to Roman Catholicism, and sometimes more specifically local to German Roman Catholicism. These local problems include, most obviously, questions of ecumenism (on the Catholic side) and questions of ecclesial authority. The second reason is that Rahner investigates the relationship between objective truth-claims and subjective experience, and the theories of truth with which he operates are no longer persuasive either to Catholics or Protestants. Whether one favours "linguistic" (Schleiermacher, Heidegger, Wittgenstein), or "pragmatic" (Peirce, Dewey, Rorty) tools, the theories of truth upon which Rahner depends fail to persuade contemporary theologians. Rahner is, like any theologian, a thinker of his age. Even Catholics who wish to learn from and use his theology will need to repair his philosophical apparatus.[2]

If Rahner's theology may not be directly influential on Protestant thought, his indirect influence is indisputable. Rahner is deeply concerned with questions of doctrinal development and revisability, especially in the context of his own tradition which uses adjectives like "irreformable" or "infallible" to describe the status of certain utterances or uttering bodies. This question is of interest to all theologians, even if the particular local context is not shared and thus not so urgent. George Lindbeck's short and sharp *The Nature of Doctrine* is explicitly worked out in response to Rahner's theology, and in a "companion" to Rahner of this kind is sufficiently important to merit rehearsal. The next generation of Protestant theologians are likely to encounter Rahner through Lindbeck, and it is thus important to know what kind of Rahner they are likely to meet.

I do not propose to defend Rahner against Lindbeck's criticisms. The question is not the defense but the *repair* of Rahner's philosophical shortcomings. By philosophical shortcomings I mean the technical apparatus he uses as "second-order" reflections upon doctrine, as opposed to the primary business of elaborating particular doctrines for particular historical purposes. An appropriate response to Lindbeck is not to try to undermine his attempts at repair, but to identify problems with Lindbeck's own approach, and to try to repair those. I shall not attempt that in this essay, however, as our focus is on the reception of Rahner; and our primary purpose is to understand how Lindbeck reads and corrects him. Nonetheless, I shall certainly try to assist the reader in determining whether Lindbeck's criticisms of Rahner hit the mark.

Lindbeck's own influence is due to his attempt to change how theologians from all Christian denominations think about doctrines. He has bequeathed two principal tools for doctrinal discussion: a threefold typology of doctrines, and the notion of a "rule theory" of doctrine. The threefold typology divides doctrinal accounts into "cognitive-propositional," "experiential-expressive" and "cultural-linguistic," and for Lindbeck all accounts of doctrine fall under one of these headings. The "rule theory" of doctrine is Lindbeck's preferred version of a "cultural-linguistic" account of doctrine. These terms will be explained in what follows. For the moment, the important point is that the reader of Lindbeck is invited to do three things: first, to accept that this threefold typology is adequate to all relevant cases; second, to accept the superiority of the "cultural-linguistic" model; third, to adopt a "rule theory" of doctrine as the most appropriate form of "cultural-linguistic" thinking. It is for this reason that terms like "cultural-linguistic" and "regulative" are interchangeable in his account. Lindbeck's reading of Rahner is placed in the service of this threefold invitation.

Lindbeck claims that Rahner's approach to doctrine is a combination of cognitive-propositional and experiential-expressive types. These are technical terms which need explaining. By cognitive-propositional, Lindbeck means a "preoccupation with the cognitive or informational meaningfulness of religious utterances." By "experiential-expressive," he means interpretations of doctrines as "noninformative and nondiscursive symbols of inner feelings, attitudes, or existential orientations."[3] The first is about information; the second is about feelings. To treat doctrine in a "cognitive-propositional" way is to think of doctrine as providing information that one does not already have. To treat doctrine in an "experiential-expressive" way is to think of doctrine as expressing inner feelings that are common to people. Lindbeck claims that these two approaches, which he distinguishes from each other, are combined in Rahner's work. Lindbeck reads Rahner's philosophical theology as an attempt to get beyond the opposition of these two types of approach, and he concedes that combining them really is an advance and an improvement. Nonetheless, Lindbeck insists that what is needed is a model that does not combine them, but overcomes the duality they express, even when combined, and this model he names "cultural-linguistic." This latter approach does not treat doctrines as propositional truth-claims, nor as expressions of inner psychic states, but as *grammars* for guiding practices of thought and action. To treat doctrines in a "cultural-linguistic" way is to think of doctrine not as specifying beliefs and actions but as *guides for communities to make judgments* about what they believe and what they should do. Lindbeck wants to do full justice to the fact that the historical circumstances in which Christians formulate their beliefs and justify their practices change radically over time and space. The "when and where" of Christian life is almost unrecognizably variable. For Lindbeck, doctrines are best seen as "rules" for guiding Christian thought and practice under different historical conditions. Lindbeck also wants to do justice to the Roman Catholic notion of "irreformability" or "infallibility." He does so by suggesting that while the historical conditions of Christian life, and thus the content of Christian beliefs and practices, change over time, some of the rules for guiding such beliefs and practices do not. Lindbeck has many examples to demonstrate and test this.[4]

Why should a "cultural-linguistic" model be necessary? After all, most philosophy since Kant has indeed struggled to do justice to "subjective" and "objective" dimensions of knowing and doing. *Subjective dimensions* draw attention to the role of the interpreting subject, who builds an ideal model of the world and places all particulars in this imagined whole. The subject is conscious of its own activity, is alert to the possibility that it might be deceived or deceive itself, and is spontaneous and free, at some basic level. It is also embroiled in philosophical conundrums relating to the impossibility of reflecting upon its own thinking while simultaneously doing that same thinking. *Objective dimensions* draw attention to the resistance that objects exercise on the subject. They stress the independence of systems of language, which transcend the subject, and insist on the fact that it is the world, and not some fantasy, that is interpreted by the subject. At their best, approaches to the objective dimension of experience stress the impossibility of grounding any metaphysical claims about "the world" or "language," while acknowledging that such forms of metaphysics are always already presupposed and operative in all forms of subjectivity. Subjective and objective dimensions cannot be separated from each other, because all objective dimensions are "thought" subjectively, and all subjective thoughts are "about" some object, and "formed" in some "objective" language. Nonetheless they can be distinguished for the purposes of analysis, and that is what most philosophies aim to do. To say that a "combination" of objective and subjective approaches is deficient would surely be a mistake.

Lindbeck's criticism of Rahner is *not* that Rahner combines objective and subjective approaches. This can be difficult to see in *The Nature of Doctrine* because of the use of terms like "propositional" and "experiential-expressive," which might seem to suggest that this is indeed the criticism. Rather, Lindbeck is critical of *certain ways of characterizing* the objective and subjective approaches. "Propositional" is not identical to "objective," and "experiential-expressive" is not identical to "subjective." Again, this can be difficult to see, not least because Lindbeck traces back "experiential-expressive" approaches to Schleiermacher, and associates "propositional" approaches with Anglo-American analytic philosophy. As any student of Schleiermacher or analytic philosophy should know, things are not so straightforward. Schleiermacher was a brilliant *critic* of the kind of thinking Lindbeck calls "experiential-expressive," especially in his hermeneutics and his dialectics. Analytic philosophy has itself frequently acknowledged the ways in which propositional models of truth fail to do justice to the range of truth-claims raised in ordinary language. Both these points have been persuasively argued, at length, by Andrew Bowie.[5] *The Nature of Doctrine* was published in 1984, at a time when these concerns were debated mostly only by specialists in these fields, and were not so widely known to theologians. One should perhaps make allowances for Lindbeck's rather hasty characterizations, and it is undoubtedly on this question that some repair of Lindbeck's thinking would need to take place. But do these observations ruin Lindbeck's reading of Rahner? We shall see.

Lindbeck's criticism of Rahner is that he combines propositional and experiential-expressive modes of philosophy, whereas what is needed is a "cultural-linguistic" model. He does not suggest that Rahner should himself have provided this. Such a claim would fail to take into account the philosophical tools available to Rahner in the 1960s. Instead, Lindbeck takes Rahner's thinking seriously, and tries to repair the problems that arise in it.

We need, therefore, to have a better idea about the two modes that Rahner allegedly combines, in order to determine whether Lindbeck is right that Rahner indeed combines them. Once this has been done, we can evaluate whether Lindbeck's criticisms are appropriate, and whether he does justice to Rahner's approach. It is quite possible, of course, that Lindbeck does not go far enough.

Lindbeck is not primarily concerned with Rahner. He is concerned with "doctrine," and his reading of Rahner is situated within this wider concern. Rahner thus serves as a "type" of approach. The reader needs warning of this, because Lindbeck's goal is not to produce a sensitive reading of Rahner, but to advance his own project over and against the "type" that Rahner embodies, at least in his view. This is a perfectly appropriate approach, given Lindbeck's own ends, but compensations would be needed if one *were* to do justice to Rahner's theology. For our purposes, we simply need to be aware that Lindbeck is not claiming to read Rahner attentively in *The Nature of Doctrine*; we would need to look elsewhere for that.

Lindbeck claims that propositional and experiential-expressive approaches do not share the field equally. He claims that propositional approaches have been dying out, and have found themselves on the defensive, whereas experiential-expressive approaches have been in ascendance, and are correspondingly confident.[6] His models for the cultural-linguistic approach are social anthropologists and sociologists, such as Clifford Geertz, Peter Winch, and Peter Berger. However, Lindbeck's actual practice is not to treat a linear development from propositional through experiential to cultural accounts of doctrine. Instead, he thinks of propositional approaches as deficient, and as raising the need for a different approach. Experiential approaches are one such different approach, but Lindbeck rejects them because "they make meaningless the historic doctrinal affirmations of unconditionality, irreversibility, or infallibility," and for this reason all the interesting debates Lindbeck wants to have with Roman Catholics simply disappear.[7] Cultural-linguistic or rule-theory approaches are another way of repairing problems with propositional thinking. For this reason it is arguably better to read Lindbeck as addressing the breakdown of propositional thinking and treating experiential-expressive and cultural-linguistic thinking as two rival responses to this breakdown. This, I think, does better justice to the fact that Lindbeck spends most of his time debating the problems of propositional thinking.

Lindbeck describes Rahner as a "two dimensional" existential-expressivist.[8] He attempts to do justice to two aspects that characterize Rahner's approach to religion. The first is his talk of "subjectivity" and "reflection." The second is his appeal to "transcendental experience." Lindbeck suggests that the themes of subjectivity and reflection deal with the question of *how traditions change* and produce many different regional ways of speaking; this gives rise to the existential-expressivist tendency. The theme of transcendental experience treats the question of *how a tradition is a unity over time*, rather than a series of discrete traditions; this gives rise to the propositional tendency.

Lindbeck's account is very abbreviated here, and it is worth expanding a little on Rahner's language, and the purpose it has in his thinking. Rahner has learned from Kant that any good account of judgment must acknowledge a turn to the subject. It is precisely the subject who judges; the subject is not an effect of the world, but an agent with its own spontaneity and freedom. To deny the turn to the subject is to deny the reality of freedom as in accounts like Spinoza's *Ethics*. Rahner has learned from Hegel that cultural values arise precisely within a culture, and that reflection on this state of affairs makes the subject aware that, because different cultures have different values, her own culture's values are relativized. This is familiar from Hegel's discussion of the "unhappy consciousness" in the *Phenomenology of Spirit*. The turn to the subject, and the result of reflection, are significant enough for Rahner that he begins his discussion in his *Foundations of Christian Faith* with an elaborate rehearsal of the main arguments.[9] At the same time, Rahner recognizes that these discussions cannot be adequate. There needs to be some way of acknowledging the *objective* dimensions of experience: otherwise there is no way to distinguish between a paranoid subject, which thinks only its own internal thoughts about its own internal world, and a being truly "in the world." Kant and Hegel do have resources for elaborating the objective aspect of experience. Kant talks about the "synthetic a priori" of concepts and the "thing in itself." Hegel identifies change as itself the changing of a self-identical Spirit, known in philosophy, whose self-consciousness takes the form of human thinking. However, these are not available to Rahner because he accepts Heidegger's critique of both Kant and Hegel. Heidegger subjects the turn to subjectivity and the logic of reflection to a critique whose basic insight is that beings in the world are conditioned by being that is in principle unknowable, and with which the subject is always already involved. Rahner is persuaded by this critique (having attended Heidegger's classes) but he adapts some of Heidegger's analysis of *Dasein* and casts it in Christian theological language. It is worth observing how this is undertaken.

First, Rahner gives an account rooted in the German philosophical tradition: "Man is a transcendent being insofar as all of his knowledge and all of his conscious activity is grounded in a pre-apprehension (*Vorgriff*) of 'being' as such, in an unthematic but ever-present knowledge of the infinity of reality."[10] This is a familiar strand of the tradition. It tries to articulate the conditions for thinking: What does there have to be, in order for people to be able to think at all? Rahner rehearses the approach he has learned from Heidegger. The conditions or "grounds" for thinking (the German *Grund* has a wide range of meanings including "reason," "condition," and "ground") are a prior grasping, at some level, of reality, which is not yet the explicit focus of thinking. The question, of course, is: What kind of grasp is this? Rahner takes an approach developed in scholastic philosophy and developed by Descartes and Leibniz. Roughly, the subject is finite, and yet is capable of grasping the idea of infinity. This idea cannot arise from something finite; nor can it arise from "nothing." It must therefore originate *outside* the subject. This is an argument famously developed in Descartes's *Meditations*. Rahner builds on this, in a manner typical of one strand of German philosophy, by insisting that although one has to acknowledge the ground of thinking as *external* to thinking, nonetheless it cannot be grasped conceptually in a manner *internal* to thinking. It remains at some level *unthinkable*. Rahner speaks of it as "never captured by metaphysical reflection," "approached asymptotically," a "secret ingredient," a "mystery."[11] This he learns from Heidegger, which in turn is developed from arguments in Schelling's *System of Transcendental Idealism*. The main point is that the "ground" of thinking is itself unthinkable, yet must be presupposed if one acknowledges that thinking nonetheless happens.

It is important to notice that Rahner speaks not only of a *Vorgriff* but of an *experience* of the ground of thinking. This is unusual. The classic figures in German philosophy from Kant to Heidegger would say that the subject "experiences" objects in the world, but "presupposes" or "posits" the ground of thinking. They would not say that one "experiences" the "ground." Rahner is innovating when he says "It is an *experience* because this knowledge . . . is a moment within and a condition of possibility for every concrete experience of any and every object."[12] Figures from Kant to Heidegger would claim that this makes no sense at all. It is true that the subject experiences objects. It is true that there must be a condition for that experience. It is true that the subject can, in philosophy, grasp that there must be such a condition. It is *false* to claim that, because the subject has this knowledge, the subject therefore experiences something. Quite the reverse: Such knowledge is purely speculative.

Whatever the sources for Rahner's claims, there are three important points. (1) The ground of thinking is external to the subject; (2) the ground of thinking is unthinkable; (3) the subject's activity is thus grounded objectively and obscurely.

We can now return to Lindbeck's critique. It is important to recognize that he could have chosen to criticize Rahner using the very tradition on which Rahner draws. There are, for example, critiques of Kant that draw on the significance of language (Herder, Hamann); there are critiques of Hegel that stress the "mystery" of grounds (Schelling, Schleiermacher).[13] Instead, Lindbeck identifies a question that for him nicely frames the matter: Does experience shape religion, or does religion shape experience? This is a "Which comes first?" kind of question. Rahner's argumentation *starts* with experience. More specifically, it opens with familiar arguments in German philosophy about the unthinkable ground of thinking, but with a distinctive (and strictly speaking meaningless) Rahnerian emphasis that one somehow "experiences" this unthinkable ground. It moves *subsequently* to identify religious practices as expressing this "transcendental experience" in particular cultural languages. Lindbeck reverses things. His argumentation *starts* with languages. More specifically, it suggests that people learn languages and through them come to describe the world to themselves and to each other. It moves *subsequently* to identify particular experiences which such languages make possible. Lindbeck thus denies that there can be any "transcendental experience" that can be discussed in advance of its possible expression in particular languages. Language comes first, and experience arises within an already learned language which itself shapes the experiences people have.

We can now see why Lindbeck finds fault with Rahner's combination of existential-expressivist and propositional approaches. On the existential-expressivist side, Rahner emphasizes the turn to the subject, and the relativity of cultural values. Lindbeck finds no fault with this. Instead, he draws attention to the fact that this cannot be satisfactory for Rahner: there needs to be an objective dimension. On the propositional side, Rahner speculates about a "transcendental experience." Lindbeck finds the fault precisely *here*. There is no such experience. What Lindbeck argues for in the light of this is a way beyond the two-dimensional combination of existential-expressivist and propositional arguments, toward one more firmly rooted in language, where there is neither objectivity beyond language, nor a subjectivity behind it.

Does Lindbeck do justice to Rahner? To ask this is different from asking whether Lindbeck's arguments against Rahner are sound. Lindbeck criticizes Rahner for combining cognitive-propositional with experiential-expressive approaches. But he does not ask *why* Rahner does so. Lindbeck might give the unwary reader the impression that there is a kind of *histori-cal progress* from cognitive-propositional, through experiential-expressive, through combinations of the two, to cultural-linguistic approaches. He cer-tainly claims that developments in social anthropology have not yet been assimilated by theologians.[14] In Rahner's case, however, things are not so simple. Rahner's situation was quite particular: Dominant voices in his tra-dition advocated a strong identification of church teaching with truth, which were couched in such a way as to imply that the *only* access to such truth was via acceptance of official church teaching. The problem with this is not that it is "cognitive-propositional" (which it is), but that it casts the truth-seeker as purely passive, and utterly reliant on an external source not only of authority but of truth itself. Rahner's so-called "transcendentalism" may be philosophically questionable, but it makes more sense when understood as a response to one-sidedly "external" models of truth. Rahner's "both-and" approach to subjective/objective dimensions in cognition and perception is not merely "an approach" to the question, but a thoughtfully worked-out response to a particular problem: the need to articulate the subjective dimension of experience of God in a context which heavily emphasizes the objective (ecclesial) mediation of that experience. Its philosophical short-comings are real, and thus stand in need of correction, but any serious engagement with their intent has to take into account their ecclesial con-text. Lindbeck's cultural-linguistic model is intended to assist in Rahner's project of casting Christians as active "hearers" and not just passive recipi-ents of official teaching. This dimension – the importance of active hearing – is arguably much more important than Rahner's failure as a "type" of second-order discourse about doctrine.

Properly to understand Rahner's approach in *Foundations*, one must pay attention to its wider purpose. It was published in 1976, and was designed not as a scholarly tome for theologians, but as an introductory book for young men entering the priesthood. Its explicit context is the need for accessible and reliable theological education in the wake of the Second Vatican Council, with the aim of addressing obstacles to theological learning that are commonly encountered among those training for ordi-nation. It is striking that although the early discussions carry the subtitle "Preliminary Remarks on Methodology," from the very first sentences it is obvious that the main problem the book addresses is not the need for yet another fundamental theology, but the existential needs of seminary students. Rahner complains that too many textbooks avoid confronting the difficulties faced by seminarians by focusing on dryly presented scholarly problems:

It is ridiculous for theology professors to set up as their highest ideal the attempt to demonstrate before the young theologians right at the beginning their scholarliness in the problematic of their learned discipline . . . They are too much scholarship for its own sake, they are too splintered and fragmented to be really able to respond in any adequate way to the personal situation of theology students today.[15]

This is striking enough, but it is even more remarkable when one draws attention to the fact that it is this situation that prefaces Rahner's concern with the "turn to the subject" and "transcendental experience" – a discussion that begins less than ten pages later. Rahner's purpose in using such concepts is to address a problem: "theology students today live in a situation of crisis for their faith."[16] What is this crisis? Rahner does not say directly, and this too is worth noticing. Rahner draws attention to problems that were familiar in the early 1970s: the fragmentation of theology into an unmanageably diverse field; the plurality of philosophical models which cannot be harmonized; the power of natural science as the dominant explanatory discourse for human life. These are not really a "crisis," however: they are part of the normal cultural background for discussion in any discipline at this time – not just theology. The crisis is left unspecified, and perhaps the reader is expected to know what is being referred to. Is it too bold to suggest that the crisis in question is the difficulty of knowing how to reconcile the demands of free theological inquiry with the requirements of ecclesial discipline in matters of teaching and learning? Perhaps it is against this background that Rahner seeks, in *Foundations*, to present a well-argued model of theological inquiry which addresses the needs of the wider Church, in both its dimensions of genuinely needed ecclesial discipline and scholarly inquiry.

Lindbeck is quite aware of such concerns, having been an observer at Vatican II, and having formed many friendships with Roman Catholic theologians. It is striking to most Protestant readers just how much effort is made in *The Nature of Doctrine* persuading the reader that his "cultural-linguistic" model will be acceptable not just to his own Lutheran tradition, and will not only be of interest more broadly in Protestant thought, but will be compelling especially for Roman Catholics. It is for this reason that he devotes precious space, in this short book, to discussion of topics such as Mariology and infallibility. It would be a mistake to assume that Lindbeck is unconcerned with intra-Catholic concerns. Rather, although he acknowledges that the combination of propositional and existential-expressivist approaches is a genuine advance over one-sided methods, Lindbeck finds them inadequate not only for Protestant theological use, but even in the Roman Catholic context.

Lindbeck does not draw attention to Rahner's attempt to mediate the needs of ecclesial discipline and theological inquiry, but he is certainly aware of it:

> Theories of the third type, which utilize both cognitivist and experiential-expressive perspectives, are equipped to account more fully than can the first two types for both variable and invariable aspects of religious traditions but have difficulty in coherently combining them. Even at their best, as in Rahner and Lonergan, they resort to complicated intellectual gymnastics and to that extent are unpersuasive. They are also weak in criteria for determining when a given doctrinal development is consistent with the sources of faith, and they are therefore unable to avoid a rather greater reliance on the magisterium, the official teaching of the church, for decisions in such matters than all Reformation Protestants and many Catholics consider desirable.[17]

In other words, Rahner's approach has two weaknesses: (1) it is more intellectually complex than the problem requires; (2) it fails adequately to specify criteria for judging which doctrinal developments are orthodox, and relies instead on official teaching to decide matters. This is the closest Lindbeck comes to acknowledging the difficult context in which Rahner is writing.

Lindbeck's critique of Rahner is interesting because it focuses on the relationship between subjectivity and objectivity, and tries to offer a better account. It does not hold Rahner to ransom over his philosophical claims but instead tries to grasp the intention that lies behind those claims – namely, the desire to combine cognitivist-propositional objectivity and existential-expressive subjectivity. Karen Kilby, one of Rahner's most sympathetic and attentive recent interpreters, has suggested that the best readings of Rahner not only acknowledge the inconsistencies internal to his philosophy but allow Rahner's theology a certain degree of independence from the philosophy which often seems to underpin it. Kilby's argument, in summary, is that Rahner's philosophy does not underpin his theology, but accompanies it in a fashion that is difficult to specify.[18] Lindbeck's reading, likewise, is not so fixed upon the philosophical shortcomings of Rahner's approach to doctrine, but judges it by its fruits. Rahner adopts a "two-dimensional" approach in order to mitigate the "propositional" (magisterial?) voice with an "existential-expressive" (community?)

voice. Lindbeck's critique is designed not to prevent this approach, but to improve upon it. The cultural-linguistic approach advocated by Lindbeck is, he thinks, a far better tool for addressing problems that arise in questions of authority.

The problem to be solved is this: How can one best describe the relationship between an "objective" and "propositional" voice of a tradition's authority and a "subjective" and "expressive" voice of a tradition's small community? Rahner, in a complex and difficult way, recasts matters by trying to characterize the two poles as an "objective" dimension rooted in the "transcendental experience" of all human beings and a "subjective" dimension characterized by the Kantian subject and the Hegelian historically situated community. The purpose of this recasting is to address a "crisis" confronting young people undertaking theological training. Its effect is to place the relationship between objective and subjective truth-claims not in the opposition of magisterium to community, but in the interplay of "universal" human experience (especially self-consciousness) and "subjective" communal languages for describing it concretely.

Lindbeck suggests that, apart from the philosophical problems, Rahner leaves the important matters so vague that magisterial authority is required after all, and not only to settle debate, but to make any judgment at all. His alternative is a model based on language. Lindbeck wants to do justice to the importance of communal voices, but instead of imagining the two parties as magisterium and individual, his ideal types come from grammar: "experts" versus "ordinary users" of language. Lindbeck suggests that grammarians typically have a far more explicit and reflective account of the rules of a language than ordinary users who have grown up using a language. Experts are better able to reconstruct the rules that are operative in a language and, if they identify errors, they are better able to specify which rules have been broken when an error is made. Nonetheless, there are crucial limits to a grammarian's expertise:

> . . . every formulated rule has more exceptions than the grammarians and the theologians are aware of . . . The deep grammar of the language may escape detection. It may be impossible to find rules that show why some crucial usages are beautifully right and others dangerously wrong. The experts must on occasion bow to the superior wisdom of the competent speaker who simply knows that such and such is right or wrong even though it violates the rules they have formulated.[19]

In the context of a discussion which has been sharply critical of magisterial authority in matters of judging theological rightness, this model is more than merely suggestive. Lindbeck's cultural-linguistic model is designed to do justice to the genuine expertise of theological experts, while emphasizing the possibility that ordinary believers are sometimes the ultimate authority on whether certain beliefs or practices are theologically right or wrong. On Lindbeck's model, magisterial impositions resemble attempts to specify "proper" use of language or pronunciation on communities that have their own dialects and regional accents. This is, however, not to suggest that such forms of authority are unnecessary. Debates arise in communities which threaten the integrity of theology, and which call for adjudication. Truly to repair Rahner's account, one needs to find a way to acknowledge the authority of those whose task is to end disputes. Lindbeck puts the matter starkly: "Yet, despite these inadequacies, the guidance offered by the grammar or the doctrine of the textbooks may be indispensable, especially to those who are learning a language, to those who have not mastered it well, or to those who, for whatever reason, are in danger of corrupting it into meaninglessness."[20]

What kind of Rahner is encountered in Lindbeck? On the one hand it is the Rahner of the "two-dimensional" approach, whose arguments Lindbeck wishes to repair. On the other hand it is the Rahner of Vatican II, whose concern is to do justice to the insights of "ordinary users of language." These two Rahners are, of course, one theologian, and it is no easy matter to separate things out. Rahner's more philosophical speculations – the "two-dimensional" Rahner – are unlikely to be generative of developments in Protestant theology, and Lindbeck's criticisms are difficult to answer. Rahner's concern with ordinary users of language, however, is of more enduring interest, and Lindbeck seems to have learned a lot from him. Questions of authority are not peculiar to Catholicism, and so long as they continue to be raised in classrooms and in ecumenical discussion, there will perhaps always be a place to remember a German Jesuit who devoted his life to grappling with such problems.

Notes

1 G. Lindbeck, *The Nature of Doctrine: Religion and Theology in a Postliberal Age* (Philadelphia: Westminster, 1984).
2 For one such attempt see F. Kerr, *Theology After Wittgenstein*, 2nd edn (London: SPCK, 1997).
3 Lindbeck, *Nature of Doctrine*, 16.
4 Ibid., 91–111.
5 For the most accessible discussion of these issues, see A. Bowie, *Introduction to German Philosophy* (Cambridge: Polity, 2003).
6 Lindbeck, *Nature of Doctrine*, 19.

7 Ibid., 91.
8 Ibid., 24.
9 *FCF*, 1–43.
10 Ibid., 33. I leave to one side the problems associated with "*Vorgriff*"; for discussion see K. Kilby, *Karl Rahner: Theology and Philosophy* (London: Routledge, 2004), 19–31.
11 *FCF*, 35.
12 Ibid., 20.
13 See Kilby's exploration of Rahner's "transcendentalism" which, instead of using German philosophy, explains matters by using tools from the analytical tradition: Kilby, *Karl Rahner*, 32–48.
14 Lindbeck, *Nature of Doctrine*, 19–25.
15 *FCF*, 6.
16 Ibid.
17 Lindbeck, *Nature of Doctrine*, 17.
18 Kilby, *Karl Rahner*, 70–99.
19 Lindbeck, *Nature of Doctrine*, 81–82.
20 Ibid., 82.

Further reading

Bowie, A., *Introduction to German Philosophy* (Cambridge: Polity, 2003).
Kilby, K., *Karl Rahner: Theology and Philosophy* (London: Routledge, 2004).
Lindbeck, G., *The Nature of Doctrine: Religion and Theology in a Postliberal Age* (Philadelphia: Westminster, 1984).
Rahner, K., *Foundations of Christian Faith: An Introduction to the Idea of Christianity*, trans. W. Dych (Darton, Longman & Todd, 1978).

14 Karl Rahner: toward a theological aesthetics
GESA ELSBETH THIESSEN

It may come as a surprise to include an article on Rahner's contribution to a theological aesthetics in this *Companion*. This theme in Rahner has hitherto received only little attention. However, it seems timely to consider this aspect of his writings here, as it will throw new light on Rahner's theology as such and demonstrate his continued relevance in theology and, in particular, in the current development of the dialogue between theology and the arts.

The quest for a theological aesthetics, including a theology of art, has become a significant theme in theology since the early 1980s. The numerous publications on theology and art, literature, music, and film, etc. and the setting up of whole programs and departments in theological faculties witness to this development. The overall aim in such endeavors is to investigate how the arts are sources of, and can play an active role in, theology. It is precisely such questions that Rahner addressed in his articles on the arts.

Rahner was in many ways a prophetic voice in twentieth century Christianity. His idea that the Christian of the future would need to be a mystic is reflected in today's interest in diverse forms of spirituality, i.e., in the search for and reflection on religious experience in an age of pluralism. Rahner's *leitmotif* is the God who reveals Godself in all realms of life, in human experience, as holy mystery, the God who communicates Godself through grace, yet who remains always wholly Other. Rahner saw the whole of human existence and of history as embraced by God's transforming love and presence. In his many essays, meditations, and sermons he tried to bring across to the most diverse audiences, including those with serious doubts about Church and faith, this mystery of a loving God. In this context it does not surprise that he would engage with the question of the arts as sources of revelation and meaning and their role in theology. Rahner was fully aware of the pluralism which had become a characteristic of modern culture, and more particularly of theology itself. Although he lived his own faith firmly in adherence to the tradition of his Church, Ignatian spirituality, and prayer, his openness to people of other faiths and other denominations, to questions of modern science and culture, are manifested throughout his work. It is this fundamental openness, his prophetic voice and mystical awareness, which also holds true in his reflective and at times deeply felt engagement with the arts. For the most part his writing on the arts and their relationship with theology is on a broader level, as opposed to discussions of specific works of art, music, or literature. As he considered himself an "amateur theologian," he also felt he had little to say on the arts. Far from it, his views are astute and relevant as he addressed issues that continue to be central to this day. He devoted several articles to the non-verbal arts, i.e. to music and fine art, and also to poetry for which, like his teacher Heidegger, he appears to have had a special love.

BEYOND A VERBAL THEOLOGY

Rahner emphasized that fundamentally theology must not and cannot be reduced to verbal theology. Given that only a small number of theologians have *explicitly* noted that our theological ideas and concepts must include the non-verbal, this simple statement deserves further scrutiny.

Theology, as Rahner reiterates, is to be understood as the total and conscious self-expression of the human being, insofar as this self-expression arises out of God's self-communication to us through grace. In also taking this idea as his point of departure in the dialogue of theology and the arts, he maintains that theology can therefore only be regarded as complete if it includes the arts as an integral part in its own life. Indeed, the arts ought to be nothing less than an intrinsic moment of theology. This integration he considers essential since art is a deep, authentic expression of the human person and because theology and the arts both refer to the transcendental nature of the human being. This, Rahner holds, not only applies to verbal art, i.e., literature, but to all the arts. All arts are forms of human self-expression. He notes: "If theology is simply and arbitrarily defined as being identical with verbal theology . . . we would have to ask whether such a reduction of theology to verbal theology does justice to the value and uniqueness of these arts, and whether it does not unjustifiably limit the capacity of these arts to be used by God in his revelation."[1] Hence for him the idea of art being a source of theology is ultimately based on his theology of revelation. It also hinges on his anthropology, i.e., his view of the human being as a creature of transcendence always directed to the experience of the mystery and transformed by grace. He emphasized that art, due to its revealing dimension, is *not* to be understood merely as an *ancilla theologiae*, as an aid or an illustration of a religious truth, but can in itself become a *locus theologicus*.[2] Rahner thereby implicitly recognized the modern aesthetic criteria of originality and autonomy of a work of art, while at the same time valuing its theological relevance. This idea of the work of art as an important source of, rather than a mere illustrative help in, theology has become foundational to the dialogue between theology and the arts, e.g., in John Dillenberger, Horst Schwebel, and Richard Viladesau, to name but a few.

Rahner further examined the relationship between image and word. In the context of the interpretation of art, he opines that one ought to be aware of and respect the fact that non-verbal art can never be fully captured in words. If one were to attempt such a translation, the uniqueness and autonomy of the non-verbal arts would lose their whole *raison d'être*. Yet, Rahner is aware that despite the autonomy and uniqueness of visual art, interpretation of works of art, including those with Christian subject matter, are necessary in order to bring out more clearly the message contained in the works. In this way, then, the visual and the verbal can complement each other.

ART AND RELIGIOUS EXPERIENCE

A work of art, Rahner asserts, in order to be experienced as spiritual, must not necessarily contain religious subject matter. Today this view no longer seems particularly remarkable. Yet it was another fundamental insight, first voiced by Paul Tillich, who initiated the dialogue between theology and modern art in numerous essays and talks. Whether Rahner was aware of Tillich's writings and appropriated them cannot be ascertained. It may well have been the case that he read Tillich, yet there are no direct references to the latter in this context.[3] Tillich was the first theologian who explicitly made this momentous observation in his analysis of expressionist and abstract art and thus recognized modern art without explicit Christian iconography as a relevant source of and for theology.

Rahner stressed that in both hearing and seeing we can have sensory experiences of transcendence and that these experiences may become genuine religious experiences of divine self-communication. In emphasizing seeing as an irreducible and fundamental element in the totality of religious acts, he takes up an important issue, running through the whole of Christian theology and based on the Gospels, namely the search for the vision of God. In fact, given the diversity of writings on the vision of the divine, it constitutes one, possibly *the* most prevalent, theme in theological aesthetics throughout Christian history. Rahner himself wrote on the beatific vision. Moreover he pointed out that the Christian must learn to see, indeed that it is an "elevated task" and a "sacred, human and Christian art to learn to see" with loving eyes if we confess Christ not only as the Word but also as the image of God.

Thus, since it is the whole person who is involved in a religious or in another type of experience, it always concerns body, mind, and soul. Rahner states that it would be theologically naïve to think that only explicitly religious acts will be conducive to a salutary relationship with the divine. A painting or a symphony, he argues, may be so inspired by divine revelation and by God's gracious self-communication that it conveys something about the human being in the light of the divine. When a work of art reaches and is revelatory of the depths of human existence, it reaches the realm where true religious experience takes place. While he is aware of the possibilities of religious experience through art, he does, however, concede that there are works of art that may not be very conducive in evoking spiritual and religious depth, i.e., well-intended but sentimental, pious, works of little artistic merit. As he notes: "When I paint the crib with Jesus, Mary and Joseph, using aureoles to show from the outset what is being presented, I have, objectively speaking, a religious picture. It may, in fact, not be very religious, because it is unable to evoke in those who see it a genuine and deep religious reaction. There exists what we call religious *Kitsch*."[4] On the other hand, a work by Rembrandt, for example, – even without any specific religious theme – may still confront and affect the whole human being in such a way that she is faced with the ultimate meaning of existence. He asserts that this is, in fact, in a most fundamental sense a religious image. His analysis here is not only important concerning what constitutes genuine art, but addresses one of the central questions regarding a theology of art, namely how religious or spiritual experience happens through the work of art, with or without Christian iconography.

Yet, Rahner acknowledges that in Christianity and in our personal-spiritual life we also need specifically religious images that are easily understood by all. These help us to grasp the message of the Bible, and they remind us of the Gospel stories. Images therefore also have a didactic role. Ultimately word and image should be seen as complementary in our spiritual life and knowledge. Images have an aesthetic, epistemological, mediatory, and meditative function, not only in the more secular spheres of life but also with regard to the Christian message, thus they are not to be undervalued. In this context we are reminded once more of Rahner's anthropology with its emphasis on the unity of sense knowledge and spiritual-conceptual knowledge. Senses, intuition, emotion always play their part in human understanding and knowledge. Rahner repeatedly insisted that real human knowledge, including religious knowledge, cannot be achieved merely by concepts and speculation. While books can help us a little on the way, knowledge is gained through experience, through joy and suffering in everyday life. It is in this way that the person gains hope and wisdom and comes to know God. God cannot be approached as an object to be mastered by systematic argument; rather, it is through the experience of the all-embracing love of God as mystery, that we know something of the always greater and hidden divinity. It is in this way, too, that the work of art, with its concrete, experiential, intellectual, and aesthetic dimension, reveals to us glimpses of the divine and can play a relevant role in the work of theology.

THEOLOGY AND ART: SUBJECTIVITY, PRAYER, TRANSCENDENCE

Rahner insisted on many occasions that theology must be subjective in that it begins with subjective experience; it must be concerned with faith, hope, and charity, with our personal relationship with God. However, subjectivity here does not mean subjectivism and relativism, but rather the human being as a free and responsible agent in the light of faith. (Earlier in the volume Francis Fiorenza discussed the criticism of Metz and others of Rahner's notion of subjectivity and its apparent lack of concern for the social. Here I consider his stress on the subjective in relation to the dialogue between theology and the arts.) Art, Rahner acknowledges, is also essentially subjective and offers the possibility of transcendence. "Whatever is expressed in art is a product of that transcendentality by which, as spiritual and free beings, we strive for the totality of reality . . . [I]t is only because we are transcendental beings that art and theology can really exist."[5] Further, he points out that art is always historical, and is thus situated in particularity. True art is the result of a particular historical event of human transcendentality. Historicity/particularity and transcendence enjoy an essential mutual relationship. Rahner's affirmation that theology must be subjective because it speaks of our personal and particular relationship with God thus parallels his views on subjectivity and historical particularity in art.

Theology, like art, cannot simply be developed through abstract concepts but, Rahner maintains, must be mystagogical. Mystagogy implies that people must be encouraged not to learn the catechism by heart but rather to genuinely experience what underlies the more abstract concepts. Human beings through their life experience and faith can be led into the depths of self. This may happen when a person is wholly absorbed in hearing or seeing and, more specifically, in prayer. Prayer is not understood simply as words of petition, but in a wider sense of being open to the presence of God in the individual's life, both inside and outside the Church. From Rahner's whole conception of art as a *locus theologicus* we could surmise that he might have been aware that artists like Rouault and Kandinsky perceived their work in terms of prayer and religious vocation.

It is significant that Rahner discusses art not only in the "horizon of theology" but also in the "horizon of piety." Conscious of the spiritual in non-religious subject matter in modern art, he concedes that, in a wider human context, we may speak of an "anonymous piety" even in an Impressionist work of art. Rahner explicitly referred to piety *outside* the Church, which, he held, has its primal ground in, and is sustained by, the experience of God.[6] Piety does not simply arise in the specific sphere of the Church but connotes the fundamental relatedness of the human being to God, and his/her witness to sincerity, truth, and love, all actions founded on and pointing to God's universal grace. This witness includes authentic artistic creation and commitment. His notion of an anonymous piety in art thus directly corresponds to his idea of piety outside the Church and indirectly therefore to his view of the "anonymous Christian."

PATHS TO THE WORD OF GOD – POETRY

Among Rahner's articles on the arts, those which concentrate on poetry and the relationship between poetry and Christian life are particularly numerous and written with profound empathy and insight. Rahner was deeply aware of Christianity's intrinsic relationship with the word, and hence with the poetic word. Given the vast range of his own writing in different genres – meditations, prayers, sermons, dictionary articles, essays, systematic theological writings – he appears to have felt a particular affinity with the possibilities of language and with literature, in particular, with poetry as an art form. Indeed, his considerable ability of self-expression through the spoken and written word was recognized when he was awarded the "Sigmund Freud Prize for Scientific Prose" from the German Academy for Language and Poetry in 1973. Many of his writings have a decidedly poetic dimension, such as *Encounters with Silence* and the prose in articles such as "Priest and Poet."

In "Poetry and the Christian," an article on the relationship between poetry, theology, and Christian living, Rahner asks – in the context of the decline of Christian themes in literature (and in art) in modernity – whether, on a more fundamental level, this decline has actually taken place. Perhaps it is simply through new and renewed symbols, forms, and images that something of the spiritual and/or religious is expressed. Poetry, especially great poetry, is important, because it takes shape where the human being radically faces who he or she is.[7] Such facing oneself includes sin, guilt, hatred, deep pain, and failure. But in such authenticity, Rahner asserts, the "happy danger" of meeting God is more likely than in the philistine avoidance of all the chasms in human existence. If one prefers to live at a superficial level, one is likely to meet neither doubts nor God. Great poetry – as also great art and music – and "great," that is authentic, Christian living have an "inner kinship." In Christian existence, as in composing and listening to music or through writing and reading great poetry, the individual is led into the heights and depths, into hope, doubts, and moments of despair. Both the poetic word and the theological word can reach the human heart, which in turn may encourage and enable one to open up to the divine mystery.

In this context Rahner mentions four preconditions which need to be fulfilled in order to hear especially the *word* of the Christian message. First, the human being must open her or his ear, to hear *that* word which speaks of "the silent mystery as the ground of our being." Secondly, we must develop the ability to hear words which hit the center, the human heart. The third, and especially important, precondition is the ability to hear the words that *unite*. Usually words are used to distinguish, to isolate. The ultimate words, however, Rahner emphasizes, are those that unite, reconcile, and liberate. The ultimate words unite, as they express *the* central Christian message, of love, which is not some kind of feeling, but the true substance of reality, that desires to become manifest everywhere. The fourth and final precondition is to perceive in the individual word the unutterable mystery, the ability to hear the incarnational and incarnate incomprehensibility, indeed, to hear the word that became flesh. For this reason, Rahner concludes, we must become open to the Word, to the word made flesh, since through and in this word the human word is filled with truth and grace.

In this way, then, to perceive the poetic, the primordial word becomes a precondition of hearing the word of God. The individual does not thereby necessarily have to be particularly gifted, musically, artistically, or poetically. We need only to become receptive and learn to hear those words that are able to hint at what is deepest and unutterable, the words which convey something of the silent, eternal mystery of the divine. Thus, Rahner concludes, the question of how we as Christians deal with poetry becomes a "very serious and truly Christian question."

Rahner referred approvingly to von Balthasar's comment that today we lack a "kneeling theology" (*knieende Theologie*), adding that we also need a "poetic theology" (*dichtende Theologie*), understood as mystagogical theology, i.e., a theology based on and leading to the experience of the mystery of God. In "Priest and Poet," a poetic and moving essay, he examines the relationship of the priest and the poet. The true poet, "driven forward by the transcendence of the Spirit," speaks the primordial words; he or she speaks of what is deepest within, of what springs from the heart, of longing, a longing that touches on the horizon of the incomprehensible mystery.[8] The priest also speaks the truth of God; he [or she] does so even if they have failed to personally and existentially appropriate this truth. Rahner concludes that the future fulfillment, to which our pilgrim path is leading, assures us that the perfect priest and the perfect poet will be one and the same.[9] Such rare moments when the word of God and the word of poetry become one are moments of redemption.

Poetry therefore for Rahner is no optional extra, it is "essential." Written a few decades ago, his love and defense of poetry is poignant and prophetic: "In periods when humanism and poetry seem to be dying, buried under the achievements of technological skill and suffocated by the chatter of the masses, Christianity must defend human culture and the poetic word . . . We Christians must love and fight for the poetic word, because we must defend what is human, since God himself has assumed it into his eternal reality."[10] Here again Rahner's basic premise of art as an essential source of human self-expression is evident, along with an urgency to protect and foster poetry as a source of meaning and truth, and as a path to the holy mystery.

CONCLUSION

"Has theology become more perfect because theologians have become more prosaic?" Rahner asked with some urgency, adding, "What has become of the times when the great theologians also wrote hymns?"[11] He recalls Paul's great hymn to love, the Psalms, the account of creation, Methodius of Olympus, Augustine, Bonaventure, Aquinas, John of the Cross, Meister Eckhart, Angelus Silesius, Dante, Brentano, Annette von Droste, and "many, many other poets." Perhaps their poetic word was "more original and comprehensive, more alive than that of those theologians who are proud of the fact of not being poets."

Prosaic and at times dull language and jargon have made inroads into theology. But here and there we find a voice like Rahner's. Rahner, in an age of secularism, was still able and not ashamed to address God as a Thou (*Du*), not in any sentimental or overly pious way, but in a genuinely humble, sometimes poetic, fashion. His personal integration of life, spirituality, and theology, of head and heart, of the systematic-conceptual and the meditative-poetic dimension, is reflected in and indeed enabled his profound empathy for poetry and the other arts.

Theologians through the ages have acknowledged that all theology ultimately issues in doxology. In some this is more obvious than in others. Rahner's theology, with its emphasis on God as mystery, and on the God who is love and encountered in freedom, his stress on the universality of revelation, his love of the early Christian writers, and his openness to contemporary people and issues, may have contributed to his own poetic sensibility and his love and understanding of the arts. His insistence on dialogue within and beyond the Church in an age of pluralism, on the need for theologians to take risks and not simply regurgitate traditional formulas, may have further enhanced this intellectual openness and love for the arts, not only for themselves, but also as *loci theologici*.

For Rahner then all art – literature, theatre, film, music, architecture, painting, sculpture, etc. – has the potential to speak, paint, or sound of what concerns us profoundly in our human existence, of what brings great happiness or deepest sadness into our lives, of what makes us ecstatic, calm, empathetic, or even apathetic. The arts are therefore existential and part of what it means to become truly human. It is in this way that they point us toward ultimate meaning and reveal glimpses of the mystery of the unfathomable divine. The arts can provide us with moments of genuine seeing, hearing, tasting, and feeling, and thus understanding. In so doing they further our knowledge and faith through a unity of sensory-spiritual-intellectual perception.

Human existence and transcendentality, and God's self-communication through the cross and the hope for redemption, can be revealed and expressed in both art and theology. To conclude with Rahner: "[W]hen listening to a Bach oratorio, why should we not have the impression that, not only through its text but also through its music, we are in a very special way brought into a relationship with divine revelation about humanity? Why would we not believe that this too is theology?"[12]

Notes

1 K. Rahner, "Theology and the Arts," *Thought – A Review of Culture and the Arts*, 57/224 (1982), 25.
2 "The Theology of the Religious Meaning of Images," *TI* xxiii, trans. J. Donceel (London: Darton, Longman & Todd, 1992), 155–56.
3 See the first chapter of my book *Theology and Modern Irish Art* (Dublin: Columba Press, 1999), which deals extensively with Tillich's theology of art.
4 "Art against the Horizon of Theology and Piety," *TI* xxiii, 167.
5 Ibid., *TI* xxiii, 165.
6 "Religious Feeling Inside and Outside the Church," *TI* xvii, 233.
7 "Poetry and the Christian," *TI* iv, 365. See also "The Spirituality of the Church of the Future," *TI* xx, 143–53.
8 "Priest and Poet," *TI* iii, 316.
9 Ibid., *TI* iii, 294.
10 "Poetry and the Christian," *TI* iv, 364.
11 "Priest and Poet," *TI* iii, 316.
12 "Art against the Horizon of Theology and Piety," *TI* xxiii, 163.
 * *I would like to express my gratitude to the Tyrone Guthrie Centre at Annaghmak-errig, Ireland, for a privileged time of intensive work on this article.*

Further reading

Rahner, K., "Priest and Poet," *TI* iii, 294–317.
 "Poetry and the Christian," *TI* iv, 357–67.
 "The Task of the Writer in Relation to Christian Living," *TI* viii, 112–29.
 "Religious Feeling Inside and Outside the Church," *TI* xvii, 228–42.
 "The Religious Meaning of Images," *TI* xxiii, 149–61.
 "Art against the Horizon of Theology and Piety," *TI* xxiii, 162–69.
 Everyday Faith (New York: Herder and Herder, 1968).
Thiessen, G., *Theological Aesthetics – A Reader* (London: SCM, 2004; Grand Rapids, MI and Cambridge, UK: Eerdmans, 2005).

15 Rahner and religious diversity

JEANNINE HILL FLETCHER

It is hard to name a theologian who has singularly influenced the contemporary discourse on religious pluralism more than Karl Rahner. In the 1960s and 1970s his writings on the topic gained wide appeal and his thoughts enjoyed popular exposure through public sermons and radio addresses. Throughout the last quarter of the twentieth century and into the new millennium, his theological project has so influenced the discussion that many of today's major voices on religious diversity present their theologies in direct conversation with his. Rahner's ideas have even elicited responses from notable spokespersons of the religions of the world. Thus, in examining Rahner's theology of religious pluralism, we can gain insight not only into his own influential thinking, but into the contours of the conversation today.

At the forefront of Rahner's work was a concern that theology speak to people. And so, he explained Christian doctrine in a way that connected with lived experience. As people embedded in a complex and diverse world, Rahner recognized that the encounter with the religious "other" would be among the challenges Christians would face. Religious diversity was not merely an abstract theological concern, but one that grew out of an increasing awareness of and engagement with people of other faiths. He writes:

> The society in which the Catholic Christian of today lives is a complex and heterogeneous one. He lives in the closest proximity to, and has the closest personal connections with, non-Catholic Christians. The sphere in which his life is passed is no longer a country which in its social, cultural and even civic aspects, is homogeneously "Catholic." Indeed, where formerly the individual nations were independent of one another in their lines of historical development, nowadays these lines are tending to become fused into a single great world history. And the result of this is that the non-Christian religions and philosophies of life such as Islam, Hinduism and Buddhism, no longer

constitute an area of foreign folklore which has no bearing upon the
course of life modern man maps out for himself and raises no radical
problems for him. Instead of this, these non-Christian religions have
come to be regarded as the philosophies of life of men who have
become neighbours to modern man, men in whom he cannot fail to
recognize just as high a degree of intelligence as that with which he
credits himself.[1]

Anticipating some of the globalization discussion that would come to dom-
inate late twentieth century political and social thought, Rahner sketches
a world where the encounter with difference repeats locally and globally.
Our world has indeed become a single place where "the lines of historical
development" have "become fused" through the interconnected systems of
economics, information, travel, and immigration. The movement of persons and ideas through these systems has created living contexts where
cultural and religious differences are not contained in discrete nations, but
disperse through fluid boundaries. In many parts of the world, one's neighbors are as likely to be members of diverse faiths as they are to be Christian.
But unlike the "clash of civilizations" posited by some theorists of religious
encounter, Rahner navigates the terrain of religious diversity by envision-
ing fundamental similarities that cut through whatever differences might
be encountered.

The most basic similarity Rahner asserts is that all humanity is the
creative work of the one God. He interprets the doctrine of creation to
underscore how all humans are intimately related to God as the site of
God's indwelling. God is the incomprehensible mystery of existence that is
sufficient unto itself, but chooses to come into expression through the multiplicity of created realities. God's overabundant nature courses through
the universe rendering all creation graced. Yet, in order for the communication to be complete, there must be a hearer who receives it. Human
nature is the only created reality with the freedom to accept God's self-
communication in grace. When humanity accepts this self-communication,
God's purpose in creation is complete as God's fullest self-expression can be
manifest in the world. Humanity is the site of God's greatest self-disclosure;
or, as Rahner explains, "[the human being] is accordingly in the most basic
definition that which God becomes if he sets out to show himself in the
region of the extra-divine."[2] While this concept leads naturally to a discussion of the incarnation in Jesus Christ, Rahner understood it also to be
reflective of a more widely recognizable presence of God in all humanity.
"Really and radically," he wrote, "*every* person must be understood as the

event of a supernatural self-communication of God."[3] Regardless of cultural and religious location, all human beings are the site of God's indwelling in grace.

Building on the foundation of humanity's common status in creation, Rahner insists further that every person has the opportunity to experience God. When a sceptical conversation partner once said to Rahner, "I have never had an experience of God," Rahner simply replied, "I don't believe you; I just don't accept that. You have had, perhaps no experience of God under this precise code-word *God* but you have had or have now an experience of God – and I am convinced that this is true of every person."[4] Rahner saw the most basic human experiences – the ability to know, to love, and to make free choices – as indicating an experience of God. Each and every time the human person goes beyond him or herself in growth or love; or pursues a life path not bound by the gains of a material world; or recognizes the incomprehensible in the process of learning; that individual extends beyond the limits of what he or she presently is and creates something new. As the individual oversteps the boundaries which define the present self, he or she has the experience of reaching into that which is not the self, and encountering the boundless range of possibilities contained in the ever-receding horizon of transcendence. He or she is opened up to the absolute fullness of being. When the individual realizes that the self's extension is limitless and that the ultimate term toward which we reach can never be grasped or even understood, s/he has the opportunity to recognize the infinite mystery that is God. Reflecting on the connection between the inexhaustibility of human growth and that which makes this endless growth possible, Rahner names God as "precisely that mystery of the incomprehensible, the inexpressible, toward which at every moment of my life I am always tending."[5] God exists as the source and sustenance of human growth and transcendence, whether humans recognize it or not, whether they name it or not, and most importantly, whether they are Christian or not. In fact, for Rahner, "there is no form of human living in which an encounter with God does not take place at least anonymously, non-thematically, and transcendentally."[6] In the very structure of human knowing, willing, and loving, God is present to all persons who remain open to the grace-filled movement into ever greater becoming. Furthermore, it is in the response to grace in the process of transcendence that the human person finds fulfillment. This response is neither an optional addition to human nature, nor is it an external demand from God imposed as law. Rather, participation in grace, through growth and transcendence, is "stamped on humans at creation" and "determines" human nature itself.[7]

These essential similarities – being created as the self-communication of God and experiencing God in the process of personal growth – sustain Rahner's belief in the universal call to communion with God that is salvation. When we are fully human, when we become precisely what we were created to be, we are in communion with God. By engaging in the dynamism of transcendence, the human person participates in the being of God – the holy mystery of human existence. Responding to the deepest sense of their humanity, persons are responding to God and opening themselves up to salvation. Rahner writes:

> Salvation here is to be understood as the strictly supernatural and direct presence of God in himself afforded by grace . . . The fundamental proposition which is the proper subject of theological investigation refers therefore to the universal possibility of supernatural salvation for all men after original sin. This possibility must really be given to *all*. By this is meant all those throughout human history who have come to a free realisation of their existence.[8]

As persons are in relationship to themselves in growth and love, they are realizing the foundational mystery of their existence and are in relation-ship to God. Understood as the completion of human becoming in grace, salvation is the culmination of the process of transcendence, begun in life and fulfilled beyond the boundaries of our material existence. The ultimate goal of salvation is achieved by all persons who remain open to growth and transcendence, or in Rahner's own words, "Anyone who does not close him [or her] self to God in an ultimate act of his [or her] life . . . this person finds salvation."[9] Rahner envisions that all persons can enjoy salvation by virtue of the intimate relation to God endowed through the grace of creation and witnessed in the ongoing process of love and transcendence. He goes even further to describe this process of salvation not limited to a person's spiritual development, but as the fulfillment of the whole person[10] from his/her historically concrete "existential standpoint."[11] A "yes" to personal growth in transcendence is a "yes" to the fulfillment of one's own human nature; this is also a "yes" to God and a "yes" to salvation.

This understanding of salvation is prior to any religious categorization and thus God's free offer in the self-communication of grace is not lim-ited to Christians. There can be transcendence and salvation everywhere in human history. Rahner concludes, "As God's real self-communication in grace, therefore, the history of salvation and revelation is coexistent and coextensive with the history of the world and of the human spirit, and hence also with the history of religion."[12] Being historically situated in a tradition other than Christianity does not rule out experiencing the deep relationship that is salvation. In fact, Rahner allows for the religions to be contexts for the human encounter with God in history. Because we are social beings, our human becoming is nourished in living communities. Therefore, Rahner defends the proposition that, "when a non-Christian wins salvation through faith, hope and love, the non-Christian religions cannot be thought to have played no part, or only a negative one, in this winning of justification and salvation."[13] Here, we see that Rahner is not only reinterpreting the doctrine of salvation (away from the idea of "no salvation outside the Church" that has dominated Christian thinking), he is allowing for the possibility of a positive role the religions might have in sustaining human growth toward God. In each of the world's religions, there will also be moments when people will be self-consciously aware of God's presence and will articulate the unthematic experience of transcendence in the expressions of their distinctive religion.[14] In the close joining of theology and anthropology, all humans, in whatever religion they might find themselves, can be aware of God's offer of grace and open to the salvation it brings.

But Rahner does not join only theology and anthropology (that is, the doctrine of God and his understanding of the human person). He links the theology–anthropology connection distinctively *through* the person of Jesus Christ. As we have seen, for Rahner, the fulfillment of human nature in the acceptance of grace is simultaneously the fulfillment of God's self-communication to the world. As humans respond to their own nature, God's self-communication becomes manifest and the incarnation of God in and through human nature completes the intention of creation. But it is only the perfect reception in humanity that can complete God's communicative action making it a reality; otherwise it remains merely a possibility. Or, as Rahner describes, "God's self-communication must have a permanent beginning and in this beginning a guarantee that it has taken place."[15] For Rahner, the universally available self-giving of God is activated precisely when the perfection of human nature takes place; that is, when God's self-communication meets with the most perfect human acceptance and transcendence. If persons today experience God's grace in the transcendence of knowledge, will, and love, then the self-communication of God *is* a reality. This means that at some point the fullness of God's self-communication has been made a reality in and through its perfect human reception. Searching history to find the one in whom God's self-communication was made complete, the Christian finds Jesus Christ.[16] Christians find in Jesus of Nazareth the perfect human being who made God fully incarnate in his life. Jesus Christ was the one who was fully open to the mystery of God, whose self-consciousness was consciousness of the human participation in God, and who achieved the fulfillment to which human nature calls all persons. In Jesus Christ, persons can see "the explicit statement of the revelation of grace which humans always experience implicitly in the depths of their own being."[17] This means that in the explicit witness of Jesus Christ, humanity can see its own true nature revealed. In and through Jesus Christ, we can see that each of us is called, through an openness to God, to a life of growth and transcendence. Or, as Rahner writes, "the incarnation of God is the uniquely supreme case of the actualization of man's nature in general."[18] The witness of Jesus reveals to humanity its fundamental connectedness and dynamism toward God. Rahner explains, "Through the Word of God, we learn that deep in our own nature God dwells, and that this is no mere metaphor for the reflection of the infinite things within us, but the expression of a literal truth."[19] As Jesus perfects human nature he simultaneously incarnates God's own being in the world and reflects back to human beings the reality of God's grace within them. Jesus is the model of what human nature is called to become, and the real symbol of God's presence in the world.

What takes place in Jesus Christ has significance on an ontological plane – that is, the event has to do with being itself and completes the very structure of existence. As Rahner writes:

> The Incarnation of the Logos (however much we must insist on the fact that it is itself an historical, unique Event in an essentially historical world) appears as the *ontologically* (not merely "morally," an afterthought) unambiguous goal of the movement of creation as a whole, in relation to which everything prior is merely a preparation of the scene. It appears as orientated from the very first to this point in which God achieves once and for all both the greatest proximity to and distance from what is other than he (while at the same time giving it being) . . .[20]

In completing the structure intended in creation by fulfilling the self-communication of God in humanity, the incarnation is seen as the very perfection and climax of creation. And since the incarnation is the fulfillment of human nature in general, the Christ event is seen also as the goal of human being and becoming. Perfecting the structure of human being in the world, Christ becomes "the very thing towards which [hu]mankind is moving."[21] The goal of union with God in grace has been *fully* actualized by Christ, making Christ the mediator who effects God's salvation for humanity. Through the perfect acceptance of God's self-communication of grace, Jesus Christ fully extends the process of transcendence into fullness of union with God, making God's gift of grace irreversible. The completion of the offer of God's self-communication in Christ stamps the rest of humanity with the possibility of transcending toward God. As the goal of human becoming, Christ is the effective cause of all transcendence and therefore of *all* salvation. Jesus Christ is the ontological reality that makes possible the growth and transcendence that is salvation. Therefore, "the achievement by any man of his proper and definitive salvation is dependent upon Jesus Christ."[22] As an ontological reality, Christ remains effective of universal salvation regardless of whether or not the individual recognizes Christ as the source of the transcendence that leads him or her to God. Thus, Rahner does not require explicit confession of Jesus Christ or baptism in the Christian Church as prerequisite for salvation. Yet, while the human expressions of relationship with God are diverse, they are, as Rahner understands them, "basically the same" in being ultimately related to God through Christ. In his description, "the relationship of God to man is basically the same for all men, because it rests on the Incarnation, death and resurrection of the one Word of God made flesh."[23] When a person of another faith tradition has a successful moment of articulating the experience of God in transcendence, that person is implicitly articulating that which was perfected in Christ. So, although framed in the idiom of a non-Christian religion, nevertheless, that individual is intending the mysterious reality of Jesus Christ. Furthermore, when persons in other faith traditions experience the growth and transcendence constitutive of salvation, they are encountering Christ within their non-Christian religion. In fact, for Rahner, saviour figures in other traditions can be seen as signs that anticipate and/or point to the fullness of the saviour Jesus Christ.[24] Thus, "salvation" as an existential reality is singularly focused on the person of Christ, who has actualized union with God as a human possibility. All those who follow the path of accepting the self-communication of God (made possible by Christ) achieve "salvation in the proper and Christian sense of God's absolute self-communication in absolute closeness, and hence it also means what we call the beatific vision."[25] Just as Christ constitutes salvation for Christians, so too does Christ constitute the salvation of all persons. Regardless of one's religious tradition, "salvation" as personal union with the triune God is achieved through acceptance of God's self-communication. While the Christian is explicitly aware of this, the non-Christian has only an implicit understanding. The non-Christian is understood to participate anonymously in the mystery of salvation made real by God's offer in Christ and witnessed in the Christian faith. This is the reasoning behind Rahner's famous phrase, "anonymous Christian." Rahner coined this term to describe the ontological status of all persons who fulfill their human nature through the acceptance of God's offer of transcendence while they remain unaware of its source. In Rahner's own words, ". . . anyone who has let himself be taken hold of by this grace can be called with every right an 'anonymous Christian'."[26] This identification of persons as "anonymous Christians" allows Rahner to cut through the differences of religion and cultural context to envision the ultimate unity among human beings. Moving away from exclusivist theologies that barred non-Christians from the fullness of salvation, Rahner's inclusivism sees all humans offered the opportunity for participating in the grace of Christ. All humanity is "included" in the saving work of Jesus Christ (hence the designation of Rahner's theology as "inclusivist"). The essential link between anthropology and theology *through* Christology thus opened the way of salvation beyond the bounds of the Church for all who could be seen as "anonymous Christians."

Rahner's innovative stance moved away from the exclusivist theologies of his day. His project represents a groundbreaking response to religious difference attuned to the mindset of his audience. The theological framework of the "anonymous Christian" allowed contemporary Christians to affirm the goodness of diverse religious traditions and to see in them an inherent sameness with their own Christian pursuit. Yet, while Rahner acknowledged reasons for adhering to diverse religious faiths and defended the human right to do so, he nevertheless saw a preference for moving from being an "anonymous Christian" to full membership in the Church. Because Rahner has identified that the proper relation to God in transcendence is made possible by Christ, and it is the Spirit of Christ as an ontological reality within non-Christian religions that allows these traditions to be contexts for salvation, he argues that implicit forms of being a Christian (i.e., the anonymous Christian of another tradition) have as their goal an explicit form of Christianity. In his understanding, only the explicit form of Christianity can fully speak to humanity's lived experience of transcendence. And so, he argued that if someone of another faith truly understood the Christian revelation, they would prefer its revelatory power over that of any other religion. In his own words, "wherever in practice Christianity reaches man in the real urgency and rigour of his actual existence, Christianity – once understood – presents itself as the only still valid religion for this man, a necessary means for his salvation."[27] In essence, Rahner saw the diversity of religions as stepping-stones to the fullness of expression in explicit Christianity. In describing how the term "anonymous Christian" implies this dynamism, Rahner writes:

This name implicitly signifies that this fundamental actuation of a man, like all actuations, cannot and does not want to stop in its anonymous state but strives toward an explicit expression, towards its full name. An unfavourable historical environment may impose limitations on the explicitness of this expression so that this actuation may not exceed the explicit appearance of a loving humaneness, but it will not act against this tendency whenever a new and higher stage of explicitness is presented to it right up to the ultimate perfection of a consciously accepted profession of Church membership.[28]

Since transcendence for all human persons is made possible by Christ, the recognition of that transcendence and its "true" source should (according to Rahner) eliminate all "anonymous" experiences of Christ in favor of a professed form. He argues that there is a "basic and indisputable vocation and duty of every individual to become a Christian in a sense that is manifested at the historical level, having an explicitly creedal force and social dimension . . . the doctrine of anonymous Christianity is reconcilable with the doctrine of the duty of every man to become a Christian in an explicit sense."[29]

It is perhaps not surprising that some pluralist theologians who see diverse religions as distinctive paths toward God are critical of Rahner's privileging of Christianity in his concept of the "anonymous Christian." John Hick, for example, responds to Rahner's program with the concern that "anonymous Christians" is an "imperialistic-sounding phrase" and in its place encourages the acceptance of all religions as sources of salvific transformation.[30] Just as Jesus Christ provides the pattern of transcendence in the turn from self-centeredness to God-and-other-centeredness (so Hick's argument goes), figures of other religions also offer this same moral pattern, thus making those religions salvific as well. In essence, Hick removes Rahner's christological link between God and humans and replaces it with the diversity of religious figures from the various religions of the world. In a similar vein, Paul Knitter presses Rahner directly on the point of Jesus as "the culmination of human nature." While agreeing with Rahner that "the incarnation resonates with human experience" Knitter calls into question the emphasis on the singularity of Jesus. He feels that Rahner holds back from facing the implications of the intimate joining of God and humanity, namely, "that there can be *other incarnations*, other individuals who achieved (or were granted) the same fullness of God-human unity realized in Jesus."[31]

If pluralists argue that Rahner is too christocentric, there is a way in which another set of critics argue that Rahner is not sufficiently christocentric in that he allows Christ to be at work without any specific features recognizable to non-Christians. Concerned to safeguard the particularity and distinctiveness of Jesus Christ, these theologians see the concept of the "anonymous Christian" as missing the fundamental content of the historical person of Jesus and the Christian story as it might distinctively inform patterns of thought and action. For example, the liberationist perspective of Johann Baptist Metz is concerned that the "anonymous Christian" does not fully incorporate the Christian narrative which provides the dangerous memory for a praxis of following Christ.[32] George Lindbeck similarly argues that it is not "human nature" generally, but precisely and uniquely the categories made available in Christian Scripture, that shape persons for an encounter with the God whom Christ reveals. These critiques represent a desire to safeguard the distinctiveness of Christianity from a universalism that would erase its particularity.

As these responses show, it can be difficult to "fit" the reality of religious diversity into the framework of the Christian tradition, as Rahner attempts to do when he works within the boundaries of Christian doctrine. But Rahner's systematic project is enduring precisely because he is able to maintain two essential teachings: God's universal will of salvation and the christological affirmation of Jesus' role as mediator of that salvation. These same two doctrines serve as cornerstones in Vatican II's Declaration on Non-Christian Religions, *Nostra Aetate*. In this text, the Catholic Church affirmed:

> Humanity forms but one community. This is so because all stem from the one stock which God created to people the entire earth (see Acts 17:26), and also because all share a common destiny, namely God. His providence, evident goodness, and saving designs extend to all humankind (see Wis. 8:1; Acts 14:17; Rom. 2:6–7; 1 Tim. 2:4).

And:

> The Catholic Church rejects nothing of what is true and holy in these religions. It has a high regard for the manner of life and conduct, the precepts and doctrines which, although differing in many ways from its own teaching, nevertheless often reflect a ray of that truth which enlightens all men and women. Yet it proclaims and is in duty bound to proclaim without fail, Christ who is the way, the truth and the life (Jn. 1:6). In him, in whom God reconciled all things to himself (see 2 Cor. 5:18–19), people find the fullness of their religious life.[33]

Just as Rahner's work does, this declaration identifies all humanity as the creative work of the one God and sees religions as communities that positively shape diverse peoples. Simultaneously, it identifies Christ as the one who decisively brings people to God. This conciliar statement remains normative for the Catholic Church, binding even on later magisterial declarations, so that even more recent writings, for example *Dominus Iesus* (2000), maintain an essentially inclusivist position whereby all salvation comes through Christ, even if in ways not fully understood to humanity. The creative engagement within the boundaries of these two doctrines and his systematic explanation of them are among the reasons why Rahner's inclusivism has remained in the mainstream of theological thinking from Vatican II to the present. It is also the reason why many contemporary theologians continue to use Rahner's framework as their guide. For example, Jacques Dupuis's reconstruction in *Toward a Christian Theology of Religious Pluralism* (1997) takes Rahner as model in articulating a vision of the many paths of the diversity of religions that lead ultimately to the salvation constituted by Jesus Christ. Dupuis explains that "the person of Jesus Christ and the Christ-event are 'constitutive' of salvation of the whole of humankind; in particular, the event of his death-resurrection opens access to God for all human beings, independently of their historical situation."[34] A trinitarian theology of religions enables Dupuis to envision the presence of Christ in the diversity of religions through the power of his Spirit. Similarly, Gavin D'Costa's christocentric trinitarian theology is indebted to Rahner. Holding the revelation of God in Christ as normative, D'Costa's inclusivism "facilitates an openness to the world religions, for the activity of the Spirit cannot be confined to Christianity."[35] One might say that this new trend builds on Rahner's work to employ an inclusivism rooted in the Trinity that identifies not so much "Christ" present in the other traditions, but the work of the Holy Spirit constituting the mysterious connection among all faiths. In maintaining a doctrinal Christian position, many theologians use a modified form of Rahner's inclusivism to speak to Christians today.

While a theological response guided by Rahner explains religious diversity from a Christian doctrinal perspective, his inclusivist position raises some interesting issues when viewed through the eyes of other faiths. Turning the table on his project, the Japanese philosopher and head of the Kyoto school, Nishitani, once asked Rahner, "What would you say to my treating you as an anonymous Zen Buddhist?"[36] Ovey Mohammed asserts that from the perspective of Hindu faith, Christians can be seen as "anonymous Krishnas" since both Jesus and Krishna are recognized as incarnations of God.[37] These examples demonstrate that Rahner's influence has been felt beyond the boundaries of the Christian conversation as his theory is reinterpreted and applied from these new perspectives. More importantly, perhaps, these examples reveal how a self-referential construction of the "other," such as Rahner employs, erases the differences among religions. Just as Rahner identifies a sameness rooted in Christ and names others as "anonymous Christians," these representatives from Buddhism and Hinduism name their "Christian others" with the categories of their respective traditions. In these self-referential constructions of otherness, the other is not allowed to be distinctive, but is named with reference to one's own categories and judged on the basis of one's own self-identity. Many Christians might wonder how their faith in Christ constitutes membership as an "anonymous Zen Buddhist." Or, they might be puzzled as to what it means to be called an "anonymous Krishna" since they are unfamiliar with the Hindu tradition and the role Krishna plays in it. The experience of seeing things from the perspective of other faiths helps to clarify why naming the other as an "anonymous Christian" might be problematic when taking into account the details and differences of the traditions. Returning to one's own Christian perspective with new eyes, one might really have to ask how "Christ" is present in a tradition that appears so different in its very fundamentals. For example, if Christ is understood as the salvific mediator of union with the one God, how does this translate into the religious tradition of Buddhism with its radically different concepts of Ultimate Reality and salvation? How can Christians respond to their Hindu neighbors who see Jesus Christ as one among many of the manifestations of God in the world? As Christians become increasingly aware of the differences among neighbors of other faiths, they will continue to inquire whether a concept like the "anonymous Christian" can accurately reflect their lived experience, or whether new theological representations are needed. And as Christian theologians look ahead to new formulations that continue to speak to people, those who consider a theological response to religious difference surely will stand on the shoulders of Rahner to see where we have been and to think our way forward.

Notes

1 "Church, Churches and Religions," *TI* x, 30.
2 "Anonymous Christians," *TI* vii, 393.
3 *FCF*, 127.
4 "Interview with K. H. Weger for Radio Austria," Vienna (March 2, 1979), in *Karl Rahner in Dialogue: Conversations and Interviews 1965–1982*, trans. and ed. H. Biallowons, H. D. Egan, S.J., and P. Imhof, S.J. (New York: Crossroad, 1986), 211.
5 "Interview with K. H. Weger and H. Lüning for South-German Radio (SDR)," Stuttgart (March 19, 1979) in *Karl Rahner in Dialogue*, 217.

6 "Theological Considerations on Secularization and Atheism," *TI* xi, 176.
7 "Anonymous Christians," *TI* vi, 393.
8 "The One Christ and the Universality of Salvation," *TI* xvi, 200.
9 *FCF*, 143.
10 "The Hermeneutics of Eschatological Assertions," *TI* iv, 331.
11 "The One Christ and the Universality of Salvation," *TI* xvi, 203.
12 *FCF*, 153.
13 "Jesus Christ in the Non-Christian Religions," *TI* xvii, 41.
14 *FCF*, 173.
15 Ibid., 193.
16 Ibid., 211.
17 "Anonymous Christians," *TI* vi, 393.
18 Ibid.
19 K. Rahner, *On Prayer* (New York: Paulist, 1968), 28.
20 "Current Problems in Christology," *TI* i, 165.
21 *FCF*, 170.
22 "The One Christ and the Universality of Salvation," *TI* xvi, 200.
23 "Christianity and the Non-Christian Religions," *TI* v, 118.
24 "Jesus Christ in the Non-Christian Religions," *TI* xvii, 50.
25 *FCF*, 147.
26 "Anonymous Christians," *TI* vi, 395.
27 "Christianity and the Non-Christian Religions," *TI* v, 120.
28 "Anonymous Christians," *TI* vi, 395.
29 "Anonymous Christianity and the Missionary Task of the Church," *TI* xii, 162.
30 J. Hick, *A Christian Theology of Religions: The Rainbow of Faiths* (Louisville, KY: Westminster John Knox Press, 1995), 20.
31 P. Knitter, *No Other Name? A Critical Survey of Christian Attitudes Toward the World Religions* (Maryknoll, NY: Orbis, 1985), 191.
32 J. B. Metz, *Faith in History and Society: Toward a Practical Fundamental Theology* (New York: Crossroad, 1980), 165. See also "An Identity Crisis in Christianity?" in W. J. Kelly, ed., *Theology and Discovery: Essays in Honour of Karl Rahner, S.J.* (Milwaukee, WI: Marquette University Press, 1980), 169–88.
33 *Nostra Aetate* (*Declaration on the Relation of the Church to Non-Christian Religions*), in A. Flannery, ed., *The Basic Sixteen Documents of Vatican Council II* (Northport, NY: Costello Publishing, 1996), 569 and 570–71.
34 J. Dupuis, *Toward a Christian Theology of Religious Pluralism* (Maryknoll, NY: Orbis, 1997), 387.
35 G. D'Costa, "Christ, the Trinity, and Religious Pluralism," in G. D.'Costa, ed., *Christian Uniqueness Reconsidered: The Myth of a Pluralistic Theology of Religions* (Maryknoll, NY: Orbis, 1990), 17.
36 "The One Christ and the Universality of Salvation," *TI* xvi, 219.
37 O. N. Mohammed, "Jesus and Krishna," in R. S. Sugirtharajah, ed., *Asian Faces of Jesus* (Maryknoll, NY: Orbis, 1993), 13.

Further reading

D'Costa, G., "Karl Rahner's Anonymous Christian – a Reappraisal," *Modern Theology* 1:2 (1985), 131–48.

Kelly, W. J., ed., *Theology and Discovery: Essays in Honor of Karl Rahner, S.J.*
(Milwaukee, WI: Marquette University Press, 1980).

Rahner, K. "Christianity and the Non-Christian Religions," *TI* v, 115–34.

"Anonymous Christians," *TI* vi, 390–98.

"Anonymous Christianity and the Missionary Task of the Church," *TI* xii, 161–80.

Foundations of Christian Faith: An Introduction to the Idea of Christianity, trans.
W. Dych (New York: Crossroad, 1978).

"Jesus Christ in the Non-Christian Religions," *TI* xvii, 39–52.

Vass, G., *Understanding Karl Rahner* (London: Sheed & Ward, 1985), 3 vols.

Vorgrimler, H., *Understanding Karl Rahner* (London: SCM Press, 1986).

16 Political and liberation theologies

GASPAR MARTINEZ

There is a wide consensus among theologians that Rahner was a turning point in Catholic theology, paving the way for a fruitful dialogue between modernity and Catholic theology and opening countless doors to further theological enterprises. A very fruitful Rahnerian heritage can be found in the work of two theologians who have developed their own theological projects in two different cultural and social contexts: Johann Baptist Metz in Germany, and Gustavo Gutiérrez in Peru. Political theology has developed in Germany through the works of Dorothee Sölle, Jürgen Moltmann, and Johann Baptist Metz. Of the three, Metz is the key figure to capture some of the potentialities and problems in the theology of Rahner, of whom Metz was a student, a collaborator, and a friend. Liberation theology is a way of doing theology that originated in Latin America in the late sixties and is currently widespread throughout the world. Gustavo Gutiérrez is widely regarded as the father of that theology, since he has been one of its most consistent proponents, and the first who formulated it formally.

Gutiérrez and Metz, as well as the theological currents they represent, relate to Rahner in a different way. Whereas Metz studied under Rahner, Gutiérrez's main exposure was to *la nouvelle théologie* during his studies at Lyon. However, Rahner's theology plays the role of starting or referential point in both political and liberation theologies, which, therefore, present continuities and discontinuities in relation to Rahner. Among the continuities, these post-Rahnerian theologies seek the meaning of faith and the role of theology in relation to the situation from which they stem and to which they relate, thus following the Rahnerian drive toward a pastorally focused theology that is meaningful to those Christians who want to live out their faith in the midst of their culture. In that sense, they are pastoral-correlational theologies. Metz and Gutiérrez also share one of Rahner's main tenets, namely, the intrinsic correlation that exists between human history and the history of salvation. In other words, what happens in human history is relevant for salvation. Therefore, salvation, although always beyond historical reach, must be acted out in history. The obvious corollary is the relevance of Christianity for public ethics and politics, something liberation and political theologies emphasize, reacting strongly to the process of privatization that has developed hand in hand with modernity. These two theologies are also, like Rahner's, apologetical in a positive way because they endeavor to show both the legitimacy and the relevance of Christian faith for human life.

The crucial discontinuity in relation to Rahner lies in the fact that these post-Rahnerian theologies want to be anchored in the social and historical circumstances of the reality they address. In that respect, they distance themselves from the relative a-historicity of Rahner's transcendental reflection. Rahner seemed to theologize in the midst of a culture that was modern but had no further specification. His theology is basically a metaphysical (transcendental, existential, and mystical) reflection, which, although aware of and committed to history, is not grounded in the concrete conditions of any particular history. Rahner's crucial turn to the subject consisted in exiting the barren dogmatical approach of the schools to enter the domain of the subject and of historicity understood as an existential dimension of that "subject." This crucial turn allowed Rahner to link dogma with experience; revelation with historicity; and theology with anthropology, hence establishing an inner relationship between grace and nature. The post-Rahnerian theologians intensify Rahner's method, moving further from an understanding of historicity as an "existential" to an emphasis on the concreteness of history; from the abstract Rahnerian subject to the concrete subjects and non-subjects in their particular societies and cultures; and from the transcendental identity found in the original experience to the concrete experiences of non-identity found in those particular histories, societies, and cultures. The catastrophes in history, the real presence of evil, and the experiences of discrimination and systemic injustice are the challenges that function as *loci theologici* in these post-Rahnerian theologies.

Political theology, born in the particular context of the highly developed and historically complex German society, seeks to respond to the privatization of religion typical of the developed societies of Europe. Moreover, it seeks to formulate Christian theology in a way that accounts for the concrete experiences of non-identity in the history of those societies in general and of Germany in particular, namely the Enlightenment, Auschwitz, and the Third World. By responding to those challenges, political theology tries to help both theology itself and the Church to overcome the danger of being co-opted by modernity, and aims at rescuing the subject from its loss of identity in a society that has colonized reason and separated it from its own history.

Liberation theology was born as a theological response to the experiences of systemic poverty, death, and non-personhood in the context of a society founded on the grounds of colonization, dependence, and underdevelopment, in which the excluded, the non-persons, have started to make their voices heard. In this respect, liberation theology represents a radically new kind of theological voice further developed in the manifold Third-World theologies. Liberation theology seeks to formulate Christian theology from the perspective of the non-person, responding to the experience of suffering and death and interpreting Christianity in a way that is relevant to people's liberation from all kinds of exclusions, dependencies, and exploitations.

THEOLOGICAL METHOD

Political and liberation theologies born in late modernity value the emancipatory drive of the Enlightenment, and seek to formulate Christian theology in a positive and critical dialogue with modernity. This gives these theologies a correlational character. In the case of Rahner, correlation is made explicit in the anthropological grounding of his theology, that is to say, in the inner link he establishes between theology and anthropology, between revelation and human experience, between grace and nature, and between human history and the history of salvation. The correlational role of theology, however, is different in each of the two post-Rahnerian models. Metz seeks to relate the Christian message to the situation created by a colonizing, evolutionistic-triumphalistic, and oppressive modernity that does away with the subject and causes massive suffering and sheer annihilation. The experiences of non-identity are the ground upon which Metz wants to formulate a post-idealistic theology that does not reflect on God abstractly but on the basis of concrete realities and the experiences of history.

His is also a practical theology, a theology that, like Gutiérrez's, recognizes the primacy of praxis as well as its epistemological correlate, namely, that truth must be done. The main problem for Metz is not the cognitive crisis of Christianity vis-à-vis modernity but its privatization, thus losing its constitutive social-political-practical dimension, and the fact that the Church, as the primary Christian subject, is utterly unable to do the truth and unwilling to pay the price of its orthodoxy in the practice of its life because it has been co-opted by modernity. Consequently, praxis and subject constitute the two central concepts of a political theology understood as a practical hermeneutics of Christianity.

Gutiérrez's theology wants to relate to the situation of the poor, of the non-persons in the concrete Latin American situation, in which certain conditions obtain: massive poverty, pervasive religiosity, the highly relevant presence of the Catholic Church, and an "irruption of the poor" in the life of the region, demanding that their voices be heard. It is from this particularity that he wants to make a public and universal claim as regards both the Catholic Church and world society at large. His theology, therefore, entails an interpretation of the situation from the perspective of "the underside of history" and an interpretation of the Word of God that can relate to that situation. This correlation has a denouncing-prophetic-transformative character, vis-à-vis both the Church and society.

One of the main traits of his theology is its crucial grounding in spirituality. This spirituality, made up of the silence of contemplation and the practice of following Christ in the community of the Church, is the *actus primus* of the Christian. Only then does theology take place as an *actus secundus*. As such, theology becomes a critical reflection on Christian praxis in the light of the Word. The Word and liberating praxis disclose each other in a dialectical way. This is the key hermeneutical principle of liberation theology and implies the theologian be a member of the Church, a follower of Christ within a community committed both to its own permanent conversion and to the transformation of society in the light of the Word.

Rahner and other theologians who brought about a radical revision of Catholic theology insisted on the necessity of using social sciences as partners of theology. For both political and liberation theologies, social sciences and critical social theory play an indispensable role in interpreting their social settings. In the case of political theology the main partner is the critical social theory of the Frankfurt School with its insistence on negative dialectics. The main partners of liberation theology are the theory of dependency and some aspects of Marxism. They play an especially important role because one of the main practical aims of that theology is to transform reality, doing away with poverty, discrimination, and early death. However, Gutiérrez has been insistent on the theological centrality of his enterprise, claiming that the role of social theory in his theology is important and relevant but not foundational. Theology has its own sources of which the Word of God and the life of the Christian Church in following Christ are the central ones.

With regard to the use of the Jewish-Christian Scriptures, modern theology has approached them with the tools of critical interpretation. Both literary and historical-critical methods have played a crucial role in understanding biblical texts in a way that could relate to modern critical reason.

Rahner followed, albeit in his own terms, this modern trend in interpreting biblical texts. The two post-Rahnerian theologies have developed their own approach to scriptures and, also on that score, mark a difference with Rahner. Although they take critical methods for granted, their main approach to the Bible does not depend on the results those methods may offer. Critical methods have a corrective and auxiliary character but in no way can have a substantive character in reading scriptures theologically because they simply do not approach them from a salvific viewpoint but only from a scientific perspective. Both theologies approach the texts, therefore, in a rather straightforward manner as inspired texts in which the believers have recognized a salvific truth, which is paradigmatic for the Christian community.

Metz has stressed more and more the importance of the biblical narrative and of its grounding character as regards theological reason. In keeping with the theological centrality of concrete history and concrete social-cultural environment, he stresses the narrative structure of the theological argument, arguing that Christianity is not a community of interpretation and argumentation, but a community of memory and narrative in a practical way. This stress, in turn, relates to Metz's insistence on the theologically grounding character of the category of memory.

Gutiérrez uses scriptures continually and systematically in his theological work. Therefore, his theology is pervaded by an ongoing, meditative-reflective reading of the Bible from the perspective of a communitarian-ecclesial Christian praxis of following Jesus under the circumstances of poverty, injustice, and death in Latin America. Reading the scriptures is not a pure search for the meaning of the text but rather a dialogue of the community of the Church that follows Jesus with the God that is the avenger of the poor and the oppressed, the God of life, history, and creation.

THEOLOGICAL CONTENT OF POLITICAL AND LIBERATION THEOLOGIES

Theologically speaking, the development of both political and liberation theologies is a journey toward a decreasing positive theological content; a journey in which the more they become genuinely "theo-logical," the more also they become negative theologies; in short, a journey of intensification down the *via negationis* toward the mystery of a God whose hiddenness must be taken with full seriousness. As regards their theological core Rahner, Metz, and Gutiérrez favor a given moment or symbol of Christian salvation. Although the Christ event plays a central role in all of them, Rahner's understanding of salvation is rather protological, Metz emphasizes eschatology, and Gutiérrez stresses Christology. Since the crucial theological shift of political and liberation theologies has been to make historical, concrete experience the main entry to "theo-logy," the classical themes of creation, fall, redemption, Church, and eschatology are analyzed in the light of the concrete historical experiences of "non-identity."

Because of this theological location, creation will not be primarily understood by Metz and Gutiérrez as the protological salvific act of God in which grace, that is to say, God's own self-communication, once and for all is "always-already" present. Rather, creation is historicized and thus is understood as the stage in which both the presence of evil and suffering, and the salvific action of God, take place. From his existential-personal perspective and in the framework of his transcendental argument, Rahner understands sin as a sort of historical, pre-existent, co-determination of freedom; and the existence of radical evil as a mysterious reality which, in any case, does not compromise the abiding sovereignty of God. For both political and liberation theologies, the presence of evil in history is a major issue and, therefore, becomes theologically crucial. History cannot be either easily read as a triumphal progression toward freedom and justice, or rendered theologically irrelevant through a transcendental analysis for which grace is necessarily "always-already" present. Such optimistic or transcendental views either contradict the facts or do not take them with theological seriousness. If suffering, poverty, evil in its different expressions, and death are not to be forgotten and suppressed by a history read with the eyes of the victors or by a theology that runs so high that it does not touch them in its development, then history must be reread from the perspective of suffering and Christianity must be reinterpreted also from that perspective.

For Metz, history is not primarily the stage of action and progress; rather, it is the phenomenon of unredeemed suffering (*passio*) that becomes the main hermeneutical criterion and judge of history. This *conversio ad passionem* is the central perspective from which all Metz's theology stems. Creation and history, therefore, must be understood, on the basis of the biblical narrative that brings to the fore the memory of suffering, as ultimately being in the hands of a God whose acts remain always hidden to human categories. Any triumphalistic understanding of history must be interrupted by the memory of suffering. Indeed, history itself must be understood precisely on the basis of the interruption caused by the memory of suffering; the interruption that results from heeding the "authority of those who suffer." Human action in history, then, must be led by that memory of suffering to the practice of universal solidarity with all those who suffer, ultimately understanding history in the light of the definitive eschatological interruption through which and in which history is constituted and the dead and forgotten of that history are rescued. This memory of suffering is not primarily a category of the past but an eschatological category, a memory that represents the active, salvific presence in history of God's eschatological salvation.

For Gutiérrez, the history of Latin America and the fact that the vast majority of people in the world belong to the mass of the poor witness to the fact that history has been built upon domination, inequality, exclusion, oppression, and, finally, death. History, however, is not the realm of evil, but the stage in which, through salvific acts, God's self-manifestation takes place. Human history and destiny are ultimately dependent on God's gratuitous purpose, not necessarily coincident with human pursuits. In recognizing this, human behavior is not limited to ethical-prophetical action but essentially turns to the mystical-contemplative acknowledgment of God's sovereign gratuitousness.

Not only creation and history but Christology too is reinterpreted by political and liberation theologies. Metz's Christology, like the rest of his theology, seeks to establish an inner link between the Christian message and the historical situation in an eschatological key. Jesus Christ's salvific power is intrinsically united with his *memoria passionis, mortis et resurrectionis*. Christ, consequently, cannot be understood either as a triumphant victor or as a purely religious redeemer. Metz wants to preserve both the constitutive *passio* character of the Christ event and the political-historical dimension of his redemption. The memory of suffering and death cannot be annulled by the memory of resurrection but becomes a constitutive part of that memory. They belong together. There is no "Easter Sunday-Christology" without "Holy Saturday-Christology." In this respect, the Christ event, as a foundation of hope in history, must be interpreted as a dangerous memory of suffering that proleptically announces a definitive eschatological salvation. This proleptic announcement both prompts a solidary historical response in favor of all the oppressed and forgotten in history and interrupts any easy affirmation of intra-historical salvation.

Christ appears closely united in Gutiérrez to his idea of integral liberation. Within liberation theology's understanding of God's salvation in history, Christ is *el liberador*. In this respect, although Gutiérrez's theology is also aware of the importance of eschatology, it has a markedly christocentric and intra-historical character. More to the point, the intra-historical dimension of salvation on the basis of Christ's integral liberation is crucial for this theology that seeks to expose both the inner link between Christian salvation and the political-ethical transformation of society, and the historical role of Christians in bringing about this transformation. Christology, therefore, is primarily understood in its salvific-redemptive character but bearing in mind that the idea of Christ's action as liberator in history is complemented by a view of the suffering Christ as radically solidary with the poor. In this way, using Metz's terms, the Christ of *actio* becomes also the Christ of *passio* in the suffering faces of the poor. In this scenario, the ethical-historical dimension of salvation in Christ is interpreted under the light of God's sovereignty and gratuitousness.

The Church, although it plays different roles in Metz and in Gutiérrez, is for both the community that, following Christ in history, announces his truth and bears his hope under the conditions of history. For Metz, the Church must embrace radical discipleship and its ensuing costs in order to witness to God's liberating message and action. Christ followers must be prophets whose life refers constantly in practical terms to the dangerous and subversive memory of Christ. The Church's clearly prophetic role must serve both to make Christianity understandable and credible in practical terms and to rescue the subject in a society in which an instrumental reason reigns overall and has converted the self into a passive practitioner of the ways and aims imposed by this reason. The truth of Christianity can only be relevant when the community of believers pays the price of its orthodoxy through the dangerous orthopraxis of living out in history and society the implications of Christ's *memoria passionis, mortis et resurrectionis.*

In the case of Gutiérrez, the experience of the church that follows Jesus Christ in the Latin American situation of suffering and injustice is both the matrix of his theology and its main practitioner. His can be properly named both a pastorally driven church theology and a theology of the Church and for the Church. The Church is the people of God in history whose task and main purpose is to bear eschatological hope. This mission in Latin America does not consist in the purely religious announcement of an a-historical message of salvation but rather in reading politically "the signs of the time" and announcing its message of Christian liberation, actively aligning itself with the poor and their liberation struggle. It is the poor who, far from being mere recipients of the aid of the Church, are both subjects of their own liberation and evangelizers in and of a Church which, being a disciple of Christ in history and society, does the truth. Performing this orthopractical task in Latin America under difficult and dangerous conditions, the Church pays the price for its orthodoxy with the fertile blood of the martyrs.

For both political and liberation theologies, eschatology is the final horizon of salvation. However, their stress on this theological category is different. As stated above, eschatology is Metz's key theological category and, as such, pervades his theology to such an extent that every other category or theological statement must be understood from a radically, indeed interruptive, eschatological stand. One of the most important theological paradigms in the late twentieth century has been the classic "already-not yet" paradigm. Both Rahner and Gutiérrez formulate their theology within this paradigm that tries to make explicit the necessary balance and radical tension between the historical presence and actuality of salvation and its final, eschatological nature. Metz, however, wants so much to stress the radical nature of eschatology that he is suspicious of this "already-not yet" formula. He fears that the "already's" strength may silence the experience of non-identity, the memory of suffering that belongs to the experience of Jesus himself and to the core of biblical religion. He also fears that the radical eschatological dimension, indeed interruption, of Christianity may simply be seen, in practical terms, as the final or definitive step of a salvation that "already" is at hand and grows in history. The question for him is not how much salvation we "already" have and how much "not yet," but how much eschatologically understood time do we have at all? Metz insists constantly that eschatology must be understood as the end of history, as the total and final interruption of history; so total and final that such an interruption is best understood in the biblical category of apocalypse. Because this interruption marks the definitive end of history, it is at the same time the point from which both history and historical action are, in a way, constituted. Without either memory or interruptive end, time and history become just mere repetition of an empty sameness, lacking, in the last resort, both identity and true existence. This apocalyptical-eschatological dimension of Christianity constitutes the very foundation of hope. This hope includes on the one hand the historical signs of salvation manifested through and in the resurrection of Christ, while preserving on the other hand the experiences of non-identity, the unresolved questions concerning the passion and death of Jesus Christ, and, in general, suffering and evil in history. In the last analysis, Christian hope can only exist as imminent expectancy of the final coming of the Lord.

This radical-apocalyptical eschatology has its consequences for the importance of both human action and human responsibility in history. In this regard, Gutiérrez and Metz are somewhat different. Both stress historical responsibility and transformative action concerning the pursuit of justice, peace, and freedom. However, their different social contexts and concerns prompt them to put different accents on that common transformational thrust. For Metz, because every historical achievement is under eschatological judgment and must be interrupted by the memory of suffering, liberating action is understood rather in terms of Adorno's negative dialectics. Although this action is intrinsic to Christian praxis, its practical content will always be provisional and ambiguous. Metz's corrective stress on the *passio* component of Christian praxis stems from his concern to differentiate it from the action-driven, domineering, social practice common in developed societies. Gutiérrez's concern is different, namely, the need to accompany the poor in their pursuit of liberation and justice. Stressing the *passio* element may be adequate in those societies to which Metz refers but it could be misinterpreted and lead to resignation and passive acceptance of suffering and injustice in a society like the Peruvian one. This in no way implies that Gutiérrez has disregarded that *passio* element entailed by discipleship and actualized by so many Christians who, in Latin America, have suffered persecution, torture, and even death for their commitment to the poor and to the pursuit of justice. Rather, it means that Metz's and Gutiérrez's emphases on *actio* and *passio* are somewhat different within their common theological framework.

THE MYSTERY OF GOD AS THEOLOGY'S ULTIMATE WORD

The last, and indeed only, word of "theo-logy" is about God. Every theological system must have a notion of God that coheres with all the other elements in the system. Conversely, every element depends on the notion of God that sustains the whole system. Rahner recapitulates his entire theology in his notion of God as the incomprehensible "holy mystery." This notion is rooted in the divine action that constitutes the only Christian mystery, i.e., God's free and loving self-communication as it is unthematically affirmed in any meaningful human act, and fully disclosed in Jesus Christ. The Rahner who starts with the analysis of the transcendental experience from a philosophical perspective, and who historicizes it, opening it out to existential dimensions of humanness other than knowledge, and to social-political dimensions that belong to it, ends with a meditative theology based on the experience of God and centered on the mystery of God, where, finally, everything coheres. This recapitulation of everything else in God as "holy mystery" fully coheres with Rahner's theological will and aim, namely to give the ultimate answer to existence from within, showing that such an answer cannot be other than the incomprehensible God ever present in human existence as its innermost constitutive element and fully disclosed in Jesus Christ.

Like Rahner, Metz and Gutiérrez have also evolved in a strictly "theological" way, coming to consider the question of God the fundamental, indeed only, question of their theologies. This question comes to the fore in these theologies not because they have suddenly converted to speculative theology, but because they need to find their own way of talking about the God they have encountered in the concrete history in which they have developed their theological enterprises from the perspective of the "underside," the vanquished, and the dead. Theology, as *Gottesrede*, as *un hablar de Dios*, is directly challenged to reinterpret history, reason, and everything that exists, adopting a critical approach, changing perspectives, widening the limits of reason, opening the doors to the repressed others, bringing new voices to the theological task, and challenging the "official" ways of imagining and representing reality. Metz wants to change the terms in which both classical and transcendental theologies have imagined God: a strong God who remains unchallenged and untouched by the tragedies and contradictions of history, and who, in the end, is invincible. In a God so rendered, the experiences of non-identity have no relevance and go theologically unnoticed. Faced with those experiences, the question "Who is God?" must be reformulated as "Where is God?" This way, the question about God becomes totally practical in the face of the actually massive suffering in the world and issues in a negative theology that seeks an answer not on the basis of God's presence but, so to speak, by "missing" God in the midst of suffering and by asking, "crying and hoping" like Christ on the cross, about God's whereabouts.

Thus, the language of theology is transformed. God-talk becomes primarily a "talking to God," before being a "talking about God," firmly anchored in prayer as a form of speech free enough to express the *leiden an Gott*, that is to say, free enough to question God, to complain to God, to show anger and frustration for the inexplicable existence of evil and suffering. This theology is, therefore, a reflective language of prayer, a reflection on God that starts with prayer and keeps using that language throughout, because, ultimately, there are no answers to the questions, to the complaints, and to the suffering. Ultimately, God cannot be properly described with "strong" categories. Rather, these categories must be "weak," mirroring the "vulnerability" of God vis-à-vis the presence and "power" of evil and suffering. These "weak" categories are the biblical categories of the beatitudes, of the sermon on the mount; the categories of poverty, mourning, and "hunger and thirst for justice"; those categories that express the reality of suffering and longing, and the inability to be consoled and to triumph, while at the same time expressing eschatological hope. Even the

Johannine "God is love" must be "weakly" understood. God's love is not invincible; it bears the marks of the "wound" caused by suffering and sheer destruction. A God who is discovered and remembered in a memory of passion is always a "poor," "endangered," "weak," "vulnerable" God. The God of Israel is "poor" because such a God does not console; does not take away the contradictions, suffering, and anxiety always present in history. Israel remains always an eschatological "land of screams," a land of memory and expectation, and, therefore, absolutely incapable of imagining God in either mythical or idealistic terms. Such negative-theological *Gottesrede* seeks to express all the tensions involved in the *Gottespassion* concerning the God of biblical monotheism. The believer, together with Israel and with Jesus of Nazareth, the crucified and resurrected Christ, is passionately attracted to the God of the promise, the only and true hope for life and liberation, while at the same time enduring a *passio*, an inexplicable suffering, *leiden an Gott*, full of questions without definitive answers. God is not a human-made myth whose function is to console either with answers or with power and strength. God is both irritatingly eschatological and "weak," a vulnerable and suffering God with open flanks. Therefore, the *Gottesrede* is a constitutionally negative language to and about God, only ultimately possible in and through prayer.

Gutiérrez's *hablar de Dios*, his God-talk, is also essentially an *hablar con Dios*, a talking to God. It is not possible to talk about God without being befriended by God, without going through all the experiences of a true and deep, close relationship with the God of the Bible, including not only obedience, confidence, praise, and love, but, as in Job, also rebellion, betrayal, grievance, and estrangement. Gutiérrez's main aim is to speak of God as a loving God in the midst of innocent suffering. In doing so, his *hablar de Dios*, his theology, is an *hablar con Dios*, that is to say, a prayer. Gutiérrez refers to his theological method as "a talk enriched by silence," very close to Metz's "reflective prayer-talk" based on contemplation, discipleship, and praxis. For both, true theology stems from and issues in a prayer that is always accompanied by the praxis of discipleship in history.

History is also Gutiérrez's locus for encountering God; a history from which to establish a dialogue with the experience of God conveyed by the biblical narrative. This narrative, now read through the eyes of the poor and the oppressed, reveals the face of God in the face of the poor, as in the works of Arguedas, and in the experiences of estrangement, absurdity, and lack of hope encountered in that history, as in Vallejo's poetry.[1] In fact, Vallejo and Arguedas are powerful voices that express the way history is read in

Peru from the perspective of the oppressed and the poor and try to relate that history to the experience of the presence-absence of God. Their literary-mythical-poetical language provides Gutiérrez with a powerful instrument to overcome the strictures of a purely discursive language, opening the theological language to the intuitive and meaning-excessive language it needs to suggest and somehow express the inexpressible.

In this "Peruvian" God-talk, Metz's memory of the dead in history becomes Gutiérrez's current awareness of those presently dead-alive. Theology can be carried out only if rooted in the mystery of God, that is to say, in the paradoxical experience of seeking a God who seems not only to neglect the creature and to remain hidden but also to persecute this creature. It is in the midst of this painful experience that Gutiérrez seeks, with Job, with Arguedas, and with Vallejo, to talk to and about God. Faced with the suffering of the masses of the poor, the reigning social inequalities and injustice, and the death of innocent people, Gutiérrez insists on affirming that the Christian God is the God of life and the God of love of the letter of John. God, to begin with, is not a consoling God of the poor, but the foundation of their hope, resistance, and struggle. The consoling idol must be unmasked and replaced by the biblical, liberating God, who is paradoxically manifested in all those who have been rejected in society – the "Indians," the poor, the despised, the fools, the malformed, the unadapted, and the socially incorrect – and who, therefore, becomes a different, "underside," "fool," "irrational," and "malformed" God. This "weak" God is the God of hope, resistance, and liberation.

Gutiérrez's dialogical commentary on Job is his most elaborate work on God, whose central question is: how to talk about the God of love and justice in the midst of poverty, oppression, and the suffering of the innocent? As in Metz, the question is: "Where are you, my God?" However, Gutiérrez's reading of Job is not centered on the mystery of evil and suffering in history. Gutiérrez's Job is the Job who, despite every counter-evidence, aims at believing in God as the God in whom he can trust in a totally gratuitous way. Ultimately, therefore, the subject matter of the book of Job is not, according to Gutiérrez, the theodicy question but the question of the nature of the God–creature relation as a totally gratuitous relation. The conversation with God, through Job and with Job, is the way by which Gutiérrez discovers the utterly gratuitous love of God in the midst of the suffering of the innocent in Latin America.

Gratuitousness in Gutiérrez means the absolute lack of motive and reason. In this sense, gratuitousness is a negative concept, a way of referring to the radical "emptiness" of God's love. Gratuitousness, therefore, is the name of God's mystery in Gutiérrez; that which has no reason or motive, and, therefore, cannot be explained. The way to discover the gratuitous love of God is, ultimately, the way of mystical language. This way, however, is preceded by the discovery of the poor and oppressed; by the commitment to justice and to the cause of the poor; by the prophetical language that demands that justice be done in history. Job's final dialogue with God, his listening to God, is his route to contemplation. Job begins to understand that God cannot be comprehended in human categories. God's plans and ways, designs and justice are not the same as those of the creatures. God's justice, plans, and ways completely exceed any reason; they are reason-free; they can only be understood within the "emptiness" of God's absolute gratuitousness. God is beyond categories and beyond any logic other than sheer gratuitousness. It is in that beyond-ness that Job meets, discovers, and enters a new relation of gratuitousness with God.

CONCLUSION

Whereas Rahner seeks to make sense of the experience of the modern self, Metz wants to rescue and to find a firm foundation for the dead and forgotten of history, while Gutiérrez seeks to liberate and to find hope for the poor and for all those who suffer innocently. In this sense, the three of them, each one by his own route, come to discover and to affirm God as the holy, non-identical, and gratuitous mystery. Hence, political and liberation theologies, after moving from Rahner's transcendentality to history and society – in order to place the discussion of God on the level of the conditions of history and the experiences of non-identity found in it – retrieve the hiddenness and the incomprehensibility of God, thus returning, in their own way, to the mystery of God in which Rahner likewise encapsulated his entire theological enterprise.

Note

1 Jose Maria Arguedas (1911–69). Peruvian anthropologist and writer. His works explore the subjugated indigenous Peruvian culture and its relationship with the domineering colonial culture, paying special attention to the ambiguous role of religion in that relationship. He and Gutiérrez became friends shortly before Arguedas' death.

Cesar Vallejo (1892–1938). Peruvian poet. He left Peru in 1923 for Paris where he spent the remainder of his life. He developed contact with avant-garde artists, such as Artaud and Picasso, and with the political Left. His poetry reflects the many hardships in his life, and reflect a desperate reaching out for hope in the midst of darkness and intense suffering.

Further reading

Gutiérrez, G., *On Job: God-Talk and the Suffering of the Innocent* (Maryknoll, NY: Orbis, 1987).

    Theology of Liberation: History, Politics and Salvation, 15th edn. (Maryknoll, NY: Orbis, 1988).

    Las Casas: In Search of the Poor of Jesus Christ (Maryknoll, NY: Orbis, 1993).

    The Density of the Present: Selected Writings (Maryknoll, NY: Orbis, 1999).

Metz, J. B., *Faith in History and Society: Toward a Practical Fundamental Theology* (New York: Seabury, 1980).

    A Passion for God: The Mystical-Political Dimension of Christianity, ed. and trans. J. M. Ashley (Mahwah, NJ: Paulist, 1998).

    Poverty of Spirit, ed. and trans. J. Drury (Mahwah, NJ: Paulist, 1998).

    Love's Strategy: The Political Theology of Johann Baptist Metz, ed. J. K. Downey (Harrisburg, PA: Trinity Press International, 1999).

If the title of this essay is taken at face value, by all rights it should be very short. While Rahner's life spanned the twentieth century, with the rapid and irreversible change that century has brought to our understanding of "female," Rahner's observations about the changing status of women do not refer to the movement of feminist theology, a movement that was well underway by the time of his death in 1984. At the outset, then, we must state clearly that Karl Rahner was not a feminist (indeed, not even an "anonymous" one). Nevertheless, Rahner's twin expositions of the hearer of the word and the mystery of God, his searching method, and, perhaps most importantly, his insistence that these ground a dynamic re-framing of the Christian, and particularly the Roman Catholic, tradition, have proven to be a rich resource for Catholic feminists.

Following the vision of Vatican II, and responding to the needs of a church faced with rising numbers and declining vocations, an unprecedented wave of lay women and men began graduate-level study in theology in the 1970s, readying themselves for a variety of positions in parish ministry and education. Many of those studying were women, women who were experiencing simultaneous social and ecclesial revolutions.[1] For many of these, Rahner's voice shaped their theological study, providing a theological framework for questions about doctrinal change, masculine symbolism, and the status of the human person before God, as well as a pastoral voice that took seriously their experience of profound change, with its shock of freedom and decision.

Feminist theology is a scholarly movement that brings the critical lens of gender analysis to bear on the methods, doctrines, themes, texts, and practices that shape theological reflection. As this analysis demonstrates a pervasive androcentric bias in theological reflection, feminist theology generally proceeds with a "hermeneutic of suspicion" that seeks both unrecognized oppression and uncelebrated grace in the long tradition of Christian women's religious experience and reflection. Feminist theology often uses the analytical tools of liberation theology, with its well-developed resistance to the intellectual, linguistic, and social tools of oppression. In a critical mode, however, feminist theology also reflects (perhaps only implicitly) the broader lens of modernity, asking, with Feuerbach, if religious symbols are not simply projections of the values of a given (patriarchal) social order. More recently, a "third wave" of women theologians from outside of the white academic feminist establishment has asked feminist theology the same questions, calling for a stronger sense of the "world Church" that Rahner envisioned.

As questions of theological anthropology are central to both Rahner's work and that of Catholic feminist theology, this chapter will first focus on the resources for feminist anthropology offered by some fundamental themes in Rahner's work. The middle part of this essay will highlight Rahner's treatment of three specific topics: the changing role of women in society and Church, the question of women's ordination, and the post-Vatican II understanding of Mary. Rahner recognized and positively grounded the changes he saw taking place with regard to the role of women in society and in ecclesial life, and directly addressed the question of ordaining women as prompted by these changing conditions. In a similar practical fashion, Rahner called for women themselves to name how the figure of Mary would appropriately function for Christian women. The chapter concludes with some further directions and critical questions which might come to bear in future feminist appropriation of Rahner's theological vision.

"STARTING WITH THE HUMAN": A STARTING POINT FOR FEMINIST THEOLOGY[2]

Rahner's most fundamental theological commitments are those which reflect his understanding of the graced human person. For Rahner, the human person has an inner orientation toward the divine, a fundamental capacity for the self-communication of God. This positive valuation of the human capacity to know God grounds Rahner's turn to human experience in his "indirect method" and is given theological expression in his theology of grace. Most importantly, Rahner's assertion of the human capacity for the self-communication of God opened the door for women to claim their experience as a starting point for theological reflection.

A representative exposition of "mainline Christian feminism" is Anne Carr's 1988 study, *Transforming Grace: Christian Tradition and Women's Experience.*[3] Speaking from within the Catholic tradition, and grounded in post-Vatican II theology, Carr draws on Schillebeeckx, Tillich, and Tracy, but returns most consistently to the theological insights of Rahner. Carr had claimed earlier that Rahner's work proceeded methodologically as a "theological anthropology"; in *Transforming Grace* this starting point is a feminist imperative, recognizing the necessity of bringing women's experience to bear in critical fashion on the construction of Christian theology. Moreover, Carr also follows an important nuance in Rahner's "turn to the subject" in that, like Rahner, she finds human experience to be a starting point not only for the various systematic treatises (anthropology, Christology, etc.); human experience also serves, for Carr and Rahner, as the starting point for understanding the more fundamental theological horizon of God's incomprehensibility.

Like many feminist theologians, Carr is more interested in developing the constructive possibilities of the feminist critique as it cuts across the discipline than in positioning herself vis-à-vis the lineage of a great (male) theologian. So while Carr acknowledges her use of Rahner, it is always in company with his theological contemporaries; it would thus not be correct to name her a "Rahnerian," in the way that such usage might apply in other cases. It seems more accurate to say that Rahner's theological perspective is a profound influence on Carr's thought, and can be seen as an impetus for at least four key assertions in her feminist theology.

First, Carr draws on the methodological insights of Paul Tillich (and later David Tracy) in company with Rahner's theological perspective to develop a method of correlation. Taking as a starting point the task of correlating "the kerygma with the 'situation' in theology,"[4] Carr names "the situation" in theology to be "patriarchal," and thus one which requires that the critical claims of the feminist movement be used to question the beliefs, texts, and practices of Christian theology. It would not be sufficient for feminist purposes, however, merely to correlate current insights with Christian belief, as the goal of feminist theology is not the full realization of the anthropological status quo, but a this-worldly realization of its redemption. Such a prophetic stance requires a similarly oriented anthropology, which Carr finds in Rahner's critique of the standard theological treatment of human nature as a "static essence." Thus, in a second assertion, Carr highlights Rahner's emphasis on human self-determination, which pairs both freedom and responsibility "in the determination of what human being is and will become."[5] In Rahner's hands, Thomas' optimistic view of human capacity is reinforced by an Ignatian sense of the Christian life as a calling. For Carr, this open-ended but urgent anthropology theologically grounds an invitation for women to claim their agency in creating the human future.

Third, Carr follows Rahner's retrieval of God as mystery. While Rahner describes humanity as the place where God reveals Godself, what is revealed is God's essential incomprehensibility. For feminist theologians, this retrieval frees the symbol of God from multiple layers of androcentric projection, allowing the symbol to speak anew, with new effects. And fourth, Carr develops Rahner's understanding that this God, while remaining incomprehensible, comes close to us by sharing in our humanity, an understanding of the incarnation that rejects dualistic notions of nature and supernature: "God is self-limited in a way that allows creatures, especially humans, their own autonomy . . . the more autonomy creatures possess, the more dependent they are (precisely through union) on God."[6] Divine immanence and divine transcendence are seen here as interdependent, not competing, concepts, illustrated in Rahner's "searching Christology" with its "emphasis on the truly human Jesus."[7] Women's experience of the "truly human" is validated, in Carr's feminist appropriation of Rahner, as a properly theological resource; in other words, in the form "female" we know God directly, not in relief.

In early 1993, sensing an at least provisional consensus among Catholic feminists, Catherine Mowry LaCugna edited a collection of essays on themes from revelation to Christology to spirituality, intended to present a feminist overview of systematic theology. Titled *Freeing Theology: The Essentials of Theology in Feminist Perspective*, the collection illustrated the reach of a common formation among Catholic feminists who shared a liberal/liberationist and often Rahnerian post-Vatican II theological sensibility, very much in the trajectory of Carr's "mainstream Christian feminism."[8] In various ways, the echo of Rahner is found: in Catherine Hilkert's presentation of an experiential understanding of revelation; in Mary Hines' tracing of the shift in ecclesiology from static models to a dynamic sense of a pilgrim people, and in Susan Ross' discussion of the profound shift in understanding of sacramental theology, particularly in the role of the symbol, after Vatican II. Anne Carr's opening essay for the volume details the use of "women's experience" in the methods of feminist theologians Rosemary Radford Ruether and Elisabeth Schüssler Fiorenza, finally arguing for a feminist norm that would address the "whole of Scripture and tradition" while offering "an interpretation of the meaning of that whole" (citing Rahner and Schillebeeckx as models).

In a well-known essay, Rahner argued that "dogmatic theology today must be theological anthropology" (paralleling and amplifying this point by also arguing that a similar interpenetration pertains to "philosophical" and revealed theology).[9] While theological anthropology has been a starting point for many feminist theologians, some have also engaged Rahner's thought in works that begin with a feminist rethinking of the doctrine of God. Catherine Mowry LaCugna uses Rahner's trinitarian theology to support a revitalized approach to both the understanding of God as triune mystery and the theological treatment of human personhood, an approach which is shaped by feminist concern.[10] In *She Who Is: The Mystery of God in Feminist Theological Discourse*, Elizabeth A. Johnson extended an explicitly feminist exploration of the image of "Sophia" as a lens for the doctrine of God and retrieved the thought of both Thomas and Rahner. While Johnson's starting point in that study is a commitment to "the flourishing of poor women of color in violent situations . . . women with their dependent children," her theological agenda is focused on a constructive response to the problem of idolatrously androcentric God-talk.[11] In true feminist fashion, her next large study addresses the relational reality of Christian community in a work on the communion of saints, and only after that does she present, through her own very decisive "turn to the subject," a pneumatological study of the theology of Mary that will certainly provide a Rahnerian perspective for future feminist theological anthropologies.[12]

In addition to providing a theological scaffolding that has proven fruitful for feminist constructive theology, Rahner also treated "women's issues" at several points in his long career. His systematizing vision is discernable in these treatments, as he dealt with these issues in ways that are illustrative of, rather than exceptions to, his theological vision as a whole.

THE CHANGING ROLE OF WOMEN

Rahner wrote on the Christian life from many perspectives, from theological articles on anthropology, grace, and the sacraments, to more pastorally oriented essays on prayer, confession, and spirituality, to programmatic pieces on the priesthood and the laity. In all of these, one imagines that the "man" he had in mind is male, yet his essays are strikingly free of "feminine" and "masculine" stereotypes. Instead, his focus is consistently on the inner integrity of being human, as he wrote directly for Christians about the need to engage patiently with their own humanity in all its weakness and darkness and confusion.

Yet, on a few occasions, he did address the question of women's changing social role, and the ramifications of this for their life as Catholic Christians.[13] A 1964 address to the Convention of the Union of German Catholic Women, on the topic of "women in church and society," could well be reconsidered today. In this address, Rahner asserted that, since women and men are equal, the Church must understand "layman" as pertaining to men and women equally. He called for the Church to value the work and lives of all women, asking that women themselves help the Church's ministry to "take into account the unmarried, independent and professional woman no less than the mother and the housewife."[14] He also encouraged women to come forward in the life of the Church because of the declining numbers of ordained priests. While hardly a flattering rationale, the ranks of female parish workers that did emerge in the wake of Vatican II would be pleased to note that his support for their work is paired with the charge that those lay people who participate in the "apostolate of the hierarchy" need to be understood as "having a dignity and personal responsibility" that is not dependent on "the short-sighted caprice of the individual parish priest".

But what is most striking about this address, at a distance of forty years, is his approach to the topic "women in church and society," an approach which contrasts powerfully with how one might expect this topic to be treated today. Much of his address is devoted to a description of the "situation" in the Church, with speculative digressions into topics such as the role of the West in salvation history. Little of his address is devoted to telling his listeners how they should perceive themselves, other than to warn them of the dangers of living their lives as women according to a "folklore" model that may not be appropriate for their own "situation." While he does mention "feminine qualities," he does so only to ground his claim that women themselves will have to find the appropriate Christian "concrete pattern of life for women today," adding that this would be not a single "pattern" but "a whole range . . . and these must be of various kinds." Most importantly, in Rahner's view, how to be a Christian woman "is for the Christian woman herself to decide . . . as her primary, proper, and inalienable task."[15]

The "nature of woman" is also often addressed in a theologian's writings on marriage. Once again, Rahner presents both pre- and post-Vatican II accounts that stand in contrast to contemporary magisterial treatments that increasingly feature rather specific gender roles, particularly for women.[16] In 1936, near the end of an essay titled "The Consecration of the Layman to the Care of Souls," Rahner turned to the question of the marital relationship. Without placing complementary understandings of gender in the forefront, Rahner presented the theological significance of married love, arguing that the sacramental understanding of the conjugal union matters because it is in this union that the inexhaustible love of God can be encountered: "Love for a man for the sake of God does not lead out of the beloved man but into him. God is not another 'alongside' man. He is what is most intimate . . ."[17] Rahner seems to think that married love can be treated as on a continuum with the love of neighbor, as it is merely "a new consecration to the care of souls because it is an increase of supernatural love for God and for men."

Forty years later, in his 1976 *Foundations of Christian Faith*, Rahner again refuses to present male–female complementarity as the primary interpretive framework for the sacrament of marriage. Commenting on the nuptial metaphor in Ephesians 5:22–23, he suggests that the author of Ephesians is focused not on prescribing gender roles, but rather on describing the "unity of the love itself in one flesh and in one body [that] constitutes the parallel between Christ–church and marriage."[18] Echoing the continuity between marriage and the love of neighbor from forty years earlier, Rahner further claims that in this "genuine relationship of participation," a relationship that characterizes all of the graced relationality of the created order, the "church becomes present." This approach to the question of male–female roles in marriage, an approach that both prizes relationality and sets that relation in continuity with others, offers a helpful focus for feminist reflection.

THE ORDINATION OF WOMEN

The disjoinder between social and ecclesial roles for Roman Catholic women is most clearly marked by the Roman Catholic Church's continued refusal to ordain women; a disjoinder exacerbated by the acceptance of women in ministerial roles (including ordination) in other Christian churches. Rahner seemed to think that the social movement of women called for a far different ecclesial response than was offered.

Writing directly on "Women and the Priesthood," after the 1976 publication of *Inter Insigniores*, Rahner rejects that document's use of a gendered theological anthropology that claims that only a male priest can stand *in persona Christi*. Without elaboration, he simply says that such "an anthropology . . . would again threaten what the Declaration recognizes as the equal dignity and equal rights of women."[19] Moreover, Rahner also finds those portions of the CDF (the Vatican's Congregation for the Doctrine of the Faith) statement that rest on historical claims to consist of unsupported assertion. In Rahner's evaluation, Jesus and the disciples acted in a manner consistent with their historical and cultural context; he concludes that it "does not seem to be proved that the actual behaviour of Jesus and the Apostles implies a norm of divine revelation in the strict sense of the term."[20]

Although they already addressed questions about biological sexuality and social roles before the publication of *Inter Insigniores*, that document's problematic assertions certainly encouraged the efforts of Roman Catholic feminists. At first, the discussions featured a contrast between traditional theology's dual-nature model of humanity, for which biological sexuality was determinative, and a liberal proposal of a single-nature model of humanity, to which biological sexuality was incidental. In response to these, Mary Buckley presented a third, more person-centered, model, one which Anne Carr found to be congenial to Rahner's open-ended sense of human possibility.[21] Buckley's articulation of the notion of trans-formation presented a fertile common ground for Rahner's anthropological insights and the critical and prophetic character of feminist theology in the liberationist mode.

In a later interview (1981), Rahner again observed that the 1976 dec-laration "failed to convince me" but he also recognized that the official treatment of the topic was becoming even less amenable to dialogue.[22] Not only were the parameters of the discussion about the "nature of male and female" changing, the tenor of doctrinal discussion in general was rapidly becoming more rigid as the reforming directions of Vatican II were increas-ingly seen as in need of dialogue-ending "clarification," or even "definition." Rahner argued against this direction, not only for pastoral reasons, but to protect the notion of doctrine itself from misunderstanding. As Richard Lennan notes, Rahner did not find development to be antagonistic to doc-trine, but rather to be part of what doctrine is; Rahner's understanding of development is not "something that might occur only under fortuitous cir-cumstances, but . . . something that [has] its roots in the characteristics of doctrine itself."[23]

A final resource for thinking about Rahner's perspective on the question of women's ordination is the rich archive of his writings on the priesthood. In his latter years, he argued that the priesthood should change and develop to respond to a living Church, and it is noteworthy that his understand-ing of responding to change in this area is not unlike his understanding of an appropriate ecclesial response to women's changing social role. In both cases, Rahner did not advocate specific changes for the world-wide church, but, rather, promoted a broader and more flexible ecclesial frame-work in which a variety of forms for the exercise of the priesthood might be permitted, in the same way that he promoted a variety of patterns for women's social and ecclesial self-understanding. This perspective, rather than a positive championing of any particular remedy, is consistent with his approach to the question of women's ordination, as he notes that any such "development" might be more appropriate in some regions than in others ("my principle – namely, the Church is not meant to be a centralized, homogeneous, holy state").[24] Mary Hines points out some evolution in Rahner's own thought on doctrinal development, arguing that in his earlier work any impetus for development was fairly "in-house," emerging from discussions among theologians and the magisterium. Later essays, however, turn more toward the "faith of the people," even suggesting that this *sensus fidelium* has the status of a theological norm.[25] Rahner's support for ecclesial diversity certainly reflects the diversity of a Church that would take the "faith of the people" as an ecclesial template.

THE THEOLOGY OF MARY

Rahner's early impetus, in his writings about Mary, was doctrinal, as his concern was to curb what he saw as a problematic momentum in the proliferation of Marian dogmas. Illustrative of his approach to a wide variety of doctrinal topics, the early essays on the Immaculate Conception and the dogma of the Assumption reject the deductive approach of manual theology in favor of a starting point that asks what proper theological role this belief plays in the life of faith and the whole of Christian theology.[26]

Prefiguring the general contours of what will be Vatican II's understanding of the role of Mary in Catholic theology, Rahner treats Mary's "consent in faith" as central to salvation history, presenting it thus as "public" rather than "a pious, edifying idyll from someone's private life."[27] Mary's role is central to ecclesial self-understanding, not under the pall of submission, as the self-effacing, humble virgin, but as the one whose "consent" meets the fullness of the Word. In Rahner's understanding of the sweep of salvation history, *this* moment is the definitive act, as it is here, "in reply to this assent of the Virgin, God spoke his definitive word to the world as a Word of salvation and not of judgment."[28]

Rahner traces a fine line in these reflections, amplifying Mary's response as iconic but without reifying her (female) person. In a later essay, employing the language of the "perfect image," Rahner seems to accept the traditional linkage between Mary and the Church and Mary and "woman." Yet he rejects the notion that she should be a "model for believers in general," and professes "great embarrassment" at the treatment of "woman" in the tradition:

> Such concrete descriptions of woman's religious existence are based often and hastily on characteristics which really do not belong to the external, authentic nature of woman, but are historically, culturally, and sociologically conditioned. The charge might be made today that these descriptions purporting to be a theologically guaranteed

understanding of her nature are really opposed to woman's emancipation. The danger then arises that Mary's image will be drawn with the aid of such an historically and culturally conditioned image of woman and then used theologically to sanction and perpetuate this older and today in many respects dubious image.[29]

In a more specific example, the feminist reader is astonished to find Rahner producing an entire essay on Mary's virginity without once raising the question of gender.[30] Admittedly, Rahner's stated focus was less on the content of the debate about Mary's virginity before, during, and after the birth of Jesus, and more on the question of the need for a careful theological treatment of dogmatic claims. It must also be noted that the question of Mary's virginity is, for the Catholic tradition, not merely prurient speculation but a question that has been construed to have profound christological resonance. Nevertheless, while Rahner's avoidance of the kind of discussion that seemed overly focused on a fetish-like fascination with Mary's "bodily integrity" seems helpful, a feminist reader wonders how the question of gender could have escaped Rahner, with his keen eye for what was really at stake in doctrinal issues.

Rahner's focus on the human person rather than on biological sexuality led to a presentation of the theology of Mary that consistently set aside her maternal role in favour of her role as a graced human person. Elizabeth Johnson's study of the theology of Mary takes up Rahner's claim that Mary is "entirely one of us" as an invitation to reconstruct the figure of Mary of Nazareth as a historical person, and to present her Spirit-filled life in a way that "would integrate Mary back into theology." Johnson's feminist critique of the theological tradition about Mary, and her historical reconstruction of the likely shape of Mary's life as a poor woman in first century Palestine, fully exploits both Rahner's theology of grace and his anthropology of human freedom and self-determination.[31]

RAHNER AS A RESOURCE FOR FEMINIST THEOLOGY TODAY

This essay has already noted Rahner's call for women themselves to address their ecclesial self-understanding, a call used, to some extent, as a "warrant" for the work of Catholic feminists. Yet Rahner's call was not intended as a gratuitous invitation but was rather a corollary to his theological understanding of the human person. In the same spirit, future feminist retrievals of Rahner's theology might do well to focus less on what he did or did not say about female persons or "women's issues," and focus more on a critical retrieval of his theological work as a partner for the fundamental theological questions raised by feminist theology. In particular, the systematic interrelation of questions that drive feminist theological anthropology will come into play: questions of a fully contextual reading of human personhood, questions of the significance of gender for embodiment and social roles, and questions that engage the ecclesial context of theology.

With others, feminist theologians have asked whether Rahner's anthropology overly emphasizes the person as a decontextualized individual, seen as an isolated and autonomous "hearer of the word," a view rejected by contemporary relational models. Feminist moral theologian Lisa Cahill, for example, finds the "turn to the subject" too individualist a perspective for a contemporary ethical perspective.[32] On the other hand, Kevin Hogan suggests that discussion of Rahner's emphasis on the individual person's agency needs to take into account Rahner's emphasis on the historicity of the subject.[33] Such an understanding of agency is illustrated in an evocative 1972 essay, "Theological Observations on the Concept of 'Witness'," as Rahner brings forward the "public and political character" of human activity, speaking of the act of witness as not reducible to concrete factors, but "a total human act."[34]

On the other hand, feminists do have a specific agenda for social change. While Rahner has in mind a more flexible ecclesiology, open to the movement of the Spirit, feminist theologians in general do not see the basic feminist claim – even in various formulations – as a movement of the Spirit that may be more "appropriate" in some arenas than in others. Rather, they see their claims as appropriately calling the entirety of Catholic Christianity to self-scrutiny, particularly as these claims are formulated in the language of liberation. At the same time, feminist theologians have found their analysis to be inadequate if not developed in company with womanist, mujerista, and Asian feminists, whose theological work reflects the extraordinary struggle for Third-World women to claim and speak their experience. María Pilar Aquino argues that "[t]here is no need to suppress what is different; on the contrary a multidimensional anthropology accepts the challenge and mystery of our extraordinary diversity."[35]

"Feminist theology," as a term, can be seen as problematically universalizing the concerns and experiences of women, papering over their real differences and ignoring the way in which social and economic location, among other factors, condition the very "female" for whom feminist theology purports to speak. Susan Abraham, utilizing a post-colonial analysis to critique the possibility of retrieving Rahner for those who are socially marginalized, asks whether Rahner's spirituality moves too quickly toward a vision of unity. Justice, in this vision, might not be justice for the marginalized, she suggests: "Becoming one with the other for gendered subalterns is a terrifying proposal, because it asks such subjects to participate in the very systems that relegate them to near invisibility."[36] Abraham suggests that *difference* cannot be resolved, that "difference itself must become the universal that it is."[37] Yet, while emphasizing irreducible plurality, this analysis also questions some common theological distinctions, as socially marginalized women now question what seems to be a false ecclesial distinction between "pastoral" and "theological" questions.

For Roman Catholic feminist theologians, the question of whether ecclesial theology can be self-critical is of central importance. Rahner found such self-criticism necessary, as he saw any role for the Church as a critic of society to be based on the possibility of the Church's capacity for self-criticism.[38] For Rahner, this issue is posed as the question of secularity, as secularity calls for the development of a theological framework that would allow the theology of the magisterium to recognize a voice it does not call its own as authoritative. Viewed as such a "secular" critique, feminist theology represents a profound challenge to the integralism that Catholic theology has yet to fully overcome. Others might reply that feminist criticism, for Christian theologians, represents a more complex story, as its claims are both corrective, recognizing the already present but unnamed authority of women in historical or biblical contexts, and genuinely novel (secular). Feminist theology thus presents a twofold critique, as feminist criticism is always both "from the margins" and "deeply intimate" to every social order.

Feminist theory is well aware of the "bifocal" character of its critique. Feminist theologians also recognize that the question of alterity is a properly theological question, as questions of difference and gender very clearly mark many of the classic "treatises" at levels other than their androcentric symbolism. With regard to trinitarian theology, for example, the God–world relationship that is presupposed is a presupposition about difference. For Rahner, the God that is incomprehensible mystery is the same God that is triune in self-communication. How, feminists might ask, does this distinction-in-unity that grounds the created order give rise to fundamental presuppositions about the relationship between the self and the (potentially gendered) character of the other? Is a modalist model, as Rahner's, a helpful model for feminists? With regard to method and questions of identity and difference, feminist theologians might ask if the insights we have gleaned thus far from Rahner would be deepened if we allowed the critical value these have yielded to come into play in an approach that is more dialectical than correlational.[39] And both of these questions might be further illumined by a careful retrieval of Rahner's pneumatology, as he argues for the Spirit as a source of genuine novelty. While these questions do not immediately raise "women's issues," nevertheless, in their often-gendered presuppositions, they certainly require the lens of a feminist analysis.

Finally, Rahner's theological direction, evident after the Council and deepening through his later works, pointed to the plurality of scholarship as a call for an ecclesial modesty rather than dogmatic proliferation. Indeed, while feminist theory or the insights of gender studies did not seem to cross Rahner's desk as he surveyed the disciplines that rightly shape philosophy and theology, his recognition of the plurality within these disciplines required an open-ended approach. Given the explosion of expertise in fields such as archaeology, history, literary criticism, and philosophy, and the increasingly global context for Christian theology, Rahner called for theology conceived as a "new task" for a "future horizon."[40] Feminist theologians, inspired by Rahner's theological unfolding of the graced hearer of the word and the abiding mystery that is God-with-us, have every reason to turn more deeply toward his work as a resource for the needs of a world Church that will be liberating for both women and men.

Notes

1 C. M. LaCugna, "Catholic Women as Ministers and Theologians," *America* 167 (1992), 238f.

2 A. E. Carr, "Starting with the Human," in L. J. O'Donovan, ed., *A World of Grace: An Introduction to the Themes and Foundations of Karl Rahner's Theology* (New York: Seabury, 1980), 17–30.

3 A. E. Carr, *Transforming Grace: Christian Tradition and Women's Experience* (San Francisco: HarperSanFrancisco, 1988).

4 Ibid., 117.

5 Ibid., 132, citing Rahner, "The Problem of Genetic Manipulation," *TI* IX, 225–52.

6 Ibid., 150, citing Rahner, "Theology of Incarnation," *TI* IV, 177.

7 Ibid., 112.

8 C. M. LaCugna, ed., *Freeing Theology: The Essentials of Theology in Feminist Perspective* (San Francisco: HarperSanFrancisco, 1993).

9 "Theology and Anthropology," *TI* IX, 28, 34.

10 C. M. LaCugna, *God For Us: The Trinity and Christian Life* (San Francisco: Harper-SanFrancisco, 1991). See also E. T. Groppe's excellent critical introduction in "Catherine Mowry LaCugna's Contribution to Trinitarian Theology," *Theological Studies* 63 (2002), 730–63.

11 E. A. Johnson, *She Who Is: The Mystery of God in Feminist Theological Discourse* (New York: Crossroad, 1993), 11.

12 E. A. Johnson, *Friends of God and Prophets: A Feminist Theological Reading of the Communion of Saints* (New York: Continuum, 1998); and *Truly Our Sister: A Theology of Mary in the Communion of Saints* (New York: Continuum 2003).

13 Perhaps Rahner's long friendship with the political activist and writer Luise Rinser shaped his relatively progressive understanding of the role of women. While his letters to her are unavailable, she has published her letters to him in L. Rinser, *Gratwanderung. Briefe der Freundschaft an Karl Rahner 1962–1984* (Munich: Kösel, 1994). An overview in English is available in Pamela Kirk, "Reflections on Luise Rinser's *Gratwanderung*," *Philosophy & Theology* 10 (1997), 293–300.

14 "The Position of Woman in the New Situation in Which the Church Finds Herself," *TI* VIII, trans. D. Bourke (London: Darton, Longman & Todd, 1971), 83.

15 Ibid., *TI* VIII, 89.

16 "Marriage as a Sacrament," *TI* X, 199–221; "What Makes a Marriage Christian? in *Karl Rahner in Dialogue: Conversations and Interviews 1965–1982*, trans. and ed. H. Biallowons, H. D. Egan, S.J., and P. Imhof, S.J. (New York: Crossroad, 1986), 117–122; "Priesthood, Celibacy and Marriage," in ibid., 29–34.

17 "The Consecration of the Layman to the Care of Souls," *TI* III, 270–71.

18 *FCF*, 419.

19 "Women and the Priesthood," *TI* XX, 44.

20 Ibid., 45.

21 The development of feminist theological anthropology in Roman Catholic circles is well documented in M. A. Hinsdale, "Heeding the Voices: An Historical Overview," in A. O'Hara Graff, ed., *In The Embrace of God: Feminist Approaches to Theological Anthropology* (Maryknoll, NY: Orbis, 1995), 22–48.

22 *Karl Rahner in Dialogue*, 271–72.

23 R. Lennan, "Rahner's Theology of the Priesthood and the Development of Doctrine," *Philosophy & Theology* 12 (2000), 166.

24 *Karl Rahner in Dialogue*, 272.

25 M. E. Hines, "Karl Rahner on Development of Doctrine: How Relevant is Rahner Today?" *Philosophy & Theology* 12 (2000), 111–30.

26 See "The Immaculate Conception," *TI* I, 201–13; and also "The Dogma of the Assumption," *TI* I, 215–27, and "The Dogma of the Immaculate Conception in Our Spiritual Life," *TI* III, 129–40.

27 "The Immaculate Conception," *TI* I, 203.

28 Ibid., *TI* I, 205.

29 "Mary and the Christian Image of Woman," *TI* XIX, 216.

30 "Mary's Virginity," *TI* XIX, 218–31.

31 E. A. Johnson, *Truly Our Sister*, 124–25.

32 "Mary and the Christian Image of Woman," *TI* XIX, 218.

33 K, Hogan, "Entering into Otherness: The Postmodern Critique of the Subject and Karl Rahner's Theological Anthropology," *Horizons* 25 (1998), 181–202.

34 "Theological Observations on the Concept of 'Witness'," *TI* XIII, 164. Feminist theologians might find this essay, in dialogue with an examination of Rahner's theology of the symbol as a public and social theology, to be of interest.

35 M. P. Aquino, *Our Cry for Life: Feminist Theology from Latin America*, trans. D. Livingstone (Maryknoll, NY: Orbis, 1993), 89.

36 S. Abraham, "The Caress of the Doer of the Word: A Postcolonial Critique of Miguel Díaz's *On Being Human*," *Philosophy & Theology* 16 (2004), 48.

37 Ibid., 50.

38 "The Function of the Church as a Critic of Society," *TI* XII, 229–49.
39 See L. O'Donovan, "A Final Harvest: Karl Rahner's Last Theological Writings," *Religious Studies Review* 11 (1985), 357–61.
40 "Yesterday's History of Dogma and Theology for Tomorrow," *TI* XVIII, 34.

Further reading

Carr, A. E., *Transforming Grace: Christian Tradition and Women's Experience* (New York: HarperCollins, 1988).

Johnson, E. A., *Truly Our Sister: A Theology of Mary in the Communion of Saints* (New York: Continuum, 2003).

LaCugna, C. M., *God For Us: The Trinity and Christian Life* (San Francisco: HarperSanFrancisco, 1991).

LaCugna, C. M., ed., *Freeing Theology: The Essentials of Theology in Feminist Perspective* (San Francisco: HarperSanFrancisco, 1993).

Rahner, K., "The Position of Women in the New Situation in Which the Church Finds Herself," *TI* VIII, 75–93.

"Theology and Anthropology," *TI* IX, 28–45.

"Mary and the Christian Image of Woman," *TI* XIX, 211–17.

"Women and the Priesthood," *TI* XX, 35–47.

Part IV

Retrospect and Prospect

18 Has Rahnerian theology a future?

PHILIP ENDEAN

The reputation of great figures is often eclipsed in the generation after their death, and there is no lack of commentators who regard Rahner's achievement as *passé*. At the end of this collection of essays on Karl Rahner, compiled in the year when he would have been 100 years old, an obvious question arises about the kind of significance Rahner's theology has for us now. Is Rahner's achievement now primarily a matter of cultural and intellectual history? Does it amount simply to a set of ideas highly influential on Roman Catholicism in the historically rather unusual situation of the 1960s? Are Rahner's lessons something we need to *outgrow*, whether in gratitude for what they have helped us to accomplish, or in repentance for the errors into which they once seduced us? Or do they still hold a message for the future? Is there still life in Rahnerian theology?

There is no doubt that Rahner's work enabled official Catholicism rather belatedly to engage with modernity – a modernity of which it had been decidedly wary for four centuries, whether in its initial appearance as a Lutheran appeal to the individual conscience, or later in various forms of Enlightenment emancipation. For many thinkers both in Rahner's own time and on the contemporary scene, there was something ignoble and mistaken about that engagement. Moreover, it appears ironical that Catholicism should have been trying to catch up with modernity just as the secular world was moving into something different, something so elusive that we can only call it "post-modernity." It might easily appear that Rahner's theology is at best an anachronism, and at worst a heretical muddle.

My intent in this essay is to make a case for a more positive reading, in particular with regard to the needs of theology into the future. What Rahner's theology accomplished in the middle decades of the twentieth century was necessary, generally beneficial, and historically significant. Nevertheless, the critics have several valid points that still need to be addressed.[1] More importantly, the particular, liberalizing import of Rahner's message in the Roman Catholicism of the Council period is only one expression of a far more important intellectual achievement, an achievement that needs to be articulated rather differently in the twenty-first century, an achievement that the theological establishment has still not really appropriated. The case I want to make could be summarized in terms of what Chesterton once said about Christianity: It is not that Rahner's theology has been tried and found wanting; it has been found difficult and therefore not really tried.[2]

The discussion about Rahner still centers too much on the conflicts between tradition and inspiration inherent in the way children of modernity spontaneously imagine what it is to be a Christian. We tend simply to see Rahner as a participant in these conflicts, on the "liberal" side, and not to recognize that he was also subverting the conflicts. We need to learn that Rahner was – without in any way denying the cognitive and ethical gains that have come to us from the Enlightenment – also teaching us that the natural-scientific models of truth and knowledge taken as normative in modernity inevitably distorted Christianity; of their nature, they falsified the reality which is God-among-us. Moreover, Rahner was offering us alternatives. The texts in which he was doing this are often piously quoted, but rarely appreciated for what they really are. We need to recognize Rahner as anticipating what is sane in the approaches to theology current today that are concerned to offer a critique of modernity, while at the same time admirably avoiding what is fideist and merely pretentious. Whereas Rahner often appears as a typically "modern" figure, he is more properly understood as 'post-modern' and 'liberationist' *avant la lettre*. Only when that point is understood can we properly address the question of this theology and the future.

This essay, therefore, falls into three main parts. First, I shall try to show how the image of Rahner's theology as a liberal "corrective" to standard post-Tridentine Catholic theology and practice has widely influenced the way in which his achievement has been received. Secondly, I want to suggest that this immediate impact was only one possible manifestation of an achievement that was far deeper, far more subversive of standard ways of thinking. Finally, I shall address directly the question of whether and how Rahnerian theology might develop into the future.

EXPERIENCE AS A LOCUS OF GRACE

Readers of this *Companion* will by now be well aware of the central features of Rahner's theology: an insistence that the word of revelation must find a correlative in the hearer, and hence that claims about the unique status under God of the Church's message must stand in correlation with realities in human consciousness at large. Clearly, too, such theology therefore challengingly qualifies any claims that mainstream Christianity represents the unique truth of God, and leads us to nuance significantly the triumphalist, threatening theologies of Church and mission implicit in much standard Christian proclamation. Rahner was presenting human experience as a *locus theologicus*, a source of theological authority.

The kinds of conflict surrounding mainstream Rahnerian interpretation can be well evoked by two quotations. The first is from Anne Carr in 1973, who is appreciative of Rahner, and who was perhaps the author of the first serious scholarly study of him in English:

> . . . his own original position on the supernatural existential . . . ultimately leads Rahner to insist on the universality of transcendental revelation; the fundamental mystery of human existence is the Christian mystery, and it is anonymously present wherever a man (*sic!* – Carr is now a leading feminist theologian) lives authentically, no matter what words are used to describe and define it. Thus, he apparently relativises any theological language, including his own . . .
>
> In his formal discussions of theological method, Rahner insists that theology is not to be deduced from experience; rather the correspondence between dogma and experience is to be discerned . . . The Christian revelation, then, would provide normative interpretation of experience. On the other hand . . . wherever human experience is authentic, it is always anonymously Christian.
>
> These two radically different perspectives, which seem to be at odds with one another in Rahner's thought, reflect in a significant way the current ambivalence in Catholic theology. In the dialectic between past and present experience, Rahner seeks to maintain the continuity that for him is the Roman Catholic tradition. One recognises him as the bridge or transition figure between the old in Catholic thought and the yet unformed new.[3]

The second comes from Hans Urs von Balthasar, writing for the English-language edition of *Communio* in 1978:

> Today, Rahner seems to stand undecided at crossroads: his thoroughly Catholic heart wants him to be faithful to the visible, official and sacramental Church, but his speculative bent demands the relativisation of everything ecclesiastical in the name of an all-pervading grace.[4]

The implicit evaluations are different here: one derives from a doctorate seeking to expound Rahner, while the other – notoriously – is expressing a vehemently felt suspicion of his project. But Carr and Von Balthasar are broadly at one on what Rahner's achievement consists in. Rahner has claimed an authority for the presence of God in human experience at large, and therefore relativized – which is a polite word for "undermined" – the authority claims of the visible Church. Whether this achievement is to be regarded as creative or as confused, whether it represents a renewal of Catholic identity or a seductive threat, Rahner appears as a man struggling to hold together two potentially competing values: a grace present universally in human experience at large, and the external authority of the Church and its tradition. Rahner is caught with a tension between autonomous and heteronomous conceptions of theology. Von Balthasar blatantly and Carr implicitly both suggest that Rahner's allegiance to the Church is somehow tribal, pre-theological. The logic of his theology is reductive and idealist. We can take another illustration, put in more philosophical terms, from the Scottish Dominican theologian, Fergus Kerr:

> Rahner's consistently individualist presentation of the self emphasizes cognition, self-reflexiveness and an unrestricted capacity to know. It rapidly leaves time and place behind. It is not surprising if this mentalist-individualist conception of the self seems difficult to reconcile with the insistence on hierarchy and tradition that marks Rahner's Roman Catholic ecclesiology.[5]

This general picture clearly owes much to Church politics, and to the different interpretations current among Roman Catholics about what was at stake in Vatican II. There are obvious and serious problems with the disjunction between Church and grace, tradition and experience implicit in all three of these quotations. Nevertheless, this picture is surely right in its general claim that Rahner is challenging an excessively heteronomous view of divine revelation and Church authority.

Rahner's central contribution to *ressourcement* surely consists in his recasting the idiom of the Tridentine theology of grace. In response to how they perceived the challenge of Protestantism, the fathers at the Council of Trent had wanted to assert the authority of the Church and the normative status of Church practice, especially sacramental practice. In understandable reaction to Protestant claims about an experience of justification, they had marginalized talk of the indwelling of the Spirit. They had focused on the change which grace brings about in the creature as it does churchy things, rather than on the gift of God's own self; they had presented the grace through which even the heathen could, in principle, be saved, as an episodic summons. Subsequent scholasticism had radicalized these positions. It had claimed that grace could not, even in principle, be experienced by Christians at large – even at a time when the mystical life was flourishing throughout the Catholic world. Grace was present within the self, of course – one's own grace, as the Council of Trent would stress. But one's only way of knowing about it was through the Word externally proclaimed. As Rahner developed his key positions in the theology of grace – grace as a formal object of experience, albeit never clearly distinguishable; the grounding of the effects of grace (created grace) in the imparting of God's own self (uncreated grace); the supernatural existential – he was drawing both on scholastic logic and positive sources, both biblical and later, to develop a theology that presented experience as a genuine source of revelation and of theological authority.[6]

Karl Rahner wrote within and for a Church conditioned by the Counter-Reformation. At least as far as theology was concerned, Catholic theology reacted defensively against the Reformers, with little comprehension of the serious issues that the Reformation was raising.[7] The pattern was repeated in the Enlightenment, and with many of the intellectual discoveries and political emancipations that came in the nineteenth and twentieth centuries. The immediate effect of Rahner's work was thus liberating. The Church had seen fidelity in terms of maintaining tradition *over against* an individual creativity and freedom all too corrupted by sin: there was a conflict between experience and authority, and fidelity consisted in obeying authority. Rahner's work on grace and Church offered ways of moving beyond the dishonesty, repressiveness, and bad faith inherent in this dysfunctional construction of holiness and of Christian belonging. Thus he naturally appeared as a much needed "liberal" counterbalance: for this way of thinking, Rahner may have been historically more fortunate, conceptually more careful, and politically more astute than those whom papal paranoia had denounced as "modernists" half a century earlier, but his project was fundamentally the same as theirs.

Within this pattern of thinking, Rahner's account of grace and revelation seems marked by two poles of authority: the experience of believers at large, and the external authority represented by the official Church. The question then arises as to the proper relationship between the two. The obvious temptation is to suppose that one has to be given systematic preference over the other. I want to suggest below that a correct reading of Rahner depends on recognizing that this temptation is to be avoided. But the Church for which he was writing was influenced by a "modern" obsession with certainty of a kind that sound theology needs to avoid. In such a climate, any suggestion that the authority of external tradition is to be relativized inevitably appeared as an advocacy of an alternative source, namely the experience of believers at large. Rahner thus appeared in religious journalism as an advocate of "liberal" positions, and often an adversarial, provocative one. At the same time, given that what he was really teaching did not fit within this framework of thought at all, he could also appear ambivalent and confused, in ways that unsympathetic critics could easily exploit.

THEOCENTRIC THEOLOGY

Rahner's maturity coincided with Vatican II. There was therefore a widespread openness for what he had to say, and indeed a great group-psychological need for an intellectually authoritative voice that could give a hitherto unenlightened Church permission to explore new possibilities. It is this version of Rahner that contemporary commentators – at least outside specialist circles – either revere or deplore. Much, indeed, was achieved by this Rahner of the 1960s; much, sadly, remains outstanding, or has been betrayed. At the same time, this particular image of Rahner can be misleading: it fails to bring out how radical his intellectual project was.

Both Carr and von Balthasar understand the problem with Rahner's theology in terms of where ultimate authority lies. Does it lie with the subject or with the external object? The implication is that a correct answer to that question would yield, in some uncomplicated, almost positivistic sense, assured knowledge. Were we so inclined, we might even use the unhelpful smear-word, "foundationalism." Part of what is at stake at the Reformation is the question of whether valid knowledge comes from inner testimony or external authority; the same pattern runs through the tedious and fruitless debates about "conservatism" and "liberalism" that seem currently to bedevil all developed forms at least of Western Christianity. The instabilities in Rahner's theology about conscience and authority then appear as a symptom of a deeper incoherence: that between a new-fangled project of *aggiornamento* and the rejection of modernity that had become all but constitutive of Catholic identity.

Rahner was not always a careful writer, and when he was focusing on one particular problem, he had the habit of presupposing conventional positions (what he disparagingly called *die durchschnittliche Schultheologie* – "average academic scholastic theology") on other problems. This he could do, even when he himself had elsewhere criticized these conventional accounts radically. It follows that a hostile critic could certainly find evidence to make a case for incoherence in Rahner's writings regarding experience and authority.

Biographically, however, it is an error to see Rahner's most characteristic insights as a response to the "problems of the modern world." Such a label may describe liberal Protestantism or so-called 'modernism', but it tells at most half the story about the movement of *ressourcement* that informed the renewal of Roman Catholicism in the second half of the twentieth century. Though Rahner certainly was impressed and influenced by the difficulties of faith in a secularized society,[8] he had developed his most creative theological insights as a young man, in isolated academic and seminary settings. His achievement emerged from awareness of deep contradictions in the decadent Tridentine theology of grace into which he was educated, from reading of positive sources, and – though the point should not be overstated – from his own experiences in prayer.

The conventional picture of Rahner obscures how he was trying to move Christianity forward from the deficient epistemology which gave rise to a sense of inevitable conflict between tradition and innovation. As a Roman Catholic, Rahner was theologizing from within a system that was rather proud of never having explicitly accepted the "modern" project. Whatever the faults of Counter-Reformation Catholic theology, and however much it was informed by a regrettable insensitivity to legitimate concerns, it had at least to some extent kept its distance from the Enlightenment, and recognized that the construction of rationality dominant in the Enlightenment was in some ways problematic for theology of any kind.

The *ressourcement* theologians in general, and Rahner in particular, drew on pre-modern traditions to subvert patterns of theological thought that set in with early modernity, and to point us all beyond the limitations of the construction of holiness and Church that prevailed throughout the Enlightenment period. As much as any liberationist or post-modern or "radically orthodox" theology – and without any trace of the irrationalism and pretentiousness that can mar such writing – Rahnerian theology is profoundly influenced by a sense of how "modern" patterns of thought and affiliation distort the reality of Catholic, Christian, truth.

One reason why Rahner's achievement has been difficult to interpret is that he himself never presented an adequate synthesis. Only in the 1970s did he begin to articulate how the experience of God, which at least in his mind was associated in a special way with Ignatian spirituality, was the central, integrating principle of his achievement – far too late to influence the structure of the *Grundkurs* (which largely reproduces lectures given at Münster), or for him to begin another large-scale systematic work. He may, indeed, have been influenced by the early major commentators, notably Klaus Fischer.[9] Subsequent researches, notably those of Nikolaus Schwerdtfeger (now a bishop in Hildesheim) – who admittedly was drawing on unpublished material produced in the 1960s by the Finnish Lutheran theologian Tuomo Mannermaa –, have brought home the central importance of Rahner's lecture codex on grace, a text which he never published, and the analysis given therein of the experience of grace, of the "supernatural formal object."[10] The results of these studies have certainly not been absorbed fully outside the German-speaking world, and it may be that even within it they are well known only among a relatively small range of specialists. But they enable us to see that Rahner's account of how we know God's grace privileges neither subject nor object. Our discoveries in knowledge are essentially interactive: the external object can affect us only if there is a disposition within us; and this disposition becomes conscious only when the object affects the human mind from outside.[11] The fundamental reliability of the system is not directly accessible either through the subject or the object, but rather through a God who is source of both and works through both in ways that are quite mysterious.[12]

When, therefore, Rahner was exhorting the seminarians in Innsbruck in the 1950s in a Christmas talk to the effect that "the heart's experience enables you to understand the message of Christmas properly,"[13] he was not saying that the heart's experience or insight is in any strong sense epistemologically prior to the word. The priority comes with the initiative of a God beyond comprehension who sustains a charismatic interaction: "The experienced reality from within and the message from without move towards each other, and where *each understands itself in the other* the feast of Christmas takes place, because faith comes not only from hearing but also from the grace that arises in the inmost centre of the heart."[14]

What is important is that the relationship should be maintained in openness to a transcendent power that lies beyond both subject and object, not that either pole should have priority. Sometimes, confrontation with the Gospel word leads us radically to reconstruct our sense of self; at other times, a change within the self leads us to read the Gospel with radically new eyes. There is place in the Church of God for both sorts of narrative, because it is God's action which is foundational for theology. This word is active among us, but there is no simple, universally valid, account of how this is the case. Jesus' resurrection guarantees *that* his kingdom preaching will ultimately come to fulfillment, but the ways and means remain to be disclosed and discovered. Moreover, precisely because the kingdom is universal, this relational process of growth in grace can and must occur in secular form, outside the Church. But the secular form of the process remains radically relational: there is never any question of the human subject possessing the fullness of truth in itself, prior to any engagement with the external world.

Rahner's constant references to the category of mystery are organically part of his intellectual achievement: They are not merely pious decoration, nor are they expressive of some devotional sphere into which heavy-footed speculation should fear to tread. Authority and certainty lie with God, a God who is mystery, who is mediated to us only through other objects in the world – a God about whom we inevitably ask questions (and therefore about whom we know enough to ask meaningful questions, about whom we have a *Vorgriff*), but questions to which our answers are permanently open to subversion. We may in some sense know that God exists, but what that existence amounts to needs constantly to be rediscovered. If we hold Christian truth in such a way as to prevent us from further learning, we are misconstruing that truth, and indeed behaving in such a way as to contradict its nature. And whereas the forms of knowledge characteristic of modernity prize above all the knowledge of what can be grasped as certain – forms of knowledge which Catholicism took on, particularly in its rationalist fundamental theology, even as it was fulminating against the errors of "modernism" – Rahner's theology suggests that the highest forms of knowledge are of a different kind. The faculty of reasoning indeed involves "the faculty of grasping an object and bringing it under submission . . . the faculty of directive judgment, of encompassing and grasping." But this style of reasoning is only secondary. Reason in its full sense is also "the faculty of accepting something greater that is not judged, of simply being apprehended, of handing oneself over, of submitting oneself, of a loving moving outwards." Mystery is the most proper object of reason. To invoke "mystery" is precisely not to claim that reason is somehow incomplete and deficient, but rather "just the point which knowledge reaches when it attains its perfection."[15]

Importantly, the divine self-gift in grace, the gospel of divine intimacy and solidarity with the creation, does not amount to an abrogation of this principle:

> This self-communication does not suspend or deny what has been said previously about God's presence as that of the absolute mystery, essentially past all grasp. In grace too, even in the immediate vision of God, God remains God: the first and last standard which cannot be

measured against anything else; God remains the mystery which alone
provides its own explanation . . . God who can never be grasped – and
therefore not even through His self-communication in grace and in
immediate vision; God who is never subject to humanity, who can
never be fitted into calculations and systems of human knowledge
and freedom.[16]

It is a commonplace in modern accounts of Christianity for our situation to be presented as somehow fragile, sin-conditioned, uncertain, and then for the gospel to be seen as providing us with stability, grace and certainty. Once again, the paradigms of knowledge proper to Enlightenment science are being uncritically adopted, in ways that quite disastrously falsify the reality of which theology speaks. Rahner's epistemology is akin to Wittgenstein's critique of the view that ostensive definition is the normative way in which language refers. While not denying that epistemologies of control and grasping have an important and even fundamental place, Rahner refuses to accept this paradigm as normative for theology. Even the human Jesus lived in the same kind of darkness as we do; even the three divine persons adore each other as *unbegreifliches Geheimnis*.[17]

> My Christianity, when it understands itself aright, is the act of letting
> myself go into the mystery past all grasp. My Christianity is therefore
> anything but an "explanation" of the world and of my existence; it is
> rather the prohibition against regarding any experience, any
> understanding (however good and illuminating they may be) as
> finally and definitively valid (*endgültig*), as completely intelligible in
> themselves.[18]

The obvious question then arises: If Christian revelation does not overcome the problems of finitude and uncertainty, what does it provide for us? A way of thinking centered on knowledge as clear comprehension presents Christian revelation as some special, guaranteed knowledge, which then stands in more or less problematic relationship with what we might know already from our ordinary resources. Rahner's epistemology of self-disclosing mystery enables him to resituate this well-known problem of nature and grace. That the positions he developed in so doing have been consistently misread as intrinsicist reductionism, and as tantamount to a denial that church tradition has any special role, is a powerful indication of how poorly his achievement has been understood. Jesus, and the tradition which stems from him, does not represent any kind of unique divine interruption within the problematic human condition, but rather, in his resurrection, a divine promise that the graced union between God and humanity has already been inaugurated and that it will therefore, in God's good time, come to completion. But the how remains obscure. The assent of faith is a surrender to mystery, a patient willingness to let life unfold.

The problem of nature and grace is insoluble when considered in terms of the natural knowledge of God amounting to perspicuous content. Rahner's philosophy of mind and God is, however, purely formal: it asserts that the human mind is open to whatever is the case regarding God, without in any way specifying what that case might be. As such, it provides a version of natural theology that does not constrain the freedom of God's grace – it merely asserts the near tautology that God's gracious action in the human must touch the human. If the supernatural exists, if the gospel of grace is true, then this supernatural reality must also be an existential, something that touches *us*. There cannot be any absolute disjunction between the orders of knowing and being; the question we inevitably ask about what makes things be is a question worth asking, albeit not one to which we have any final answer.

Rahner does theology by challenging the fundamental assumptions shaping the whole academic enterprise, notably as regards truth and certainty. The success of natural science has conditioned us to construct a religion with all the answers. Rahner insists that the reality of God will always be falsified when presented through such an epistemology. That which is highest is most mysterious; trust and patience are epistemological as well as moral and spiritual virtues. Thus Rahner subverts conventional divisions between disciplines – not only between philosophy and theology, but also between academic theology and practical specialisms such as pastoral theology and spirituality. Rahner's analysis of the incoherence in conventional accounts of the relationship between philosophy and theology at the outset of *Hörer des Wortes* is still astonishingly contemporary – both our university politics and our *Wissenschaftstheorie* (theory of academic disciplines) are still bedevilled by the dialogue of the deaf between rationalists and fideists that Rahner sketches so trenchantly at the outset of that work.[19] Rahner's attempt to move the discussion forward remains unappreciated – not least because there is not even in English a word to name the genre of *Wissenschaftstheorie* in which he was writing.

There is a story about a distinguished Irish theologian who used to say: "In all his voluminous works, Rahner has really only one thing to say – but it is maddeningly difficult to name what that one thing is." One possible gloss on this story is to see it as pointing to the interplay between system and chaos in Rahner, between the simplicity of the one single mystery of a self-communicating God within human experience on the one hand and on the other the pluralism and untidiness of the human race which receives this divine self-gift. Another interpretation is that Rahner is trying to say something which does not fit easily within the canons of rationality dominant in modernity. Both interpretations have their cogency.

Rahner's "conservative" critics are right to insist that there is a contradiction in Christian theology conforming itself to models of truth and rationality established independently of Christianity: rather, if theology truly refers to God, then theology must, by the logic of its subject matter, claim the right to specify *what counts as* truth and rationality. Their error – one which they share with many who applaud Rahner – lies in the failure to see that such a claim lies at the heart of Rahner's work. The real argument between Rahner and his more conservative critics is not about faith and reason, but rather about whether the subversive freedom of God (understood by Rahner in a way that incorporates all the legitimate concerns of a Barthian) can occur also outside conventional church structures, and in ways not recognized by conventional constructions of Christianity.

THE FUTURE

The question about whether Rahnerian theology has a future depends on what is meant by Rahnerian theology. I have suggested that Rahner's earliest interpreters read him as a critical, balancing force within a particular construction of theology. This reading of Rahner still has a valuable function. Most of the Church and of wider society is still stuck in positivistic ways of thinking, and in such a world liberalism is healthier than authoritarian repressiveness. But it remains the case that this way of looking at Rahner's achievement inevitably situates him within a particular cultural setting, and suggests that only within that setting is his work of value. There are, however, other ways of reading Rahner's achievement, at once more fruitful, more accurate, and more promising for the future.

What forms might the future of Rahnerian theology take? There is a desperate need for Rahner's insights about the nature of religious truth to be translated into an idiom comprehensible today. The primary texts presuppose an education in scholasticism; their key terms often defy straightforward translation; and the additions made by Metz to the second editions of both *Geist in Welt* and *Hörer des Wortes* have made Rahner's thought less rather than more accessible. Closer attention to the linguistic structures of human experience might enable us to overcome tensions both in Rahner's fundamental theology and in his dogmatic theology of the Church; his work in ethics and eschatology needs to be developed.[20] That said, the future of this theology probably lies with people other than theologians, at least in a narrow, professional sense. Rahner has taught us how to take secularity seriously as source for theology without compromising our commitment to Christian tradition. The future of his approach to theology will lie, I suspect, largely in the practical sphere, as people find Rahner a helpful resource for the theological interpretation of different life situations.

The question as to whether this Rahnerian theology will last can be understood in different ways. It can be taken as a sociological question about the forms of Christianity that will last into the future. It can be taken as a question about the intrinsic value of Rahner's speculations. It can even be taken as a matter of theological faith and hope.

From empirical and sociological points of view, the prospects may well not be hopeful. Perhaps the post-Conciliar experience shows that it is not possible for a church to sustain itself on the tentative, questioning theology offered by Rahner, particularly as the subcultures that nourished him and many of his readers crumble. Perhaps the Christian Church can only maintain its cohesion and identity if it develops a clearer sense of boundaries between those within and those without than an apophatic, mystical approach to theology like Rahner's can possibly yield. The spiritual maturity towards which the Spirit was calling the Roman Catholic Church through the Vatican Council, and through the theologies that contributed to it, does not seem to be one that can easily be sustained culturally and institutionally: it is threatened both by the fundamentalist sectarianisms of the Right and by the woolly liberalisms of the Left.

If the judgment here is negative, however, the grounds for the no should be seen clearly as residing in human limitation, in particular truths about the human condition that cannot easily be avoided, rather than in any divinely sanctioned imperative or in any theological inadequacy in Rahner's vision. An example may illustrate the point at issue. Perhaps there are good reasons for Christians to have reservations about a homosexual lifestyle, and good reasons too for saying that practising homosexuals cannot properly exercise the ministry of unity proper to an Anglican bishop. It may well be appropriate for the authority which the Church must have, and which is therefore at least indirectly divinely sanctioned, to insist on those arguments. But such cases need to be made empirically; great harm is done by those who bring the Bible into disrepute by insisting that such claims can simply be read off from Christian tradition. Firm government may be necessary, and this tentative, questioning theology in no way denies that possibility a priori – it simply insists that there is an enormous difference in status between the tentative, time-conditioned judgments about what the good order of the Church requires, and the law of God. We must do what is necessary for maintaining the Church's identity without insisting that God straight-forwardly legitimates those mechanisms. Indeed, such an insistence risks cutting us off a priori from any new possibility of growth, any possibility that our religious identity be enriched. A religion which takes that path is dead. But, empirically speaking, such may be our future.

If the question about the future of Rahnerian theology is one about the permanent value of his insights, the answer can be much more confident and positive. This theology certainly should have a future. There is a tension in the Christian message between the particularity of God's election of Israel, of Jesus, of the Church, on the one hand, and on the other the universality of a message addressed to all nations, correlated with a goodness in the creation as a whole. The tension is to be found in literary form in the Bible – Matthew's Gospel may indicate that it was a psychological reality for Jesus himself as his focus changes from the lost sheep of the house of Israel to the whole world to which he sends his disciples after the resurrection.

Rahner's general approach to theology presents the tradition of Jesus as offering an indispensable symbol of the kingdom, but not the full reality: that has to be discovered in dialogue and in ongoing experience. His heart remains, in von Balthasar's tendentious phrase, "thoroughly Catholic" – but that commitment to a universal Catholicity entails a denial that the Church's particular construction of Christianity here and now exhausts the truth of God's grace. A Rahnerian theology and epistemology, centered on promise rather than achievement, offers possibilities for holding tradition and openness together that the alternatives do not – those which simply subordinate Christian truth in revelation to a secular analysis of the human or vice versa. For that reason alone, it deserves to survive.

The question about the future of Rahner's theology is ultimately the question about the future of Christianity. Will the believers of the future still opt to live with the tensions in the biblical picture of God, between a God who chooses some and not others, and a God who has no favorites? Though a case can certainly be made for theological hope, its grounds are neither empirical nor speculative: rather, they lie in divine promise. To argue in this way is to echo Rahner himself, as he ended the piece he called his spiritual testament, "Ignatius of Loyola Speaks to a Contemporary Jesuit."[21] Such conviction is not easily shaken by futurological argument, and its distinctive logic needs to be acknowledged. On less elevated, purely speculative, grounds, we may be able to argue that Christian theology cannot survive with integrity without being at least anonymously Rahnerian. But it would be untrue to Rahner's spirit to insist on that point too strongly. It may be more prudent simply to refute facile arguments about Rahner's datedness, not to invest too heavily in any one account of how the theology of the future will turn out, and simply to insist that Rahner's questions will always be worth asking.

Notes

Translations of primary sources are my own; page citations follow published English translations.

1 For a helpful survey, see D. Marmion, "Rahner and his Critics: Revisiting the Dialogue," *Irish Theological Quarterly* 68 (2003), 195–212.

2 G. K. Chesterton, *What's Wrong with the World* (London: Cassell, 1910), 39.

3 A. Carr, "Theology and Experience in the Thought of Karl Rahner," *Journal of Religion* 53 (1973), 359–76, here pp. 375–76.

4 H. Urs von Balthasar, "Current Trends in Catholic Theology and the Responsibility of the Christian," *Communio* 5/1 (1978), 77–85, here p. 80. To my knowledge, this piece was never published in German.

5 F. Kerr, *Theology after Wittgenstein* (Oxford: Blackwell, 1986), 14.

6 For an overall account of Rahner's theology of grace in these terms, see P. Endean, *Karl Rahner and Ignatian Spirituality* (Oxford: Oxford University Press, 2001), 33–54.

7 For the purposes of this essay, a conventional account of early modern Catholicism in terms of "Counter-Reformation" is appropriate. On the complexities of the issue, see J. W. O'Malley, *Trent and All That: Renaming Catholicism in the Early Modern Era* (Cambridge, MA: Harvard University Press, 2000).

8 See K. H. Neufeld, *Die Brüder Rahner: Eine Biographie* (Freiburg: Herder, 1994), 159–77 for some provocative and insightful material on Karl Rahner's experiences in wartime Vienna.

9 K. P. Fischer, *Der Mensch als Geheimnis: Die Anthopologie Karl Rahners. Mit einem Brief von Karl Rahner* (Freiburg: Herder, 1974).

10 N. Schwerdtfeger, *Gnade und Welt: Zum Grundgefüge von Karl Rahners Theorie der 'anonymen Christen'* (Freiburg: Herder, 1982), esp. 150–60; Endean, *Karl Rahner and Ignatian Spirituality*, 35–41, 56–59.

11 *De gratia Christi*, 1st edn. (lecture codex: Innsbruck, 1938), p. 308: *Haec tendentia aprioristica obiective illimitata intellectualitatis naturalis insuper per se solam nullum potest sibi dare obiectum concretum. Ut tale detur (in quo cognito ipsa haec tendentia solum conscia fit), requiritur determinatio ab extra, causa aliqua quasi materialis, i.e. obiectum sensibile, seu saltem species creata limitata. Cum qua determinatione simul tendentia aprioristica (tamquam quasi-forma eius) intelligibile actu constituit.*

12 For an English-language study that gets close to the substantive position here, see T. M. Kelly, *Theology at the Void: The Retrieval of Experience* (Notre Dame: University of Notre Dame Press, 2002). Kelly reaches his position by careful comparative readings of Rahner, Schleiermacher, Wayne Proudfoot, George Lindbeck, and the literary theorist George Steiner.

13 "On the Theology of Christmas," *TI* III, 29.

14 Ibid., *TI* III, 28.
15 "The Concept of Mystery in Catholic Theology," *TI* IV, 43.
16 *FCF*, 119–20.
17 "The Concept of Mystery in Catholic Theology," *TI* IV, 49.
18 K. Rahner, "Why Am I a Christian Today?" in K. Lehmann and A. Raffelt, eds., *The Practice of Faith: A Handbook of Contemporary Spirituality* (London: SCM Press, 1985), 6–7.
19 *HW*, 16–22.
20 Some of this agenda is addressed in the "constructive interpretation" attempted in the later chapters of Endean, *Karl Rahner and Ignatian Spirituality.*
21 *Ignatius of Loyola*, trans. R. Ockenden (London: Collins, 1979), 38.

19 Experiences of a Catholic theologian

KARL RAHNER

Translated by DECLAN MARMION and GESA THIESSEN

TRANSLATORS' INTRODUCTION

Shortly before his death in March 1984, Karl Rahner offered this brief retrospective on his life's work as a theologian in which he focused on four "experiences" which, as he approached the end of his life, he considered crucial to any form of theological reflection. With characteristic modesty he uses these experiences as a way of critically reviewing his own theological work. These experiences appear to us to be in order of priority for Rahner. Pride of place goes to what he calls the analogical nature of all theological assertions, since Rahner always favored an apophatic way of speaking about God. Yet this God does not remain distant but has communicated God's very self to humankind. This self-communication of God, an experience of grace, is the second experience discussed here and constitutes for Rahner the core of the Christian message. A third retrospective experience is that as a Jesuit his theology has some affinity with the spirituality of his religious order. At least, that was his hope – that he would be able to incorporate some of the "existentialism of Ignatius" into his own way of theologizing. A fourth and final experience is the "incongruence" of theology with the other sciences. Nevertheless, if theologians are not to preoccupy themselves with a purely abstract concept of God, they will see the various natural sciences and artistic expressions such as music, visual art, and poetry as revealing the hand of God.

The experience of "not-knowing," of not being able to provide any clear answers to a multitude of problems and questions, led Rahner to plea for a greater modesty in theological discourse: "A theology that wishes to answer all questions clearly and thoroughly is guaranteed to miss its proper 'object'."[1] This experience, in turn, is linked to a central tenet of Rahner's theology, namely, to the God of incomprehensible mystery, who cannot be explained with rationalistic clarity. Rahner concludes his retrospective by returning to a familiar emphasis on God as the absolute future, a future which can be reached only through the medium of death. Death and eternal life constitute radical caesurae, which he can describe only in the paradoxical language of emptiness and fulfillment, darkness and light, question and answer.

RAHNER'S TEXT

After having received so many *laudationes*, I feel somewhat anxious as I now rise to speak. But I will do my best. In the program for this conference my topic has been given as "Experiences of a Catholic Theologian."[2] I am not referring here to very personal or intimate experiences that make up one's biography. Such experiences will never find their way into print. Nor am I referring primarily to experiences with the Church, with ecclesiastical politics, or to my experiences as a cleric. I do not regard these experiences as that important, and so I will not dwell on them today. What I am referring to are the experiences of a theologian, or better yet, experiences of someone who was given the task of being a theologian, but who is not quite sure whether he has done justice to this task. This doubt stems not so much from a general sense of human limitation but rather from a sense of being pushed to the limit – something essential to any theological effort, since one must speak of the incomprehensible nature of God. If, therefore, my talk here is about "experiences," it should be noted from the outset that, although we are dealing with theological statements intended as objective, this is not to deny that there is undeniably present a subjective dimension in the way I have selected these experiences.

ANALOGICAL AFFIRMATIONS

The first experience I want to talk about is the experience that all theological statements – even if this is manifest in a variety of ways and degrees – are analogical statements. This goes without saying for any Catholic theology. It is explicitly stated, on one page or other, of every theology and, since Erich Przywara, has become even more self-evident for theologians. Nevertheless, my conviction is that this principle is continually overlooked in individual theological assertions. I want to share my alarm about this kind of oversight.

Let me begin in a rather simple way. A very basic, simple understanding of the concept of analogy runs along the following lines: an analogical way of thinking is characterized by the fact that, with the help of such an approach, an assertion about a specific reality is legitimate and unavoidable. However, at the same time, the assertion must always be negated in a certain sense. Were we merely to apply this concept alone to the reality at issue without negating it, without acknowledging this strange and uncanny back and forth between affirmation and negation, we would be mistaking the real object and end up in error. But this mysterious and uncanny negation necessary for the truth of an analogical statement is more often than not left unclarified and forgotten. It is not possible here to develop an actual metaphysics of knowing (*Erkenntnismetaphysik*) analogical statements. By so doing, we could counter the unsophisticated and naïve belief that an analogical term is simply an amalgam between an ordinary univocal utterance on the one hand and an equivocal utterance on the other. A true understanding of analogy, however, would acknowledge the fact that analogy comprises a fundamental and basic structure of human cognition.

Here I touch on the essence of analogy – something too frequently overlooked and, in particular instances, altogether ignored – namely, the negation of an affirmative statement of conceptual content precisely in its affirmation. The Fourth Lateran Council clearly stated that from the perspective of this world, that is from any starting-point we might conceive of based on human knowing, nothing substantial of a positive nature about God can be stated without, at the same time, perceiving the radical inadequacy of such affirmative statements. Yet time and again in our theological praxis we forget this. We talk about God, about God's existence, characteristics, about three persons in God; we speak of God's freedom, of God's binding will, and so forth. Of course, we need to proceed in this manner; we cannot simply keep silent about God. Indeed, it is only after we have first spoken that it is possible – really possible – to be silent. But in such discourse we usually forget that any statement made about God is legitimate only to the extent that it is always simultaneously negated. It is a question here of enduring the uncanny suspension between affirmation and negation as the true and only fixed term of our knowledge. In so doing, our theological assertions descend into the silent incomprehensibility of God's very self. Our theoretical statements then share the same existential destiny as we do, namely, that of a loving, trusting self-surrender to the unfathomable reign of God, to God's merciful judgment and sacred incomprehensibility.

I think – I hope – that no theologian will seriously dispute what I have just said. But at the same time it is so often the case with us theologians that this single, formal proposition is simply mentioned somewhere in our theology alongside other things. This theological truism is hardly a vital force that really radically and inexorably pervades our entire theology in all of its statements. So often from our lecture podiums and our pulpits and from the Church's sacred dicasteries our pronouncements do not give the clear impression that they are replete with the complete humility of a creature. Only with such humility can one truly speak about God. Only then does one recognize that all discourse about God can only be the final moment before that blessed silence that fills the heavens with the pure vision of God face to face.

Of course, we cannot always append to each theological statement that it is meant only analogically and note that there is in fact greater dissimilarity than the explicitly stated similarity. Still, it should be recognized more clearly that in theology, when we make specific statements, we have not forgotten what we maintain in general and in abstract realms about the analogical nature of theological terms. If this basic principle, this theological axiom, were radically put into practice, then those hearing theological pronouncements would realize that vast dimensions of divine and created reality are not covered by such statements but remain silently empty. For example, we say that in death the human being reaches the definitive point of one's moral state, one's relationship with God; that the human being comes before the judgment of God. All this is true, but it really says incredibly little about the concrete reality that is meant – partly because of the use of a very formal and abstract way of speaking, and partly because of ways of thinking that may be moving but really are naïve.

We should certainly not try to fill the lacunas in our knowledge and faith with the simplicities of modern spiritualism, if for no other reason than that such attempts are uninteresting. But we should also realize that in making these kinds of theological affirmations what is revealed to us are the empty spaces, the gaps in our knowledge. Yet at the same time these lacunas, in many respects, remain hidden to us – something we are aware of, but overlook. Although we fill in these gaps in our knowledge, they still remain a mystery for us. For example, what does it actually mean to say that the Son of Man will return again on the clouds of heaven, that he truly gives himself to us – body and blood – in the Eucharist, that the pope is infallible in *ex cathedra* decisions, or that hell is eternal? More fundamentally, what does it mean to say that the human person could in one's puny creatureliness seriously have something to do with the infinite, unutterable reality of God's very self – something that transcends all infinite distances?

In theology we talk about many things and, when we have finished, we think – although this goes against our basic convictions – that we have really reached the end and that we can draw things to a close. We think that the few affirmations we have made will quench every metaphysical and existential thirst, not realizing the challenge (as we really should) that after making all these affirmations we are destined finally to reach that *aporia* that, according to Paul in 2 Corinthians 4:8, characterizes our human existence and that does not provide us with any answers. Here I do not want and I am unable to talk in greater detail about God's incomprehensibility and hence about the true object of theology. I want only to confirm the experience that theologians are worthy of the title only when they do not seek to reassure themselves that they are providing clear and lucid discourse, but rather when they are experiencing and witnessing, with both terror and bliss, to the analogical back and forth between affirmation and negation before the abyss of God's incomprehensibility. I want only to confess that as a mere individual theologian I give too little thought to the analogical nature of all my theological assertions. As theologians we devote too much time to *talking* about this issue and in all our talk we basically forget the very subject of our discourse.

GOD'S RADICAL SELF-COMMUNICATION

A second experience that follows naturally from what we have already mentioned is the fact that in our theology we often – or almost always – overlook the real core of what we have to address. Since the Second Vatican Council there has been much talk about the hierarchy of truths of the Christian message. Lazy and short-sighted theologians, when they get into difficulties with regard to individual questions in theology, like to get out of these situations by saying that, in regard to this or that individual question, it is not really all that important what is and what is not true. We give far too little thought to what constitutes the real core of the Christian message. It can certainly and rightfully be said that Jesus of Nazareth is this focal point, the One who was crucified and rose again, and after whom we call ourselves Christians. But if that is true, and if it is to be of help, then it needs to be said why and how this Jesus is the only one to whom we can entrust ourselves in life and in death. What kind of answer can we give to this question? The answer can only be the confession that the actual self-communication of the infinite God, transcending all creaturely reality and any finite divine gift, is given in Jesus and in him alone, and is promised, offered, and guaranteed to us through him. If this were not the case, then the reality of Jesus could perhaps ground *one* religion, perhaps the best religion, namely, the Jesus-religion. But it could not be the absolute religion solemnly pledged to all humankind, because the reality of Jesus and its message would remain in the realm of the finite and the contingent.

For me, therefore, the true and sole centre of Christianity is the real self-communication of God to creation in God's innermost reality and glory. It is to profess the most improbable truth, namely, that God in God's very self with infinite reality and glory, with holiness, freedom, and love can really and without any holding back enter the creatureliness of our existence. Everything else that Christianity offers or demands of us is by comparison only provisional or of secondary importance.

What I am talking about here can also be expressed in another way. If I were to deny this, I would be contradicting what I have already stated about the analogical nature of all theological statements. For me, all of the most pious enthusiasm for Jesus (*Jesuanismus*), all involvement for justice and charity in the world, all humanism that wants to use God for the human being rather than casting the human being into the depths of God, would be a religion characterized by an unbelievably modest humanism. Such a humanism is simply not an option given the immense might of God's love, a love whereby God truly pours out divine love. We can want either everything, namely the pure divinity of God, or we are condemned, that is we are buried in the prison of our own finitude. In Catholic theology one may speculate whether a "pure nature" could be happy and complete in itself under the distant sovereignty of God. In truth, however, reality is constituted in such a way – and this precisely because of the relentless draw of grace – that we either suffocate in our finiteness or come to where God, God's very self, is. Of course, it could be held that the only claim we can make here is the rather sober one that, with the possible exception of a few saints, this thirst for the absolute, the relentless draw of the unconditional, and this ecstasy [*ecstasis*] of the finite spirit into God is not to be found among ordinary persons. Even if it is the case that, for the most part, in our theologizing we focus only on how those who are cared for by the Church and the sacraments come before the face of God, we should reflect much more on how we could imagine the journey of all peoples – even the most primitive human beings a million years ago, as well as non-Christians, and even atheists – in such a way that this journey leads to God's very self.

Of course, one can say – though I find this a bit weak and rather facile – that actual divine salvation is possible everywhere and for all peoples throughout history, and that this happens in ways known only to God. This is all very true. So much so that I, together with all Christian theology, must in the end leave things to the unfathomable judgment of God who is really able to penetrate with liberating love the crevices in this fierce concrete bunker that is our egoism. But in a time when Christianity really could and should be presented in a way that it can be offered to people of all cultures and in every age, so that it might become their earnest religion, then in general and in every age we need to devote more thought to "anonymous" Christianity, even if the controversial term as such is not so important for me. It may well be a gross presumption on the creature's part if an individual does not want to let oneself be saved, when one cannot see how one's neighbour is being saved. But it can also be a sublime act of love of neighbour – one required ultimately from each Christian – when one hopes for oneself only within the framework of a universal hope, a hope for all people. This line of thought then gives rise to a view of how God's grace – which in the final analysis is God's very self in self-communication – is really poured out on all humanity and not merely on the few who have been sealed by the sacraments.

My contention, moreover, is that a Christian theologian is not prevented from thinking that the theme of human sinfulness and forgiveness of guilt through pure grace is, in a certain sense, somewhat secondary compared to the theme of God's radical *self*-communication. It is not as if we do not get caught up time and again in our egoism because we are sinners. It is not as if we are not in need of God's forgiving grace, something we need to accept as pure grace – without our thinking we have any personal claim on God. It is not as if God's self-communication does not always take place in fact by way of forgiveness. It is not as if our fundamental experience of sinfulness – a despairing experience as far as we are concerned, but one in which we initially experience our freedom in a concrete way – does not correspond to the actual situation in which a person truly begins to reach out for God. Christian experience has given concrete witness to this fact down through the ages. But today we see how difficult it is for people to accept justification simply as forgiveness of sin. Moreover, for a Catholic theologian, God and God's promise of self to humanity (in whatever way this is understood in greater detail) already exists as pure grace prior to sin. This is the sheer and unexpected miracle of God, a God who bestows God's very self and who turns such a love into the adventure that is God's own history. If we accept this, then I think we can easily hold that God's self-communication to the creature is more pivotal than sin and the forgiveness of sin.

I know that such a claim is highly problematic, especially when placed under the judgment of Scripture. But even if we basically cannot think about sin in any way outside of the framework of God's love for the sinner, there is also at least the danger of *hubris* that we might take sin too seriously. By doing so, we could forget perhaps what most shocks us about the appalling aspects of the history of humanity, namely, that, in spite of everything, this is more the result of the creatureliness of humans in all their innocent stupidity, weakness, and the domination of their instincts than real sin for which a true account will have to be given before the judgment seat of God.

And therefore I believe from a thoroughly Christian perspective – and not simply from an inflated kind of humanism – that belief in God's free self-communication in grace should be prior to any confession of humanity's sinfulness. Moreover, a study of the history of faith clearly shows how our knowledge is historical and undergoes continual changes and shifts of emphasis. If this fact has been recognized explicitly since the era of historicism where such changes were actually made and endured, we can thus legitimately claim the right to critically make such shifts in emphasis today too. Indeed, one might suggest that it is only by incorporating such changes that one can make the Christian message plausible and coherent to modern men and women.

As far as the reflections in *this* talk are concerned, it is not just a question of naming and describing this Christian reality as such, but rather of trying to say something about the experience one has had of this reality, however "subjective" this may seem. And therefore it must be conceded here, even with a little trepidation, that the notion of sin and the forgiveness of sin – and this is certainly problematic – are less prominent in my theology than the theme of God's self-communication. But surely theologians – within their own limited subjectivity – cannot hope to encompass every possible experience of what it means to be Christian. Thus if people hold these limitations against me, then I can rejoin by asking them whether they do not need to take into account the weaknesses of their own unavoidably subjective theology. Such limitations are inevitable if we want to express our basic theological position clearly.

SCHOOLS OF THEOLOGY

A *third* experience also selected rather arbitrarily can be mentioned. In the past, when a theologian practised theology as member of a religious order, that is, as a member of a congregation formed according to a certain spirit distinguished from that of other orders, this theology bore the distinct and tangible imprint of the theology of that order. The major orders such as the Benedictines, the Dominicans, the Franciscans, and the Jesuits each had their own style of theology, a fact that was acknowledged then. Each order cultivated its own specific theology and each distinguished its theology from that of other religious orders. They were proud of their respective theological traditions and they even had their own officially recognized doctors of the Church as well as key figures in the various theological "schools." In all of this, there is nothing objectionable provided, of course, that these differences do not degenerate into stubborn conflicts along party lines – something that occurred quite often in the past. Nowadays I think this is no longer the case. As far as legislation of my order is concerned, I ought to teach, for example, the so-called *scientia media* and consequently should oppose and reject the Thomistic theology of grace as expounded in the Baroque era. Today, such clearly distinctive theologies associated with religious orders no longer exist and can no longer exist. A number of factors now make it simply impossible for a member of a religious order to advocate among reasonable people such a specific school theology handed on from one generation to the next. These factors include: the manner in which theological questions are nowadays formulated, the wealth of theological material that has to be considered, the sheer weight of contemporary biblical scholarship, and the more objective conclusions of dogmatic and historical theology.

The genuine differences evident in theology today cut right across the orders. This does not mean, however, to belabour the obvious, that the theology of a member of a religious order has nothing to do with the distinctive character of the life and spirituality of that order. For example, I would hope that Ignatius Loyola, the great founder of my order, would recognize something of his own spirit and spirituality in my theology. At least I would like to think that that is the case! If one can be so bold, I would argue that in one or another point I am actually closer to the spirit of Ignatius than was the notable Jesuit theology of the Baroque era which sometimes did not pay sufficient attention to what I might call the existentialism of Ignatius. A few years ago on the occasion of one of my birthdays, the communist Ignatius Silone autographed one of his books for me with the hand-written inscription "unum in una spe: libertas." This inscription reminds me as a Jesuit of that simple but magnificent closing prayer of the *Spiritual Exercises* where Ignatius entrusts himself totally to God without reservation and where the notion of freedom holds pride of place over the Augustinian triad of memory, understanding, and will. I do not believe that this choice of words and way of speaking were simply by chance. I also do not believe that the traditional Jesuit theology took this fact seriously enough; I am not convinced that I have done a better job in my own work. But at least I have tried to move in that direction.

At any rate, as a Jesuit I do not consider myself bound to any narrow school theology. This is even the case in regard to adherence to a particular philosophical school. On the whole, I also developed a greater appreciation for Thomistic philosophy as interpreted by [Joseph] Maréchal as opposed to Suarez's interpretation on which I had been trained initially. Of course, the type of contemporary philosophy and theology that I have tried to practise can be criticized as not having moved beyond a certain eclecticism. But where in the world is there a systematic philosophy and theology that cannot be suspected of eclecticism – since philosophy and theology are clearly derived from various sources and backgrounds? How can we do theology today except in as wide as possible confrontation and dialogue with the enormous variety of contemporary anthropological sciences? How can theology – one that wants to listen in all quarters and to learn from various sources – avoid this accusation of eclecticism? Of course, I know that in my theology there is perhaps quite a lot that does not fit together in a clear and unambiguous manner. The reason for that is the original pluralistic character of the sources of our knowledge, which makes very difficult any attempt on our part at an adequate and all-embracing reflection on the coherence of our statements. Therefore, a theologian can only request from both supporters and opponents that they approach one's theology with gracious goodwill and regard one's starting point, basic orientations, and formulation of questions as more significant than the "results" which, all things considered, can really never be conclusive.

THEOLOGY AND OTHER SCIENCES

A *fourth* and final experience can be mentioned, although this is already implicit in the previous experiences, and is certainly not as such the most important for theology. I am referring to the lack of congruence between theology and the other sciences. By this I am not referring to the subtle issue of a theological theory of knowledge or a general epistemology. What I mean is the simple fact that I know and have experienced only a very small amount of humanity's experience and knowledge as explored in all the sciences, but also in poetry, music, the fine arts, and even in the history of humanity in general – though as a theologian I should be well informed about all of this. If as a theologian I inquire not about an abstract concept of God, but wish to approach God directly, then absolutely nothing of what God has revealed as Creator of the world, as Lord of history, should be uninteresting to me. Naturally, it could be piously claimed that everything that is necessary for my salvation is contained in Holy Scripture, and that one needs to know nothing beyond this. But if I wish to love God for God's own sake and not only for the sake of my personal salvation, then in order to find God I cannot restrict my interest to Scripture alone. Rather, everything through which God permits God's very self to be perceived in this creaturely world will be of interest to me. This is especially the case for the theologian whose task it is to intellectually oppose every kind of false egoism relating to salvation. Although I would like to know more about the variety of human experiences as explored in the sciences, the arts, and historical events, I am quite ignorant of much of this. For the theologian all these human experiences speak of God even if the individual theologian knows very little about them. Thus one's theology – despite all existential engagement theologians like to refer to – is so abstract, so colourless, so far removed from revealing the human person and the world. To be sure, the theologian has in the last analysis, only one thing to say. But this one affirmation should comprehend that mysterious core of all reality. Yet, as a theologian, every time I open a book on modern science, I become quite panic-stricken. Most of what is written in these books is quite foreign to me. What is more, really, I am more than likely not capable of understanding their content. Hence, as a theologian, I feel somewhat compromised faced with this reality. Then the pale abstraction and hollowness of my own theological concepts hits me with a shock.

As a theologian, I maintain that God created the world but, since I know so little about the world, the notion of creation remains strangely empty. As a theologian, I also proclaim that Jesus, as well as being human, is Lord of all creation. Then I read that the cosmos extends thousands of millions of light-years and I ask myself somewhat fearfully what my previous statement actually means. St. Paul still knew which sphere of the cosmos belonged to the angels. This is something I do not know.

I ask myself with trepidation whether about half the souls in the kingdom of God have ever had a personal life history. I ask this since authentic Church teaching holds that a personal, spiritual, and eternal soul exists from the moment of an egg's fertilization by sperm and that any other view is simply not acceptable. How is the fact of the countless number of spontaneous abortions reconciled with this notion of a personal history of freedom right from the start? I find no clear answer when I ask myself what is the precise meaning of the claim that the first humans over two million years ago constitute the first subjects of salvation history and revelation. I let secular anthropology teach me to be more careful about differentiating between body and soul – something that continues to be problematic. This implies that I can no longer interpret the teaching contained in the encyclical *Humani generis*, namely, that the human body derives from the animal kingdom whereas the soul is created by God as dualistically as it initially appears. I even ask myself, since this could be quite pertinent, whether a pope could resign from office because of an illness that rendered him incapacitated. I could continue along this line, noting problems that modern science puts to theology, without theology having yet come up with any very clear answers to these kinds of questions.

On the one hand, there is the so-called permanence and clearly unchanging character of human nature, as this is presumed by moral teaching on the laws of nature. On the other hand, we try to reconcile this with the fact that human beings with their constantly developing and changing genetic structure are to be situated within the whole history of evolution. Is it not surprising then to be rather taken aback at times by the unambiguous and unchangeable tone of the Church's moral promulgation given that such certainties are not that obvious within human beings? Given this situation, theologians need to be careful and modest, but they must have the courage to proclaim their message and retain their own convictions.

As a theologian it is possible to console oneself in all of this with the observation that no clear synthesis exists even among the natural scientists, namely a harmony between what they postulate *as* scientists regarding their work and what they experience over and beyond these individual items of scientific knowledge, for example, issues such as human freedom, responsibility, and questioning. If theologians have these bitter experiences of "not-knowing" and courageously and without prejudice accept them, then they could serve as an example and stimulus for other scientists to manifest a similar modesty and awareness of the limitation of their own knowledge. In this way, tensions between the sciences are not only not removed, but become even more accentuated because they are acknowledged. Moreover, the unavoidable conflict between the different scientific disciplines and theology could be embraced by that peace that reigns among those who in their own particular ways have an inkling and an experience of the mystery we call God.

WHAT IS TO COME

There would be many more similar experiences to recount and those we have been describing are certainly not the most important. I could relate my experiences with my colleagues at the universities in Innsbruck, Munich, and Münster. I could speak of my sixty-two years' experience as a Jesuit in my order. I could recount both pleasant as well as less happy memories of experiences with Rome. And so on. Life is certainly rich, even if with age it gradually slips away into a mist of forgetfulness.

But I would still like to try to say something of an experience which runs at an angle to all that I have recounted so far, and thus cannot be numbered with all these other experiences. I am referring to that experience of waiting for "what is to come." When as Christians we acknowledge an eternal life which will be given to us, it seems that this waiting for what is to come, initially at any rate, is nothing particularly special. Hope for eternal life is normally spoken of in rather unctuous and consoling tones. Far be it from me to disapprove of such language provided it is meant sincerely. But I must personally confess to feeling a little uncomfortable when I hear such talk. It seems to me that the conceptual models used to clarify what is meant by eternal life are for the most part insufficient to deal with the radical break that takes place at death. Eternal life – strangely described as continuing "beyond" and "after" death – is clothed too much with realities with which we are familiar. Eternal life is thus imagined along the lines of continuing to live on, or as a meeting up with those who were close to us, or as friendship and peace, or as a banquet and a celebration. These and similar conceptions focus on the never-ending and ongoing character of eternal life.

Yet I fear that the radical incomprehensibility of what is really meant by eternal life is in this way trivialized. What we call the direct vision of God in eternal life is downgraded to one pleasant activity alongside others that go to make up this life. What is not properly perceived is the unspeakable enormity of the fact that the absolute divinity, God's very self, stoops down naked and bare into our narrow creatureliness. I admit that it seems to me to be both an agonizing and an always-incomplete task for the contemporary theologian to come up with a better model for understanding the notion of eternal life – a model that would exclude these difficulties from the outset. But how? But how? The angels of death will gather up all that trivia that we call our history from the rooms of our spirit (though, of course, the true essence of our active freedom will remain). The starry ideals with which we have rather presumptuously adorned the higher spheres of our life will have faded away and gone out. Death will have erected a huge, silent void. And we will have silently accepted this state in a spirit of faith and hope as corresponding to our true destiny and being. Our seemingly long life then appears as a single short explosion of our freedom like an extended replay, an explosion in which question is transposed into answer, possibility into reality, time into eternity, potential freedom into exercised freedom. Then within that immense terror that is death will come a cry of unutterable joy which will reveal that the immense and silent void we experience as death is in reality filled with the primordial mystery we call God. It is filled with God's pure light, with God's all-absorbing and all-giving love. Perhaps there in this incomprehensible mystery we can catch a glimpse of Jesus, the blessed one who appears to us and looks at us. It is in this concrete figure of Jesus that all our legitimate assumptions about the incomprehensibility of the infinite God are *divinely surpassed.* I would not like to call what I have just said a description of what is to come. Rather I have merely offered, however falteringly and provisionally, an indication of how one might expect what is to come, namely, by experiencing the descent that is death as already the ascent of what still awaits us. Eighty years is a long time. For each one of us, however, the life span apportioned to us is that brief moment in time which will be what constitutes our ultimate purpose and meaning.[3]

Notes

1 "Why Doing Theology Is So Difficult," in *Karl Rahner in Dialogue: Conversations and Interviews 1965–1982,* trans. and ed. H. Biallowons, H. D. Egan, S.J., and P. Imhof, S.J. (New York: Crossroad, 1986), 216.

2 Rahner's address was given at a conference of the Katholische Akademie, held on February 11–12, 1984, in honour of Karl Rahner's 80th birthday. It was published in German in *Vor dem Geheimnis Gottes den Menschen verstehen: Karl Rahner zum 80. Geburtstag,* ed. K. Lehmann (Munich: Schnell & Steiner, 1984), 105–19. The English translation first appeared in *Theological Studies* 61 (2000), 3–15, and we gratefully acknowledge the editor, Michael A. Fahey, S.J., for permission to reproduce it again here.

3 Our special thanks to Dr. Roman Siebenrock, director of the Karl Rahner Archives at the University of Innsbruck, who drew our attention to some brief spontaneous remarks that Rahner made immediately following his presentation. Not all of his words are decipherable on the video recording, but what follows is our translation of what is clear on the tape. Rahner commented: "Honoured guests, after this celebration I do not want to rise to speak again, except for a few words at the very end. Now I want to thank you for listening to this little story . . . written for an 80th birthday [?]. I thank you from my heart, and I would kindly ask you not to have me expand any further on this, nor to dwell on what has already been said. I thank you sincerely. As an ordinary Christian, as one who knows what really matters, I would ask you to say perhaps a little prayer to God for me so that at the end God will grant me love and mercy."

Appendix: reading Rahner: a guide for students

DECLAN MARMION and MARY E. HINES

Rahner's literary output was prodigious – even by 1974 it had reached almost 3,000 publications, including translations – and for the student approaching his work for the first time it can be a daunting task to know exactly where to begin. It is with this problem in mind that the following comments and selections have been made.

One danger for students approaching Rahner is that his often dense writing style will prove off-putting and result in a reliance solely on the extensive secondary literature. Such an approach, however, only leads to an impoverished understanding of Rahner. Moreover, it overlooks the fact that underlying the myriad of theological themes that he explores are a few basic convictions. Some of these are articulated in the last public address he gave prior to his death in March 1984, "Experiences of a Catholic Theologian," included in this volume.

Rather than beginning there, an easier place to start is with a series of interviews he gave over a number of years (*Karl Rahner in Dialogue: Conversations and Interviews 1965–1982*, trans. and ed. H. Biallowons, H. D. Egan, S.J., and P. Imhof, S.J., New York: Crossroad, 1986). These interviews comprise an overview of many of the themes in Rahner's theology in an engaging style. The passion and personality of Rahner come more to the fore than in his *Theological Investigations*. A further series of interviews towards the end of his life is contained in *Faith in a Wintry Season: Interviews and Conversations with Karl Rahner in the Last Years of his Life, 1982–84* (trans. and ed. H. Biallowons, H. D. Egan, S.J., and Paul Imhof, S.J., New York: Crossroad, 1990).

Another way to begin reading Rahner is to start with his prayers and meditations, for example, *Encounters with Silence* (Westminster, MD: Newman Press, 1960), first published in 1938, and one of his most success-ful works. For Rahner no gap existed between doing theology in the context of church, on the one hand, and the life of prayer, meditation, and com-mitment to people, on the other. Indeed, many of his theological concerns (e.g., the experience of God, the God of Mystery, grace in everyday life, etc.) are found in his spiritual writings.

Readers approaching the twenty-three volumes of his *Theological Investigations* for the first time will find the later writings less daunting than many of the earlier pieces. They are also generally shorter. Not that the earlier volumes should be overlooked. "Thoughts on the Theology of Christmas," (*TI* III, 24–34), for example, depicts in a meditative way a number of foundational Rahnerian themes, including prayer, the experience of God, and anthropology, and serves as an excellent introduction to what lies at the core of Rahner's theology, namely, the experience of the personal self-communication of God or grace. Though the various volumes of the *Investigations* are each given a thematic subtitle, many of the articles were originally talks he gave for a particular occasion. Rahner preferred to stress the ad hoc nature of his work – describing himself as a *dilettante* – rather than offering a fully developed systematic theology along the lines, for example, of Karl Barth.

The themes covered throughout the *Investigations* span the whole gamut of Rahner's output including spirituality, anthropology, theological methodology, ecclesiology, Christology, and the sacraments. In the "Further Reading" section at the end of each chapter of this book, readers are directed to pertinent articles in the *Investigations* as well as to important secondary literature, so there is no need to repeat that work here. Nevertheless, for the beginning student some articles in the *Investigations* are more "user-friendly" than others and provide a helpful access into his thought. For those interested in Rahner's view of spirituality, for example, there is "The Spirituality of the Church of the Future" (*TI* xx, 143–53). The key ideas underlying his theological methodology are contained in "Some Clarifying Remarks about My Own Work" (*TI* xvii, 243–48), "A Theology That We Can Live With" (*TI* xxi, 99–112), and "Intellectual Patience with Ourselves" (*TI* xxiii, 38–49). Substantial and significant earlier articles dealing with methodology (e.g., "The Theology of The Symbol," *TI* iv, 221–52), and the nature/grace problematic (e.g., "Nature and Grace," *TI* iv, 165–88), however, presuppose a good grasp of Thomistic metaphysics and epistemology. On Christology, readers will find a distillation of Rahner's views in volume xxi of *Investigations*, while in volume xx he voices his concern for the future of the Church.

Rahner's style was more suited to the article format rather than to the formal book. His theological synthesis, *Foundations of Christian Faith* (1978), opens with a condensed form of the philosophical underpinnings of his anthropology before dealing with specific theological themes (salvation, revelation, Christology, ecclesiology, spirituality, and eschatology). New students will find it easier to start with the more digestible and expansive treatments of these themes both in *Hearer of the Word* (for the philosophical part) and in the *Investigations*.

In terms of more recent publications on Rahner, the Karl Rahner Trust in conjunction with the Herder publishing company has begun the task of gathering all of Rahner's writings into one complete series. This project, *Karl Rahner: Sämtliche Werke*, comprising approximately thirty-two volumes, a third of which have already been published, also contains hitherto unpublished material. It will likely be the standard work of reference for the future. The centenary year of Rahner's birth in 2004 also saw numerous congresses and symposia on both sides of the Atlantic devoted to his work and his ongoing legacy. In Ireland, the Centre for Culture, Technology and Values, in association with the Department of Theology and Religious Studies at the University of Limerick, produced a CD-ROM of the twenty-three volumes of Rahner's *Theological Investigations* to mark the occasion.

There are a number of helpful bibliographies of Rahner's works, the most comprehensive of which exist in German. In English too there are some useful bibliographies arranged both chronologically and thematically. Bibliographies of the secondary literature also exist. Some of these are listed below:

Bibliographies on Karl Rahner
Bleistein, R., and E. Klinger, *Bibliographie Karl Rahner 1924–1969* (Freiburg: Herder, 1969).
Bleistein, R., ed., *Bibliographie Karl Rahner 1969–1974* (Freiburg: Herder, 1969).
Imhof, P., and H. Treziak, "Bibliographie Karl Rahner 1974–1979," in H. Vorgrimler, ed., *Wagnis Theologie: Erfahrungen mit der Theologie Karl Rahners* (Freiburg: Herder, 1979), 579–97.
Imhof, P., and E. Meuser, "Bibliographie Karl Rahner 1979–1984," in E. Klinger and K. Wittstadt, eds., *Glaube im Prozess* (Freiburg: Herder, 1984), 854–88.
Pedley, C. J., "An English Bibliographical Aid to Karl Rahner," *The Heythrop Journal* 25 (1984), 319–65.

Bibliographies of secondary literature on Rahner
Raffelt, A., "Karl Rahner – Bibliographie der Sekundärliteratur 1948–1978," in H. Vorgrimler, ed., *Wagnis Theologie: Erfahrungen mit der Theologie Karl Rahners* (Freiburg: Herder, 1979), 598–622.
Raffelt, A., "Karl Rahner – Bibliographie der Sekundärliteratur 1979–1983 und Nachträge," in E. Klinger and K. Wittstadt, eds., *Glaube im Prozeß* (Freiburg: Herder, 1984), 872–85.

Raffelt, A., and R. Siebenrock, "Karl Rahner – Sekundärliteratur 1984–1993," in A. Raffelt, ed., *Karl Rahner in Erinnerung*, Freiburger Akademieschriften, Band 8 (Düsseldorf: Patmos, 1994), 165–205.

Tallon, A., "Rahner Studies, 1939–89: Part 1, 1939–73," *Theology Digest* 36:4 (1989), 321–46.

Tallon, A., "Rahner Studies, 1939–89: Part 2, 1974–89," *Theology Digest* 37:1 (1990), 17–41.

Tallon, A., "Rahner Bibliography Supplement," *Theology Digest* 38:2 (1991), 131–140.

The above bibliographical information in relation to both the primary and the secondary literature is also available on the web. The US-based Karl Rahner Society (http://www.krs.stjohnsem.edu) provides biographical, bibliographical and other information about Rahner. It also contains links to comprehensive bibliographies, archives, publications, and databases on Rahner. Two of the most important of these include the Karl Rahner Archive at the University of Innsbruck (http://theol.uibk.ac.at/) and the Rahner Databank at the University of Freiburg, the town of Rahner's birth.

Index

ightning Source UK Ltd.
'ilton Keynes UK
KOW04f2115020316
69463UK00001B/142/P

9 780521 54040